Ephemeron

Memoirs:
Fragments from a life
(Thripsala Tis Zois – Greek language edition)
Fragments that remain
Ephemeron

Fiction:
Convergence — Aspects of the change
A Floating World

Non-fiction:
Cinematography Underwater
Aikido – Basic and Intermediate Studies
Aikido – Beyond questions often asked
Attributes a writer needs

Ephemeron

John Litchen

Fragments of my Life – with Science Fiction

Yambu

All rights reserved. No part of this publication may be reproduced by any means including photocopying or in other information storage and retrieval systems without written consent of the publisher. except for small portions which may be quoted for the purpose of reviewing the work as a whole.

Ephemeron
First edition: 2017
Copyright © John Litchen 2017

National Library of Australia Cataloguing-in-Publication entry
Creator: Litchen, John, author, photographer.

Title: Ephemeron : fragments from my life with science fiction / John Litchen.

ISBN: 9780980410488 (paperback)

Subjects: Litchen, John--Childhood and youth.
 Litchen, John--Travel.
 Litchen, John.
 Men--Australia--Biography.
 Coming of age--Australia.

Published by Yambu
PO Box 3503 Robina Town Centre QLD 4230
Contact: John Litchen 07 55788748 jlitchen@bigpond.net.au

Ephemeron:
a: a thing (especially a printed item) of short-lived interest or usefulness.
b: a short-lived thing.
The Australian Oxford Dictionary.

Acknowledgement:
Thanks to Bruce Gillespie who has been a friend for more than 45 years for publishing parts of this volume in his various fanzines.

Scratchpad 74, February 2010,
From Melbourne to Tennant Creek, My life and Science Fiction part 2.

Scratchpad 76, February 2011,
Travels to the Top End, My life and Science Fiction part 3.

Scratchpad 79, December 2011,
Dancing on Sand, My life and Science Fiction part 4
(*These were online magazines, some of which were print copies with the title of BRG which were essentially the same as the online Scratchpad version.*)

Treasure 1, June 2013,
The Sound of Different Drums, My Life and Science Fiction part 5.

Treasure 3, November 2014,
An Innocent Afloat, My life and Science Fiction part 6.

Fragments of my Life – with Science Fiction

— *Ephemeron* —

Foreword...

Everyone is an amalgam of all the things that happen to them in life, and in my case it seems I lived separate yet parallel lives simultaneously.

For example I was a dry cleaner, while at the same time I was a musician, playing in nightclubs and later on the Don Lane Show as a fill in percussionist when Gary Hyde (the regular percussionist or his cousin Barry Quinn) were not available because of other commitments. And during the early 60s I also played percussion on some other TV programmes, (The Peter Couchman Show on channel 10, as well as sometimes with the Young Talent Time orchestra), shows at Festival Hall (Gladys Knight and The Pips) and recordings in Studios.

I was also involved in scuba diving and underwater photography, fascinated by film making and just loved reading science fiction.

In 1964 I went overseas by passenger ship, taking my drums with me and spent 5 months in Paris playing with a Cuban band, (Los Matecocos) then worked in a kitchen in London, drank too much booze in Seville, Spain, and laid around on a beach in Greece reading Report to Greco by Kazantsakis — in my view, the best of all his books — while soaking up the sun and sipping Turkish coffee.

In 1968 I went to Mexico where I stayed for almost a year, coming back to Australia in 1969.

But it all began in 1952 when I was twelve years old...

Science Fiction and a Sense of Wonder

In 1952 when I was 12 years old and attending an intermediate level high school (year 7 and 8) in Hyde Street Footscray. There was a Milk Bar in Hyde Street right on the corner of a side street opposite the front entrance to the school. For those who don't know, a Milk Bar was not a piece of chocolate but what we called a shop that today would be like a 7/11 store minus the service station and petrol sales. It sold groceries pies and pasties and sausage rolls as well as ice creams and lollies, and soft drinks and milk shakes and all those things that we see now as separate franchises endlessly repeated in shopping centres around the country. It also sold some fresh fruit and vegetables and like a general store it even had small range of hardware items. They sold newspapers and magazines and paperback books; books like Carter Brown detective stories, Westerns, Romances, and Science Fiction and Fantasy novels — an endlessly changing selection. These books were all short being no more than between 98 and 128 pages. Only rarely did one of them have something like 180 pages.

It was in this little shop that I discovered SF, books often with lurid covers depicting half naked maidens being rescued by men in space suits wielding of all things medieval swords from attacking alien monsters with ray guns. If not that the covers often showed weird spaceships battling each other with vast energy rays or destroying major landmarks in London or New York.

To a 12 year old, these books appeared wonderfully exciting. There was no TV, only radio which I listened to sometimes, and picture shows (movies) to which I sometimes went usually with my brother and one sister, (the other was still too young) on Saturday afternoons at the St

Georges Theatre in Yarraville near the station. What we had for entertainment were the games we played in the streets we lived in and what we could conjure in our imaginations as we read books.

The lurid books in that little corner shop certainly fired my imagination and I saved up as much as my lunch money as needed to buy at least one of them each week. It very quickly became two a week and I discovered my preference for Science Fiction far outweighed fantasy but if it wasn't SF then Science Fantasy would do. I didn't mind space men battling with swords no matter how incongruous it seemed. I also like Edgar Rice Burroughs books and just loved the Mars and Venus novels. I was a fan of Tarzan as well, and read every one of those books. I guess I liked adventure stories.

It seems strange though that the books I bought and collected apart from Edgar Rice Burroughs were the pulp novels of Vargo Staten and Volstead Gridban of which there was a new one almost every week. I even had a copy of the novelization of *The Creature from the Black Lagoon* by Vargo Staten. If I remember right that one had 180 pages —a long book in those days! This was my first awareness of a movie-book tie-in. I had seen the movie before the book was published but I read the book anyway and enjoyed it immensely as it brought back images in my mind from the film. I kept these for many years. To make room for more books I eventually sold for me at a national SF convention.

I had so many books mounting up in my room (a veranda that had been converted into a sleep out) that I went to the local greengrocer and asked him if I could have some boxes. Fruit used to come packed in wooden boxes about two and a half feet long by a foot deep and a foot high, a perfect size when stacked sideways to make bookshelves. All my books went into these improvised shelves.

The power of words to create worlds within one's mind is profound. And people of today who get their entertainment passively from watching TV or playing video games, or attending the latest movie will never understand, because they didn't grow up in a time when those things didn't exist and all we had were books, and radio dramas, of which the key ingredient was our imagination. From time to time SF movies appeared in the city cinemas and seeing one of those was heavenly.

I loved those stories. They transported me to worlds far more real and exciting than the reality of Melbourne's western suburbs in the early 1950s. The writing was no doubt awful, corny, and ridiculously over the top, with totally unlikely situations — isn't most SF like that? — Yet for all that it captured my imagination as films and radio never could. I spent hours absorbed in these books. I couldn't get enough of them.

In 1954 I went to University High School in Parkville where I was to continue with years 9 to 12. To get there I took busses from Yarraville to Footscray, then a tramways bus from Footscray to Queen Street in Melbourne. I would walk a block to Elizabeth Street where I could take a tram up to Parkville and the University High School which was situated just off Sydney Road behind the Royal Melbourne Hospital.

It didn't take long for me to discover McGills and the fine selection of SF books right by the front entrance as you walked in. McGills was the very first real bookshop I ever went into and the array of books I saw there was astounding. But I rarely got past the section where the Science Fiction books were displayed.

Usually standing near that selection was Merv Binns. He might have been the manager of the book shop but he probably spent more time in the science fiction section that anywhere else in the shop, at least it seemed like that to me. It didn't matter whether I walked in on my way to school or on my way home again later in the afternoon, he was always there, ready to recommend and sell me the latest SF book.

I discovered authors I had never heard of and found magazines I never imagined existed; *New Worlds, Nebula, Galaxy, Astounding*, and many others. I didn't know what to choose, but Merv was there to tell me the latest news, what the plot of each novel displayed was about, even to the plots of some of the short stories in the various magazines. He must have read everything. It's hard to believe that today but back in 1954 it was certainly possible, and I reckon I made a good effort to do just that.

What I loved about these books was the sense of wonder, the adventure, the weirdness of other worlds, the technicalities of space travel, the delusions of hyperspace and faster than light travel, matter transmission, telepathy, telekinesis, longevity extending over centuries and all those other almost impossible ideas. I loved every one of those books and continued to buy and stack them up in my makeshift box-bookshelves.

I had no idea there was science fiction club behind McGills in Somerset Place. If Merv at some stage mentioned it, and I'm sure he would have, I don't remember, but not knowing about it I never went there.

— *Ephemeron* —

Underwater swimming the hard way

In the summer of 1956 I was sixteen and my friend Brian Mealy was seventeen and a half and we were full of restless energy. For us summer holidays meant riding our bikes to Williamstown Beach, swimming and experimenting with the new sport of skindiving.

We had both read *Diving to Adventure* by Hans Haas, and couldn't wait to try this business of underwater swimming. Masks, snorkels and swim-fins (now called flippers) could be bought in some of the sports stores, but they were by no means common. You could even buy dry rubber (frogman type) diving suits from Pirrelli, if you could afford it. We couldn't. We went snorkelling with our masks and fins, breathing through the long snorkels with bent ends after having removed the useless ping pong balls meant to stop water flooding into the snorkel. We wore several old jumpers and T shirts to keep warm.

People who saw us thought we were mad.

We had homemade spear guns and we used to go in a lot at a place called the Crystal Pool, just by Williamstown beach a bit past the life saving club. There were lots of fish there in those days, mostly butterfish (banded morwong) and brightly coloured leatherjackets. We often saw pike and barracuda, and schools of garfish would scatter as we blundered into them, re-forming behind us to continue happily on their way. Tiny squid and cuttlefish would hover in gullies between large rocks covered with undulating green sea lettuce, vanishing in an instant if we moved too close.

If you looked at the weed-covered rocks there were heaps of small clams, pippis, periwinkles, mussels, small and large abalone (or mutton fish, as we derogatively called them), a huge number of crabs, shrimps, sea-urchins, anemones, ascidians and many other weird living things we had no names for. There were various starfish, from the ubiquitous biscuit stars to the monstrous eleven-armed Cosinasterias calamaria, the dreaded shellfish predator.

Sometimes we even bumped into a Port Jackson shark, and on rare occasions a carpet shark. We often swam over sinister-looking stingrays lying on the bottom partly buried in sand. We could see their eyes follow us as we swam by. If they felt threatened they would lift up off the sand and with a snap of their wings shoot towards us, making us frantically backpedal to get out of their way. The ray would then veer off to fly across the bottom and disappear into the murk beyond our visibility. Some of those rays were as big as two metres across, and were a magnificent sight, if not downright scary.

After a hard day of swimming and snorkelling, if we sat quietly on the promenade by the Crystal Pool and waited till the sun had set, as the sky slowly darkened we would see the big butterfish come up into the shallow water to feed. They would slowly work their way along the rocks near the edge nibbling at the sea lettuce. It was like watching tame fish in a giant fishpond.

The area was so full of life we could not imagine it being any other way. Just getting into the water was exciting, never knowing what we would see, but knowing that there would always be something interesting to see.

Now forty-four years later, it is difficult to imagine what it was like then, all that time ago. The seaweed is still there, and the tiny things like shrimp and little fish, but it is rare to see anything bigger than a few centimetres. The butterfish have gone, the leatherjackets too. There are no mussels, or abalone, or clams and pipis on the rocks. They have been stripped bare by voracious humans and predatory starfish, though I think the humans did most of the damage. There are signs screwed to the poles along the foreshore prohibiting the taking of shellfish. $500 is the fine if you are caught.

To me the gullies between the rocky reefs now look devoid of life, but I suppose to the kids of today it is probably as exciting as it was to Brian and me back in the late fifties. I took my own son Brian into the Crystal Pool to teach him how to skindive, and he loved it in there. The water is shallow, but still deep enough to swim in and dive. Lots of large rocks are exposed at low tide. If there is a problem with the mask or snorkel, you can simply stand on a partly submerged rock and be almost completely out of the water, or you can walk over the exposed rocks back to the foreshore. Access is simple: walk down the steps or climb over the rocks to step straight into water no more than a metre deep. The Crystal Pool has been extremely popular with generations of kids over more than half a century.

As soon as I had saved enough money I bought a sealskin. This was a black rubber vest that wrapped around the body from the neck to the crotch. There were holes for the legs and arms and a buckle at the front held it together. I wore a jumper underneath the sealskin and around the waist I had to use a belt with lead weights to counteract the buoyancy. Like a modern wetsuit, though nowhere as efficient, the sealskin allowed water to enter and become trapped against the body. This trapped water was warmed by body heat, and so after an initial few minutes of coldness you then swam about with a thin layer of warm water against your skin. This increased the time you could stay in the water before getting too cold.

Of course Brian thought this was fantastic. He tried it, but because he was a taller than I a lot of cold water came in under the arms. The sealskin didn't work as well for him as it did for me.

We all know that throughout history, when the time is right for an idea to present itself, for something particular to be invented, it will occur to many people in widely different parts of the world. Often the person who gets credit for the invention is not the first one to invent it but simply the first to patent it or produce it commercially. Whoever first started manufacturing wetsuits is a mystery, but Brian would have been among the first to come up with the concept. He loved the idea of swimming in cold water with a fine layer of warm water against the body, so he thought of making a vest like the sealskin only from sponge rubber.

Brian's stepfather worked for an oil company and they manufactured sheets of sponge rubber. We spent many nights cutting these 5 mm thick sheets of sponge and experimenting with different glues to see if we could get the pieces to stick together to make a jacket. Nothing seemed to work and it never occurred to us to stitch it together. In the end we made a vest similar to the sealskin. It wrapped right around and was buckled at the front. It worked, and was infinitely warmer than my flat rubber vest, and Brian was as proud as could be every time he wore it.

Neither of these vests was that efficient, and after a time we still got very cold and had to come out of the water. We used them for a while because we had nothing better. Once we had saved enough money however, we bought the real thing — Pirreli dry suits.

The dry suits were absolutely fantastic. They came in two halves: a pair of legs you stepped into, and a top that was pulled down over head and arms. Soft surgical rubber sealed the neck and the wrists. It took some getting used to because at first it felt like you were strangling. The suit sealed at the waist. The bottom half came fairly high over the waist and was folded down. The top half came down over this and the two pieces were folded up several times and sealed over a hoop around the waist. You had to wear long underwear and maybe a jumper under the suit, as all the suit did was keep you dry.

I remember how strange it felt the first time we tried them. When you jumped into the water they ballooned up and you had to let the bulk of the trapped air escape by pulling the neck out. Swimming around and feeling the water against you while remaining absolutely dry was deliciously exhilarating. The really marvellous thing was we could stay in the water for hours and hours on end without any discomfort other than wrinkled skin on our fingers and a very cold face.

Not long after we got these suits we started using simple aqualungs. We never went to a diving school because there weren't any. We were on our own. Learning to scuba dive for us was a trial-and-error effort combined with common sense. Technical knowledge was obtained from a US Navy manual for divers, a book by Hilbert Schenk Jr and Henry Kendall called Shallow Water Diving and Spearfishing, and from books by Hans Haas and Jacques Yves Cousteau.

Apart from entertaining us splendidly, a careful reading of these books taught us a lot. We learnt about air embolism, nitrogen narcosis and decompression sickness, about bottom times and decompression stops. We found out about buoyancy control, buddy breathing and how to take a mask off and put it on again underwater, about not holding your breath and breathing naturally underwater. We practised these things in the shallow waters of the Crystal Pool once we had obtained our aqualungs.

We also discovered that panic can be a killer and that you should be absolutely familiar with your equipment, so you don't have to think about it and can simply enjoy being underwater. We had a wonderful time teaching ourselves those things you now must learn at a diving school. It was the best summer we ever had.

As our confidence increased we became more daring and looked for deeper water to dive in. Barwon Heads was our first choice. We had often camped there and knew the area around the cliff quite well. There is always a swell and the reefs drop away into deeper water. There is some current but it's not too dangerous. We got heaps of crayfish. Apart from the fact that it was unsporting — no one thought about that back then in the fifties — it has been forbidden for a long time to hunt crayfish with aqualungs and spear guns. You are supposed to grab them by hand while holding your breath. There was plenty of everything to take, and access was good. Sadly, for many years now all these spots have been fished out. All of us, those early over-enthusiastic divers are to blame.

Brian was eighteen months older than I and the moment he turned eighteen he bought a car. It wasn't much of a car and he was constantly fixing it, but when it did run well it got us to places like Phillip Island where the diving was excellent.

We were very confident in our ability to dive anywhere, so we chose a spot that looked terrific. It was an inlet not far from The Nobbies with a rocky black lava beach. As we looked down from the top of the cliff we saw a rocky kelp-covered ledge uncovered by the outgoing tide. This ledge extended some ten metres out into the sea and we thought it would be a good spot to dive from. Because this ledge was uncovered we had assumed that the tide was out. This was a stupid assumption, as I soon found out.

The cliffs here were all black, and though it was a beautiful day with not a cloud in the sky, the water surging about the edge of the rocky ledge also appeared black. In retrospect it looked ominous, but at that moment to us it looked exciting. We couldn't wait to get in.

We got our gear out of the car. The paths down the cliff would have challenged a mountain goat so we decided the easiest way to get everything down to the bottom was to put it on except for the flippers and spear guns. We did this and half slid, half scrambled down the cliff with showers of small dislodged pebbles and rocks accompanying us. It was a wonder we didn't puncture our dry suits. When we got to the bottom we were so hot, and sweating so much inside our dry suits, that we had to sit in the water by the small beach to cool off.

Now that we were on the beach we could see there was quite a swell. Each wave surged up the beach rolling tiny black pebbles forward then sucking them back out with considerable force. The water was absolutely clear. It had only appeared black from the top of the cliff because all the rocks under the water were black, the same volcanic rock that made up the cliffs on either side of this inlet.

We put our flippers on, cleaned our masks by spitting into them and rinsing them in the sea — this stopped them from fogging — checked that our tanks were turned on and air was released when we breathed through the regulator, then we floated out and emptied the air from the suits.

The water got deep very quickly as we swam past the end of the rocky ledge. Visibility was exceptionally good. We swam through the heavy brown kelp growing up from the base of the ledge and came out onto a sandy bottom. Strangely enough I didn't see any fish; no kelpies, no toadies, no leatherjackets or anything else. Once out of the kelp I could see giant sandy ridges extending down and disappearing into the murky distance thirty or forty metres away. I drifted down and swam along the top of the ridges. I could see the sand trickling over the top of each ridge as the motion of the swell above pushed the sand towards the beach then drew it back again. It brought to mind the image of wind blowing sand off the top of giant dunes in the Sahara. It was fascinating to see this same action underwater, though on a smaller though no less monumental scale. I let the water carry me across the ridges, not needing to swim at all. It was an exhilarating feeling.

I suddenly realised I was alone. Brian had stayed close to the cliff edge as we swam down. He was looking for something to shoot with his spear gun. I was just looking. I had even forgotten that I had the spear gun with me and had not pulled the rubber back to load it.

I looked back, then spun around in a circle. Brian was nowhere to be seen. I couldn't even see the cliff or the rocky ledge that marked the spot we had entered the water. There was nothing but ridges of sand as far as I could see in all directions. I could feel the pressure of the water. The suit was pinching so I knew I was much deeper than I had ever been before. And to make matters worse I was drifting at an ever-increasing rate. I tried to swim against the current but could make no headway.

Damn. Don't panic. But that was exactly what I could feel myself doing. My heart raced, and my legs ached from that short spurt of trying to swim against the current. I started to sweat inside the dry suit.

I forced myself to think. How long had I been in the water? I looked at my diver's watch. Only ten minutes! Seemed longer than that. I had plenty of air so that was not something to worry about, but the drifting out was. Then I noticed the current was not constant but moved in and out, as did the swells above. I would drift forward over a ridge, pause for a moment, only to be sucked back over two or three ridges by a stronger outgoing current. It suddenly occurred to me that if I could hang on to something I could stay in the same spot while the current sucked past me. When the swell pushed shoreward I could swim with it to gain a few metres then hang on once more while the current again sucked out.

But hang on to what?

There was nothing but sand everywhere. No rocks, no kelp, only ridges of shifting sand.

The spear gun! I could dig it into the sand and hang on.

As soon as the next swell stopped pushing me forward, I dug the gun into the sand in front of the ridge beneath me. Then the outgoing water surged past me. Now that I wasn't drifting it was obvious just how strong that current was. No one could swim against that. I could see the sand around the spear gun ripped away by the outward surge. It disappeared underneath me to run down the ridge behind me. As soon as the surge from the next swell started to come forward, I pulled up the spear gun and swam as fast as I could with the water. As the forward momentum slowed I again dug the gun into the sand, having gained two ridges.

Now I knew I could get back. But where was I? Had I drifted down the coast towards the Nobbies and Seal Rocks? Or had I gone straight out away from the spot where we entered the water? There was only one way to find out. I would have to give up what I had gained and swim up to the surface.

At the surface I realised how lucky I was. The beach in the tiny inlet where we climbed down the cliff was right in front of me, but such a long way away. It seemed like a kilometre, but it was probably only two hundred metres. I rose up and down with the swell. I tried to swim towards the inlet but gained nothing. The swells were too high. The water smashing against the aqualung on my back was too strong. I thought briefly about dropping my lead belt and aqualung and swimming in, but then I remembered how strong the outward surge and the current was. I could not swim against that in any case even though the dry suit would keep me on the surface.

There was only one way to get back. Reluctantly I pushed down to the sandy bottom. Again, using the spear gun as an anchor, I laboriously worked my way across the sand ridges, alternately swimming in, then hanging on against the outward current. It seemed to take forever, and just when I started to worry about having used all the air, I felt the pressure of the current lessening. Black rocks appeared, sticking up through the sand. Then I saw the edge of the kelp by the cliff wall and the rock ledge. With a huge feeling of relief I pushed through the kelp and swam towards the beach.

When I crawled onto the beach I saw Brian sitting there, his aqualung, lead belt, mask snorkel and flippers beside him.

'A lousy spot,' he said. 'Nothing but kelp and sand.'

'It wasn't much of a dive,' I agreed as I pulled off my mask.

'What took you so long?'

'I don't know. I just wanted to have a look around.'

There was no way I would admit that I had been dragged out by the outgoing tide.

Climbing back up the cliff was the worst part of the whole day. Wearing lead belts, carrying aqualungs and the other bits and pieces made it a hard slog. We must have dislodged half the cliff face as we struggled to climb back up.

Later, after a long rest we dived again on the other side of the island. We snorkelled out from the beach where there were no big swells. A couple of hundred metres offshore were some nice reefs full of butterfish. Brian shot a couple, which we took home and had for dinner that night.

I never shot anything with my spear gun. I carried it into the water with me at first because everyone who went skin diving had one.

The only time it was of any use to me was when It stopped me from being carried away by the outgoing tide in the channel between Phillip Island and the mainland.

The wonder is that so many of us early skindivers survived, not knowing what we were doing, learning things the hard way. They were good times and I will never forget them.

Nor will I ever forget Brian who was my closest friend. He died from a heart attack at 42 brought upon by the stress of modern living.

— *Ephemeron* —

My close friend Brian wearing a Pirelli dry suit, climbs out of the water at Phillip Island.

He is carrying the same kind of speargun I used to help me swim back in against the outgoing tide.

He had stayed close to the edge of the drop-off and so wasn't affected by the pull of the outgoing tide.

I wanted to go to Tibet

I have already mentioned that we are an amalgam of all the things that happen to us in life and that we live – or at least some of us do – separate but parallel lives.

There are also certain moments where possibilities collide, and nodes are formed from which numerous life streams can evolve, where a choice is made usually without thinking and life goes on in a particular direction. That branch evolves while the others wither, disappearing forever into the realm of vague possibility, or perhaps into an alternate universe where that happened while this didn't.

Sometimes I wonder what I would be like had I made different choices than the ones I did make at various points in time. What would my life be like now all these years later? I can only assume that as an individual I probably would be much the same — one's character is formed at a young age and rarely changes much no matter what happens — but the life I live could have been very different. Not that I regret the choices I made, well most of them anyway… But who knows?

Looking back more than 50 years later it's just possible that I can see these nodal points and wonder what could have happened, where as a 17 year old I wouldn't have been able to see those nodes if I bumped into them. The problem with looking back is that unless you have an eidetic memory most of what you remember is coloured by later experiences and knowledge you couldn't possibly have had at the time, and so those memories are not as accurate as they should be regardless of how accurate and true to life you think they are.

Upon reflection, I don't think my decision to go to Darwin was the result of guilt over giving up playing the violin, which my father wanted me to do, and of using the broken little finger of the left hand as an excuse; it was that I had this sense of wonder engendered by the reading of Science Fiction and adventure stories like *John Carter on Mars*, *Pellucidar* and the Tarzan books, and that I felt I had to escape from the boring existence of the years spent in high school.

Besides, I was sick of standing in the kitchen every night practicing violin while all the other kids in the street were outside playing games. Apart from that I thought it kind of useless playing music that to me was dead and mechanical. It had been created and written down hundreds of years before and it couldn't be changed or improvised upon in any way. I was rebelling against the strictness and the restrictiveness of it more than anything else, which was probably the real reason for giving up the violin.

Prospects did not seem to be very exciting, going to university (more school and I'd had enough of that), or alternatively, working full time in my father's dry cleaning business. I knew this business quite well having grown up with it, and having already worked part time on Saturday mornings and Friday afternoons at the shop and the factory — this didn't seem like anything I wanted to spend a lifetime doing. Yet strangely enough by the time I was nineteen I was working in this business and would go on to spend more than 35 years in it with my brother Phillip, though for many years it was our business and not our father's.

I wasn't that keen on school over the last two years, finding most subjects boring other than English literature and expression where we got to read a varied selection of books in year eleven. I had endless discussions with my teacher over what I thought were great stories and why we didn't get something better to read than *Catcher in the Rye*, which I though was a drag, along with others which I cannot and do not particularly want to recollect. But there was *Seven Years in Tibet* by Heinrich Harrer, the only book that impressed me from those I had to read at school. I thought it was fantastic. The way the people lived, the places described could well have been on another world. It was for me like reading a science fiction adventure story.

If I couldn't go to another planet then I wanted to go to Tibet.

Years later a spectacular film called *The Horsemen*, starring Jack Palance and Omar Shariff reminded me of how it could have been a few hundreds or a thousand years ago. It could have been set on another world. In my eyes Afghanistan was literally another world.

The story revolved around the game of *Bushkazi* where horsemen dragged around the carcass of a calf with the intention of putting it in a place where there were goal posts while other horsemen tried to stop it from happening. They could use whips, or any physical violence needed to make the person with the calf drop it so someone else could get it and drag it to their goal posts.

It was a fascinating film that had nothing to do with any reality I was familiar with, which made it quite alien. It made me think of a book by Jack Vance, *Trullion: Alastor 2262*, which was also built around a planet wide game called *Hussade* that the whole world played. There was a lot more to the film than the game of *Bushkazi*. It was about tribal life, training to be a warrior, and a good horseman whose prowess could be put to the test in the game because there were no more battles to be had in a world that was irrevocably changing. Obviously this was before the Russians went into Afghanistan and long before the present day.

Outside of school I also came across several other books that fired up my sense of adventure. These were books written by remarkable people who did incredible things. *The Silent World* by Captain Jacques Yves Cousteau, *Diving to Adventure* and *Beneath the Red Sea* by Dr Hans Haas, *The Blue Continent* by Falco Quilici, (which was also a wonderful full length documentary film) and the *Kon Tiki Expedition* by Thor Heyerdahl, were books that opened my eyes to the world and the wonderful adventures that could be had.

Now I wanted to sail to the South Sea Islands, and in particular Tahiti. I wanted to dive beneath the sea and discover the world Hans Haas was writing about. In fact I could hardly contain myself. I spoke to my friend Brian Mealey and together we found a place that catered to people interested in the new sport of Skin Diving where we could get masks, snorkels and flippers, and we headed straight to Williamstown and the rocky foreshore beyond the beach where we plunged into the underwater world with much excitement and lots of awkwardness.

When I suggested to my teacher that *The Weapon Shops of Isher* and *Slan* were great books he asked me to lend them to him so he could read them. They were infinitely better than the Vargo Statten or Volstead Gridban paperbacks I had bought and read while at Footscray intermediate School in Hyde Street, and which I never mentioned to the teacher. I had bought these from Merv Binns at McGills bookshop and they were nice hardcover books and I was proud of them. Well, he read them, and when he gave them back to me he said they were absolute garbage. I was stunned. They were two of my favourite books. He had nothing good to say about any part of them, the writing, the plots, the characters, none of it was any good as far as he was concerned. I dreaded to think what he might have said about Isaac Asimov or Arthur C. Clarke who's *Sands of Mars* I enjoyed but found rather stilted.

Of course he was right, but it was not something I wanted to hear at that age. For a long time I still thought they were fantastic books. In retrospect what attracted me to them was the imagination that could think up the strange and wonderful things that happened in those books. It was the sense of wonder generated in my mind that attracted me to them, not the quality of the writing.

Needless to say that spoilt my English expression and literature classes. I decided I would not go to them for a while and instead I used to sneak off into town where I wandered in and out of bookshops and very soon discovered early sessions at movie theatres in Bourke Street.

I went to early morning demonstrations of Cinemascope at the Regent theatre in Collins Street, and was stunned at how fantastic *The Robe* looked.

Not long after that at the MGM theatre in Collins Street which was just up the hill a short distance from the Regent there was a demonstration of Vista-Vision, Paramount's answer to 20th Century Fox's Cinemascope. I can't remember what film they showed but it was equally as stunning as *The Robe*. Both of those films were in colour which in itself was unusual in the early fifties.

The other theatres in Bourke Street often showed SF films; *Them, The Creature from the Black Lagoon, It came from Outer Space, Forbidden Planet,* (in colour and Cinemascope! And with weird electronic sounds instead of awful music. How far ahead of the pack was this film?) Then there was *20,000 Leagues Under The Sea* (also in colour and cinemascope), *War of the Worlds, The Conquest of Space* (in colour and Vista Vision), *This Island Earth,* (also in colour and widescreen), *The Day The Earth Stood Still, Godzilla,* and others as well as great westerns like *Shane,* (with Alan Ladd and a wonderfully evil Jack Palance) *Hondo* (with John Wayne) and *The Naked Spur* (with the greatly underrated Robert Ryan), Marlon Brando in *Julius Caesar, The Wild One* and *Viva Zapata* co-starring the wonderful Anthony Quinn. John Steinbeck who wrote the screenplay was nominated for an Acadamy Award for best original story and best screenplay.

There were also plenty of gangster films and one that sticks in my memory was *The Big Heat* which had Lee Marvin doing his best to be nasty and the lovely Gloria Graham who was disfigured when Lee Marvin threw a cup of boiling coffee into her face. I loved all of these films.

After a while it got to the point where instead of going to school I left home as normal and spent the day in the city wandering about or going to see the latest film no matter what it was. I saw just about every film that came on in those Bourke street theatres during that time.

For several months I watched people rushing about going to work while I strolled around with all the leisure time in the world, going to movies, wandering down to Flinders Street railway station and looking over from the Swanston Street bridge at all the lines that ran along beside the river, and wondering where the different trains went.

Eventually of course the teachers at the school noticed my absence and contacted Dad to find out why I wasn't at school. He was furious and gave me hard talking to. I went back to school without telling anyone where I had been or what I had been doing, and knuckled down to catch up on what I had missed. But it didn't stop me from dreaming about strange places and living different adventures.

Towards the end of 1955 my uncle Bill turned up in a car he had driven across Australia. One of Mum's two older brothers, he worked as a Commonwealth Agronomist and had been on loan to the United Nations Food and Agricultural Organization where he was instrumental in developing vast areas of desert in Pakistan to be used for agriculture. He spent a lot of time talking about Pakistan and what life was like there, but that part of his life was over and he was about to go to Darwin where he would oversee a huge project involving Rice planting near Darwin and Peanut growing near Katherine.

This was the first time I had heard about Darwin. Prior to that I barely knew Darwin existed, other than having seen the name on a map of Australia. Apparently he knew it well because he dropped names of important people who lived there who worked in fishing and agriculture, and spoke about pearl diving, ideas about culturing pearls, growing rice in both the wet and the dry seasons, and irrigation schemes in the Ord river area of Western Australia – stuff that sounded fantastic and adventurous to me.

Subconsciously I must have decided that I would go to Darwin although the thought never became concrete until the end of 1957.

Back in English expression my teacher encouraged me to write essays and to read books that were more adventurous and certainly different to those we were supposed to read in class.

Perhaps he saw something in me that he wanted to encourage. He suggested I should read *The Greek Passion* by Nikos Kazantzakis which was made into a film in France which I never saw. I didn't actually read that book until many years later. The first book by Kazantzakis that I read, *Report to Greco,* was in 1965 while sitting on a beach a short ferry ride away from the Greek mainland, a tiny island where few tourists went and where I could be undisturbed while reading — and drinking medium sweet Turkish coffees. I didn't read *Zorba* until after I'd seen the film back in Melbourne with Anthony Quinn playing Zorba. I still think that Anthony Quinn captured the essence of Zorba and that Kazantzakis would have been proud of Quinn's portrayal.

Report to Greco was such a profound book that I decided I would read all of that author's work when I got the chance. So my appreciation of better writing encouraged by my English literature and expression teacher was working, though of course I never thought of it that way back then. I had just discovered a writer who wrote fantastically good books. And not only did he write them in Greek which of course I read in English translation, but he wrote his earlier novels in French which were also translated into English and back into Greek.

What better place to read Kazantzakis could there be than in the country where this writer was born and where he lived while he searched his soul for explication of his own existence?

But again I digress. After the Olympic Games and all the excitement that went on with people from all around the world in Melbourne I just couldn't harbour the thought of going to university and spending another 3 or more years studying. I wanted to be free of that.

I suppose if I'd had some idea of what I wanted to do, going to university would have been easy and inevitable, but I had no idea at all. Neither Mum nor Dad had insisted on me following a specific career as many other parents of Kids at High school did, especially those of migrant parentage. They were going to be doctors or lawyers and they knew all through their school life, choosing subjects to facilitate their objective, while those who weren't really sure were going to be teachers.

But not me; none of those things interested me in the slightest. The subjects I had chosen were things I liked, art, literature, biology and geography. I avoided maths and anything related to maths, so in effect what I had chosen would lead nowhere in the career stakes, but were interesting subjects in themselves.

Back from the dead

The only other memorable event that occurred in 1956 was Mum's brother came back from the dead.

Uncle Bill's twin brother whom Mum always referred to as Jack had disappeared somewhere in New Guinea during the Second World War. No one in the family knew what had happened and for a long period Mum had tried to get the Red Cross to search for him. No records of him were ever found and after much time had passed the thought that he had died during the war finally sunk in and became accepted. Eventually his existence vanished from the thoughts of all the family. Then one day, as the Olympics were drawing to a close the phone rang and Mum answered it, as she usually did.

She let out a scream and dropped the phone. We all ran to see what had happened. She was jumping up and down with excitement, which was no easy feat because Mum was a big woman.

'He's alive, he's alive,' she managed to get out before retrieving the phone. 'Hello…' she said as she regained her breath.

We of course had no idea to whom she was referring. She spoke excitedly into the phone, almost too fast for us to make any sense at all of what she was saying. I heard her say Dad once or twice so she was speaking to Grandpa. We knew he was alive, we had seen him the weekend before; so whoever she was referring to as alive must be someone else. Someone important or she wouldn't have been so excited.

'He's coming over right now,' she told us triumphantly, a huge grin on her face. We looked blank so she added, 'your Uncle Jack who we all thought was dead.'

When she had calmed down she rang Eddie her other brother who lived in Melbourne and he said he was coming over as well. And while we waited for this mysterious uncle of ours to turn up she also called her sister Betty and Jack's twin brother Bill in Sydney to give them the news.

When she finally put the phone down she decided she had better put the kettle on so we could all have a cup of tea. She probably made a batch of scones too. She could whip up a batch of scones and have them in the oven inside of ten minutes. By the time a loud voice called out from the front door, the scones were out of the oven and on the table.

When he arrived we found he was tall and gangly, had the same deep ebullient voice that Uncle Bill had, and looked nothing like him. How could he be a twin brother? I always thought twins should be identical.

There were tears in her eyes when she brought Jack in and introduced him to us. He insisted we call him Lofty, which was apt because he was certainly taller than anyone else in our family. Not long after Lofty arrived Uncle Eddie turned up and let himself in, and shortly after that Grandpa arrived. After initially hearing that Lofty was living in Brisbane, was married and had two children, worked as a car salesman, and had come down to Melbourne to repossess a car that had been bought from him but not paid for after the first instalment, he had decided to look up Curteis in the phone book and found Grandpa listed. He had called Grandpa, and Grandpa had called Mum and that led to the excitement and the sudden batch of scones.

Lofty seemed embarrassed by the excitement and was reticent to talk about himself. He wanted to know about everyone else. But Mum insisted he tell them where he had been and what had happened. As it turned out he was working as a bank teller in Port Moresby when the war broke out. He enlisted and spent most of the war years in New Guinea and the South Pacific. He returned to Australia and settled in Brisbane because he liked the sub-tropical climate. There he worked as a car salesman and currently was the managing director of a large second hand and new Holden dealership on the northern side of Brisbane. He was married and we had two cousins we didn't know about.

There was no way he could have got in touch with anyone during the war and afterwards time seemed to fly by and he never thought much at all about contacting anyone in the family. I suppose he must have wondered what everyone was up to and where they lived, but never did much to find out. This I find is typical of many Australians of British descent. They live their lives and outside of a small circle of friends and associates there is no contact with anyone else. I have found also that as I have got older my tendency is to do the same. Once you have been away for a long time it gets harder and harder to keep in touch with people you have not seen for years, and eventually contact is lost, and you don't even think about it.

I guess we were a little different because of Dad's Greek heritage. Family and compatriots are very important to people of Greek origin and some of this rubbed off on Mum because she was the one who maintained contact with all her brothers and sisters where ever they were, and whenever any of them came to Melbourne they always came to see us, or even if they were in transit through Melbourne to or from another country they would ring from the airport to say hello and have a bit of a chat.

This was also the year my Grandfather died. It was only a few months after Lofty's reappearance and he insisted on paying for the funeral. He said he felt guilty about never contacting him for all that time, but was happy that he had finally got to see him before he died. All the uncles and aunts from all over turned up for Grandpa's funeral and that was actually the last time they were all together in one group.

Having head about Lofty's adventures in New Guinea, and Uncle Bill's work in Pakistan and North Africa and what he was doing in Darwin I began to imagine what it would be like to see a bit of the world. Geography after all had been one of my favourite subjects.

1957 was my matriculation year and about half way through the year I realized I wasn't cut out to go to university like many of the other student seriously studying to do that. If something interested me I could learn enough of it to pass a test without having to study too hard, but if I was not interested in a subject and had been required to take it as part of something needed to complete matriculation or to gain entry to university, then no matter how hard I studied it I wouldn't learn anything.

I loved Biology and Geography, English Expression, and Modern Art, so there were no problems with these. I wanted to do languages, but had chosen the wrong course subjects to include any languages other than Latin, and Latin didn't interest me at all. A dead language! How can you talk to people in a dead language? Mathematics and anything related to maths left me in a coma.

Half way through that final year it was clear I would not gain the full requirements for university, and I didn't really care. I had already decided I would do something adventurous when the school year finished, but exactly what that would be had not become clear at that stage.

The idea of being an artist cropped up. I had entered one of my paintings in an exhibition of secondary school art held in the lower

Melbourne Town Hall, and one night I received a phone call from a man who said he wanted to buy my painting and he offered me 20 pounds. I couldn't believe it. This got me thinking. Of course I immediately told him yes, you could have it for 20 pounds.

I gave him my address and within a few days the cheque arrived in the mail. I never saw the painting again because he collected it at the end of the exhibition which saved me the trouble of bringing it back home. I was so excited about that sale that I started a lot of paintings with the intention of one day having an exhibition of my own. I remember that painting. It was of a dead tree jutting up into a burnt sky out of a cracked and desiccated landscape…an image of something I had read in a science fiction story.

That image, which cropped up in several paintings I later did, had stuck in my mind and I simply had to paint it as a subject for art class. Everyone was painting pretty landscapes or classical still life images, while I was painting an image of the world shrivelled and burnt, bathed in the light of a swollen sun. Could this have been caused by the fear of a nuclear holocaust? We had all been told about the atom bomb tests and seen images of the devastation caused by these bomb blasts. Perhaps images from recent disaster stories I had read like the one where a deep crack opened up in the ocean and all the water drained away or boiled away leaving the Earth dessicated and barren had affected the way I imagined the future could be. Disaster stories of one kind or another were popular during the late fifties on into the early sixties. I read them all, so there is no doubt my imagination was affected by them.

I think it could have been Mum who reinforced the idea that travelling is a good way to learn about the world and how others lived. I agreed with her and when I said I wanted to go to Tibet she suggested that I should think about going to Darwin where she knew her brother, my Uncle Bill was presently located.

It was the end of 1957, and having finished year 12 at University High School, I decided not to go on the Melbourne University because I didn't have any idea of what I wanted to do. As Mum had reminded me, I had an Uncle who was head of Plant Industry in the Northern Territory who was instrumental in setting up the big rice growing experiment south of Darwin at Humpty Doo, so I decided I would hitchhike to Darwin.

I thought about that for several weeks after school finished – Darwin was as far as you can go while still being in Australia – and decided that

I would go there instead of Tibet.

I told Mum and Dad I wanted to go to Darwin and Mum just smiled.

I can't remember what Dad's reaction was. I'm sure it wasn't supportive at first, but Mum wasn't opposed to the idea. I heard her tell Dad later that 'Bill is in Darwin. I'll let him know John is coming and he will look after him. They get on well together so there shouldn't be any problems.'

I don't know what Dad replied to that but eventually he accepted the idea that I was going to Darwin, and didn't say anything else against it. Possibly Mum wrote to her brother and told him what I was going to do, but I'm not sure about that. She did give me his address and told me to look him up as soon as I got there. By the time the year had ended Dad was used to the idea having heard me talk about it often enough for it to be familiar and accepted.

Finally the school holidays were over and while most of my school mates waited anxiously to see their results (published in the morning newspapers) I couldn't have cared less. I knew I wouldn't have passed all the subjects required for university anyway; I'd missed too much time and had mucked about without studying, coming late, skipping classes, and so on. When it was time for them to go back to school or to move on to university I packed a duffel bag and got on a train to Adelaide.

A journey begins

It was early January 1958 with hot weather and scorching north winds blasting across the city, a typical summer day back then, and I was thinking that maybe I should have gone to the beach instead. Well the train was air-conditioned and quite comfortable, so that settled that. I was on my way. I can't remember how I got to Spencer Street station but I am assuming that Dad accompanied by Mum drove me there. I was too excited to be getting on a train and heading off into the unknown to remember any details of how I got to the station or when I bought the ticket, or any other of those mundane details. The train was pulling out of the station and I was on the first leg of my trip to Darwin.

I had to change trains in Adelaide, to take one that went north to Port Augusta, but because the train from Melbourne didn't arrive in time for me to catch that other one I would have to stay overnight in Adelaide in order to get the Port Augusta train the next morning. Again I can't remember many details about the overnight stay except that it was in a cheap room not far from the station and that it had pale green thin corrugated metal walls, with pressed tin ceiling also painted pale green. There was a single bed covered with old grey army blankets beside a small night table that had a bible on it. The pillow was lumpy but it was clean. The only light was single dim bulb that dangled from a bare cord coming out of the ceiling. It must have been only 25 or 50 watts because the light it produced barely allowed me to read. It was only bright enough to see the bed and where the door was. I didn't bother to take my book out of the duffel bag.

I think the place was run by the Salvation Army and it catered to drunks and derelicts and to travellers who wanted a very cheap room to sleep in. In any case I didn't want to read. I wanted to sleep, but sleeping proved to be difficult.

It was a noisy place and there was a lot of yelling and drunken cursing coming from a common room nearby, and the fact that the room was not all that great kept me awake for a long time. Heat radiated down from the tin ceiling because it had been just as hot in Adelaide as it had been in Melbourne. I was worried I wouldn't wake up in time to get to the station for the train to Port Augusta, and that didn't help me sleep either. Eventually I fell asleep and woke up with lots of noise as the people in the common room were making their way to a communal kitchen and dining room where breakfast was being served. I didn't want to miss my train so I didn't stay for breakfast, but I did grab a bread roll and some cheese to eat while I walked to the central station a couple of blocks away.

That morning was bright and sunny, and already warming up even though it was still early. There was a feeling of excitement within me that I couldn't keep down. I was really on my way now.

This was it. I had been to Adelaide before and was not impressed, but this time, on my own, heading into the station towards the train waiting to go north, it dawned on me that I really was venturing out into the unknown.

Because of the way Australia developed with each state defiantly independent, the engineers who designed and built the railways created different and non-compatible systems. Victoria had broad gauge railways with 5 feet 3 inches separating the rails while NSW and SA had standard gauge railways of 4 feet 8 inches (1.48 metre). Much of Queensland had Narrow gauge and parts of the NT as well as Northern South Australia had narrow gauge which was only 3 feet 6 inches. To go to or from Sydney to Melbourne travellers had to change trains at the NSW border in order to complete the journey. (*And at one stage when NSW and Victoria were separate colonies rather than idividual states, train passengers also had to pass through a customs checkpoint.*) Although a broad gauge ran all the way from Melbourne to Adelaide, all the other lines in SA used standard gauge, and going north it was standard until Maree where it changed to Narrow gauge to travel through the desert to Alice Springs. If it wasn't for narrow gauge very little of the outback would have been opened up because the cost of running a broader gauge out there was prohibitive.

The trip from Adelaide to Port Augusta was unmemorable and uneventful; through flat or undulating farmland with an occasional water tower jutting up into a cloudless sky. On arrival at Port Augusta, along with most of the people on the train, I transferred to another train almost immediately, after which we sat there at the station for what seemed like hours. I guess it was to enable the transfer of luggage and other goods which was done by uncoupling some carriages from one train and joining them onto the other one while we all sat inside waiting. Eventually this train took off but stopped not long after at a place called Quorn where we stayed for at least another two hours, again I presume to load on goods for transport further up the line. This was to be a common occurrence later in life whenever I travelled anywhere — a lot of time was spent waiting either to get started or to continue after stopping for some obscure reason.

By the time we went on up into the Simpson's Ranges, through them and down into the beginnings of the desert country and passed through Leigh Creek, it got dark. It was almost like a light being switched off. There was no long twilight like in Melbourne and it got dark much quicker than I had expected.

The moon wasn't up and the stars glittered so brightly I imagined if I had wanted to I could have counted every one of them. I had good eyes in those days. The Milky Way wasn't a smudge as it was in Melbourne, but was sharp and clear with millions of individual stars. I could even see faint specks that were probably massive stars or galaxies but they were so many light years away it was almost impossible to conceive such distances.

I tried to see Sputnik the first Russian satellite that had everyone so excited when it was launched only a couple of months previously, but there were too many bright stars and with the movement of the train I couldn't tell if any one star in particular was moving rapidly across the sky. It was up there but I couldn't see it. Nevertheless a shiver ran up my spine as I reminded myself that the space age had really begun the moment they launched sputnik. It wouldn't be too long before all the things I had been reading about in my science fiction novels would start to happen, space ships and stations, moon bases and colonies on other worlds.

What a great time to live in, I thought as I stared up at the night sky.

The Ghan

The train arrived at Maree about 10 pm. and everybody had to get off with all their luggage and wait while the other train, the Ghan, was being prepared for the rest of the journey through to Alice Springs.

I was surprised there was no station. It was exciting climbing down off the train. It made me think of all those cowboy films I had seen where the trains drove along the main street of some frontier town and there was never a proper station. Every other time I had got onto or off a train it had been on a platform and you just stepped in or out of the door. But here it was dark and all of those on board had to climb down a couple of steps onto the ground. Some people struggled with large suitcases but all I had was a duffel bag and I threw that over my shoulder and quickly jumped down.

We walked across a broad dusty expanse towards several buildings with wide verandas. It was hard to see how dusty it was but you could smell it in the air. Bright lights glared around the trains but the space between the trains and the distant buildings was black as pitch. Halfway across and away from the glare of the floodlights I could see the silhouettes of people moving about in front of the local pub where everyone was heading to for a few beers and something to eat.

Suddenly I jumped as a tall dark shape with four legs walked across in front of me blotting out the pub's lights. It was quickly followed by a man hissing at it and hitting it with a long stick. Clouds of dust swirled around as it passed and I realised it was a camel. I'd never seen a camel up close before. I wished I could see more of it but in the dark it was not possible. I could hear it shuffling away and snorting as the man with it slapped it with his stick. It didn't take long for the sound of it to disappear in the dark as well, covered up by the voices of the people walking across to the pub. I wondered if any of them had seen it.

Camels were probably still occasionally used back then to get stuff out to remote places. Trains of them once ferried goods up through the desert to Alice Springs. They belonged to Afghan keepers who were brought out along with their camels to help open up the inland desert areas. Now that the Ghan did what they used to –even appropriating an abbreviation of the name Afghan– the camels had been let loose and they ran wild becoming feral. The few tame ones left were probably used to give visitors a ride around the town.

No one could have imagined then that fifty and more years later camels would be feral pests over-running the centre of Australia and across to the far West in their millions doing untold damage to the natural environment. The government of today is talking about culling them, to bring them down to a level that isn't destructive to the environment so a balance can be maintained. But with hunters shooting up to 25,000 a year and costing millions of dollars, no headway is being made because the camels are breeding at the rate of 80,000 per year. Something else has to be done before the camels become worse pests than rabbits. Perhaps they can be harvested and butchered and sold as meat. There are lots of places that would love supplies of camel meat.

I even have a recipe in an old Greek cookbook that tells how to marinate and roast camel meat. The introduction to the recipe states: *Today the camel is a gastronomical curiosity to the Western World. Greeks no longer consider it edible, but in Ancient Greece camel meat was served to royalty. Aristophanes mentions camel meat in his writings and praises it as being tasty. (See page 17 The Complete Greek Cookbook – The best from 3000 years of Greek cooking, by Theresa Karas Yianilos, published in the USA sometime in the 1950's.)*

It was noisy and crowded in the pub and the food was terrible. I had a pie that was either dried up or made from some kind of dark meat that was dry and chewy. I didn't want to ask if it was kangaroo (*maybe it was camel!*) but put lots of tomato sauce on top of it to disguise the taste. I washed it down with a couple of beers and no one said anything to me about being too young to buy drinks. I was almost eighteen anyway. Hanging on to my second drink I went back outside because it was too noisy and smoky inside the pub.

It was dark between the pub and the train lines, but the trains were brightly lit with powerful searchlights, and this only accentuated the inky blackness of the in between space. Several trucks with cranes on them were lifting flatbed carriages that had been part of the train from Port Augusta off the standard bogies and placing them on the narrow gauge bogies. These flat-bed carriages were stacked with boxes and crates tied down to prevent shifting. Once the flatbeds were secure the carriage was shunted towards the back of the Ghan and connected.

I watched cranes lift cars and small trucks belonging to people who didn't want to risk the rough drive along the track from Maree to Alice Springs, and as they swung back and forth while the cranes drove across to the narrow gauge flatbeds already hitched to the Ghan I wondered what they would do if the chains came loose and the vehicle fell down onto the ground.

It didn't happen. Those people obviously knew what they were doing. Clouds of dust rose up accentuating the searchlight's powerful beams making the activity look mysterious. Finally, close to midnight when everything had been transferred an announcement broke into the cacophony of the pub to inform the passengers that it was time to board the Ghan.

Long lines of people straggled across the dusty expanse towards the Ghan, climbed on board and looked for seats. Some had sleeping compartments, but I didn't. I would sleep sitting up on hard backed seats, as would many others. I found a spot, tossed my duffel bag into the overhead rack and sat down thinking the train would take off soon, but it didn't. It waited and waited and still people drifted in and wandered along the carriages looking for somewhere to sit. It must have been 2 or 3 am before the train lurched and slowly inched forward. I could hear the engines up ahead roaring loudly as they slowly built up speed.

It was a very long train beyond the half dozen passenger carriages, more than half a mile long with all the goods carriages on behind. It took forever to get up speed and when it did, it wasn't very fast.

'I reckon I could get out and walk faster,' some wag sitting a few rows beyond me said. There was a bit of laughter but it quickly died away as everyone tried to make themselves comfortable. There was a lot of fidgeting because the hard wooden seats were not the best for relaxing or sleeping.

There were children complaining and mothers trying to calm them down, families on their way home after a holiday down south in Adelaide. There were quite a few younger people, teenagers like myself, also returning home after school holidays or heading north for work, adventure, sightseeing; stuff like that. Most of the passengers were probably like me and had been travelling interspersed with waiting to travel, all day. It wasn't the travelling that tired you, I decided, what did it was the waiting. It did take a long time though for people to settle down. Fortunately everyone had a seat; they had to because it was to be a long trip.

It would be at least two days before we got to Alice Springs and the Ghan would stop at lots of places to unload mail and goods to the various Cattle and Outback Stations along the way. Some people would get off and be left standing beside a sign with nothing anywhere for miles but they didn't seem the slightest bit worried. At other places there would be people leaning against a battered 4 wheel drive waiting beside the track for the train to stop so they could unload their supplies. I was thinking about that and what I would see as the light from the train windows lit the scrub beside the tracks, but found it difficult to keep my eyes open. I was hoping to see something of Lake Eyre. I knew we were going to pass right by the end of the smaller Lake Eyre South and that it stretched for miles, dead flat and blisteringly white. It was twelve metres below sea level and was very hot during the day, and that land speed records had been attempted and set on the larger lake's flat salt bed. It would have been an interesting thing to see and I thought it would be visible even in the starlight.

It seemed as if the train stood still while the scrub flitted past gradually becoming more and more blurred as I lost focus. I kept looking for the glow of the lake but after such a long and exhausting day, not to mention sleeping poorly the night before, and with a couple of beers in me I eventually fell asleep.

I woke up as the train lurched. I sat there blinking and trying to orientate myself. The train gently rocked and rattled. It made me think of a boat as it rocked one way for a moment suddenly coming to a stop with a pronounced jerk before rocking back the other way to repeat the procedure on the other side. Now I understood why there were chains linking the sides of the carriages to the bogeys where the wheels were. The carriages were top heavy with a high centre of gravity and the tracks were narrow on ground that undulated. If the train moved too fast the carriages could easily topple over, they simply didn't have the stability that the broader gauge trains had. The chains stopped side to side movement and kept the carriages more or less centred over the bogeys. The movement at first was quite unsettling, but once you got used to it everything was fine. The Ghan trundled along at the glorious speed of about twenty five miles per hour while gently rocking from side to side.

I went back to sleep and only woke up once when the train stopped beside a small shack where several mail bags were offloaded. I could see pale sand lit by the light spilling out of the train's windows, but beyond the point where the light stopped it was black. The moon had disappeared and though the stars were bright, they weren't bright enough to light up the land enough for anyone to see while their eyes were accustomed to the brightness inside the train.

After about fifteen minutes we started moving again, rattling slowly forward while rocking from side to side. I got up and went down to the end of the carriage where I could step out onto a small balcony. Beyond this carriage were the mail carriages and the other ones that carried goods of all kinds, and beyond them were the flatcars where cars and vans and small trucks were tied on with chains. As the train went around a wide but gentle curve I could see all those other carriages stretched out into invisibility in the darkness. I though the train must have been at least a mile and a half long. No wonder it took so long to get up to the cruising speed.

The air was bitingly cold, very crisp, which surprised me even though I knew from geography classes that it could get down to freezing at night in the desert while the days were incredibly hot — to actually experience it was something new to me. The air had a dry dusty smell without the slightest hint of humidity. As the morning brightened and the day began I could see out into the desert and it was absolutely beautiful with red sand dunes for mile after mile broken only by the odd scabby bush or sometimes small clumps of spindly grass that seemed too bright and green against the intensity of the red sand. On the side of one passing dune there were a bunch of pale small melons attached to a vine like shrub sprawled across the sand. It seemed so incongruous to me. A little while later I saw some more of them and was told they were poisonous. In the distance a shimmering line of faded trees marked the course of a dry creek bed. It wasn't long before they disappeared behind us as the Ghan wound along its course between endless sand dunes.

I saw little wisps of sand being blown off the top of the dunes to trickle down the sides making ripples that reminded me of the beach at Barwon Heads and Ocean Grove where the tide left a long flat area that the Barwon river water trickled over to create thousands of hard ripples. Only the sand here was red and soft and it made me think that Mars could look like this. It made me think not of *The Sands of Mars* by Arthur C Clarke but of another book where the sands were alive rather than dead. Of course Mars would have been much colder, I knew that, but that didn't seem to bother Ray Bradbury and his descriptions of Mars matched what I could see out beyond the train better than those of Arthur C Clarke. Perhaps it was the poetic visions of Mars that Bradbury wrote of that captured my imagination. I also imagined Edgar Rice Burroughs books with all the action that took place on his mythical Mars. I could see it taking place out there, in the vastness of the sand dunes that seemed to stretch far beyond the horizon.

A track ran parallel to the railway line and this was the track you would drive along if you decided not to take the train. It was covered with drifting fine sand and in some places was completely buried. It would have been impossible for anything but a 4 wheel drive vehicle to travel along it. A loose dangling wire cable slung from a series of narrow poles half buried in the drifting sand ran alongside the track on the side away from the train line. Was this the original telegraph cable that connected Alice Springs with the South and through that to the rest of the country? Or did this original cable run further to the West? The condition of the one I could see looked as if it had been long abandoned – perhaps it was only a telephone line strung up to connect a few outback stations.

One of the reasons the Ghan travelled so slowly was because the railway lines were not firmly fixed to each sleeper but only to every fourth or fifth one, and if the train moved too fast it would derail or cause the lines to shift enough to make the train to run off the rails.

I was told the rails weren't fixed because often the lines got washed away during flash floods and it was much easier and quicker to replace them if they didn't have to fix the rail line to each sleeper. That would take too much time for the few people whose job it was to look after the railway line to repair before the next train was due either coming south from The Alice or going north from Marree. There were supposed to be three trains per week but this rarely happened and usually there was only one each way each week and that was it.

I didn't know whether to believe that or not. It did sound plausible and this was borne out when we stopped later that day before a wide flat area that looked as dry as anywhere else but was supposedly a river bed. Someone said it was the Hamilton Creek and this was long past Oodnadatta and Mount Dutton where I couldn't see any sign of a Mount other than a small hill some distance away from the track across a plain covered with glistening blood-red stones. The hill looked green as if covered in grass but I suspect it was more to do with traces of copper in the stones than any grass, because there was no grass growing anywhere there.

The air rippled with heat rising off the stones. The sky was so intensely clear and blue it was hard to imagine that it could have rained anywhere nearby. But there had been a flash flood the day before and the rail lines were all over the place, broken in a couple of spots. In some places there were no sleepers; they were scattered far and wide along the broad river bed. There was no sign of water but the damage it did was easily seen.

We had to wait for a crew coming down from Alice Springs to arrive to fix it. Most of the passengers got off to sit or wander about in the shade of the train. With the Ghan not moving it was too hot to stay inside.

A couple of hours after we stopped several flatbeds loaded with spare rails and sleepers pulled by a noisy engine that belched black diesel fumes into the air arrived on the other side of the dry river bed. It took the repair crew half a day to replace the twisted rail lines and sit them onto new sleepers laid across the river bed. They left the twisted lines off to one side and didn't bother to go and collect the sleepers that had been washed down stream. The crew took off ahead of us and very slowly the Ghan moved forward down onto the newly replaced section and finally we traversed the river bed and went back up onto higher ground. There were lots of short stops at remote farms and sidings over the next two days before I saw in the distance the low line of purple hills that were the MacDonnell ranges. Alice Springs was through a gap in those ranges.

I had gotten used to being on the train and was feeling a bit nervous about what I would do when it finally arrived at Alice Springs. People very quickly adapt to routine and on a train like the Ghan routine is what you got. Three meals served in batches in the dining car, regular stops to unload and pick up mail or other goods and the camaraderie of fellow passengers all of whom were interesting or were preparing to do something interesting when they left the train. One of the many people I spoke to said he was driving up to Katherine and that if I wanted he would give me a lift. That was fantastic, because Katherine was three quarters of the way to Darwin.

'There's a light rail carriage that runs from Katherine to Darwin,' he told me, 'so you can go the rest of the way by train.'

The only problem was that this chap was in a hurry to get to Katherine and would leave as soon as his small truck was unloaded from the Ghan. I would not have an opportunity to see anything of Alice Springs, but that didn't matter. Darwin was my destination and passing up a long lift just to do a bit of sight-seeing would be silly. Besides, when I came home I would have to come back the same way so I could make up for it by staying in The Alice then so I could see what there was to see.

I watched the cars and trucks being unloaded and the people fussing about with worried looks on their faces as their vehicles were picked up by cranes and were roughly dumped onto the ground beside the train. They needn't have worried because not a mark, scratch or dint was added by the rough handling.

After about half an hour this chap's truck was unloaded and he called me over.

'Are you ready to go?' he asked.

'I sure am,' I told him.

'I need to get some diesel in the tank first,' he explained. 'Chuck your duffel in the back and hop in.'

I did this and a few minutes later we were off, leaving the bustle behind us, heading north along the bitumen. He topped up the tank at a service station after which it hardly seemed more than a few seconds before we were out of town and heading along the unbroken stretch of highway that linked Alice Springs with Darwin.

An endless strip of bitumen

As I sat back in the seat and stared at the heat waves rising up off the bitumen far ahead I finally accepted the fact that I was on my way. On the Ghan it had been different, leisurely, but this was something else, on an empty road and almost alone, hot air blasting in through the open window, tyres thrumming on the bitumen, the truck ripped along at a pace much faster than the Ghan had travelled.

All that had come before had been preliminary, now the travelling felt real.

I couldn't wait to get to Darwin.

What do I remember about the road trip? Not a great deal. Little things — like someplace on the map giving the impression it was a substantial town or place to stop, only to find when we got there it was no more than a dilapidated old pub type roadhouse that had seen better days, and nothing else. The first one of these we stopped at was at least a four hour drive north of Alice Springs.

Dust swirled around in a tight eddy as we pulled up in front of two old bowsers where the driver of the truck used one to top up his diesel tank. Just as he finished someone came out of the building to check how much he put in and to collect the money. They chatted while I went inside the old diner to see what there was to drink. It was cool inside but so dark it took a minute for my eyes to adjust. I heard the screen door slam shut behind me as the driver came in. It was just like a suburban pub only older looking, I discovered once I could see in the gloom. There were a couple of people seated at the bar and one of them turned to see who had come in while the other simply sat immobile and stared at his drink. A young girl popped her head around the edge of a door leading to a food preparation area, took a brief look and just as quickly disappeared from sight.

'We should get something to eat,' the driver said, 'because I won't be stopping until we get to Tennant Creek.'

I wasn't really that hungry. 'How far away is that?' I asked.

'I dunno…maybe another six hours driving. It's halfway to Katherine so I'll probably stop there for the night.'

'Maybe we should get something,' I had to agree.

There wasn't much to eat, just the usual crap. But the girl came back out and said she would make some sandwiches for us so we decided to have those with some soft drinks.

Not long after that we were on our way again, thundering along the endless narrow strip of bitumen. We passed a road train which was the first time I had seen a truck prime mover with several trailers coupled on behind. It really did look like a train. It looked dangerous to me. I could feel our small truck being buffeted and pushed sideways by the wind pushed aside by the road train as it roared past us heading south. We passed several more of these road trains all filled with cattle as the day progressed.

The landscape remained much the same, mostly red desert with sparkling ghost gums, white trunks glowing in clumps here and there with pale purple shaded hills in the distance to the west. There were flat topped mesas, small hills, and drifting sand dunes interspersed with Spinifex. Dust devils whipped up the bright red sand, whirling it high into the sky before dissipating and allowing the sand to rain down onto a different dune. The sky above started off absolutely clear but gradually as the day progressed it became streaky with fine wisps of cloud far up in the stratosphere. We also passed a few roadside petrol stops much the same as the one where we had refilled with diesel and some sandwiches, but we didn't stop. Sometimes there was a car or a 4-wheel drive parked beside the wide veranda that inevitably surrounded these roadside places, and sometimes there didn't appear to be anyone there. Rarely did we see anyone outside these places. If anyone was there they would have been inside where it was much cooler. It was summer and in the middle of the day, and the air that blew past us was hot, but the fact we were moving is what kept us comfortable. It would simply have been too hot to spend much time wandering about out in the open.

We did stop at Devil's Marbles just past the Wauchope Roadhouse so we could stretch our legs; have a toilet break. I think he really stopped so I could have a look at this beautiful natural rock formation. The so called marbles are huge granite boulders that have weathered over millions of years into huge round balls that seemed to be randomly

— *Ephemeron* —

scattered across the land on both sides of the highway. Some are precariously balanced on top of others, and I imagined a slight wind pressing against these might make them roll off, but this never happens. They have remained like this for as long as people passing through can remember, solidly welded together by the forces of nature. I was told the local Warramunga people consider these stone formations to be eggs of the Rainbow Serpent.

Eggs of the Rainbow Serpent – Devil's Marbles. The figure at the base gives an idea of the size of these massive granite boulders.

A split caused through natural weathering.
The contrast between boiling hot daytime temperatures and freezing night temperatures causes expansion and contraction on the surface and within the rock. Often a split will occur. Over time the edges will begin to flake off and eventually the straight split becomes rounded. Given enough time, almost perfect gigantic egg shaped rocks appear.

We spent half an hour wandering amongst the massive rock balls before returning to the truck and continuing on.

As dusk approached I could see in the distance ahead the brighter glow of lights that indicated a substantial town.

Tennant Creek is a junction, a town that evolved because of the highway that links Queensland with the Northern Territory. The Barkly Highway runs eastward to Mount Isa, the famous mining town just over the border in Queensland and splits into two different highways just past the town to become the Lansdsborough Highway going to Winton and Longreach and eventually Brisbane (retaining the same highway number) while the other one becomes the Flinders Highway linking Charters Towers and Townsville on the tropical coast.

The Stuart Highway runs north from Alice Springs to Darwin. If you wanted to go to Queensland from the Northern Territory then the Barkly Highway is the only way that is an easy drive. The two don't actually meet in Tennant Creek but do a short distance north at a place called the Three Ways Roadhouse. It is somewhat more grandiose than other roadhouses along the Stuart Highway and caters for tourists, general travellers and the truckies who take the road trains north and south as well as east and west, a very busy place at all times.

The Stuart highway is named after the explorer John McDougall Stuart who found and opened the way from Adelaide to the far north in 1860. He made it possible for the telegraph link from Australia to Europe through Asia. Most of the roadside stops were where the original wells were dug for water supplies which encouraged some sparse settlement along the route. The Stuart highway virtually follows the same route north and south. It has however in later years had some of the twists and bends taken out of it so it is a much straighter run than before.

Tennant Creek was named after the South Australian Pastoralist John Tennant by John McDougall Stuart who stopped there on his way north. In 1872 an overland telegraph station was established and this encouraged some pastoral settlement in the area. The Town just south of the creek grew rapidly especially when gold was discovered and mining commenced in 1930. Copper was mined in 1950.

I was surprised at how wide the street through the centre of the town was. There was at least 100 metres of space on either side of the bitumen strip that was the highway. There were lots of cars angle parked on both sides close to a footpath with overhanging verandas. Crowds of people were out and about now that the desert air had started to cool. As soon as the sun went down the temperature rapidly dropped with the heat of the day dissipating up into a clear sky. The first stars were twinkling as we drove into the town and pulled up in front of a hotel. This was not the kind of hotel where you stayed, but the kind where you did a lot of drinking. As we walked in it was already crowded and raucous.

'Why don't you get a couple of beers for us,' the driver said. 'I have a phone call to make.'

'Sure, not a problem.'

By the time the two beers were placed on the bar in front of me the driver was back. 'We're not staying here tonight. I have to keep going. Is that all right with you?'

It didn't worry me. As long as he was giving me a lift I would go along when he left. I wasn't going to argue about it.

'Something's come up and I have to get to Katherine sooner than I anticipated. We'll get some dinner then be on our way. Okay?'

We drank the beers and they felt terrific after a long hot drive. As soon as they were down we went outside and wandered along the footpath until we found a café where we could get something reasonable to eat. I think it was called The Acropolis Café or something Greek anyway. The owner reminded me of my uncle George who always had country cafes as long as he was working, but he never moved out of Victoria. I had steak and eggs with chips and salad, and it was fantastic, very substantial. We followed it with coffee.

We stopped shortly after driving out of town at the roadhouse where the highways met and refuelled the truck. I insisted on paying for it but he wouldn't let me telling me that if he was alone he would have to pay for it himself anyway, but eventually after some discussion he agreed to half which I gave him. Feeling much better about that I jumped back into the cabin and soon we were on our way driving into a tunnel of light spearing through the dark.

It's strange how sometimes there is no warning, no slow drifting away into unconsciousness, but a sudden switching off.

One moment I was staring ahead trying to see beyond the range of the headlights.

Then without any apparent passing of time I was opening my eyes to see luscious green grass at least a metre high whipping past us as we drove towards Katherine.

The air was hot and humid even though it was still early in the morning. There was no more of the dry dusty smell of the desert, the air here smelt of green things and rotting vegetation and the sound of cicadas waking up filled the air with their strident mating calls.

'Wow, this is certainly different,' I said.

'A couple more miles and we'll be there. How'd you sleep?'

'…pretty good I suppose. I didn't feel a thing. I don't even remember dreaming, so it must have been a deep sleep.'

'You were out like a log.'

'Sorry.'

'Don't worry. You must have needed it. We'll be in Katherine in a few minutes and I'll drop you off at the railway station. It's not really a train, but it will take you to Darwin. There's only one a day so I hope we can make it in time or you'll be sitting there until tomorrow morning.'

He was right. It wasn't a train but two carriages coupled together. Both carriages had a diesel engine at the end so there was no need to turn around at either end of the journey. The driver simply went to the driver's compartment at the end of the second carriage, switched on the engine and that end then became the front, while the previous front then became the other end. There was a single narrow gauge line extending from the station northwards and the two carriages sat at the station with the northern engine rumbling when I got my ticket and walked on to the station.

Two people sat in the back carriage and one halfway along in the front. With me on board there were only four passengers going to Darwin. It had come down from Darwin overnight and was ready for the return trip. I wasn't sure how long the small train would stay there so I boarded the front carriage straight away, and sat beside a window a couple of seats back from the engine driver's compartment. There was a doorway that joined the two carriages so I could change while we were travelling if I decided to sit elsewhere. The toilet was in the second carriage so if I wanted to use it I would have to go in there anyway.

The seats were placed across the carriage facing each other so you either sat facing the direction you were travelling or facing the other way. I preferred to sit facing the direction of travel. The backs of the seats were moulded plywood stained with a dark varnish while the actual seat part was covered with hard padding with a dark durable cover; nothing fancy.

I was starting to feel hungry and wondered if here would be enough time to go and get some breakfast. There was nothing on the station that hinted you could get food which meant I would have to go into town to see if any place was open. It was barely seven in the morning so it seemed unlikely. But before I could think much more about it a loud hoot came from in front of the train.

The man who sold me the ticket was standing on the platform and waving to the driver. Another loud hoot and the train started forward smoothly and with only a slight increase in the rumble of the diesel engine. We were on our way and breakfast would have to wait.

Through a green tunnel

The thing I remember most about the journey from Katherine to Darwin was the greenness, the train was trundling along though a tunnel of green. It was much smoother than the old Ghan to Alice Springs and the engine powering the two carriages was much quieter. On either side tall thick grass grew right to the edge of the rock base the rail lines sat on. As it whipped past some of it sometimes brushed against the side of the carriage with a soft whooshing sound. When the train crossed a creek it did so suddenly. The height of the grass along the edges of the track obscured any advance sight for someone who might be looking out of the window and when we crossed over on a bridge the appearance

of a creek or a small river was like a snapshot; a momentary glimpse of glistening water, rippling over sand and rocks, Pandanus palms hanging over with roots extending down from the underside of the branches as they reached for the water below. I caught a glimpse of a huge pendulous fruit hanging beneath a clump of Pandanus. It looked like an elongated fat green pineapple, only the segments covering it were like huge scales, and the thought that entered my mind was it looked primitive, reptilian. Can a fruit look reptilian? Then it was gone as instantly as it had appeared, leaving nothing but a rapidly fading afterimage, and we were back to tall grass swishing by as we trundled through the green tunnel.

The desert south of Tennant Creek, covered with fresh flowers, green bushes and trees.

It was as if Katherine was inside an invisible wall, a line of demarcation between two different climates. South of the wall it was a desert; dry and dusty, with stunted trees and bushes interspersed with Spinifex. The further south you went the dryer it became. It was only when an occasional shower drenched the region, which was not very often, that it would bust into life with wild flowers almost growing overnight to fill the desert with colour and fragrance and buzzing insects searching for honey. If no more rain came, it would revert back to desert sand and dry scrub within weeks.

North of the wall it was lush, wet, the air thick with entrained moisture. It was January and well into the wet season and it rained every day. Grass that had lain dormant for the dry season sprouted and grew at a prodigious pace. I was told it grew around Darwin at the rate of 5 centimetres a day. You could actually sit and watch it grow! When I first got there the wild grass along the roadsides stood waist high as I walked from the train stop into town.

Three weeks later by the end of January it was shoulder height. It took some time for me to get used to that.

Heavy wet air

The little train had been air-conditioned and I didn't really notice how heavy the air was until I stepped out of the carriage at the terminus on the outskirts of Darwin.

I walked to the end of the station and looked towards the harbour which wasn't very far away. *There was no water there!* Boats were sitting in the mud with ropes to hold them in place reaching up to the top of long poles the height of lamp posts and a jetty not far from a thin bitumen road that went to the edge of where the water should be stood way up in the air at least 30 feet above the slushy mud. (We still used feet and inches, *the imperial system,* back in 1958. The thought of using a decimal system had barely entered anyone's consciousness.) *Where did the water go?* How far out does it retreat when the tide goes out? I found out later that all across the top end the average tidal rise and fall is about twenty feet, and if the bay is shallow then when the tide goes out it goes out for a half mile or more, exposing a vast area of mud flats.

A pale glistening line almost on the horizon indicated the sea was out there somewhere. Huge cumulous clouds roiled up with massive cauliflower heads reaching far up into a deep blue sky. The flat bottoms of the clouds looked dark and ominous, deep grey with shadings of charcoal and black. They stretched in a long line from East to West as far as I could see. Beneath them what I could see of the distant sea glowed with a hint of translucent green. Closer to shore and near the high jetty there were a couple of shipwrecks, rusted jagged iron flanks uncovered and burning in the sun.

That short walk to the end of the station made me start sweating. Within a minute I was wet all over as every pore leaked fluid. I might as well have been in a Turkish bath. I had seen pictures of fat ugly men draped in towels, glistening with sweat while sitting together in the steam and it was not something I imagined I would ever want to experience, but standing there with my clothes stuck to me the image of being in a Turkish bath filled my mind. *Had I made a mistake in coming to Darwin?*

Mud flats with poles used to tie up small boats when the tide comes in. from an 8mm film.

Street scene in Darwin, January 1958.

I looked along the narrow road from the station and it went up a short rise and turned to the left. There was no one else on the platform. The few others who had boarded the train at several stops along the way had vanished. Even the driver was gone. I hadn't heard any busses or cars coming while I was looking at the distant horizon but everyone was gone. I assumed they had simply walked up the road into town, so there was nothing else I could do but emulate them.

Just picking up my duffel bag and slinging it over my shoulder made me burst into sweat again. There was no movement in the air and it seemed to cling to me like a heap of wet rags. Down on the mud flats the air shimmered as the sun baked the moisture out of it. I wondered if there were any crocodiles in the mangroves along the edge of the mud; if they came this close to Darwin I had no idea. I wasn't going to look for them, that's for sure. I started walking up the road into town.

The sun was burning into the shirt on my back as I trudged up the road and I continued to sweat. If it kept up I would soon be dehydrated. How much fluid can you sweat out? I didn't want to find an answer to that.

It didn't take long to arrive at the edge of the town. Darwin wasn't very big, at least not then. I remember walking past a few houses and building on stilts that cast deep shadows beneath them, and before long I was walking past the commonwealth bank with its brick walls with holes in it for air circulation separating the proper part of the building itself. It was the coolest building in town and it wasn't even air conditioned. I found myself in front of a hotel so I went in and found a room. This was a hotel where rooms could be had and they usually filled up for the weekends as workers came into town to spend Saturday and Sunday boozing and fighting. They would stay there and return after the weekend to their jobs in the bush. Most of the other so called hotels along the highway were really only bars. Few people ever stayed in them although I suspect they probably had to have some official accommodation to be classified and licensed as a hotel, the owners were really only interested in selling beer.

The bar was huge and was full of people drinking and talking at the tops of their voices. The barman sent me into the lounge where someone else checked me in and gave me a room. It was a Monday so there were plenty of rooms to choose from.

On my way to the hotel I had passed what appeared to be a boarding house, really a flop house where a lot of scruffy blokes were sitting under the shade drinking and smoking. I didn't want to stay there and had walked on past it. There were drunks sleeping on the footpath, half in and half out of a couple of doorways. Very dark aboriginal people congregated under a tree in a small public park. I had never seen any as dark as that. It reminded me of a documentary film I had seen in one of Melbourne's theatres about Africa and there were people in that film so black that they appeared to be navy blue and you could see nothing but their eyes and their teeth when they smiled. They were so dark in contrast to the brightness of their surroundings that the colour film used had been unable to register facial details.

All along the streets there were huge Mango and Morton Bay fig trees with gnarled roots pushing up the edges of footpaths, tall palms that brushed the bottom of the sky with lacy fronds, and sometimes a banyan tree or a clump of bamboo. The smell was like that of all tropical places; rotting plants, damp mould, sickly sweet flowers and sometimes something that smelled like dead rats. And the air was warm and thick and heavy with contained moisture that seemed to sweat out on anything smooth. The ground was dry, but the smooth side of one building I passed had beads of moisture all over it. A tiny rivulet would appear as some beads got too heavy and breaking the surface tension they would run down the wall to the ground, grabbing other beads of moisture on the way.

It was much cooler in the hotel room and although I could hear the noise from the bar I soon fell into an exhausted sleep. Tomorrow would be soon enough to go looking for Uncle Bill. I woke during the night to hear a muffled roar that echoed over the whole building. It took a few moments before I realized it was raining. It was like the whole building vibrated with the force of it coming down. It stopped after a few minutes and I went back to sleep.

In the morning it was fresh and the humidity seemed bearable. I went out and found a clear sky and the only clouds visible were far out over the sea, small clumps of cumulous. The ground in the shade of buildings was still wet with wisps of steam rising from it. The bitumen of the street and the footpath was dry. Stepping into the sun to cross the street I felt the burning intensity of it. No wonder there were wisps of rising steam as the air heated and evaporated water trapped in the shadow areas. It was stinking hot, and not much after 8am in the morning.

As I went looking for the government owned apartment building where Uncle Bill was staying I passed the Commonwealth Employment

Service building. There were several groups of people sitting and standing either under trees or under the veranda near the main entrance. Most of them looked bored and many smoked. Most were unshaven, sporting several days' growth and none of them were well dressed. Their clothes looked like they needed a wash, as did their feet. There were a few who were barefoot, but most had some kind of sandals or thongs (flip plops). They were waiting for the office to open so they could put in their applications for unemployment, or —I assumed— looking for work. Some were reading the notices pasted in the window, but most stood around looking bored as they waited. I would not have hired any of them if I was looking for workers.

It took me a couple of hours but I found Uncle Bill's apartment and after knocking on the door and going in when he called out to enter I found him reclining on his bed, shirtless, smoking and listening to the races on the radio. He had the betting pages with the races open beside him and was studying them with considerable interest. He loved the horses and betting on the races. It was a trait that ran in the family. Mum liked listening to the races and made imaginary bets for years before she opened a TAB account and made actual bets with small sums. Uncle Eddie, the youngest of Mum's brothers was an inveterate card player and race goer. He was always telling us how much he had won, but like all true gamblers he never ever told us how much he had lost in between his winnings.

A huge ceiling fan slowly rotated and the gentle downward breeze it produced made the room quite pleasant.

'Wait until this race is finished,' Uncle Bill said, not even bothering to say hello or to ask 'how was the trip?' He grabbed the phone and dialled a number, mumbled something about a pound each way on some horse's name I couldn't catch, and then hung up. There was no TAB then so he must have been ringing a local SP bookmaker who operated out of the back room of a pub. 'How's Mary?' he asked.

I was about to tell him that Mum was fine and sends him her love when he held up his hand to stop me. The race had started.

When the race was over I could see he wasn't too happy. I guess he lost and would have to pay the bookie a pound next time he saw him.

'You win some you lose some,' he said philosophically.

I didn't say anything. I couldn't have cared less. Horse racing and betting never interested me in the least.

'Well, I'd better get dressed,' he said and jumped of the bed. 'I'll take you around to the CES and get something organized. I would hire you straight out but other people might say there was nepotism involved. But if you come to us through the CES no one will question it.'

'I'm easy,' I said.

On the way to the CES we passed a stone building on a small cliff overlooking the harbour. It was the old Post Office. The roof was gone but broken stone walls stood silhouetted starkly against a sky almost too brilliant to look at.

This was the Post Office, the first buiding to be bombed when the Japanese attacked Darwin.

'That was the first building hit with bombs when the Japanese attacked Darwin,' Uncle Bill explained as we stopped to look at it.

I stared at him in surprise. I knew, as did everyone, that Sydney Harbour had been invaded by Japanese mini subs and that one of them blew up a troop ship, but I had no idea Darwin had been attacked.

'It's true,' he said when he saw my expression. 'It was a big secret. The government didn't want anyone to know or the whole country would have panicked.'

He went on to explain that 188 Japanese aircraft flew in over Darwin and bombed the place into rubble. It was the 19th February 1942 and they caught everyone by surprise. There were no air raid sirens to warn people until the bombs started falling and then there was absolute panic with the whole population fleeing into the bush. There was nowhere else to go. They took whatever they could use to get out of town, cars, bikes, horses, trucks, road graders, even the truck that picked up the shit cans. Those that couldn't ride on something fled on foot. Defences were totally inadequate as no one expected the Japanese to ever attack the Australian mainland. The soldiers were the first to go, and with them gone Darwin was defenceless. Civilian authorities were as useless as their military counterparts. Police tried to stop the drunken looting but when the military police threatened to shoot them they gave up and fled with the rest. Every building that wasn't damaged by the bombs was broken into and looted. People tried to board the train but panicked operators sealed the doors and took off with hardly anyone on board, and they didn't stop until they reached the end of the line at Mataranka, south of Katherine. No wonder the government wanted to keep it quiet.

They also kept quiet the fact that 243 people were killed and many hundreds were wounded. Four ships were sunk with crewmen killed and those ships remained for years as wrecks to remind the citizens of what had happened.

Darwin wasn't the only town attacked by Japanese bombers. Over a 21 month period 57 bombing raids were made on Darwin and during that time Broome in West Australia was also attacked with considerable damage and much loss of life. And so were other places with bombers penetrating as far south inland as Katherine, and in WA other towns such as Derby, Drysdale, Port Headland and Wyndham, while in Queensland Mossman and Townsville were also attacked.

The government never said a word about all this, nor was any of it reported in the newspapers of the day, presumably because they were censored. They also kept secret the fact that they were ready to abandon the whole northern part of Australia in a line that ran from slightly north of Brisbane right across the whole country to West Australia. They were going to let the Japanese have it all so they could save the major population centres in the South.

We stood on the headland overlooking the harbour and Uncle Bill pointed toward some darker smudges in the water. 'The sunken ships are still there.'

Beside the long wharf was also wreckage that was quite visible. It looked like a gigantic beached whale lying half way along the side of pier in water that had dropped enough as the tide went out to uncover it. Most of it would be underwater when the tide came in.

'That's the Neptuna,' Uncle Bill said. 'It was carrying a cargo of ammunition. It made a real mess when it blew up. Forty five crewmen were killed in a series of explosions.'

Fragments of my Life – with Science Fiction

Photo montage from my first 8mm film.
The wreck of the Neptuna, which carried a cargo of ammunition.
Forty-five crewmen were killed when this ship blew up in a series
of explosions after being hit by Japanese bombs.

Rusted wrecks left in the harbour and on the mudflats after the Japanese attack on Darwin.

An old pearling lugger that had seen better days exxposed after the tide receded.

Humpty Doo — beer, and rice...

Half an hour later we were at the CES office. He walked straight past the counters with me following ignoring all the other people waiting in lines or pretending to look at the jobs available signs; straight into the manager's office without even knocking.

The manager looked up momentarily startled but he smiled immediately on recognizing Uncle Bill.

'I've got a good man here,' my uncle said, 'send him out to Humpty Doo.'

'Right away.' He pulled some forms from a drawer in his desk and started to ask me some questions; when I was born and I told him April 4th, which was true, in 1937, which was not true. Uncle Bill had told me to add a couple of years so they would think I was at least 20 years old. He didn't question my statement and asked a few other things, address in my home state, educational qualifications, and so on. When all this was done he gave me a printed slip. 'Show this to the driver in an hour and he'll take you out to Humpty Doo.'

On the way out Uncle Bill said, 'The boys from the farm are in town for the weekend and they'll be going back in an hour or so with the week's supplies. They'll take you with them.'

'That was quick.'

'It's either that or you have to wait another week before anyone is going out there.'

'You'll be based at Humpty Doo which is a commercial farm. They have accommodation and a mess hall and they'll charge you for it but you won't have to pay anything until you get your first wage cheque in 2 weeks. You won't be working for them; you'll be working for us. We have an experimental farm there as well.'

'Who's us?'

'The Commonwealth Government's Department of Plant Industry.'

'It sounds important.'

'We have projects on the go all over the place. There's a peanut farm in Katherine. We could send you down there if you want.'

'So what kind of job is it?'

'Well it's not a lion tamer,' he said with a chuckle. 'It's amazing how Darwin attracts lion tamers.'

That didn't make any sense to me.

'You'll be classified as an assistant field biologist. You'll assist the other man we have out there to look after a small experimental farm where we are testing different varieties of rice for yields in both the dry and wet seasons. We can get two crops a year here because we can irrigate the paddies during the dry season.'

'Sounds good to me. What was that about lion tamers?'

'Ha! They say that because they don't want to work. They pick the most outlandish or unlikely jobs they can think of and tell the officers in the CES that that's what they want to do, what they are trained for. The climate is good up here. You can sleep out in the open so there's no rent. Mindil Beach is full of them. And with what they get for being unemployed they can buy what they need, food cigarettes, and grog, whatever... Sometimes the police round them up as vagrants and they spend a night in jail, or they get told to move on so they find another beach to sleep on. There are a lot of people here like that and you don't want anything to do with them. Remember this is the arsehole of Australia, the place where all the shit ends up.'

And with those cheery words he told me to get my stuff from the hotel and come back here in half an hour.

'The truck will have Territory Rice - Humpty Doo painted on the side, so you can't miss it. They always stop here for a few minutes in case there is someone like you to pick up.'

He started to walk off, but turned and came back. 'I forgot to tell you, it's good to see you. I'll be out in a couple of weeks to see how you are getting on.' And with that he was gone.

As I walked back to the hotel to get my duffel bag I could feel the humidity already building up. Cicadas were making noises like a chainsaw cutting through timber as I passed a park, and I could see the cumulous clouds had drifted in off the ocean and were beginning to build up over the town. I stepped around a couple of drunks sprawled in a doorway and they swore at me.

I paid my bill at the hotel, got my stuff and walked back to the CES office to wait for the supply truck. It came fairly soon and I could see there were more cartons of VB than anything else stacked high in the back amongst sacks and other boxes. The driver didn't turn the engine off while he waited. Obviously they didn't intend to wait long.

'I was told to get a lift out to Humpty Doo with you guys. Is that okay?' I asked the driver.

'Yeah, jump in.'

'You want to see the form?'

'No. Show it to the administrator when we get there. He'll tell you where to bunk. Chuck your duffel in the back okay?'

The driver appeared to be tall and lean. His arms looked as if they had muscles of knotted wire. He was sunburned to a dark mahogany so I suspected he spent a lot of time out in the open. He never said another word on the way out to the farm but let his companion who was shorter and stockier answer any questions I had.

I climbed into the cabin and the stocky young man by the passenger side window moved across to make room.

'Is there anyone else?' he asked.

'No,' I told him.

'Then we're off.'

The driver nodded and shoved the gearstick forward. There was a loud crunch somewhere beneath the cabin floor and the truck lurched into motion.

We were quickly out of town running south along the Stuart Highway towards the junction of the Arnhem Highway which was nothing more than a dirt road going north east towards Jabiru, according to the maps I had seen in the CES office.

Humpty Doo, located close to the Adelaide River on the flat plains that get flooded every wet season, was the site of the Territory Rice's three thousand hectares of Rice paddies.

We turned left onto a raised newly completed section of the highway. It had to be at least six feet above the surrounding plain and already the grass along both sides of the road was reaching level with the bitumen surface. I could see termite mounds jutting above the top of the grass on both sides of the road, but not too many trees. There were plenty of trees in the distance though.

'I didn't expect a road as good as this,' I said.

'This is an all-weather road,' the stocky man said as we started along it. 'Up until last year we would be stuck out there during The Wet. The only way in or out or to get supplies was with a helicopter. Territory Rice figured it was cheaper to build its own road rather than continue to charter a helicopter. Now we can come and go as we please.'

'Does it go all the way across to the Gulf?'

'You got to be kidding…no it only goes to the farm. Beyond there it reverts back to a graded gravel track during the dry season which is almost always underwater and impassable during The Wet, the same as this one used to be.' And he added as an afterthought, 'That's a government road. They don't give a stuff what condition it's in. No one much goes out there anyway.'

The bitumen section we were on was a beautiful road. In no time we had traversed the twenty or so miles to the ramshackle settlement that was the operating centre for the Rice farm. Farms as it turned out; the acreage was divided into 5000 acre lots, each independently subcontracted. Territory Rice managed the project and handled the polishing and de-husking, which they did somewhere in Darwin, and the marketing of the rice that was being produced. The lessees of the various lots all stayed in accommodation supplied by the company and would do so until the project was fully operational. At this stage it had only been going for a couple of years. When it was fully operational the idea was to export the rice overseas to South East Asia during their off season and to Europe and the USA. The Australia market was too small with most of the rice used coming from the Riverina and other areas in the South. There were high expectations and a lot of enthusiasm for the project.

The truck drove into the camp and circled around once. It stopped in front of a long wide building which turned out to be the mess hall, or general recreation area.

'We'll unload the supplies here,' the driver said for my benefit as he unfolded himself from the truck to stand beside it. He pointed towards a small building standing high on steel stilts. 'Operations manager is over there. He'll sort you out for accommodation.'

Several men came out of the building to lend a hand with the unloading as I walked across to the operations manager's office.

There was a burst of loud hammering and a lot of swearing coming from a workshop across the circle we had driven around. Three men were attempting to adjust the tread of a huge tractor. The top of the tread was almost shoulder height and two of the men were hanging on to the long end of a huge spanner that looked about six feet long. They braced themselves against the ground and were heaving and pushing up against the shaft of the giant spanner, trying to shift some nut somewhere in amongst the many wheels and cogs that made the tractor tread work. A third person was alternatively attacking the large nut with an oxy acetylene torch in between hammering at it with a small sledge hammer. They were covered with dust and grease and glistening with sweat.

My shirt was stuck to my back, and I could feel sweat trickling down my chest. There was no movement at all in any of the trees that surrounded the farm headquarters; the air was hot and dead. No wonder those men by the tractor were sweating and cursing.

The whole camp looked dilapidated to me. Around the broad expanse of the circle we had driven around there was the canteen where the truck was being unloaded, the workshop with the huge tractor and the noisy men, and the two story fibrocement shed that was the manager's office, beside which several cars, utilities and 4-wheel drive Land Rovers were parked. I caught a glimpse of some heavy looking equipment, big tractors and machines used for harvesting, and something that looked like a road grader in a lot partly obscured by trees between the office and the workshop. The office was downstairs so I assumed the manager lived above it.

Beyond the circle and off to one side of the canteen two rows of eight smaller huts were spread along a branching gravel road. They were all constructed of fibro-cement; the old kind that we know now had dangerous asbestos embedded in it. No one knew how dangerous it was back then, so these huts had fibrocement walls, and corrugated fibrocement rooves; cheap building material at the time. Inside the walls and ceiling were made of painted Masonite, a board made from compressed sawdust. The huts were cheap and primitively basic, two rooms to accommodate two people each divided by a shower, wash basin and toilet connected to an underground septic system. All the access to the huts and the centre of the camp were by graded gravel paths and roads.

The accommodation at Humpty Doo rice farm.

Scraggly grass sprouted between the huts and there were a few tall gum trees between the manager's office and the canteen which threw some shade under which several vehicles were parked.

There were a number of lamp posts with loose wire strung along the tops leading from the row of huts to the canteen, the workshop, and the manager's office and residence. The line of posts disappeared into the bush in the opposite direction to the way we had come in. I found out later there was a huge diesel generator located in a workshop a quarter of a mile away from the camp so the noise from the generator would not upset anyone working or sleeping. The generator was turned off at midnight and restarted at 5 am in the morning. A smaller generator running from midnight to 5am kept the refrigerators in the canteen operating so food and drink stored there would not go off. I think they were more concerned about the beer getting warm rather than the food going off. None of the buildings had ever been painted and they had that weather beaten look that only comes from alternatively being baked in the tropical sun and pounded on by torrential rains. They were streaked with dark watermarks and speckled with patches of lichen and mould.

Walking past the workshop I started to have reservations about being there. What the hell was I going to do here? I had no idea what I was supposed to be doing other than talk to person in charge of the experimental section who was actually to be my boss. He would of course tell me what I was to do each day. But I was concerned because I really had no qualifications to be doing field work that required any scientific skills. I had passed matriculation biology but that didn't mean I was a biologist. I was not mechanically minded, couldn't fix a car, didn't have a driver's licence although I had taken lessons from Dad and could actually drive a car, but not a tractor. If I was expected to fix anything that broke down in the field, I would be stuck. I would have no idea what to do. Still I was here now and would make the best of it.

I went to the cabin I had been assigned to and found a dark skinned man of European origin sitting outside it. He looked as if he might be Italian or Spanish. He had a small easel set up and was painting a picture with Pandanus palms drooping over a small lagoon. He was using oil paints and not watercolour paint. I could smell the oil and the varnish. It was a nice smell. I had experimented with oil paint at home but was still unfamiliar with it and usually used watercolour mixed with egg to simulate oil paint in the paintings I did for matriculation art. Gouache, they called it, and once dry it lasted for centuries, just like oil paint. I liked it. It was a good medium. I didn't particularly like this person's painting though. The sky was flat and lacked depth, and the water didn't look like water. It was amateurish. The Pandanus trees looked okay though.

He nodded and mumbled 'G'day' as I went inside the hut. It didn't appear that anyone was occupying this side. There were two beds and both had sheets and pillows stacked on them but were not made up. As I stood there looking around he came to the door behind me and said, 'You can have either one of these bunks. I'm using the room on the other side of the bathroom.'

'Fair enough,' I said.

'You'll be working for me. I'm in charge of the experimental farm.'

'How come you're not working today?'

He stared at me for a moment which made me realise I had asked a dumb question. It was Saturday and nobody was working.

'It's my day off. I like to paint.' he said finally. 'Most of the other men just want to drink beer and get pissed on their days off, but I like to paint. It's very relaxing.'

He had no foreign accent at all so I guess he must have been born in Australia.

Once I had made up a bed and unpacked my duffel he came back and explained that at the moment were preparing to plant a number of rows of rice. Each row was to be a different variety and the idea was to see which grew best during the coming wet season. Each row would yield a couple of bags and once it was decided which was the best to grow, the bags would be used as seed stock for planting several acres. That wouldn't happen until the next wet season. We would do the same in April after the wet season was over so we could find which grew best during the dry season under irrigation.

The wet season rice didn't have to be irrigated but the paddies had to be staggered so the water flowed continuously slowly down from the highest to the lowest, then off into the lagoon. In the dry we would pump the water to the highest and allow it to drain down across to the lowest and back into the lagoon. Once the initial acreages had been planted and harvested the best of the results would be used on a large scale and several five thousand acre lots had been prepared ready for planting which would happen this week using the seed stock gained from last year's small acreage plantings. It has to be planted before the wet season starts in earnest.

'How big is the experimental farm?'

'It's only a couple of acres so it's pretty easy to look after, but we do have 200 varieties of rice growing there.'

'200! I never knew there were so many...'

'That's nothing. There are at least 3000 varieties of rice grown around the world. Most of them are not suitable for this climate here, so we selected the most likely and will start with those and eliminate the least productive to arrive at the best to plant on a large scale. We had more last year but we are down to 200 now. We alsos cross pollinate to produce better varieties.'

He went on to explain about long grains, fat and thin, short grains fat and thin, sticky rice, dry rice, and how we kept track of them. The aim was to find the highest yielding variety of each type so they could get two or more tons per acre each season. That would be half as good as most yields elsewhere where rice was the major crop. Our responsibility was to make sure each row of different rice stayed uncontaminated and that we could definitely differentiate it from any other row.

He also explained about the magpie geese. They were a problem on the experimental farm when the rice began to mature. There were thousands of the geese all along the Adelaide river plains and they fed on wild rice which grew all over the place. They prefer our rich heavy grains because they taste better and are more nutritious than the wild variety.

'So once the rice starts growing we have to go out on goose patrol.'

'That sounds great.'

'Not when you have to get up at 4 am in the morning to be out there before dawn,' he said, resignation colouring his voice. 'We tried using cannons timed to fire off blank charges at random and that worked for a few days but the geese are clever and quickly got used to them and ended up ignoring them. The only way is to be out there early with a couple of shotguns and as the geese come in to feed we drive up or run up to them and shoot at them. If you hit one, Good! We give it to the cook and he makes a roast with it. If you don't hit one it doesn't matter; the fact that we are there and chasing them frightens them away.'

I couldn't wait to do that.

'A thousand geese will eat all of the rice in the experimental farm in half an hour. Then we've got nothing. So we have to go out there.'

'What about the larger acreages?'

'Doesn't matter; a thousand geese might eat an acre or two, but out of five thousand that's negligible. But if they eat even one row in the experimental section then we have to wait another year to regrow it. We can't afford to let them touch it.'

With the lecture over he went back outside to check his painting leaving me to sort out my stuff and make myself comfortable.

Dinner that night was a three course meal much like what you would get in a pub, and there was plenty of it. There was a lot of talk about the day's activities, and plans for the next day. A couple of people introduced themselves to me but at this stage we didn't have much in common so I kind of drifted off to one side and enjoyed the feeling of camaraderie that filled the room. Most of them finished up with cans of Victoria Bitter and I went back to my room to relax and read a bit. I wanted to turn in early because I knew it was going to be a big day tomorrow when I would go out to the experimental farm for the first time.

He gave me a small stack of time sheets in the morning and explained that I had to fill in the times I started and finished for each day and the location where I was to be working. I also had to indicate how long I took off for lunch as well. They would pay me fortnightly based on the times I wrote on the timesheets. At the end of each day I was to hand him the time sheets and he would send them in to the Plant Industry Office at the end of each week.

After breakfast at the canteen I joined him and we went out to our section in small Land Rover that appeared to be much newer than the other ones used by the private subcontractor farmers.

It was a clear morning but already warm and humid. Flies buzzed incessantly around us as we walked towards the plots where rows of rice were starting to sprout. The gum trees at the edge of the cleared area glistened, a brilliant glowing green against a deep blue sky already showing the first signs of cloud build up. I just loved the look of the green against the dark threatening shades of cumulous building up behind it. To me it epitomized the tropics.

The flies were annoying at first but after the sun got up a bit higher they all settled on our backs. I can't remember the other guy's name so I'll call him George. He told me to wait until the flies settled. 'Then you take your shirt off and hang it on tree branch, or over there on the gatepost.' He was carefully taking off his shirt as he said this. I could see it was covered with flies no doubt sucking at the sweat that had already soaked into the shirt. I did the same, holding mine up so I could see the flies well and truly settled on the back of the shirt. I hung my shirt on the other gatepost from his, and wearing our hats to keep the sun off our heads and noses we proceeded into the rows of rice.

Each row was raised slightly above the surface level and the subsequent troughs between the rows were all flooded with dirty brown water. I was good water. It was only brown because it was full of fine sediment. There were the slightest of ripples which indicated that the water was actually flowing slowly along the troughs.

George handed me a bag of rice. The bag had a name tag with the variety of the rice printed on it. With a marker pen he wrote the row number on the name tag. He wrote the same info on a small tag fixed to a metal pole which he stuck into the ground at the beginning of the row. 'Two seeds in each hole, six inches apart, all the way along the row. I'll be doing the same in the next row. There should be enough to do the whole row.'

'I'll get started then...' With a small gardening tool I poked a series of holes along the row. As instructed I put two seeds in each hole and covered them over. The sun was beginning to burn and I was thinking, flies or not I might put my shirt back on. I didn't want to get sunburnt on my first day. I don't normally burn as I have olive skin that is used to being out in the sun, but the sun here was a lot hotter than what I was used to. It didn't seem to worry George though; he was almost as black as some of the aborigines I had seen wandering about the park in Darwin, except for his face which was protected by his hat. It was tanned, but not black.

We were about half way along the row when he said, "You should put your shirt on or you'll get burnt. The flies will be gone by now."

I went back and stepped up out of the watery trough to find a dozen leaches stuck all over my legs near the ankles. Some of them were fat having sucked heaps of blood. The weird thing was I didn't feel them at all while I was in the water.

'I'm covered in leaches,' I called out to him. I hated those things. I bent down to start pulling them off when he told me to leave them alone.

'They'll fall off as soon as the sun gets on them. It burns them and they can't stand it.'

I looked at them writhing and wiggling. But I had barely taken two steps when they started dropping off and wriggling frantically back towards the water I had stepped out of. Another step and they were all gone, leaving streaks of blood running down my ankles and across my feet. It was a relief to see them gone but I didn't feel too enthusiastic about going back into that water again.

And he was right about the flies too. I found both shirts completely fee of those insidious bush flies. 'Won't they come back?' I called out as I put the shirt back on.

'It's too hot now. They'll be under the trees in the shade.'

'Do you want your shirt too?'

'Yeah bring it over.'

And that was a daily routine. Wear a shirt before it got too hot and allow the flies to settle where the back was wet with sweat, then take it off and leave it somewhere until it got too hot and all the flies disappeared. After that you could put the shirt back on and not be bothered with flies until late afternoon when the temperature dropped a little and they came out again.

I was reluctant to step back into troughs between the planted rows of rice.

'Why don't we wear gumboots?'

'Because they stick in the mud and you can't move. They fill up with water too in the deeper spots. Barefoot is the only way.'

When I still hadn't moved into the water he said with a hint of annoyance, 'Come on. They don't do much other than to suck a bit of blood. It won't do you any harm to lose a little bit of blood.'

'That's what you think...'

'Stop pissing around and get back in here.'

I stepped back in between the rows and expected to feel hundreds of the black slimy things latch on to my ankles and feet, but actually felt nothing. Not willing to look however I quickly walked along the row, handed him his shirt and continued to plant the rest of the seed. After a while I forgot about the leaches and was really surprised to find only a couple still there when I finished planting my row and we went back for some more bags.

'See,' George said, 'once they've had a feed they all drop off anyway.'

'I'm not sure I'll ever get used to them,' I said.

He just laughed.

When we'd finished the row we went back to the Land Rover and got some more bags. He had quite a lot stacked up in neat piles, all named and numbered. He made a notation in his notebook about the name and number of each bag we took out to plant.

By mid-day we'd planted all the bags he had in the Land Rover, and my back ached from leaning over. It also felt as if the sun had burned through the shirt too, but I found out after a shower that the cracked feeling across my back was from the salt dried out of the sweat. He gave me some salt tablets and told me to take one with each meal to make up for salt lost through sweating.

The boys back at the canteen joked about my bloody legs when we got back. There were dried streaks from the calf to the ankle, but the sweat and the blood and the mud all washed away with a shower. After lunch we worked in a small storage area sorting bags of seed while George made notes in his record book. We knocked off about two in the afternoon when the sky darkened with black clouds and winds blew across the space between the canteen and the accommodation, whipping up dust before a sudden heavy downpour flattened everything. Within minutes the rain stopped and the sun came out again. Wisps of steam rose up from the wet gravel and off the tops of the huts and no matter how fresh anyone had felt before the rain we all started sweating with the rising humidity afterwards. That lasted until the sun dropped close to the horizon and the air seemed a little less humid and slightly fresher.

It rained also during the night which woke me up because water was blowing in through the Louvre windows. I quickly closed the windows and went back to sleep.

The rest of the week was like that, and the only thing I noticed that was different was how quickly the rice that had been planted in the rows before I started was growing. My first row had already started to shoot with little green spikes breaking through the soil, and the grass around the huts where I was billeted grew another five or six inches.

'Next week we'll have to start goose patrol,' George told me when Saturday arrived and some of the guys had already headed off for the night and the next day off in Darwin.

George got out his painting of the banyan trees and started to work tentatively on the water beneath the trees. I dug out a magazine I had in my bag and started to read one of the stories.

It was a *New World's Science Fiction* magazine and the main story was a serial that related to the epic of Gilgamesh. The plot dealt with two characters a man and a woman who were part of a crew from an interstellar ship that got into trouble in the solar system and made an attempt to reach a planet they could live on, Earth of course. The ship didn't make it, its power plant going critical beyond earth orbit. A number of lifeboats were launched towards the earth, but only two made it safely down. One came down in what is loosely called Mesopotamia while the other came down somewhere in Central America. The crew members although having the appearance of being human were not really as human as we are. They were very long lived as would be necessary for interstellar travellers. The person who came down in Mesopotamia discovered that the people who lived there were primitives barely above the stone age and that if he wanted any chance of being rescued he would have to do something to help these people develop a better civilization. He was instrumental in helping the development of the city of Uruk and became Gilgamesh the King. He later went in search of other crew members who may have survived and over the years he heard rumours that there was someone else in a distant land, a woman, who became a Goddess.

In reality Gilgamesh and his journeys gave rise to the clay tablets that told of his voyages.

As a character in this serialized novel he also had to change identities since he outlived everyone around him which gave rise to stories about Methuselah, the wandering Jew, until finally he disappeared from sight. He made appearances at important moments in history and we get the idea that he is deliberately leading humans into the direction that will eventually create the space race and human attempts to enter space.

When the story starts he is an American astronaut who becomes involved with a female Russian whose agenda is also to somehow to get into space. She is of course the only other surviving crew member from the interstellar ship. The only way they can be rescued by their own kind is to get into space where they can send a message like an SOS, and then wait to be rescued. They still want to go home after being on earth for 4000 years. There is of course conflict between the two of them who are both enemies as well as lovers but the details of this I simply can't remember.

It was well written compared to other stories I had read up till that time. It was titled *The Time Masters* and was written by *Wilson Tucker*, and it was illustrated with the beautiful black and white ink and scraper board drawings that were always used in those magazines. Perhaps at the time the reason I thought it was so good was because the Russians had actually put two satellites into orbit and the newspapers were full of excitement about how they were beating the Americans who had so far failed to get into Space. The space race had already begun and here was a story that gave a fantastical although implausible explanation of how it all came into existence.

The interesting thing is that it inspired me to find a copy of the Penguin Classic '*The Epic of Gilgamesh*' which I did as soon as I got back to Melbourne. I thought this classic was a great story that had the ring of truth about it—after all it had been inscribed onto clay tablets thousands of years ago. I was surprised that very few people ever used it as the basis for an epic novel either historical or fantastical. *Robert Silverberg actually did use the story of Gilgamesh many years later for two novels which I have not read.*

When I finished that first episode, if I decided to write to Merv Binns at McGills book shop opposite the GPO in Elizabeth Street, Melbourne, and got him to send me the subsequent issues because I was sure I wouldn't find anything like that in the newsagency in Darwin.

I also took the time to write some letters home and one of them I wrote to my *English Expression* teacher, the one who told me that '*Slan*' and '*The Weapon Shops of Isher*' were absolute garbage. I wanted to impress him with my observations and wrote the letter in a way that was reminiscent of the essays we had studied in school towards the end of my last year there. It was about things I saw in the area around Humpty Doo, the green tree ants and the nests they build, and how they sting when they drop down on you and bite because you've you blundered through the trees and disturbed them, about how the lagoon looks when the sun comes up and the birds start foraging, the water buffalo surging through the shallow water, that kind of nature stuff. It was all new to me and no doubt there was some sense of wonder infused in the writing because he sent me back a letter asking permission (after the fact) to read parts of my letter to his current *English Expression* class to show what a former student was doing. He also encouraged me to continue writing and that one day he would look forward to reading a book published by me.

It was in this same letter that he told me he had seen the French film 'Christ Re-Crucified' based on the novel 'The Greek Passion' by Nikos Kazantzakis, and how much better the book was when compared to the controversial film that caused a stir of protests in Melbourne. He recommended that I should read that book. I did read it about ten years later after I had been to Greece and had some inkling of the passion that infuses life in Greece.

Unfortunately he would be dead long before I published my first modest effort in 1974, *'Cinematography Underwater'*, which was of course nothing like what he would have expected anyway.

I was often called on to drive this little tractor and tow around a trailer with feul drums so the bigger tractors could be refueled without coming back to base camp.

Stacking bags of rice in preparation for planting in the experimental farm section.

Goose Patrol and chasing Buffalo

George banged on my door while it was still dark calling for me to get up. I dragged myself off the bed and chucked on some shorts and a shirt, and put some boots on. Outside George had two shotguns which he held out to me. "Take these while I drive," he said.

In the Land Rover I held the guns while George drove out to the experimental farm. There was no moon and it was pitch black. Stars sparkled high above but there was no way I could see any of the sputniks moving across the sky since we bounced around too much on the corrugated dirt track to the rice paddies.

'These geese just love rice,' George told me as we thundered along the track. 'Normally they eat the grass that grows along the edges of the lagoons and the wild rice that grows everywhere here. They have a hooked beak which is unlike any other goose and a long neck so they can reach down deep underwater to rip up roots and bulbs. They have long legs and their feet are different too. They're not as webbed as other ducks and geese. They can make quite a mess scratching and digging along the rice paddies, ripping up new shoots with their beaks. And they're big too.'

'How big?'

'On average they stand two and a half feet tall.'

Suddenly we were there. George slammed on the brakes which locked the wheels making the Land Rover skid to a halt. He turned the engine off and jumped out while the Land Rover was still moving. He reached in over to the back seat as I followed him out and grabbed a handful of thick shells. He loaded both shotguns and gave one back to me.

'You go that way,' he said indicating the direction, and I'll go the other way. Don't shoot towards me, all right?'

He handed me several shells which I dropped into my pocket.

There was a faint glow behind the trees that delineated the edge of the ploughed land. A slight breeze, warm air drifting inland from the Arafura Sea, ruffled the tops of the new rice shoots.

'They should start flying in soon. They know the new rice shoots are here.'

'Do you want me to shoot at them?'

'No, just shoot up in the air. We want to frighten them away not kill them.'

He'd already taken a few steps away in the opposite direction from the one he wanted me to take, but he turned back and said, 'Besides I don't want you to accidentally shoot me. I might end up wandering half way around to the other side.'

And with that he was gone. I could hear him walking along but it was still too dark to see him. I started walking the other way along the edge of the first row. Something slithered away in the grass and I presumed it was a snake or a goanna. It was too dark to see.

I went about fifty yards along and by then the sky began to get lighter. I could hear honking noises and other bird calls from the nearby lagoon. I could clearly see the lines of rice in the experimental farm. Then all of a sudden there was the flapping of wings and a flock of dark shapes descended from over the treetops towards the rows of rice beside me.

They were big birds all right. They are unique to Northern Australia and the southern part of New Guinea. They have no other relatives anywhere else in the world.

They looked like swans as they came flapping and gliding down towards the rice. There must have been a hundred or more of them. No wonder George was worried about them eating whole rows of rice. They spread out as they came down and suddenly there was a loud explosion down in the direction George had walked. I heard furious flapping as birds down there shot back up into the lightening sky. I fired my first shot towards the birds that were coming down near me and they hardly took any notice. Perhaps they thought it was one of those cannons that had been set up to fire at random. But as soon as I started yelling and running towards them they all took off with a flurry of white wings. I fired another shot in their general direction and the whole flock swirled away in unison.

It was light enough to see them clearly now and they were beautiful birds. They had long black necks like a swan and a white body, white wings some with black tips, and a black tail. I could see why they called them magpie geese. They looked like Magpies as far as the black and white colouring was concerned. Seeing them stand in the water by the nearby rows of rice they looked tall and elegant as they waded along. When I fired above their heads they leaped up into the air flapping their wings furiously until they gained some height after which they glided and swirled away back towards the lagoons and swamps that are their natural habitats.

'That was fun,' I told George when we met back at the Land Rover once the sun started peaking above the tree tops.

Together we inspected the rows to see if there was any damage and there were a few spots where the geese had managed to dig up some shoots before we frightened them off. But overall there was hardly any predation to speak of.

'They'll be back again tomorrow,' George said, 'and so will we.'

'I'm looking forward to it.' I said enthusiastically.

On the way back to the camp so we could get some breakfast he explained that the habitat of the geese used to extend much further east and south but extensive drainage of wetlands to make farmlands has pushed their habitat back into the top end of Queensland and the Northern Territory. Their habit of digging up and eating fresh shoots made them unpopular with farmers who quite happily shot them as pests. The geese didn't distinguish between wheat or grass or rice, it was all food for them, and besides wheat and rice are only exotic forms of grasses anyway.

Since wild rice grows all over the top end the geese were happy until people like Territory Rice came along and established a series of rice plantations. The geese were ecstatic. It was like a smorgasbord of food as far as they were concerned. Plump new rice shoots, thick and rich compared to the scrawny native wild rice they were used to. There was no way they weren't going to invade the rice farms along the Adelaide river flats. We put the rice right in the middle of their natural range. What were they supposed to do?

But the geese were not the only problem. Water buffalo also were a nuisance.

There were quite a few of them in the lagoons and swamps nearby and they often trampled through new rice paddies eating the tops of the developing grain. The men from the privately contracted farm lots chased and hunted them as well. They would go out driving through the long grass looking for buffalo wallows and shooting any buffalo they could find. As a result we often had buffalo steak on the menu in the canteen along with wild magpie goose. I can't say I particularly cared for this fare, it was usually tough and strong tasting, but the other men there actually liked it. I think the fact that they had hunted and shot it had more to do with them liking it than the actual flavour of the meat.

After a week or two of chasing geese and frightening them off the experimental farm I went into town to open a bank account so my wages could be paid directly into it. I sent money to Merv at McGills for some magazines and in a few weeks a package arrived with copies of *New Worlds, Nebula, Astounding, Worlds of If,* and *Fantasy and Science Fiction*. I was in heaven! Tons of stuff to read, and a great place to be while doing it…

I soon discovered I preferred reading the English magazines in preference to the American. I guess it was the less flamboyant style, or perhaps the assumption that the future would be American is what turned me off *Astounding*, I don't really know now. I just remember I preferred the British magazines. After coming back to Melbourne ten months later I stopped buying American magazines but continued my subscription to *New Worlds* right up until it stopped publishing in the format that I was accustomed to.

I would read in the afternoons and on Sundays when we weren't working and George would work on his paintings. I told him once I thought he should add clouds to the sky to give it some background and he got pissed off. He pointed up at the sky and said, 'Do you see any clouds?'

There weren't any. It was deep blue from horizon to horizon. But even so it had depth. This is not something you can capture in a painting. Certainly not something George could do; his sky in whatever picture he was working on looked flat and dead, and in my view spoiled whatever good stuff he had in the rest of the painting.

With the heavy rainstorms of the Wet season coming in at regular intervals and dumping tons of water on top of everything, the humidity made everyone feel irritable. If you were driving the rain came down with such intensity and so thick that you could not see two feet in front of the vehicle. You had to pull over and stop, and wait until the rain eased before continuing on. I had never seen such heavy rain before. It was literally like being underwater, like standing beneath the cascading waters of a waterfall pounding down on your head.

One Sunday morning before the build-up of clouds announced the arrival of the next downpour and instead of going into town for the usual booze-up, one of the guys suggested we should go out and see how many buffalo there were in the area. I had been almost two months at Humpty Doo and was aware that during The Wet small herds of buffalo were a problem as they wandered through the fields of rice, flattening them and destroying large areas. Usually they stayed in and around the lagoons but with vast areas flooded or swampy from the constant daily rainstorms they were all over the place.

A bunch of us took two Land Rovers and headed off along the dirt track splashing through sections covered with water, slipping and sliding, until we came to the end of the area under cultivation. The moment we went off the track we were in grass that was taller than the roof of the Land Rovers, but did that slow the drivers down? Not in the least. They gunned the accelerator and with engines roaring we slammed into the grass which was like driving into a green wall that continuously disappeared as we pushed into it. I looked behind and could see the track we made where the six foot high grass was flattened and squashed into the damp ground. I didn't know where the other Land Rover was, but I could hear it somewhere nearby slamming through the grass the same as we were.

'Shouldn't you go a bit slower?' I yelled over the roaring of the engine and the swishing of the grass sliding along our flanks.

'That wouldn't be any fun would it?' the driver replied.

'What about termite mounds?'

'You can usually see them as …there's one see?' he pointed to a darker brown shadow in the grass slightly to the right of the path we were on, and swerved a little to avoid it. The rear wheel sliding sideways with the sudden shift in direction hit the base of the mound and we bounced over it.

'The thing you have to worry about,' he went on, 'is a buffalo wallow. They flatten all the grass around a hole where they sit in the mud. If you suddenly drive into a cleared space you swerve left or right immediately. Doesn't matter which way, just swerve, or you'll end up in muddy hole three or four feet deep and you'll be stuck.'

Now just as he finished saying that we shot into a cleared space.

'Shit,' he yelled and spun the steering wheel left. The rear of the vehicle skidded sideways towards a huge muddy hole, just missing it as we came to a stop, past it and against a wall of grass.

We got out to have a look. It was a huge hole about twenty feet across. There were a series of footprints leading from the hole towards the wall of grass on the other side from where we had stopped and a narrow track leading away from the cleared flattened space surrounding the wallow.

'We must have scared them off,' the driver said. 'We'll follow them and see how many there were.'

I jumped back into the Land Rover, the driver and the other two guys got back in and we drove around the wallow and slowly followed the track leading away. Somewhere in the near distance I could hear the other Land Rover crashing through the grass.

After a few minutes we came out into a broad flatter area along the edge of a wide lagoon. There were several buffalo walking through the water away from us. They didn't seem to be in much of a hurry so I guess they weren't running away from us, they were just doing whatever it is they do. Pandanus palms grew along the edge and there were trees with huge broad leaves overhanging.

'How many can you see?' the driver asked us.

'Three or four out there. There's probably more around the bend.'

'Maybe we should drive along and have a look.'

But before we could do that a loud honking came from the direction of where I assumed the other Land Rover had been. I could hear the engine revving and water splashing, so they couldn't have been too far away.

'Silly bastards have got themselves stuck,' the driver said. 'We'd better go and drag them out.'

We piled back into the Land Rover and the driver honked a few times to let the others know we had heard them as we moved cautiously into the tall grass. We found them a few minutes later and the vehicle was nose forward in a muddy hole with the level of water and slush up as high as the bonnet. The back wheels had been spinning uselessly in an attempt to drag the vehicle out backwards but they had only succeeded in sinking the rear deeper into the black mud at the edge of the wallow. The driver was still in the vehicle while the other three men were standing around covered in mud and looking useless.

There were lots of jokes about where did you learn to drive like that? ...and did you forget to swerve? City drivers don't have a clue... while we positioned ourselves and readied a cable to tie to the rear of the stuck vehicle.

It took some effort to drag the stuck vehicle out because the mud combined with air and water pressure held very firmly to the underside of the vehicle. That the engine had been submerged didn't matter much because the air filter was connected to a snorkel that allowed air in to keep the engine running, so you could drive across creeks or along them without too much trouble. Water holes and buffalo wallows were different because they were slushy mud which had been churned up by the feet of the buffalo and had a consistency like thick porridge. If you got stuck in that it was very hard to get out again.

Once the vehicle was clear we all headed back to camp where some much needed beers were in order.

'We're supposed to keep track of how many buffalo we see in the area,' I was told over a beer in the canteen. 'Some people are talking about farming them and selling the meat in Asia. Buffalo meat is pretty good you know...better than beef.'

'Sure is,' someone else added.

'It's all talk,' someone else said. 'They'll never get buffalo farming off the ground.'

'But it makes sense to farm them,' I added to the conversation. 'This environment suits them much better than it does beef cattle.'

'Hah, listen to the expert,' someone said.

'Been here two months and he knows it all.' A round of laughter followed while more beer was passed around. And so the afternoon went on.

Counting Buffalo and painting a mural

The next day it was work as usual until a car drove up and the driver was looking for me. When they came out to the experimental section and got me I was told I was to take part in a buffalo survey over Arnhem Land. The Department of Plant Industry was doing a survey of buffalo numbers and the direction they were moving in during the Wet Season. They were trying to ascertain what the numbers were and whether it would be viable to set up some scheme to capture and slaughter the animals for their meat.

'How do you get jobs like that?' George asked me, He was surprised that someone would come all the way out from Darwin to collect me to go on a survey flying over Arnhem Land to count buffalo. 'Surely there are enough people back in Darwin who could do that.'

'I guess it all comes down to who you know,' I said with a big grin as I left him there by the rows of rice and joined the man from Darwin.

We flew out from the Darwin airport in a Cessna and the idea was to zigzag diagonally across a twenty mile length gradually working our way towards Oenpelli Mission station in the Gulf country East of Darwin. I was to note the groups of buffalo, the direction they appeared to be travelling in, and their approximate numbers. We flew over them too fast to count them individually, and because they got a bit excited if we flew too low they tended to rush through the swamps milling around in a panic. I counted a small group individually and whenever I saw a larger herd I estimated the number by comparing it to the small herd I had actually counted. I marked these on a geophysical map of the area.

These water buffalo had originally been brought into the Top End from Malaysia where they are domesticated beasts of burden. It was thought they could be used in a similar way in Australia. This didn't work and they were left to run wild when the idea was abandoned. Since then they have multiplied to such an extent that they became a threat to the environment, and are now the largest free roaming herds of wild buffalo in the world, churning up mud in shallow lagoons and destroying native fish habitats during wet seasons, and trampling grasslands during the dry as they go into breeding cycles. The buffalo in Australia are definitely a problem that needs to be sorted out.

From the air it was clear to see that this was unbelievably beautiful country through practically impassable. Not even with a 4-wheel drive vehicle could you get anywhere into this area during the wet season. Flocks of cranes grazing on the wetlands took to the air in formation as we flew low and disturbed them. There were magpie geese everywhere and it was obvious to me that this was their country. No wonder we had problems with them in the rice fields. There were many other birds of exotic colours and I had no idea what kind they were, but I was not there to look at birds. It was buffalo we were looking for. And there were plenty of them too.

I saw crocodiles slither into the water from the muddy edges of creeks and rivers, several huge emu like birds with brilliantly blue coloured heads with a nondescript lump on top above brilliant black bodies. There was a splash of red, like fresh blood on the backs of their necks. They were bigger and heavier looking, more solid than emus I had seen elsewhere in Australia. To me they looked more like ancient raptors, dinosaurs, than birds. I'd never seen anything like them before and they were running across a higher dryer area of flattened grassland. They stood out in glowing colours against the intense green of the grassland. None of these giant flightless birds were together in groups like the lesser and much more drab emus I had seen. I only ever saw one at a time, but since we covered such a large area rather quickly I got the impression there were quite a few of them scattered across the country.

'You're lucky to see them,' the pilot told me. 'They are quite rare.'

'What are they?'

'Cassowaries.'

You only find them across the top end and they are the only large ground living fruit eating bird in the rainforest. They are a protected species because with the rainforest disappearing for agriculture or for running cattle their habitat has diminished and so have their numbers. There are cassowaries in New Guinea also but I'm not sure if they are the same species.

I didn't spend too much time counting buffalo. I was too interested in looking at what would one day be designated as Kakadu National Park. It was then, and probably still is one of the most spectacular and beautiful places in the whole world.

We landed at Oenpelli where I had my first glimpse of a native mission. The men and women seemed clean and well-dressed compared to those I had seen slumming around the streets of Darwin, and the children happily played football in the paddock next to the earthen airstrip where we came down. We had afternoon tea and some sandwiches with the priest and a couple of other people all of whom gave us some mail to post when we got back. We refuelled the plane and returned to Darwin, and this time I took note of the buffalo herds, marking their locations on the map.

This flight was repeated once a week for the next two months and by that time, comparing the maps we could see clearly the migration paths of all the various herds of buffalo. The numbers were increasing as they moved westward from the gulf towards the Darwin area. The idea of farming or at least hunting them for their meat was very appealing to quite a number of people. But it was like most of the ideas mooted around that time. They sounded good, but in the end nothing went ahead on any grand scale as had been envisaged, although some small buffalo hunting and processing did take place.

One day Uncle Bill turned up and came into the canteen while we were having afternoon tea. I was there with George and he came straight across to us.

'I've got a job for you,' he said to me as he sat down to have a cup with us. 'You're a bit of an artist right?'

I could see George giving me a strange look.

The half finished mural at home on the garage wall that Uncle Bill saw when he visited us, on the basis of which he decided I would be able to paint a large mural for the NT Plant Department.

I didn't say anything but waited.

'Northern Territory Plant Industry is setting up an information stand at the Darwin Show and what I want you to do is to paint a mural to go across the top of the stand which shows the history of agriculture in the Territory.'

This came as quite a shock. It was totally unexpected. I had painted a half-finished mural on the garage wall at home and of course Uncle Bill had seen that on his last visit to Melbourne, and presumably on the basis of that he figured I could paint a mural. I had no intention of saying I couldn't even though I had never done anything like he was suggesting.

'How big a mural are we talking about?'

'About four feet high by about twenty or twenty-five feet long. About that size, I'm not sure exactly. What do you think?'

'Sounds all right to me,' I said full of bravado. I could see George staring at me in astonishment. I winked at him and he glared at me. Maybe he figured that the boss of the Department should have asked him.

While we finished out tea Uncle Bill explained what sort of things he wanted me to depict in the mural. Then he stood up and said 'I'll take you there now so you can see the site and can figure out what you'll need. You can stay at the Darwin Hotel until it's done. So go and get whatever you need for a few days and we'll be off.'

I could feel George's eyes boring into my back as I left with Uncle Bill.

The stand at the showgrounds was finished but unpainted. There were a couple of bales of hay and some bags of rice there which were to be used in the display, but nothing else. A painter was painting the back of the stand a light beige colour and I asked him if he would paint the facia where I had to create the mural with a couple of layers of white paint to seal the Masonite it was made from. While he was doing that I went with Uncle Bill to a hardware store where I selected tins of paint of various colours including red, white, blue, black, yellow, and a few other earthy colours. There weren't too many shades available but with the primary colours I could mix whatever shades I needed. The paint was house paint and oil based; the stuff that had lead in it and smelled awful. This was before water based paints were being used, before anyone knew what kind of physical damage the fumes from this paint caused.

Fortunately the place where the Plant Industry Department's stand was located was fairly open and quite airy. A lovely breeze blew through the area while I was drawing and painting and I could barely smell the paint as I was using it.

First I sketched in the ideas I had showing Pandanus palms and giant termite mounds, a group of aborigines looking an early exploration boat. This was to merge with a sketch of early settlers and the type of horse drawn equipment used to plough fields, merging again into cattle grazing, Buffalo and kangaroos (I just had to have a kangaroo in there) rice being harvested with a giant harvester like we had out at Humpty Doo, bags of rice ready for export, a cargo ship loading beside the long curved pier in Darwin's Port, and in the sky an early plane, a DC3, and something that looked like a jet – I think it was called a Comet Jetliner and they were about to be introduced. I had a picture of it to work from. I added lots of storm clouds in between clear skies and in the trees a few birds like parrots. I also wanted to put some magpie geese flying over the rice field.

Once the sketch was complete I started by blocking in the sky before adding detailed definition to the clouds, and lower down the Pandanus trees, the grassed areas, the lagoon and the rice field. On the second day I finished detailing the Pandanus trees and the termite mounds. They were quick and easy…Blocked in the clouds to give depth to the sky…painted the rice field and the blocked in the base colour for the harvester. By the third day I had started working on the figures which were the hardest and took the longest time. By the end of the week it was essentially finished and from the distance where most people would be viewing it, it looked good. I didn't use artist's brushes but a variety of brush sizes used for house painting, since the areas I had to work on were large.

I do remember with pride the look of astonishment on George's face when he turned up at the weekend with a couple of guys from Humpty Doo to have a look.

'Up close it looks a bit rough,' I told George, 'but no one is going to be very close anyway.'

'It looks great from here,' George admitted, standing back about 10 yards, 'And I do see what you mean about the sky. Without those storm clouds it would lack depth. I think I'll have to rework a few of my paintings.'

Uncle Bill was happy with the mural as well. I came once while the Show was in progress with all the stands and displays completed and I must admit I thought it looked rather good. It was certainly the biggest painting I have ever done. Although I created some large paintings later, I never contemplated anything as big as that mural again.

After that it was back to Humpty Doo and the regular routine of caring for the experimental section. I forgot about the mural and years later it occurred to me to ask Uncle Bill when I saw him in Sydney what had happened to it.

'The department sent it around to the State School and it's on display in the foyer of the assembly hall.'

Birthday celebrations

The wet was in full swing with heavy rainstorms coming in at intervals so regular you could set your watch by them.

George and I were concerned that the afternoon rains would flatten the rice in the rows we had recently planted but it was fairly sturdy and had grown sufficiently enough to withstand the regular pounding. After all Rice evolved in various tropical climates like this so it was well suited to the environment. We needn't have worried. The toughest varieties, the ones best able to withstand the regular massive rainfalls while going on to thrive and produce a good crop were what we were looking for, and most of the rows that were now planted were all good. The poorer varieties had been eliminated before I got there, and of the ones we had growing in the experimental section, we were now growing to determine which gave the best yield under wet season conditions.

Some people didn't fare too well in The Wet, with constant sweating and extremely high humidity which didn't allow the skin to dry caused rashes and fungal infections, especially amongst those who had migrated from the colder European countries. It didn't bother me too much, although at one stage I did get a mild dose of 'prickly heat' which a special anti-fungal talcum powder took care of. I did hear talk of the heat and humidity driving people nuts —'going troppo' was the expression used — to the point where they committed suicide. But to be honest no one could actually tell me that they knew someone personally who had done that. It was most likely one of those kinds of stories bandied about to add colour to the environment and to impress visitors and newcomers like me who didn't know much about the place. I suspect if there were suicides they were more than likely caused by excessive booze rather than the tropical climate although that climate probably was the cause of Darwin having the highest amount per capita of booze consumed in Australia by each individual.

Darwin was famous for its giant bottles of Victoria Bitter. They were brewed locally and were the size of a wine flagon but made from the same dark glass of the standard beer bottle. I can't recall what they called them when I was there but later they became known across Australia as 'Darwin Stubbies'. I do remember however that we drank lots of them, all the time.

It was my 18th birthday in April and that coincided with the 'knock-me-downs'— the massive downpours that signalled the end of the wet season, the rains that were so heavy they flattened the previous five months of massive growth in the grasses across the plains and river flats. They also flattened poorly built houses and sheds, washed away embankments and generally caused the havoc expected of tropical storms.

A number of the blokes from the farm gathered in my hut to celebrate my birthday. There were lots of Darwin Stubbies and probably some brandy or whisky. Not everyone drank beer. We drank and told stories and got very drunk and danced to music from Elvis Presley, Bill

Haley and the Comets, Buddy Holly and so on. I had no idea where the records or the player came from. The cook had made a cake and it was festooned with 18 candles which I was expected to blow out. Well I remember blowing out the candles but not eating the cake. The only other thing I remember from that 'party' was dancing and perhaps slipping on the concrete floor that had been made wet with spilled beer. I fell against the wall and put my left arm out hand extended to brace myself. Only the wall wasn't there, the Louvre windows were. My hand slipped between the blades of glass and my wrist sliced along the edge of the glass.

Someone pulled me upright and there was blood streaming out from where my wrist was cut.

'Shit,' I remember someone saying, 'get a tourniquet.'

It was a bit hazy after that. Something was wrapped around my arm and the blood stopped flowing. My hand went white and I felt a terrible burning sensation across the wrist where the cut was. The music had stopped and people seemed to be standing around not knowing what to do. Then George distinctly said, "I've got a needle and thread in my room. I think he should have some stitches in there."

It's a good thing I was too drunk to feel much because George came back a moment later with a sewing needle threaded with cotton and proceeded to put two stitches in my wrist to pull the cut edges together. The tourniquet was released and a little blood seeped out but it seemed as if it would be okay. By this time I couldn't feel anything. Colour came back into my hand as the circulation resumed. George then wrapped my wrist tightly with a long bandage using a safety pin to hold the bandage together.

The party went on a little bit longer but the next thing I knew everyone was gone and I was half sitting up on my bed with the room swirling about in circles. Eventually I fell asleep and woke up still sitting half up on the bed. My wrist and hand throbbed and that immediately brought back the memory of what had happened to it. A little blood had seeped into the bandage but all in all it seemed okay. George came in later and removed the bandage and put some antiseptic powder on the cut which had stopped bleeding and was already crusting.

'I'll take the stitches out in a couple of days.'

'Where'd you learn this stuff?'

'First aid. I did a course when I was in the army.'

'Lucky for me.'

'It wasn't as bad as it looked,' George said. 'Somehow it went in between the veins and the tendons…a scratch really.'

'Yeah, well thanks anyway.'

'You're welcome,' he said as he replaced the bandage with a smaller clean one that wasn't so bulky.

A few days later we went out to harvest several of the rows of experimental rice. We had to do this by hand because there was so little of it compared to the larger acreages which were drying enough to be harvested using the big machines that cut off the heads, separated the grains and bagged them while blowing the chaff out the back. We cut off each head of rice with a sickle and individually bagged each several for testing purposes. The rest of that row was then put into one Hessian bag which would be sufficient if required to plant one acre. The sample bags would be sent back to a laboratory in Darwin for analysis and comparisons before deciding which one could successfully be used on a larger scale. Once the best varieties were determined, bags of the seed we collected would be handed to Territory Rice to plant one acre lots, the seed from which would be then later collected and used to plant a five thousand acre lots. I was an ongoing process that went over several seasons and there was still a long way to go before the huge area that was Humpty Doo's collective farms would be fully planted. In the meantime they were harvesting the already established acreages and sending off quite a lot of rice for de-husking at Territory Rice's processing plant in Darwin.

It was quite exciting now that the Wet had gone and the dry season was upon us. Temperatures were still warm to hot but without the humidity that permeated everything before. To me it felt like autumn, only a bit warmer. I loved the smell of autumn, the burning leaves, and all that sort of stuff; only up here it was burning grass. As soon as the grass dried it got burnt which apparently promoted some secondary growth, and prevented uncontrolled bushfires later on. Crows circled around the edges of the burning grass catching grasshoppers and other insects trying to escape the fire. They followed along behind the ploughs that were preparing the ground for the next season of rice growing gobbling up worms and insects exposed by the ploughing. A grader was used to level the fields and to give them the correct slope to allow water pumped in from a nearby lagoon to flow across the growing rice.

An incredible little camera

We went into town one weekend and I bought a Eumig 8mm movie camera which had semi-automatic exposure control and some rolls of film. I also bought an English photography magazine that was devoted to amateur film making at the newsagents. I got this magazine each month whenever I went into town. A5 sized, it was handy to keep in a pocket when I was out and about with the camera.

Through this magazine I sent for an anamorphic lens which squeezed the image while filming and which when used on the projector later would expand the image into wide screen which was double the width to the height (2:1). This was nowhere near the aspect ratio of Cinemascope (2.8:1) but was closer to Vista Vision which Paramount developed as an alternative to 20th Century Fox's Cinemascope.

Because the image was squeezed it contained twice the information of a standard or un-squeezed image. I had to allow one-stop of exposure compensation otherwise the projected image spread across the wide screen would be underexposed and consequently dull, dark and flat. It was easy to compensate for the exposure because the way the semi-automatic exposure worked was through the viewfinder. There was a tiny lever which moved in an arc from left to right, like a miniature windscreen wiper. The left side had a minus mark while on the far right there was a plus mark. There were several dots in an arc from left to right, that is from completely underexposed to completely over exposed. The dot in the middle at the apex was correctly exposed. By turning the exposure ring on the camera lens until the lever pointed to the centre dot in the arc gave me correct exposure. To compensate for the anamorphic lens I moved the exposure ring to give me a slight degree on the right or plus side which meant I was overexposing slightly letting more light into the camera because the image was to be spread over a larger area. This all sounds very primitive by today's standards but in 1958 this little Eumig

8mm camera was the epitome of the latest in photographic development for amateur film makers.

I ran around Darwin shooting film and also filmed the harvesting and ploughing. I later took a lot of film of my return trip from Darwin back to Adelaide and on to Melbourne, which I edited together in Melbourne and showed the family. We had all seen this film a few times then eventually it got put away in a can with a description scratched onto the metal cover so I would know what was in it, and it only came out on rare occasions when we had a film night. There was some really good stuff in that can and it was in wide-screen too. Finally it got put away and was stored in a box which came with me from Yarraville to Hoppers Crossing then to Williamstown and eventually to Queensland where I now live. I finally decided fifty years later I should pull this film out and have it converted to a DVD.

When I got home with the DVD I was too excited to wait and immediately stuck it in the player. When it started I was absolutely stunned to find it was not my film from Darwin but someone else's film of a trip to Fiji with people I had never seen waving at the camera and calling out Bula Bula or something like that. I have no idea how that film got into my can other than to surmise that at least 40 years ago at the last film night in Yarraville that I can recall, I didn't rewind someone else's film after projecting it and ended up putting it by mistake into my can while my film went into the other person's can. That they never called and said they had the wrong film meant that like me they simply put it away and forgot about it.

I was upset for a while after spending the money to have it digitised onto DVD, but there was nothing I could do. I have no idea who has my film or where they might be. They may have discovered it and thrown it away, or maybe they still have it stuffed in a box of old films somewhere and their descendants will one day discover it and wonder who the hell the person travelling along the highway from Darwin to Alice Springs is because it will be no one they know.

I had really wanted to see that film again and was hoping it would jog my memory of the time I spent in Darwin and the Northern Territory but it was not to be.

A Special Dinner

Uncle Bill came out to Humpty Doo on another occasion and told me he wanted me to assist the cook in preparing and serving a special dinner the following week to be held in the manager's residence.

He would be bringing with him a most exalted guest; none other than Prince Phillip who was on a special tour and visit to Australia. The Prince was most interested in the goings on at Humpty Doo and the rice farm. There would be other officials with them. When I asked why he wanted me to be there he explained that I was the only worker who was officially working for the Plant Department and that he wanted me there for that reason. The cook and the other people there would be working either privately or were not connected with his Plant Industry Department.

'What about George?'

'He will be assisting us with a tour of the farm. I don't need him to be a waiter or a chef's assistant. You on the other hand have had experience in waiting on tables and working in a kitchen.'

'Fair enough,' I mumbled without much enthusiasm.

Since we were kids we almost always spent some time at one or another of Uncle George's cafes in different country towns. He never stayed more than a few years in any town where he had a restaurant. I never knew the reason why he often moved, but I can only assume he got tired of one town, would sell up and move to another where he would either buy another café or start a new one. As kids we went to Warragul then to Moe where he stayed for several years, after which he shifted to Maryborough, the town with the largest railway station in Victoria where he stayed possibly longer than any other place, and finally he moved to Hamilton which was the last place he had a café until he retired at the age of seventy something and moved to live with his son and his family in Lygon street Carlton.

I remember Moe and Maryborough quite well since I went there and helped out in the cafes over the Christmas school holidays. By the time he moved to Hamilton I was less interested, although I did go there once, Being 15 going on for 16 there were other interests that I preferred to pursue rather than spending holiday time waiting on tables or working in a kitchen. Uncle Bill knew this which is why he asked to have me assist the cook.

The day of the visit was busy. There were lots of things to do in the kitchen to prepare the meal. I chopped onions, and made salads, peeled potatoes, cutting them into thin round slices which I later deep fried in the final cooking stages. I also set the tables with places for 10 people. Just before the guests arrived I had to dress in black trousers and a white shirt, typical waiter's clothes. I don't remember what kind of shoes I wore or if I wore any at all. I don't even remember where the trousers came from because I certainly never had a pair of black trousers. Probably the farm manager lent them to me for the occasion. I wore sandals rather than work boots. The only shoes I had were crepe soled desert boots which were popular at the time but would have stood out like sore thumbs. The sandals would not have been noticed under the black trousers.

I was not impressed by Prince Phillip at all. He was rather thin and spoke with a posh accent that had a hint of boredom and condescension in it. He never said a word to me or acknowledged me in any way. I might as well have been invisible as far as he was concerned. I simply served the meals. The farm manager, the boss of Territory Rice, Uncle Bill who was head of the Department of Plant Industry, a couple of politicians and other hangers on entertained Prince Phillip with conversation and answers to his questions about the future of rice growing near Darwin.

Once they had finished their meal and lingered over coffee for a while they got up and left for a tour of the experimental farm and those parts that were being prepared for the planting of the dry season rice. The cook and I cleaned up after they left, washed the dishes and settled down to have a couple of beers. Our Jobs were done for the day. I never saw the royal party come back although I did hear them changing cars and chatting before the flotilla drove off to return to Darwin.

Nothing much else happened after that. I read my magazines and enjoyed the stories from *New Worlds* more than I did those from *Astounding*. I kept in touch with Mum and Dad of course, and Mum told me that Dad was thinking of going back into the dry cleaning business which he had leased to her brother Eddie almost five years earlier. He had been seriously ill with kidney stones and needed a major operation. He took the opportunity to recover by taking a break from dry cleaning and after a year or so he became a Commissioner for taking Affidavits and went into a small business with a Greek man called George Bitsis involving travel and which also assisted prospective Greek migrants with their paperwork and applications to come to Australia. Mum suggested that I might consider coming back to help Dad when he resumed the dry cleaning business. I thought about this and after a while decided it would be good to return to Melbourne.

The only other thing of note was that when I turned 18 I had to register for National Service training in the state where I lived. That was Victoria so I filed the required application, but explained that I couldn't attend the compulsory induction because I was working for the government in the Northern Territory. I asked for a deferment until I returned to Melbourne the following year.

Everyone who turned 18 had to register for National Service. It was compulsory. My good friend Brian had already served his 3 month stint and was still doing the part time second 3 months which took 2 years to complete. He had loved every minute of it. I also was looking forward to doing it. I had been in the army cadets at school for a short time and it was a lot of fun once you got past the idiotic saluting discipline imposed on you by the so called 'officers'. But that was school and wasn't real whereas this was real. I knew there would have to be discipline but I looked forward to it and to the training.

A month after I sent in the application I got a letter of deferment from 1958 to 1959. I was to reapply in April 1959 when I was back in Melbourne but before I actually got to reapply I received another letter sent to my home address from the Government to tell me that I was no longer required to apply. They were phasing out National Service the following year.

It turned out that 1959 or shortly after was when the government stopped compulsory National Service training. I think I was disappointed for about five minutes, after which I was elated because by then I didn't really want to waste 3 months running around at Pukapunyal in an army uniform.

Returning to Melbourne

I decided I should return to Melbourne in October which was close to the end of the dry season. I really didn't want to go through another Wet. Since the government never fired anyone I had to put in a letter of resignation, which they had to accept before I could leave. I did this and two weeks later I was no longer working for them.

I went back to Darwin and saw Uncle Bill who said he was driving to Alice Springs on some Government business and if I wanted I could accompany him.

That was perfect timing. Or perhaps he decided he would do that then rather than later so he could spend a little time with me. Whatever the reason it was great because it meant it would cost me nothing to get all the way south as far as The Alice; the Department of Plant Industry would at least be paying for the petrol used on the trip. As far as the Department was concerned he was driving down alone, with several sample boxes of tomatoes grown in experimental farms which he was taking to the Alice for testing.

I was just tagging along like a hitch hiker he picked up along the way; only he would be picking me up in Darwin instead of somewhere along the road.

The vehicle we used was a Holden station wagon and apart from the several boxes of tomatoes he had another box with some plates, knives and forks, cooking utensils, and a small camp stove. There was also what today would be called an 'Esky' in which he had some butter, 2 loaves of bread, a dozen eggs sitting on top of a bag of crushed or broken ice. He replaced the ice every time we stopped for petrol. On the back seat there were two foldable stretchers and a couple of sleeping bags.

I was expecting to stay in pubs or roadhouses along the way but Uncle Bill had other ideas. He wanted to camp in the bush. He wanted to save money by cooking his own food and that first night we stopped he unloaded the station wagon stacking the boxes of tomatoes to one side, took out the stretchers, telling me to look for a clear spot and to set one up. He laid the back of the rear seat forward so there was a long space in the back of the wagon.

'I'll sleep in here,' he said. 'You can use one of the stretchers. There should be a mosquito net rolled up with one of the sleeping bags. You'll need to set that up otherwise you'll be eaten alive by mossies.'

'How come you get the back of the wagon?'

'Because I'm the boss and I get the more comfortable spot.'

I just smiled at that. As Children, we used to sleep on the same kind of stretchers at home in Yarraville on those stinking hot summer nights that Melbourne has when it's in the middle of a heat wave during the height of summer. We all slept out in the back yard under the stars because it was simply too hot to stay indoors. The stretchers were quite comfortable so sleeping on one again wouldn't bother me in the least. It would be much better than the hard surface in the back of the station wagon, that's for sure.

While I was setting up the stretcher and figuring out how to suspend a mosquito net over it Uncle Bill got the camp stove going and I could smell the bread toasting. Something slithered through the grass nearby. Birds called out raucously and far away I could hear cicadas searching for mates. I hoped there were none nearby because they can be incredibly loud. We would get no sleep if they started up around us.

'Bring me some of those tomatoes,' he called out.

'I thought they were samples.'

'They are, but they won't miss a few out of each box.'

'Okay,' I said and grabbed 4 from the top box.

He cooked the tomatoes and fried 2 eggs each which we had on toast. He boiled a pot with water and we drank black tea to go with it. As simple as it was, it was the best thing I had eaten since arriving in Darwin at the beginning of the year.

I had no trouble sleeping; the stretcher was quite comfortable. Before I fell asleep I could hear Uncle Bill turning and shifting in the station wagon trying to get comfortable. I had no idea how long it took him to go to sleep because I was already out like a light while he was still moving about. But then again, in those days I could sleep on a barbed wire fence if I was tired enough.

More tomatoes on toast for breakfast, and after packing up we were on our way again. The next night was a repeat of the same only we were much further south, long past Tennant Creek. The air was not so humid since it was much further inland. It was also much colder at night and I was glad I had the sleeping bag. The mosquito net also kept off some of the moisture that condensed out of the cold air during the night.

We drove not too far that day before we turned off to the left onto a graded dirt road.

'I have a friend out here who believes he has deposits of tantalite on his station. I haven't seen him for a long time and he suggested if I was coming south to drop in and help him look for it.'

As we bumped along the dirt road we threw up clouds of dust behind.

'I've never heard of tantalite, what is it?'

'It's a rare metal, very hard with an extremely high melting point. I believe they use it in rocket engines. If there's any out here it will be worth a fortune.'

What he called tantalite was in fact tantalum and was a rare metal indeed. If it was used in the production of rocket engines as a hardening agent, with the space industry just getting off the ground there would be a big market for it. Tantalum is in fact used today in the production of the capacitors in mobile phones and if this metal had been on his property he would have been a billionaire by now.

The land ahead of us was dead flat, sandy, and with tiny tufts of grass scattered across it. The track was clearly visible. Not far up ahead though it split in two. Unwaveringly Uncle Bill took the left hand fork.

'How do you know you are going the right way? I didn't see any signs.'

'There was one where we turned off the highway.'

'But not out here.'

'Doesn't matter. He told me to take the left hand track each time it splits. I spoke to him from Darwin before we left.'

The land started to undulate with sand hills more prominent on either side of the track. After another mile it flattened out into a wide area where there was not a bit of sand. It had all been blown away and the underlying surface was barren of tracks or marks of any kind. It was hard baked earth and it felt like we were driving on concrete, it was that smooth. We stopped a short distance in because we could not see where the track we were following actually went.

'This is a bit of a problem,' Uncle Bill said.

We both got out of the car and walked ahead of it looking for tracks. There was nothing there. We didn't even leave footprints on the ground it was that hard.

'Why don't I walk around this way while you go the other way,' I suggested. 'If we go right around one of us will see where the track continues on the other side.'

'That's a good idea.'

I went to the left while Uncle Bill went to the right. We made a wide circle maybe half a mile across. We could still see the station wagon far behind us sitting there with the sun glistening on it. Little gusts of wind blew wispy fragments of sand across the smooth clay pan. Eventually we both arrived at a spot just off to the left of being a straight line from the station wagon where there were tracks in the sand. The only problem was there were several tracks leading off in different directions and they were only wheel marks grooved into the sand. There was no graded track like the one we had been following until arriving here.

'What should we do?'

'Keep to the left, I guess.'

We walked along one of the tracks for a short way and it disappeared under sand. That one was no good. One of the other tracks though, we could see it went off into the sand, looked more like one that could be used. We went back to the car and took that track. The station wagon slipped and skidded in the sand but as long as we kept a steady slow pace forward in low gear it maintained traction.

The track led us towards a dry river or creek bed and there were rows of desiccated looking scrawny trees along it. No station house or farm buildings in sight though.

'I'm not quite sure what we should do now,' Uncle Bill said. This was the first time I had ever heard uncertainty in his voice.

'The track crosses over the creek bed; do you think we can get over it?'

'Of course we can, if we get up enough speed going down this side the momentum should help us drive up the other side. I can see tracks over there on the other bank so people do drive across it.' He slipped it into first gear and we started down into the creek bed.

'Don't go too fast or you'll bury the nose in the sand on the bottom if it's too soft.' I was remembering how easy it was to bury yourself in a buffalo wallow.

I had backed into one out near the experimental farm while I was driving the old army 4 wheel drive truck that sooner or later everyone had to drive. The reason I had backed into the wallow was that the truck had no brakes and whenever we wanted to slow down to stop we had to double the clutch while revving the engine to bring the lower gear revs up high enough to allow the clutch to engage, then use the lower gear to slow the vehicle down. Coming back into the main camp the driver had to double clutch down through the gears and without using the accelerator and then while in first let the truck go round the circle track at the camp until it had slowed enough to drop into neutral after which the truck eventually drifted to a stop. I was told that the front wheel drive didn't work but I tried it anyway. I didn't want to be stuck miles away from the camp and have to walk all the way beck to get a tractor to come out and pull the truck out of the ditch. I was leaning out to see if the front wheels would drive and I must have done something right because they did and they dragged the truck up out of the ditch. When I got back to camp, after stopping by circling around until it was slow enough to edge forward and bump a tree to finally stop, I told the guys the front wheel drive did work. But they were adamant that it was not connected. Well whatever, I did see the wheels spin and grip, so I know they worked at least that one time. I could never get the front wheel drive to work again though.

Although the sand here was a lot harder than the mud and sludge back in the rice fields it was still soft enough to dig into if you hit it too fast. And we were not using a 4 wheel drive so if we got stuck we would not get out easily.

'I'll be careful,' Uncle Bill said.

We went down slowly and the front wheels didn't bury themselves into the sand. It did slow us down though. I think we were lucky because the sand in the creek bed had been driven over a few times and it had been packed down hard by heavier vehicles than ours. Although sand blasted up from the back wheels as Uncle Bill tried not to rev too hard they got enough grip to push us up the other side of the creek. As we crested over the top of the bank we could see a much clearer track leading away from the creek towards a distant clump of trees about two miles away. I could see in amongst them some buildings.

'There it is,' Uncle Bill said triumphantly, and we drove towards it with a trail of dust billowing out behind us.

The man who greeted us at the station was all smiles. 'I'm surprised you didn't get lost,' he said to Uncle Bill. 'We had a dust storm a week ago and all the tracks got buried or were scoured clean.'

'We didn't have any trouble,' was his nonchalant reply before he turned to me to confirm it. 'Did we John?'

'No trouble at all,' I agreed cheerfully.

'That's odd, because we don't use the track you came in on. We have a bridge over the creek just down here a bit and we use the track from there.' He pointed towards where the bridge was somewhere behind the trees past the main station building. 'But you're here, that's the main thing. Let's get you settled and tomorrow we can go prospecting.'

He led us towards the main building where Uncle Bill would be a guest of the family. He indicated a smaller bunk room where itinerant works stay. I would have that to myself because there was no one else working at the moment. The several aboriginal stockmen I had seen with horses under the trees not too far away stay in their own camp he explained. They would be preparing a steer for the barbeque tomorrow afternoon and if I wanted I could go with them while he and my uncle went prospecting.

Over dinner that night that's all he and Uncle Bill talked about; prospecting and the chances that there really was tantalite out there on the property. I spoke to the man's wife and daughter about the shops in Darwin and what I had been doing there after which I left to go and sleep. The last I heard as I went out the door into the cool night was them still yabbering on about tantalite.

In the morning when I got up they were gone. The station master's wife called me over to have some breakfast which was quite substantial, sausages and baked beans with eggs, lots of toast with marmalade and black tea. She told me she would be busy making preparations for the barbeque and that if I wanted I could go with the boys to get the beef.

As it turned out the boys had already got the beef. They had ridden out at dawn and selected a steer and brought it back to the station. It was standing in the shade of a large tree, and the three of them were standing around smoking. I had my Eumig camera and took some shots of them moving about under the tree.

'We're waiting for you,' one of them said as I got closer. 'Boss said you wanted to see us prepare the beef.'

The other two laughed but didn't say anything.

The one who spoke picked up a rifle. 'Make sure you got the camera running,' he said as he took aim at the side of the steer's head.

There was a loud shot. The steer shuddered and I could swear its eyes rolled up. It collapsed forward onto it front legs then toppled over to one side. Instantly one of the other stockmen slashed its throat with a knife as big as a machete and thick red blood poured forth. The dry sand underneath bubbled as it absorbed the blood. Flies immediately started buzzing around. I moved around with the camera and filmed the third man slashing open the animal's gut so he could pull out the intestines, the stomach and other entrails. They worked quickly and within a half an hour they had the animal skinned and gutted and cleaned ready to take across to the barbeque area.

While this was going on one of the men had gone away and got a small trailer which was pulled along by a Ferguson tractor. They loaded the carcass onto the trailer and drove off. I don't know what they did with the guts and the intestines because I followed the trailer. Maybe they left them for the flies, or perhaps they went back later and buried the guts. I imagined they would have taken the skin away for tanning to turn it into leather.

On the other side of the station house was a big area of lawn. There were lights strung up on poles, and on the side furthest away from the house was a huge barbeque pit. Already coals were glowing throwing up considerable heat. The stockmen took the trailer next to the pit and together they poked a long metal pole through the animal's rectum, along its spine and out through the head. The pole had some spikes welded at one end which stopped it turning inside the animal and made sure the whole carcass rotated properly. They wrapped and tied some wire cables around the middle to ensure the carcass didn't come off the metal pole as it turned over the barbecue pit.

It took three people at each end to lift it and to place each end of the long pole on a special stand. One end of the pole had a flat end welded to it and this end was connected to a small machine that started the whole thing rotating.

I was told it would take at least 6 hours for it to cook, and in the meantime people would be flying in from neighbouring properties. No one would be driving in since most of the properties were so large and extensive that to drive from one to another for a visit would take at least a day. It was much quicker to fly in and since most of the station owners had a small plane that's what they did. By mid-afternoon there were about thirty people there standing around watching the steer cook, drinking beer, picking at the salads the women had prepared, and laughing and joking as they caught up with the latest gossip. There were also kids running around playing games, but they kept away from the adults.

Uncle Bill and his friend returned and unfortunately they hadn't found any tantalite. But that wasn't going to stop the station owner from looking. He was positive that it was there somewhere.

As it turned out I never heard any more about this tantalite after I got back to Melbourne so I suspect it wasn't there. It could have been wishful thinking on the landowner's part or what he had was something else entirely, and probably not worth much.

The party was in full swing with country music blasting into the night and rowdy men guzzling beer by the bucket loads while their wives sat on the veranda gossiping and drinking tea as well as the odd beer in a much more refined manner. Uncle Bill said we would be off in the morning fairly early and that I should not drink too much. I took his advice and slipped away for an early night. From the bunk house the noise wasn't so loud and I soon fell asleep.

It was a lovely morning with the sun barely peaking over the treetops when we left. The overnight chill had dissipated and the air was beginning to feel warm. After a quick breakfast in the homestead kitchen where none of the men who had been drinking appeared other than Uncle Bill's very hung over friend, we said goodbye and left.

We went the other way, past the main buildings to the low wooden bridge crossing the dry creek and followed a well-defined path back parallel to the track we had taken the day before. Arriving back at the clay pan we discovered if we had taken the right rather than the left track we would have had a better drive out to the station. Although we couldn't see the other track from there to the highway across the width of the clay pan we knew where it was and went right across to it. Half an hour later we were back on the highway, minus one of the boxes of tomatoes which Uncle Bill had given to his friend's wife, heading South at a leisurely pace.

The country seemed different to the hot dry sandy place it had been when I traversed it the other way at the beginning of the year. There must have been some rain because it seemed a little greener. I even saw some wild flowers, bright little splashes of colour amongst the endless waves of red sand. The few jagged outcrops of rock we saw in the distance had their bases shrouded in green, fresh Spinifex grasses and new shoots on the ghost gums whose stark white trunks glistened in the sun.

It didn't get so hot either, although it did get warm. It was a dry heat without any hint of any moisture. When we stopped to camp for that last night on the road the air was already cooling as the heat of the day rapidly radiated up into an absolutely clear sky.

'Make sure you use the mosquito net tonight,' Uncle Bill said as I unpacked the back of the station wagon.

'There're no mosquitoes here,' I said with the implied question being *why should I bother to string it up?*

'Just use it, trust me you'll be glad in the morning.'

I did as I was told and by the time I settled into the sleeping bag it was quite cold. I was glad I kept all my clothes on as well because within an hour or so the air temperature had dropped almost to freezing. I could hear Uncle Bill snoring happily in the back of the wagon and eventually I fell asleep.

I woke very early with a hazy glow surrounding me. I blinked a few times and tried to figure out what it was. I pushed at the mosquito net to lift it up and discovered it was frozen solid. Shit! I lifted it up and it came up in one solid piece. I scrambled out of the sleeping bag and stood shivering in the early dawn light. Uncle Bill was still asleep in the wagon. I stared at the boat shaped white frozen thing lying where I had pushed it aside. It cracked and collapsed as I watched. And as soon as the sun began to touch it the thin ice melted and the net slowly fell into a flat sodden heap.

Now I understood why he insisted I use the net. With the condensation exuded from the cooling atmosphere settling on top of the net combined with the exhalations of my breathing while asleep rising to join it, with it freezing together as the temperature dropped to zero or a fraction below, a tiny cocoon of ice formed and that acted as an insulation to stop me actually getting too cold in the sleeping bag. Nonetheless it was sufficiently cold enough that I found myself jumping up and down and running on the spot to generate some circulation and a bit of body warmth.

I had the incongruous thought for a moment that I had slept in an igloo, like the Eskimos did, but that vanished as soon as the ice on the net melted and the sun got a bit higher. Warmth started to permeate the land. Uncle Bill woke up and crawled out of the back of the wagon yawning and scratching himself. He vanished into the bush for a moment while I started the camp stove and boiled some water and we had a lovely cup of tea.

Two hours later we were in Alice Springs and he dropped me off at a travel agency where I bought a ticket to travel south on the Ghan the next morning.

That was the last I saw of Uncle Bill for several years. I heard later that he was based in Afghanistan at Kabul and regularly commuted between Kabul, somewhere in Africa that eludes my memory, and Rome. He was on loan from the Australian Government to the United Nations Food and Agricultural Organization doing *God only knows* what.

Trying not to lose face...

Humpty Doo collapsed because there turned out to be no market for the rice in South East Asia, but I suspect the real reason was economic. Territory Rice had problems trying to market the product in South East Asia. They grew their own rice there even if it was not enough, but the prevailing reason came down to the fact that if we supplied or sold rice to them they would never become independent in the growing of their own. Give them rice and it would feed them for a while. Show them how to cultivate better yielding varieties and they wouldn't need us to feed them.

That's probably what happened, but not to lose face the company Territory Rice and the Department of Plant Industry claimed the project failed because of continuous predation of the growing crops by millions of Magpie Geese and habitat destruction by marauding water buffalo. For similar reasons the proposed buffalo farming also fell through, although some small numbers of them were regularly culled for their meat which the better restaurants served. The marketers could not convince the South East Asians to buy the meat.

I wasn't the least surprised because like everything else produced in Australia the cost of the final product was always too high for countries that had low wage regimes to afford. Australians consistently priced themselves out of the markets they hoped to generate.

Five Blankets

I had five blankets on my bed in the guest house that night because the temperature in The Alice was five degrees below zero. *That was cold!*

I also took lots of film with the Eumig as the Ghan travelled south, but that was the film that mysteriously disappeared, and with it, many of the memories from that trip back home.

Oh well, C'est la vie!

Dancing on sand

One of the first things I did after coming home was to brave the freezing cold Spring weather of Melbourne and took a trip to Cape Schanck on Victoria's southern coast with my brother Phillip and sisters Zara and Christine. Icy Antarctic winds blew in off Bass Straight, but when Zara started 'tap' dancing on the hard sand at the base of a cliff Christine and Phillip with joyful zest just had to join in to prove they could also dance on sand. Years later, looking at these photos, I couldn't help writing a poem about that moment. (*I wrote the poem in Spanish and then translated it into English.*)

Bailando en la arena

Bailando en la arena
deja pisos efímeros
mudados por vientos.
Limpiados por las mareas
lo que deja de nuestro baile
es la playa inviolable
hasta al fin del mundo.

Dancing on Sand

Dancing on sand
leaves ephemeral footprints
erased by shifting wind.
Cleansed by tides
the remains of our dance
is the beach inviolate
'till the end of time.

Clouds clearing after a freezing rainstorm...

Looking across Hobson's Bay

Looking across Hobson's Bay to Melbourne from The Strand was always a favourite pass-time. I couldn't wait to see if the city skyline had changed while I was away. The white hulls and sails of the yachts moored in protected waters close to Williamstown always added a sparkle to dull days.

It was an icy Spring day and it seemed it was even too cold for the sea gulls.

They just stood there, on rocks or in the mud exposed by the retreating tide, lacking the energy to take flight.

A Bleak prospect at first...

Melbourne was miserable in October.

I arrived back in October to find icy winds blowing off the bay, which, as far as I was concerned, might as well have come directly from Antarctica. There was often rain, sleety and gusting in concert with the winds: Spring in full swing.

In my view Spring in Melbourne is the worst time of year. The best is Autumn with its lovely warm days, mild breezes, and the smell of burning leaves as people raking up fallen leaves burn piles of them. Of course this doesn't happen anymore, since burning leaves pollute the air, and there is enough pollution in cities without burning leaves to add to it. Even so, Autumn is still the most pleasant time of year.

Even early Winter can be fabulous, with frosty mornings to ice up car windscreens and turn front lawns white as if they are covered in snow, which soon dissipates and turns into glorious sunny days, although not very warm.

After almost a year in Darwin and the Northern Territory where it is always hot, where the only seasons are Wet or Dry, I couldn't adjust to the cold weather in Melbourne. I constantly shivered, and had to wear extra jumpers to keep warm.

I believe one's blood thins out in the tropics, which is the reason I was so cold after coming back from Darwin. It took about a month to acclimatise, and by that time it was November, heading towards Summer, and when the sun came out it was definitely warmer.

A driver's licence

The first thing I had to do before anything else was to get a driver's licence. I had been driving in Darwin, actually around in the bush at Humpty Doo, and nobody cared whether I was licenced or not, but in Melbourne I needed a licence, especially since I was to start driving a van to deliver and pick up dry cleaning from agencies established by my Uncle Eddie while he leased the family business from Dad.

He had let it run down a bit, because he was more concerned with running a never-ending card game — often held at the back of the dry cleaning factory — and Dad had decided he would take it back as soon as the five-year lease expired, which was at the end of the financial year in June 1959. I was to do the driving which at the moment was being done by Eddie's son-in-law, who was married to Dawn, the younger of my two cousins on Eddie's side.

Apart from driving the dry cleaning van, Dad also delegated me to drive Zara to her dance classes, which gave him some free time at home, so the sooner I got a licence the better.

Eddie spoke to a friend of his, Ivan Foley, who operated a driving school from his place in Cecil Street, and he came and picked me up. He took me around with him doing the driving so he could gauge whether

I needed practise, and we followed the course the police take the student when doing a test. He warned me of the tricks they use to see whether the student is paying attention, and after running the course a few times he decided I didn't need extra lessons because I already could drive. He booked me in, and we went to the police station in Ballarat Road in Maidstone a day or so later. We parked the car in the street a couple of hundred yards away and went inside.

The examiner told me was that he would first do an eye test. I was expecting to read the usual chart they hang on the wall with the letters in rows of diminishing sizes but he looked out the window to the street and said, 'What's the number on that car parked five along?'

I looked, and it turned out to be the same car I was using for the test. He obviously hadn't seen us arriving. So I told him. I knew it from memory anyway. My eyes were good but not that good, but he didn't know that.

'You don't need an eye test,' he said, and ticked something on the papers he held.

We went outside, and Ivan introduced me to another examiner, who would accompany us while I drove where he directed. The very first thing he made me do was to drive out into the street then back up past several cars to reverse-park into an empty spot. If I failed this we would not proceed to drive any further. I've never had any trouble reverse-parking, and this time was no exception. Once that was done we drove around for about 10 or 15 minutes, then returned to the police station, where I went inside and was issued with a licence.

After that I went off with Eddie's son-in-law on his delivery and pickup route until I knew it and could do it on my own. Dad had ordered a new Volkswagen Kombi van for me to drive. At the factory I asked them to paint it bright yellow. It took a bit to convince them because they wanted to supply us with blue or an awful burnt orange colour. At that time blue was traditionally the colour always supplied for a commercial van. But I insisted it had to be bright yellow, and in the end they complied. We then got a signwriter to use bold black letters to print the business name on both sides of the van.

WILLIAMSTOWN DRY CLEANERS

I chose yellow because it was very bright and would stand out among all the monotonous colours used on cars and vans in 1959. Bold black letters caught everyone's eye. I copped a lot of flak when people I knew accused me of being a Richmond supporter, since yellow and black were their colours, but I didn't give a stuff about football and never followed any team. In fact I have never been to a football game anywhere in Australia regardless of the code played. I chose yellow and black because of the contrast between them, and the fact that they would be instantly visible anywhere. We also changed the colours in the shop from mundane blues and browns to bright yellow with all the signage being in bold black.

A business reborn

The business was reborn. Dad started a three-hour or six-hour system of cleaning, and a same-day service to all the agencies, which meant I had to drive the route twice a day, in the mornings to pick up stuff, and in the afternoons to deliver it back, while picking up stuff for the next day. We were incredibly busy. Including my sisters Zara and later Christine, we had three girls working in the main shop serving customers, taking in orders, sorting work in the back, and six pressers working full time, with two of the presses located in the shop so customers could see their work being finished. My brother Phillip joined us, and he worked in the factory part with the cleaning and spotting along with three other people while I mainly did the deliveries. Dad, of course, sat in his office and managed the whole thing, only occasionally venturing out onto the factory floor to do some pressing if we were short of someone.

Phillip and I had to learn how to the pressing as well as the cleaning and spotting, so while everyone else more or less stuck to one role we could take anyone's place if he or she were sick or couldn't turn up or away on holidays. We also assisted in the shop if needed. Phillip went to night school and obtained a boiler attendant's certificate, and although I could operate the boiler, I didn't get a certificate. Dad did, because it was required by law to have a registered boiler attendant on the premises whenever the boiler was operational.

The boiler was the size of a steam train without wheels, housed in a special shed out the back on an adjacent block of land behind the factory: a monster of a thing that burnt tons of oil. Eventually it was replaced by a more compact 30-horsepower machine, which was housed in a special room built between the factory and the shop. This was much cleaner, and when the price of oil escalated we had it changed to burn gas, which was again cleaner and less expensive.

I loved the driving because it meant I was outside of the factory and the shop for about six hours a day. I was always driving in peak-hour traffic, in the mornings and in the afternoons. It was exciting whizzing in and out of traffic, sometimes double parking in busy streets while I raced into a shop with a load of clothes, much to the annoyance of drivers wanting to pass, but I didn't care. It hardly took any time at all to race in and out and be on my way again. I did what I had to do, and in all the years of driving fast, double parking, whizzing in and out of traffic, I was only ever booked twice for speeding, and that was some 10 or 12 years after I started doing the delivery and pick up. Both times I was tearing along Millers Road towards North Altona. When the cop said it was a bit much to be picked up twice in a year, I told him I was driving 100,000 miles in a year, and twice within that number wasn't much really. This about the time we were changing from miles to kilometres and the speedometer in the van had a transparent overlay over it to show the kilometres. I told him I had been looking at the miles — doing 60 which was really 100 kilometres per hour — while thinking it was kilometres. I didn't realise I was going fast. He didn't buy that excuse and booked me anyway. Besides, when he booked me I reckon I had by then driven almost a million miles, and all in peak-hour traffic. We changed vans every two years, having done over 200,000 miles in that time. The van was serviced every month with new spark plugs, new points, and anything that needed replacing done each time. We could not afford to have the van off the road. It was essential to keep the business and the quantity of clothes coming and going through the factory.

When it came to taking Zara to her dance classes she refused at first to be seen arriving in a bright yellow van, and I had to take her in Dad's Ford Fairlane to Spanish dance class or her jazz ballet or Indian dance classes. She did everything, having given up classical ballet some years earlier. She was a good dancer, the classical training having stood her in good stead. Her ambition was to dance in the theatre in shows at the Tivoli and in musicals, which she eventually did. In the meantime she helped out by working in the shop at the dry cleaners.

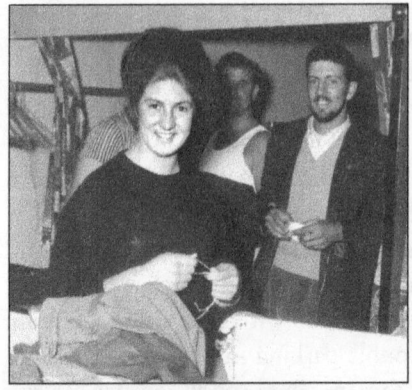

Zara and John and Christine at Williamstown Dry Cleaners.

Zara, myself and young Paul, Mum and Dad beside the yellow dry cleaner's van.

Discovering the 'clave' – the key to Afro-cuban music

I have said elsewhere that memory is elusive, and in my case often isn't there. I don't remember exactly how and when I started playing conga drums. It must have been sometime in 1959 or perhaps early 1960. I have a vague recollection of going to one or two nightclubs located in Fitzroy in Johnston Street or Brunswick Street and listening to a group of about four or five people playing Latin-American music. 'Misirlou' was one of the songs I distinctly remember, and there were others that I had heard played by Greek musicians, which I thought had been Greek songs. I was astounded to discover they were popular Latin-American songs and that they had been translated into Greek. They were boleros and cha-chas and something the band members called Afro Cuban. I loved it. The rhythms were simple compared to those in Greek music, and I was impressed with the way the drummer played the bongo and the conga drums. I thought I might like to do that, so I spoke to him and he started to teach me.

At that time night clubs were not allowed to sell alcohol. Pubs shut at 6 p.m. and any alcohol consumed in these places at night was illegal. We had to smuggle in brandy or whisky in bottles hidden in a jacket or a hip pocket — hence the popularity of hip-flask-sized bottles — and order a Coke or some other soft drink to mix the hard alcohol with. Even coffees were suffused with brandy. Those were the days!

Clubs were sometimes raided and people with alcohol on them were charged, while the club owners denied knowledge of anyone smuggling in such stuff. I remember later buying a huge overcoat with enormous pockets, which I wore when attending a ball. The oversized pockets were used to smuggle in bottles of beer or brandy to have with the dinner served. Everyone did it, and it was often amusing to see so many lumpy men wandering about with huge overcoats which they deposited at their tables and draped over a chair, instead of leaving them at the coat and hat check-in.

The name of the guy who originally taught me how to play bongos was Danny Green. His bongo playing was good, but his conga drumming was awful; I didn't know it at the time. I was fascinated by these drums, and we often jammed together. It was he who suggested we visit a jazz club called Birdland (named after the famous club in the USA), which was in St Kilda. It was the place where after-hours musicians of all kinds hung out to relax and jam and exchange ideas. This club was upstairs in Ackland Street when I first went there. Later it moved around to Fitzroy Street, where it became more commercial and less frequented by visiting musicians.

It was about this time that the Katherine Dunham Dance Theatre came to Australia, and the program it presented was all Haitian and Cuban folk music. I was blown away by the drumming and the singing, not to mention the dancing. I had never seen Afro Cuban or Afro Caribbean drumming, and had not realised that such complexity of the interlocking rhythms existed. I was drawn more towards the Cuban style rather than the Haitian, but all of the rhythms were both musically and rhythmically independent of each other, allowing dancers to dance to any of them, but at the same time they interlocked to produce

With Danny Green on my conga and myself playing bongos at a Spanish nightclub in Fitzroy Street. late 1959.
Below: roles reversed, with me on conga and Danny on bongos.

a melodic structure that overlaid the underlying rhythms. Somewhere in that mix was a beat that locked it all together, but where the count began was a mystery to me. I found out much later that the underlying beat often wasn't actually played, but was always implied, and that each drummer knew exactly where it was and how everything else fitted and blended with it. Amazing stuff!

The other thing that grabbed me was that most of the drumming was in 6/8 time, something I could feel, but something I was not used to listening to. Most European and western music fitted into simpler structures based on 2 and 4 beats to a bar or occasionally the 3/4 of waltz tempo. Not this stuff: it was 6 against 8 or 6 against 4 or 12 against 4 and it was combined with African styles of singing but with European-based melodic forms, Spanish for Cuban and Creole French for the Haitian. Often the singing was in half time to the drumming as it followed the unheard beat beneath the frenzied drumming, but whatever way it was sung it was unlike anything I had ever heard before. It was my first encounter with the syncretisation of African music and rhythms with Spanish or French melody.

My way in was the popular song 'Misirlou', played in what was euphemistically called Afro-Cuban, a rhythm that is common in many guises all across Africa and the Arabian Peninsula (actually a corrupted form or a secularisation of a religious group of rhythms played on Bata drums with three drummers, simplified so it can be performed by one drummer on conga drums), a rhythm in which the pronounced tones replicated the clave beat used in many of the slow romantic boleros, erroneously called rumbas, that were played in the night clubs.

I later discovered that the clave was the key that holds Cuban music together. It has two forms, one of which appears to be a reversal of the other, but actually isn't. There is the form used in traditional rumba groups and folkloric music that has religious significance, and the other form is used in popular dance music. They should not be confused, but they often are. The stick patterns played on the side of a drum or on a cowbell are all extensions of one or other of these two basic clave patterns, and it is these patterns that hold the group together and allow them to lock in with their various rhythms. They allow the mixing of such combinations as 6/8, 4/4, 2/4, 6/4, 12/4, 12/8, and 2/8.

The clave holds it together because it fits into the rhythms played in 6 as well as those in 4, and was for me the key to unlocking how it works. Once I knew that, I could find 1, or the first beat in first bar of the clave pattern, and the rest fell into place.

The clave always goes over two bars before repeating, so melodic rhythms always go over two or four or eight repetitions of the clave, although they could be made up of a number of one or two bar drum patterns. It sounds complicated and it is, but once you immerse yourself in it, the way it comes together becomes intuitive, and is thus not so difficult after all.

Our heart beats in 6/8 and our blood flows with the same pattern. This kind of rhythm is innate, and everyone has the ability to feel it even if they don't understand it. Even rhythms in odd metres such as 5/4 and 7/4 and 9/8 are intuitive, once you feel the melodic structure of the pattern instead of trying to count it in a rational manner.

Albert La Guerre, lead drummer with the Katherine Dunham Group when it was in Australia around 1959.

The members of the Katherine Dunham dance troupe were feted with great hospitality in Melbourne, and a few of them decided to stay in Australia when the company returned to the USA. There was Yolanda and Antonio Rodriguez, with Yolanda originally from New York and Antonio from Rio di Janeiro, Brazil, who were married but later separated, and Albert La Guerre, a Haitian drummer who was the lead drummer in the Haitian sequences. There were a couple of others whose names I can't recall. They all did floor shows in Melbourne and Sydney clubs and hotels, and eventually I got to know them quite well.

Albert I came across one night in Birdland sitting in and playing with the band. He used the drums that belonged to the club, as did I when I later played there. I was very impressed with his way of playing, which no one I had met up til then was able to do. I introduced myself and we struck up a friendship that lasted for years. He started teaching me how to play conga drums, and that's when I realised that Danny didn't know how to play them even though he was fine with bongos — in the same way that a non-Latin drummer used to playing kit drums would be if playing bongos. The riffs were drum riffs, which are not the same as those a Latin drummer or Afro-Cuban drummer would do, because of the different heritage and lineage in the evolution of the playing. Danny had no idea of the importance of the clave, and like most local musicians at that time assumed it was added in the give a feeling of something exotic in the music. The clave is fundamental to the structure of Cuban and related music. The Latin drummer's riffs are always an expansion of the clave, both rhythmically and melodically. They always think of drum patterns in terms of melody first, before thinking of them as rhythm. It wasn't until I started learning with Albert that I became aware of this.

I was fascinated by the fact that a drummer learnt his craft from another master drummer and no written music was required. A good memory was essential, along with an innate sense of rhythm and a feeling for melody. Rhythms and drum patterns are often taught by singing them, and this can be heard in every culture where drumming is prominent. Thinking of the drums as melodic instruments rather than as percussion instruments was also essential, because when you have interlocking rhythms on different drums tuned to different pitches you also get a rhythmic melody composed of the various pitches of drums that rides over all the individual rhythms being played. You have to keep in mind the melody as well as all the individual rhythms that make up the structure of the group as a whole. Once the basic structure of everything is fixed in your mind, only then can some parts of it be varied without losing the overall feel and sound. The way those parts are varied will depend on how the drummer who is playing that bit feels and reacts to what is going on within and around the group. There is a profound depth to Afro-Cuban and Afro-Caribbean drumming of both the religious and the secular styles that dates back thousands of years to mostly West African origins.

The religious styles of drumming are basically unchanged from their African origins up to and including exactly the same kinds of drums as were originally used, the same singing in the appropriate African language, and the invocation of the same deities as those in Africa, with only some of them syncretised with Catholicism and Christian saints—

but the secular music drumming (and singing) has changed radically over the years, incorporating many diverse influences from Spain, Portugal, France, and even England, as well as more recently American jazz (which itself originated from Afro-Cuban slave music via the blues) and all its various innovations.

All of this was mind boggling, and I fell profoundly in love with Afro-Cuban music. Most of the local musicians at the time were interested only in learning a few popular songs and maybe one rhythm that could generally be played with hardly any adaptation to everything they wanted to do in the clubs. Very few cared to delve into the origins and history of the music and the drumming, so in effect I became a bit of an expert. It also allowed me access to the people who were the masters of this drum music, and they were happy to teach me and have me play with them. As a result I taught other guys how to play conga drums and how they interlocked with bongos and the timbales, the three indispensable types of drums used in popular dance music that originated from the island of Cuba and for a while was known as tropical music, but for last 30 years or so has been loosely called salsa.

As a term, salsa doesn't really describe what the music is. It is a poor generic term that only means 'sauce', as in the stuff used to flavour food. How it became the word that describes an enormous variety of varying rhythms and styles all emanating from Cuba as well as including those from Puerto Rico and even perhaps Santo Domingo is totally beyond me. I do have a theory, though, which refers to a chorus, often repeated in faster tempo music, exhorting dancers to move with more excitement which says 'Put some sauce into it ... *Échale Salsa*'. When this was repeated enough, originally in New York, but soon after in many different places and in many different up-tempo songs, it may very well have become the term most associated with the music. Once some people started calling it salsa it quickly became the generic marketing term for all music played in the USA that had its origins in Cuba and the Spanish-speaking islands of the Caribbean.

How can it be used to describe mambo, guaracha, guaguanco, cha-cha, charanga, son, son montuno, guajira, danzon, changui, timba, pilon, and many variations evolving from mixing these with religious drumming and singing (of African origin), not to mention bomba and plena from Puerto Rico and merengue from Santo Domingo, cumbia from Columbia, joropo from Venezuela, and their modern derivatives mixed with other Caribbean influences?

It's not possible, and it denies the existence of some wonderful and ever-evolving music that defies description, relegating it to a single concept. It's like saying South American music or Latin American music and expecting people to know what you mean. Everyone will have a different idea of what South American and Latin American music is and whatever it is it will be limited by that person's understanding of the music itself, to what they have been exposed to and to what they may have heard broadcast commercially. South America is a vast continent that has many different countries all of which have their own musical traditions which consist of many different influences, and styles and instrumentations.

There is no term that can be used to describe all of it. How can you lump together tango, milongo, cueca, son huasteca, samba, bossa nova, chorros, and rancheras, just mention a few from some countries under the banner of a single name? For me the term salsa is as meaningless as Latin American or South American. It would be better to describe it as Cuban or Afro-Cuban music, Puerto Rican music, Columbian music, Venezuelan, Paraguayan, Argentinian, Chilean, Peruvian, or whatever the country may be, which would at least give a hint as to origin, without going into all the possible styles and rhythms employed in that country.

True, it is difficult to find much difference between a mambo, for example, played by a Cuban or Puerto Rican or Columbian or a North American New York band, or even a European or a Japanese band (such as Orchestra de la Luz). The mambo was created in Cuba by Israel 'Cachao' Lopez and his pianist brother Orestes Lopez, and has been refined over the years by Perez Prado, Tito Rodriguez, and Tito Puente, to mention a few, but a mambo is always recognised as a mambo, as is a guaracha or a bomba or a cha-cha when played by groups of various sizes. To call all of them salsa is simply erroneous and lazy and shows a lack of basic knowledge.

There was another guy, a Canadian who was in born in Hungary in the late 1930s, but after the Second World War found himself in Canada, then later the USA and in particular New York, where he frequented the Palladium during the era of the Big Band confrontations between the hot sounds of Tito Puente and the ultra-cool sounds of Tito Rodriguez, the two supreme orchestras that always had top billing at the Palladium. He learnt how to play conga drums in New York and found himself in Melbourne playing on Saturday nights at St Kilda's

Birdland. We became friends. As I became better known at the club we used to take turns playing the congas on Saturday nights. The club often featured a floor show. George preferred not to play during that time so I did it instead. The floor show usually featured singers and a dance act, or a comedy act: it was a short variety show that lasted about half an hour. Johnny Summers was a featured singer at that time, a gifted singer who unfortunately died younger than he should have, and a comedy duo called Crocker and Clarke, They were very popular, especially Barry Crocker, who went on to carve a brilliant career in show business. Kahmal also performed there. I did some shows with him as a bongo player when the calypso craze was at its height. He was singing the songs Harry Belafonte had made popular.

One night there was an exotic dancer who danced with a huge python wrapped around her. I was playing that famous rhythm based on the clave, which had a monotonous thump to it. Every time she released the python it would start crawling towards me instead of towards the audience, which is what she wanted. The constant thump and the vibration of the drums on the wooden floor were obviously irresistible to it, much to my disquiet. Fortunately, every time the python reached the drums and raised its head as if searching for the source of the vibrations, the dancer would gently drag it back and wrap it around herself again. Although this particular show went on for several weeks, I never did get used to the snake crawling towards me.

I can't remember the names of a lot of people who went on to be good musicians and great performers, all of whom cut their teeth on working the floor show at this club. Visiting musicians would drop in after their shows and jam with the band, and some nights were absolutely fantastic. There was no other place like it in Melbourne at that time.

I can't actually remember when or where or how I got my first conga drum. Like those American presidents who, when asked questions that could incriminate them, replied with 'I don't recall that' or 'I have no recollection of that', I can say the same thing: I don't remember. I suppose I would have bought it from a drum shop. I do remember decorating it with a rim of bright colours and an amoeboid-looking sun at the bottom after seeing Albert's drum painted with symbols that I assume had some religious significance to a Haitian, but which looked interesting in a primitive kind of way to the audience.

Playing my hand paited conga at Birdland during a floor show, early 1961.

At Birdland in 1963

I do remember taking it everywhere with me, as I did with other better drums later, in the yellow van that advertised Williamstown Dry Cleaners. Thursday, Friday, and Saturday nights would find that van parked somewhere in St Kilda until two or three in the morning. I cannot remember how I managed to get up at 7 a.m. to go to work, but at the time I was 18 and 19, then into my twenties, so had boundless energy. I can remember driving with Danny to Sydney on a Friday night, so we could go to a club in King's Cross called the Afro Cuban Nite Spot, which was much better than Birdland in St Kilda. We would sit in and play some Cuban-style music with its group, which played great stuff which sounded very authentic: the music you would have heard at the Palladium, but with a smaller group of six to eight people compared to the big bands in New York. There was a photographer sometimes at the club, and I got him to take some shots of Danny and me playing with the band. After the club closed we would grab a couple of hours sleep in the car, then set off to drive back to Melbourne on Sunday because both of us had to be at work on Monday. We did this quite a few times, but eventually the long drive put us off and we stopped going to Sydney.

Fragments of my Life – with Science Fiction

Above: at the Afro Cuban in Sydney Danny and I played with a member of the comedy duo The Two Earls, and below: myself at Birdland in Melbourne with a visiting guest sitting in. (c1960 - 61)

Dancing on TV

I played conga drums with lots of different people all over town. At one stage I met a trumpet player who was interested in Latin jazz. We wanted to practise, but with two very loud instruments such as conga drums and trumpet we had nowhere to practise until I suggested we do it after hours at the dry cleaning shop. A couple of times a week for a few months we went there at 7 or 8 p.m. and practised out the back of the shop in the factory area for a couple of hours. Since all the neighbours were other shops closed at night there was no one nearby to complain about the noise. Eventually we formed a small group with saxophone, trumpet, and bass, with me playing conga drums. We did a few jazz gigs, but the music was too strange for people who wanted to dance, and it was bit too far out for straight jazz fans. I can't remember who the musicians are now after all these years. Shortly after we did those few gigs we each went separate ways and I never saw them again.

In the meantime I also drove my sister Zara to various dance classes. One of her teachers, who had a studio in Elwood, organised to choreograph a show on the ABC, which had studios nearby. The group was doing a Calypso dance routine and needed a male dancer to do lifts. Zara suggested me and I just laughed at her. I'm not a dancer, but I had been doing some dance training with Antonio Rodrgiuez (an ex-Katherine Dunham dancer from Brazil), who took classes at a studio in Russell Street that was behind the cinema which showed foreign movies. I had been there to see *Orpheo Negro* starring Marpessa Dawn, which was a modern retelling of the classic Greek story of Orpheus and Eurydice, but set in Rio de Janeiro during Carnival. It was a brilliant film that introduced to the world the real sounds of samba (as distinct from the watered-down rubbish played in American and European dance bands) with all its percussive complexity overlaid with beautiful husky Portuguese singing and music. The composers of the film's music were also the creators of a new form of Brazilian music called bossa nova, which took the jazz world by storm, giving musicians a softer and more subtle form of 'Latin American' music than what they had been used to. I loved the music so much I saw that film 17 times over a couple of weeks.

Always game, I agreed to have a go at dancing in the routine set up by Zara's teacher, VijaVetra for a show on the ABC called *The Hit Parade*, where dancers mimed and danced to hit songs of the day

I discovered that if you didn't do the lifts correctly it was damned hard to lift the girl up and make it look effortless and graceful. It was all about timing. You had to lift just as the girl met you and made a slight jump. You had to catch the upward movement of the jump and using your whole body rise up into the lift as you lifted the girl. Then it was easy, and almost effortless.

Once she was up and sitting on your shoulder or supported at the apex of the lift it was easy to move around, then carefully bring her back down again. We rehearsed a few times, then went to the ABC studios in Elwood and rehearsed some more. Finally the show went on live, as these shows did, so there was no room for mistakes. None of us ever did get to see how the show looked to viewers because we didn't have video recorders then. One of the girls did manage to get a couple of shots during the studio rehearsal: the photos featured here. I never did one of those shows again. Dancing was not something I aspired to, although Zara did do other shows on TV, similar to *The Hit Parade*,

I was not the only male dancer in this routine, but I was the one who attempted the lift. My sister Zara is the one bending backwards.

Preparing to lift Vija Vetra during a calypso dance routine broadcast on the ABC from their studios in Elwood. 1959.

In the photo the lift looks awkward but in reality it went smoothly and I had no trouble getting the dancer up to have her sitting briefly on my shoulder.

I wasn't only into Cuban and related music; I was also an avid fan of rock and roll music. I had every record of Bill Haley and the Comets, Elvis Presley, Buddy Holly, Gene Vincent, Little Richard, the Platters, and whoever was the latest sensation at the time.

Mum and Dad didn't mind us playing this music at home, and Mum encouraged us to bring our friends home. This started before I went to Darwin. It began right after the astonishing sounds of 'Rock Around the Clock' filled the theatre that showed the film Blackboard Jungle (in 1956). We had lots of parties. Mum always made heaps of food so none of us got drunk on the beer we had. We danced like crazy until eventually we wore out the carpet in the lounge room. We saw all the movies that featured rock and roll, we went to the concerts at Festival Hall, the only venue big enough to accommodate the screaming fans that flocked to see whoever they idolized at the time, and we all tried out the dance steps with varying degrees of success.

We even had pyjama parties. They were all the rage at one stage. I had Mum make me a special pyjama set that was bright blue. My friend Brian had selected bright red, which Mum made as well. We would rock into a party with our bright pyjamas and it was sensational.

Brian would insist on me playing my drums to the music and nobody minded. It was the days of hippies who played bongos. Even famous actors, such as Marlon Brando, played conga drums. I was right up there with the latest fashion.

When we wanted to slow down towards the end of a party Brian would bring out a record of the George Shearing Quintet and we would quieten down to his romantic jazz interpretations of popular Latin American (Cuban) music.

Armando Peraza

George Shearing's Cuban drummer was Armando Peraza who, in my opinion then and still today, was and is the greatest Cuban drummer ever to have lived in the USA. They talk about Chano Pozo and the stuff he did with Dizzy Gillespie, and he is a legend still revered in Cuba, but in my view there are others who have long surpassed what he was doing in the forties up until he was killed in New York: people such as Tata Guines in Cuba and Armando Peraza who moved to the US in the forties. They speak of Chano with great respect, but I think both of them are far better than he was. There are many others who are also better who are probably unknown outside of Cuba.

Unlike Mongo Santamaria, Francisco Aguabella, and Patato Valdez, who were contemporaries of Armando, he is not as well known as them. For years he worked with George Shearing, and sometimes with Cal Tjader, and later with Carlos Santana, but in my view, in ability and technical prowess he outshone his contemporaries while maintaining a low profile. There is a recording made in the early fifties called *Artistry in Rhythm*. It features several different drummers, mostly jazz drummers, but one track is an extended solo with Armando Peraza accompanied by Ray Mosca, both of whom were with George Shearing at that time. Peraza takes the lion's share of the solo, which extends over about 12 minutes. It's an amazing recording of Armando in his prime. There was also, much later, a live recording of him playing 'Caravan' with George Shearing, where he plays another amazing solo beginning with three conga drums and bongos simultaneously before shifting across to the bongos for the main part of the solo. You can hear the audience going wild in the background. There are other later recordings with Santana that are brilliant, but these two early recordings stand out in my memory. When George Shearing visited Australia in the late 1950s Armando was with him. Armando was a friend of Albert Laguerre, and naturally Albert went to see him. It was with Albert that I met Armando, and the three of us jammed a bit on congas at Albert's place. Armando loved the way Albert played, because Haitian drumming is very different to Cuban drumming, and Albert likewise loved the way Armando played. Armando was more a bongocero than a conguero, but on either instrument he was brilliant. I only wish I had been able to understand more at that time. I would have learnt so much.

Armand Peraza in 1978

Books and other stuff

What has the above got to do with science fiction?
Absolutely nothing. It shows that in those days I lived different lives simultaneously, that's all.

Surely readers of science fiction don't spend all their time reading their favourite literature. Even in the early 1950s when there was no such thing as television (*it was introduced in 1956 to coincide with the Olympic games in Melbourne*), no one spent all their time reading. These days with with digital widescreen TV, DVDs, Blueray discs, video games, Internet, Facebook, Twitter and all that interactive stuff some people probably don't do any reading at all, unless they are texting each other with mobile phones. Even e-books haven't proliferated to the extent it was thought they would. There are simply too many choices today. But when I was a boy there was none of that. I had the radio which was fine when I was very young, and books and magazines. As much as I enjoyed outdoor activities as a teenager like skin-diving (*a relatively new sport introduced in the early 1950s*), riding bikes with friends, and going to movies, I enjoyed reading my SF books more than anything else.

That habit stuck with me even after TV was introduced. When I came back from Darwin I discovered Mum and Dad had bought a 22 inch 'Admiral' TV that was encased in a monstrous piece of furniture which seemed to dominate a third of the lounge room. It displayed a flat grey image that was uninteresting to me, but at least they liked it.

Most of the people I interacted with in the music field had no idea what I did at other times, except for George, who I discovered loved skin diving, after which we often went diving together, and Gary Hyde — son of Billy Hyde, a great drummer and showman — who I taught to play basic conga drum patterns. I got on really well with both him and his father and often went around to their place to socialise and play drums.

While I was playing music in night clubs around Melbourne and driving a dry cleaner's van I was also reading SF stories. I read whatever was available, which I invariably bought from McGill's Newsagency in the city. Then there was not a lot of stuff available, so I managed to read everything that was imported into Australia: novels, story collections, and the English magazines. I wasn't too fond of the American magazines, and only read the odd one when nothing else was available. I wasn't very fond of short stories, but that was all that was available at that time. Short stories generally left me dissatisfied, but at the time I didn't know why. I simply preferred longer stories and novels, and read every one that appeared. You could do that then — read everything that was published — because the field wasn't large. As more and more novels appeared I read fewer and fewer short stories. The novels kept me enthralled in ways the short stories never did.

However, just to contradict myself, one of my all-time favourite books was published in 1957. It would have been one of the first books I bought after returning from Darwin. It cost me 31 shillings and 9 pence (31/9), which was probably expensive then although it doesn't sound much now. ($3.19) It was alled *Famous Science-Fiction Stories*, subtitled *Adventures in Time and Space: 35 Great Stories of the Worlds of Atomic Power, Rockets, Robots, Time and Space Machines, etc*, edited by Raymond J Healy and Francis J McComas. No better collection had been published before then. It was originally published in 1946, so the most recent story in the collection was from 1945. My edition was a re-published Modern Library edition from Random House 1957. I loved most of the stories in this book even though they were all American. It had such masterpieces as *Nightfall*, by Isaac Asimov, *The weapons Shop* and *Black Destroyer*, both by A. E. Van Vogt, *Symbiotica* by Eric Frank Russell, *Requiem* by Robert Heinlein, *Nerves* by Lester Del Rey, and, among many others, *Who Goes There?* by Don A. Stuart and *Farewell to the Master* by Harry Bates, most of which were novellas or novelettes rather than short stories, which at least allowed room for some development of story and character along with a good idea.

Farewell to the Master was done by Hollywood as *The Day the Earth Stood Still* and was a pretty good film, whereas *Who Goes There?* was turned into the atrocious mishmash of *The Thing from Another World* which is still regarded as better than the 1980s remake, John Carpenter's *The Thing*. At least the remake was filmed in Alaska, even though it was reset in Antarctica instead of the Arctic, whereas the original version was filmed on a back lot in Hollywood with cold interiors shot inside a freezer room. The remake went back to the idea of the story in having the Thing being a shape-shifter able to change into the appearance of another living thing in order to blend in, but Carpenter in my opinion went overboard and turned the idea into ridiculous horror and gore that completely destroyed any credibility the film may have started with. Though they were both awful films I enjoyed them immensely, and think perhaps now is the time to have another look at the story and do a film that is worthy of it. I thought that was the case when a new film of the same name was released in 2010 but this turned out to be prequel to the Carpenter film and as such was very similar in mood and effects. It actually finishes where the Carpenter film begins so the two together make one longer continuous story, which is interesting in itself. I am still waiting to see a remake of the original story which if done right would be far more scary than showing lots of gore and blood.

I also liked the remake of *The Day the Earth stood Still* with Keanu Reaves, whose wooden performance seemed suitable for an alien trying to mimic a human without any understanding of human cultural heritage, or should I say American human cultural heritage? I didn't like the giant robot, which seemed a little too big and ridiculous even though it was scary enough, and I would have preferred a flying saucer rather than the glowing, semi-translucent sphere, but none the less I enjoyed the film.

Taking this book down from the shelf after all these years I am very tempted to start reading the stories again to see how well they hold up today, but perhaps I might be disappointed. Maybe what would have been a sense of wonder and astonishment to me back then would only appear trite and perhaps a little melodramatic nowadays. I wouldn't want to be disappointed, and thus spoil the fond memories I have of those stories.

Perhaps today I expect too much from a story. There is so much to choose from and so little time to read all that is worth reading, that to spend time going back over something written more than 60 years ago seems kind of pointless. I am not the same person now as I was then, and I fear my jaded self would not find the sense of wonder, the excitement and adventure my imagination conjured up when I first read those stories as a young teenager. So perhaps I will leave them alone and rely on my memories of them.

There were three authors who were my favourites at that time:

Arthur C Clarke, Isaac Asimov, and Ray Bradbury. I bought and read every book of theirs that I could get my hands on.

Before I had finished school and gone off to Darwin I had read Bradbury's *The Silver Locusts* in paperback (the English edition of *The Martian Chronicles*), *The Illustrated Man* (three of whose stories were later filmed starring Rod Steiger as The Illustrated Man quite a few years later, but this film vanished into that space where they send dead and unsuccessful films, never to be seen again), and *The Golden Apples of the Sun*, also in paperback. I don't think I read *Fahrenheit 451* until after I came back from Darwin, when I bought a hardcover copy. I also found a beautiful illustrated (by Joe Mugnaini) copy in hardcover of *The October Country*, which I found to be creepy, and didn't like as much as Bradbury's science fiction stories.

One of my favourite short stories of all time is *There Will Come Soft Rains* which resonated with me on a deep level and has probably influenced how I see possible futures.

Although I was turning away from short stories, I always made an exception for Bradbury: he was a master of the short story and could evoke wonderful moods and strong impressions with a minimum of words. He wrote only a few novels that were actual novels rather than collections of linked short stories, and apart from *Fahrenheit 451* the other I most remember is *Something Wicked This Way Comes*, published in 1962. The edition I have, which cost me 22/6, is the English hardcover from Rupert Hart Davis published in 1963.

In 1973 I replaced my copy of *The Silver Locusts* with a special hardcover edition of *The Martian Chronicles* illustrated by Karel Thole which contained two extra stories. I must have been impressionable, because one story in that edition had me dreaming at night of lying in bed while not quite asleep, with tendril-like things coming out of the bed to invade my body in order to turn me into a Martian. I would wake up shivering and reluctant to go back to sleep. I thought it was a beautiful and creepy story but it gave me awful dreams. Eventually that passed as I put Bradbury aside and started reading other stuff.

In those days Arthur C. Clarke was my all-time favourite author.

I recently opened a box of books that had not seen the light of day for almost 20 years. There are 17 such boxes stacked in my garage because I have not yet had the space or the time to build bookshelves to house them. Expecting schools of silverfish to escape when I opened the box I was pleasantly surprised to find no such creatures. But the books did appear to be stained a bit as the paper had begun to darken on some of them. The dustjackets were also a bit battered, showing me I had not been as careful with them years ago as I thought I had been. I found a bunch of books by Arthur C. Clarke and some by Bradbury. Looking at them brought back lots of memories, so I thought I would take a peek at *Childhood's End*.

I bought this at McGill's for 13/3, probably in about 1955 or 1956. It was published in 1954 by Sidgwick and Jackson. I have never seen the original American edition. In Australia then we could only buy books that had been published in England. I had not looked at this book since then, about 55 years ago. I have just read the first 25 pages, and I am astonished at how prescient Clarke was. The opening scene describes two giant rocket ships powered by atomic engines almost ready for launching into space. The man in charge of the presumably American effort is wondering how his old associate, who had chosen to join the Russians at the end of the Second World War, was managing and if their project is as advanced as his. The other man, somewhere on the shores of Lake Baikal, is wondering the same about his American counterpart in the Pacific. Each is thinking that the other is about to start a space race as they attempt to rocket off the Earth.

And this was before the Russians launched Sputniks 1 and 2 to launch the space race between the Russians and the Americans in 1957.

The American man in charge of the project is wondering whether the Russians have subs offshore monitoring their activities — shades of the Cold War, which must been in progress at the time this was written. Then what happens almost immediately before they are both ready to launch? The sky is blotted out by huge silent circular space ships that descend and travel across every country, coming to rest where they hover over every major city in every country. No one sees what the inhabitants of those ships look like, but there is no doubt about their obvious power. And that is the end of humankind's hopes of getting into space.

Does this remind anyone of the beginning of the TV series **V**, both of them and especially the recent remake where the huge ships drift down and hover over the most important cities in every country? Surely the writers of that series must have been influenced by Childhood's End's first few pages. I will have to re-read this book to see what happens, because I'm sure it's nothing like I remember. Damn it!

What I do remember though is that Clarke wrote two kinds of

stories: those that were mindboggling and always thought-provoking, in which grand ideas of humanity's future were depicted in ways that seemed magical, yet we knew were grounded in pure science; and more pedestrian adventures that involved explanations of technology and future lifestyles, most often mingled with drama on a smaller scale, that preached to younger readers like myself. As he grew older, Clarke's second type of story became incresingly pedestrian, and he probably lost many readers other than those hard-core followers who would stick with him no matter what. It wasn't until *Rendezvous with Rama*, years later, that he recaptured that enigmatic sense of wonder he exhibited in his earlier novels, such as *Against The Fall of Night* and *The City and The Stars*, both of which are the same story, with the latter written years later while he was living in Australia and exploring the Great Barrier Reef, of which he also wrote a book about called *The Coast of Coral*.

In 1935 Clarke was influenced by Olaf Stapledon's magnificent *First and Last Men* and its coverage of millions of years of human history, so he wanted to do something like that. He wrote many versions, and even though the story was rejected by John W. Campbell at Astounding as being too downbeat, Clarke eventually found a place in Startling Stories in 1948 for this story, only to be disappointed by the fact that the editor used a very sexy magazine cover that had nothing to do with his story.

He couldn't get the story and its millions of years of history out of his mind, so when some time became available while he was living on the Great Barrier Reef he rewrote this story, producing what he considered a better, although longer story. He was surprised when many readers said they preferred the earlier version, but I'm sure there were many like me who liked both versions, and would find it hard to choose between them.

Two other books that Clarke wrote as a result of his time on the Great Barrier Reef were T*he Deep Range* (1957, published by Frederick Muller and sold in Australia for 17/-), and a juvenile novel called *Dolphin Island* (Victor Gollanz, 1963, for 15/6). I liked them both, but *The Deep Range* was probably the first novel to depict undersea farming and whale herding. Whale herding, like cattle herding, he got wrong. *Dolphin Island*, however, was not a bad story. It dealt with communications between dolphins and humans, all cutting-edge research in 1963, with lots of underwater information that fascinated me at the time because I was also into skindiving and scuba diving.

Islands in the Sky is one of Clarke's earliest books. It is illustrated with a cover that looks very technical, like a black and white photo taken in space as a space station is being constructed (by R. A. Smith and originally used in Clarke's book *The Exploration of Space*) and with black-and-white scraper board illustrations (typical of the 1940s and 50s SF magazines) scattered throughout the book. There is no publication date on the book, but it had been reduced from 10/- to 5/- at McGill's, so I must have bought it around 1955 when I first started buying books there. As a fifteen-year-old I enjoyed it immensely, although now it is dated, and although probably technically accurate in how it describes the effect of no gravity in a space station, the way it describes life on board a space station it is woefully inaccurate, to judge from what I have seen of the Russian and American programs as well as images from the ISS. (*International Space Station*).

Probably such old books are better left in boxes in a garage.

Besides, who am I to talk about these books?

I'm not a scholar or an academic who specialises in SF or literature, but simply a reader who enjoys a good story that can transport me to another realm or another world, or into some place I would not normally see or find, that can entertain me as a movie does and probably better than a movie can because it gives my imagination space to roam alongside that of the author.

That's all I ask of a book.

Isaac Asimov was another author I was fond of. Such books as *Pebble in the Sky* and *The Currents of Space* were two that I enjoyed immensely. And then there were the Robot stories in the collection *I Robot*. I didn't discover his '*Foundation*' volumes until the early 1960s. I found them a good read but not up to what I expected after hearing so much about them. They were all written in the 1940s, with the first collected volume being published in 1951, and they were bestsellers everywhere. They were full of good ideas, as was everything he wrote, but those two first-mentioned books had more sense of wonder in them than did the '*Foundation*' stories. Nevertheless, when my paperback copies wore out I replaced them with a hardcover edition. I did like the robot stories, and when *The Caves of Steel* appeared, a novel that combined robots and humans living in sealed cities and a murder mystery that involved the murder of a human by a robot which was thought impossible because of the three laws of robotics, which were supposed to prevent such things from happening, and to have a robot police inspector investigate—

wow! —this was something different.

For years they talked about making a film of this story. I even heard some time ago that Jack Nicholson was to star as the robot detective, but nothing eventuated. There was a recent fabulous film called *I Robot* starring Will Smith, which looked spectacular, but had very little to do with Asimov's *I Robot*, other than the name and perhaps the names of some of the characters from those robot stories.

There was a lot of friendly rivalry between Isaac Asimov and Arthur C. Clarke, since they both were scientists and both wrote SF stories as well as scientific and technical articles. Asimov was the more prolific writer, though probably 80 per cent of his output was in the field of dumbing down science so the average reader could understand it, whereas I think Clarke's scientific articles were often more technical when they weren't strictly speculative.

On the other hand, Asimov's fiction was in general more exciting for me than Clarke's, which often was filled with too many technical details, but when Clarke wanted to do so, he could transcend pedestrianism in books like *Childhood's End, Rendezvous with Rama,* and, many years later, *Songs of Distant Earth.*

Nightfall was probably the greatest story Asimov wrote. It was a novelette, the one I remember and have read a few times, and was much better than the expanded version written by Robert Silverberg 40 or so years later.

I have heard it said that Clarke's *The City and The Stars* was his answer to Asimov's *'Foundation'* series, with its idea of an immensely old city or place where knowledge of all humankind was kept so it could be used to help civilisation, or successive civilisations, to recover after a massive collapse, but I don't see that as a viable comparison. Clarke's book was generated by his reading of Stapledon's *Last and First Men*, a massive history of humankind from its beginning to its end when the world is swallowed by the sun billions of years in the future, whereas Asimov's *'Foundation'* stories looked for their inspiration to the past, as shown in *The Rise and Fall of the Roman Empire*. For me, Clarke's book generated more excitement and feelings of wonder than did Asimov's series.

James Blish blew them all out of the water with his *Cities in Flight* series. While other writers were thinking of faster-than-light travel and explanations of how it might work in order to get mankind to the stars, along came Blish, with his gravity-neutralising device called a spindizzy, which enabled him to have huge cities of millions of people take off and leave Earth to wander among the stars.

What an idea that was!

These days it belongs to another alternate universe, because in this one it is pure science fantasy. It could never happen, any more than flying cars zipping about in the airspace of cities could. Can you imagine the chaos if you translated the traffic problems every major city has from the ground into a three-dimensional space above a city? It's bad enough at major airports with planes coming and going only minutes apart. To have every Tom , Dick, and Harry, with a personal flying car zipping up and off anytime they felt like it, would be nothing short of disastrous. It's a fantasy, a nice one, but nevertheless a fantasy, and it could never happen without some kind of gravity-neutralising drive.

One of the most memorable stories for me that Blish wrote was *Surface Tension*, a novelette I first read in a small Australian magazine, and later when it was collected with a group of stories in a volume called *The Seedling Stars*. They were all about humans being adapted to live on different planets and in different environments. They were wonderful stories, but the most outstanding was *Surface Tension*. They say that every author has at least one masterpiece in them, and this one is Blish's. If you haven't read it, please do: the twist at the end is stunning.

My cheap hardcover copy of that collection turned dark brown as the paper oxidised and it started to fall apart, so reluctantly I had to throw it away some years ago. If James Blish is remembered for anything, it has to be for that story, and for his marvellous novel *A Case of Conscience*. He is also famous for his commentaries on science fiction, but not under the name of James Blish. He used the pseudonym William Atheling Jr, in whose name an annual Australian award on SF criticism and commentary was established in 1976.

There were so many writers, and I read most of them. Most are now long forgotten, but some stand out, such as those already mentioned. I didn't like Heinlein because I thought he was too jingoistic, although I did read him later and found some good stuff. There was Murray Leinster, A. E. van Vogt, whose stories were often creepy, or convoluted to the point of not being comprehensible, Vargo Statten and Volstead Gridban, made up names for many different authors who put out a line of pulp paperbacks from England that disappeared by the mid 60s as more publishers saw the potential with the SF genre and started putting out both hardcover and softcover books. I had them all, stacked in makeshift shelves in my sleepout, my own room that had once been the veranda.

I had my drums in that sleepout as well as books. I had a turntable with a small amplifier and some good speakers so I could play records. Often while Mum and Dad were in the lounge room watching that huge Admiral television set I would practise conga drums in my room. They are quite loud, and the stuff I practiced was basic: just sounds initially, how to slap, hit an open tone, a closed tone, a bass sound, and so on. Then basic rhythms and counter rhythms, sometimes to music, sometimes not. It must have driven my parents nuts because they couldn't escape the sounds.

Once, the girl who lived across the road made a recording with her portable tape machine from inside her lounge room at the front of their house of me playing drums in my room at the front of our house. The recording was clear and it was easy to distinguish the various rhythms and sounds I played. So the sound of my playing must have been very loud in our lounge room, which was behind the windows that once opened onto the veranda which was my room.

Later I used the records to study what the conga drummer did at different points. Since recordings of the music I was interested in were not available in Australia I had to send to the USA for records, and in quite a short time had a large collection of fantastic material that no one else in Australia had heard at that time: recordings of Mongo Santamaria, Tito Puente, Tito Rodriguez, Rene Touzet, and many Cuban groups that played authentic Cuban music, records that I played so often I wore them out.

Having had some lessons at this stage from Albert as well as Armando, I found it easy to figure out what was being played and could separate the sound of the drums from the other sounds of the music, and could thus study those parts and learn to play them. I could also hear how the bass lines and the piano lines were actually extensions of either drum tonal melodies or the extended form of the clave pattern played by the sticks on the timbales and kit drums.

I would study and learn specific drum solos, then later in the clubs where I played I would try and replicate those solos. Sometimes it worked. Sometimes I got lost and quickly had to revert to a basic pattern to find where I was. Eventually I didn't need to replicate other drummers' solos, because I began to understand that they are made up of short melodic riffs that you can combine in many different ways, depending on how you felt at the time. You could evolve a solo using a short stated theme, then expand on that before returning to the same or a similar theme. It was almost as if you were writing a short piece of music. It wasn't and shouldn't be a lot of fast noisy playing to show off, but it should have space and structure, theme and resonance, before coming back to submerge into the general song or piece being played. The master conga drummers do this, which is why they can sit out on the stage as Armando Peraza did when Santana was here. They all walked off the stage and left him there with four conga drums, which he played for almost 15 minutes, creating one of the most incredible solos ever performed live. When he finished there was a standing ovation, which only stopped when the rest of the band returned and they continued whatever it was they had been playing before.

No one had seen conga drumming like that before in this country. Armando was so far above the others that he set the standards to which a lot of younger drummers aspired. But I already knew that long before he joined Santana and came back with him to Australia.

When I was 14 and 15 I also read westerns and private investigator storie,s such as the Carter Brown series. These seemed exciting at first, but soon they seemed to lack any depth. Perhaps the writing was atrocious, although I would not have known at the time. More than likely it was because the backgrounds were so ordinary, so familiar, that no imagination went into delineating them, and unless the story dealing with the characters was very good the whole thing would be bland and uninteresting. As a contrast I loved Western movies, which were often filmed in magnificent places like Monument Valley or the Painted Desert, or the Sierra Nevadas when they weren't shot on a back lot in Hollywood, like most of the interiors. The better movies had an otherworldly appearance,which hinted at a very different life style and set of rules that had to be followed. The westerns as books were often filled with local vernacular, which I found more off-putting to read than when you heard it spoken in a movie.

Those books were often found at the back of the newsagent's shop, where there were comic books, of which Superman, Batman, The Phantom, and other superheroes I liked dwelled among other ordinary characters such as Archie and Jughead, Mickey Mouse, Donald Duck, and that spinach-eating naval hero, Popeye the sailor man. I lost interest in comics and westerns and detective stories when I started reading the weekly supply of SF books.

As a contrast, SF stories were well delineated because their backgrounds were so different— alien, or technical — that a lot of description was needed to set the scenes in which the usual very human and ordinary actions took place. As I grew older, and especially after I came back from Darwin, I discovered other authors, such as Poul Anderson and Jack Vance, whose stories set on other worlds or on far future ancient Earth were for me mindboggling. Anderson has such a beautiful way of describing background, and blending it with story and action, that for years his work surpassed all that I had come to expect from SF stories. Jack Vance, also in later years, was an all-time favourite. His stories set in the most bizarre worlds had that sense of adventure and excitement that I craved, but also he was an engaging writer who often used the most unusual words which I had to look up in a dictionary to see what they meant or if they were being used in the right context. Often they seemed out of place, but thinking of them in the context of the time they became a part of the English language, they were not out of place at all, and they gave a whole different perspective to the scenes Vance was describing.

With all my reading and drum playing there was no time for watching TV. During the first two years after returning from Darwin I virtually never looked at the TV set that sat so prominently in the lounge room.

Into the Unknown

My other great interest was skin diving. With my friend Brian we had been venturing into the ocean since we were 16 and 17 respectively. We had made our own wetsuits and spearguns, and we ventured out initially from the back beach at Williamstown, or out from the Crystal Pool, which in those days was full of fish. As we became braver and more confident, we would go to Barwon Heads or Queenscliff to dive in the ocean, which was a much more dangerous and exciting place than the Bay behind Williamstown. For some reason I could not manage to shoot a fish. I always missed, but Brian didn't. He kept both his parents and mine with a good supply of fish to eat at the weekends when we went diving.

One of the boys from our next door neighbour's house, Peter Fanning, was also into skin diving and surfing. I never became interested in surfing, but it was he who gave me a copy of *Diving to Adventure* by Hans Haas, which I devoured with enthusiasm. I immediately went and bought a copy of this book for myself.

It was this book that initially inspired me to shoot film underwater. The other inspiration was a 26 episode documentary series produced by Hans Hass (who had a doctorate in marine biology), which he filmed in the tropical seas aroung The Maldive islands, The Nicobar islands ,Singapore, Malaysie and Indonesia. (*He later published a book about this called Expedition into the Unknown.*)

He had a magnificent sailing ship (*Xarifa*) filled with laboratories for film processing as well as marine research. It was what made me watch TV whereas before I wasn't interested.

Not long aftert that came a series called *Sea Hunt* starring LLoyd Bridges. This was not documentary but was a series of adventure and mystery stories all involving scuba diving. And not long after that another series starring David Hedison (whom I remembered from the original version of *The Fly* with Vincent Price) that involved water police and lots of diving sequences.

I had recently obtained a 16 mm Bolex camera with three lenses, but no housings were available, so the only solution was to make my own. Hans Haas had to make his own housings. Cousteau also did the same, and it was their original designs that became the models for first commercial manufacturing when diving enthusiasts demanded cameras they could use underwater. But this wasn't to happen for some time, so I had no recourse other than to make something I could use myself.

After much thought, I came up with a solution. It was very simple. Stick the camera in a bag of some sort that was waterproof as well as pressure proof to a degree, because water pressure increases very rapidly the deeper you go. What was strong and flexible and could withstand pressure? An inner tube was made of strong flexible rubber, but it would have to be a big inner tube like those used in truck tyres rather than the smaller ones used in cars. They were very expensive, so I put that idea on hold. Then I had another idea: what if I used a tube that had been punctured and was basically only good to throw away? I didn't need the whole inner tube, only a small section that wasn't punctured. I went back to the garage and asked what they did with punctured tubes. Could I have one? 'Why not?' the guy told me. 'There's a heap of them outside. Help yourself. They're no good to us. Someone comes and takes them away to a factory in Geelong Road where they shred them and use them in making re-treads.'

Out the back was a pile of old inner tubes and bald tyres, but only a couple of the inner tubes were big enough for what I wanted. The Bolex had to sit up in the tube, so the tube had to have at least 10 inches of height. I took my two tyre tubes home, but only one was big enough. I cut off a section a few inches longer than the length of the camera and stuffed the Bolex inside to see how it fitted. So far so good. I had already decided I needed some plate glass to seal both ends so I could hold the camera in the tube in front of my face as I swam along and could see through the tube to what the camera was pointing at. I found a glass factory in Footscray, and got the people there to cut me two oval pieces of heavy plate glass. At a hardware store I found a couple of those flat wire clips with a screw head built into them that a plumber would use to join a rubber hose to a metal pipe by screwing the metal clip tight with a screwdriver. It turned out they did make them big enough to join large drainage pipes together using a rubber seal so I bought a couple of these.

I fitted the first piece of glass to the tube, slipped the camera in, and made sure the wide-angled lens (set at its widest aperture and with an fstop of f8) sat tight against the front glass. I then fitted the back piece and tightened it to a good seal. After testing it in the bathtub so see if any water leaked in, and whether the thick rubber was flexible enough so I could depress the button that made the camera run, I undid the back, took the camera out, and wound up the spring as far as it would go. It looked like it would work fine.

I headed to the beach. With the camera all set up and ready I ventured out into the shallow water at the Williamstown backbeach, which was clear and easily accessible from the rocks along the shore. The makeshift housing didn't leak, and I shot 40 seconds of film before the camera had to be rewound.

I had to come out of the water, dry off the housing, undo it, and remove the camera to rewind it again for the next 30 to 60 seconds of filming. Replacing it back into the housing I ventured again into deeper water and shot another minute of film while swimming among schools of tiny fish and a flotilla of baby squid. I shot some images of scallops snapping and bouncing along the bottom as they tried to escape the menace I represented. This was fantastic stuff: I was excited even though I had to exit the water after every minute of filming, dry the housing, take the camera out, and rewind it before replacing it in the housing and again enter the water.

I couldn't wait to see the results. As soon as I could I sent the film off to the Kodak processing plant in Coburg to be developed.

In the meantime I scribbled some notes for a documentary on basic skindiving and got hold of my brother-in-law Fred. We headed off to the beach around the Bay near Mout Martha where the water was deep enough, but close to the beach so I could get out every time I needed to change a roll of film, or more specifically, to rewind the camera, because it was a springloaded mechanism and each wind only gave a bit over a minute of filming. With four minutes on each roll of film, that meant at least four trips back to the beach for each roll of film shot.

It took such a long time, however, to shoot a really short piece of film that this idea for a documentary about the basics of skindiving never got finished. I ended up with about 10 minutes in total after a whole afternoon of in and out of the water and most of it was shot after we came out of the water with a bag of scallops. We barbecued them on the beach and ate them with great relish.

There had to be a better way of filming, a way that enabled me to rewind the camera every time it needed without having to exit the water to do so. And that of course meant money to have an underwater housing designed that enabled me to use the camera more efficiently.

And that was something that would have to wait awhile.

I *am on the right wearing my old 'sealskin' wraparound suit. My brother inlaw Fred is wearing a wetsuit.*
We are carrying a bag of scallops we collected off the beach at Mt Martha, which we barbequed and ate on the beach.
a screen shot from a 16mm movie film. c1961.

The first scallop cooking... Zara adds worchestershire sauce to the rest. Almost always when we went diving we would bring up something to eat. Scallops, sea urchins, abalone... all of which we generally cooked on the beach.

Cameras and housings and underwater films

Diving in deeper water immediately presented a problem with the camera the way it was housed. The rubber was pushed inwards by water pressure and my fear was that it would leak in and flood the camera. The solution was the remake the rubber part by using a part of the tyre tube that had the valve used to pump air in. Once this was done, I could use a hand pump to pump some air into it which made the tube bulge as the pressure increased but as soon as I got into the water it came back to normal as I dived below the two metre mark which allowed me to push the shutter button to shoot film. But of course it was ridiculously limiting because every time I had to rewind I had to exit the water, and sometimes that was quite a swim back to the beach or the shoreline. It would have been easier from a boat but none of us had boats at that time.

Although I was happy with the results of the little filming I had managed underwater, I was nevertheless unsatisfied in general because none of what I shot matched the underwater sequences from a recent cinemascope film I had seen at the Regent theatre.

It was called the *Twelve Mile Reef* or *Beyond The Twelve Mile Reef*, and it starred the famous Gilbert Roland (a great Mexican actor) and a very young Robert Wagner.

It was a story about Greek sponge divers off the Florida coast and their rivalry with American conch divers who worked the same area some twelve miles offshore. The Greek divers used old fashioned helmets and hoses connected to the surface while the brash Americans used SCUBA as developed by Captain Jacques Yves Cousteau. In 1942 he went to an engineering friend Emile Gagnan and asked him to design something that could regulate the air intake while under pressure. He wanted air to be delivered at whatever the ambient pressure of the water was so it would be easy to breathe. Cousteau outlined his idea to Gagnan who had already been working on a reduction valve to feed fumes from burning charcoal or natural gas into car engines because there was no petrol available. It was the early stages of the Second World War and there was no petrol in France. It took Gagnan only a few weeks to modify his design and build a working model in metal which could be attached to the twin tubes of compressed air Cousteau called an Aqualung. Modern scuba diving was born.

SCUBA is an acronym that means self-contained underwater breathing apparatus.

It was no doubt coined by Americans who love acronyms. The term Aqualung was registered and couldn't be used except under licence, so anyone making a similar device came up with their own names. Eventually the description of the device, (any device that was a self-contained underwater breathing apparatus), was simply shortened to Scuba, and all of them have been called that ever since.

The Twelve Mile Reef film opened in Cinemascope with an unbelievable close up shot of a gigantic vicious looking Barracuda, a very dangerous predatory fish. It floated across the screen in magnificent colour with the sunlight glistening off its scales and I swear it sparkled once on the fish's needle sharp teeth. The camera panned down to the depths below to find a diver with heavy boots and weighted to stay on the bottom, clumping along, disturbing clouds of sand with each step, breathing noisily through a long tube that connected his helmet with a boat on the surface, but he was only wearing the helmet and not a full diving suit. The diver was Gilbert Roland and he was collecting sponges.

I don't remember much of the story which was the usual forbidden romance between the strict Greek family's beautiful daughter, and the brash young American Scuba diver the son of a Conch shell diving family. There was rivalry between the divers using old fashioned ways and those using the new aqualungs, someone got killed, someone got beaten up, but in the end love prevailed and two rival families ended up grudgingly respecting each other and uniting as the two children, one from each family publicly proclaimed their love, etc. etc.

I can't remember who the patriarch of the American family was, but I have a vague recollection it may have been Robert Ryan or perhaps that actor who went on to be the lead in the original Mission Impossible series on TV. But what I do remember is half of the film had been taken underwater in the clear seas off the Florida coast and it was absolutely outstanding. It made me want to be able to shoot film like that underwater, and it also made me painfully aware that I could never do it with a camera housed in a rubber tyre tube with pieces of glass at either end.

Cousteau of course had similar problems with taking photos and shooting movies underwater, but because he had financial backing or at least had the ability to generate money through his articles and his underwater archaeological work, he could have camera housings custom made. Eventually finding these inadequate and time consuming he developed the concept of a self-contained underwater camera which was a camera sealed and waterproofed so he didn't have to worry about housings, but could simply jump straight into the water with it. It would operate in the same way any land camera still or movie would with the exception that once loaded with film he could go straight into the water with it. He had enough engineers or skilled people who could build anything he envisioned. The Calypso (*named after his research and dive boat*) underwater 35mm camera was his design and it was later manufactured in France for general sale as well as licenced to Nikon after which it became the famous Nikonos camera. I wasn't to see one of those for a few years but in the meantime I had to manage as best

I could with my rubber bag housing. Much later a German company (Ewa) developed flexible camera housings which were in effect clear rubber bags with perspex fronts into which a camera could be placed. All the controls were accessible because the rubber was so soft. They called their housings marine bags and they were popular for a while, but you couldn't take them too deep.

The Creature from the Black Lagoon had quite a bit of underwater photography in it but somehow it didn't seem exciting. In that same year (1954) we saw Walt Disney's version of *20,000 Leagues under the Sea* with James Mason and Kirk Douglas and Peter Lorre in diving suits that were self-contained yet had a reasonable 19th century primitive look to them. A kind of retro-diving suit that somehow looked modern but wasn't. And the submarine was fabulous too, with its 'steampunk' gothic appearance that really did give the appearance that it would work. There was some great underwater stuff in this film, but some awful effects that almost spoiled it. It was an enjoyable film overall, and it still holds up pretty good against some of the other filmed stories involving Captain Nemo and the Nautilus.

When I did finally get the first model of the Nikonos released in Australia I remember we had loads of fun on the rocks by the crystal pool or on a beach wherever we went. I would take some photos on land usually of us getting ready to go in for a dive and there would always be people around watching with great curiosity. When we were ready to go in I would leave the camera hanging by a strap around my neck and climb down the rocks to get into the water, or if we were going in off a beach I would just wade in. The consternation this caused when people saw a camera hanging around my neck was priceless. They would run after me and yell out stuff like: You've got a camera around your neck, or they would gesture with wild exaggerated movements as if taking a picture and then point at their chest or point at me, waving their arms to get my attention, and when I obviously didn't get what they were trying to say they would throw their hands up in despair. It would be the last thing I saw as I slipped under the water, camera and all, smiling inwardly, because it's hard to smile physically with snorkel or a scuba mouthpiece in your mouth.

There were so few underwater cameras around, and what there were often had enormous housings so they were unmistakable, but the Nikonos looked exactly like an ordinary 35mm camera, and people would panic when they saw me entering the water with it strapped around my neck. I usually explained to them when I came back out (if they were still there) what kind of camera it was. It didn't take long though before more people had these cameras — they were brilliant completely sealed all weather cameras that could be used in snow or in sandy dusty conditions as well as underwater down to at least three atmospheres — that the novelty of seeing someone take one underwater soon wore off.

But it was fun for a while…

Eventually I met another photographer who had a camera housed in a clear Perspex casing through which there were controls sealed with tiny O-rings that allowed him to wind the film on, to push the shutter button and to change the focus. His camera was a Hasselblad, and expensive, so I'm sure his housing worked perfectly. In America there were some manufacturers making housings for various cameras as the idea of underwater photography became popular, but they were too expensive to import. This guy had not imported his housing but had it made locally. I got the name of his manufacturer and went there and got them to build me a similar Perspex housing for my Bolex. At last I could stay underwater and work the controls of the camera, only surfacing to change rolls of film. The beauty of a transparent housing was that I could see in and if even the slightest drop of water got in I could surface immediately and remove the camera before any damage could be done. I shot quite a lot of film on Abalone diving with this housing.

Filming with my first real housing made of clear perspex.

Filming with my third housing, a pressurized metal housing that certainly wouldnt leak like the perspex one did. Here I am shooting shellfish predation by the eleven armed costinasterias Calamaria starfish which caused enormous problems in Port Phillip Bay. Some of this film aired on Channel 9 news with Eric Pearce , a highly respected newsreader explaining.

Syncronicity

It's strange how similar ideas come up more or less simultaneously. Perhaps it has to do with research and the fact that many science fiction writers also read science journals and whatever popular science magazines they could get their hands on because these were full of new ideas and cutting edge research. In 1957 two books came out in that same year, Arthur C Clarke's *The Deep Range* which I have already mentioned, and Kenneth Bulmer's *City under the Sea*.

Both novels dealt with similar subject matter; exploitation of the undersea realm through farming, herding, mining, and colonization. To quote from the blurb to The Deep Range...*an exciting story of the not far distant future, when Man begins to cultivate the untouched two-thirds of this globe, and to fence the Oceans so he can herd his greatest cattle—the whales* It goes on to say: *Walter Franklin and undersea warden who goes on to become Director of the Bureau of Whales discovers that despite all the resources of science and technology, there are times when man is helpless against the sea, and that it still holds many mysteries. He also learns at the risk of his life that the ocean's ultimate depths hide creatures that match even the whales in size.*

The publisher claims that he (Clarke) is the first novelist to write a story based on the fascinating theme of organized cultivation of the sea's vast food resources.

A very similar claim is made for Kenneth Bulmer's City under the Sea, stating that it is *more than a spellbinding futuristic novel of adventure and survival that is the first to incorporate the ideas of undersea farming—and its chilly implications in a world desperate for alternative food sources—into the realm of science fiction.*

Set in the far future, when mankind owes its survival to a vast network of ocean farms it tells the shattering story of a man doomed to mindless, anonymous serfdom in a colony of underwater slaves…controlled by savage armed overseers and squadrons of man controlled killer fish. Escape seems impossible but Jeremy Dodge is a man driven to survive—for the only alternative is living death.

Two very different books in structure and tone and plot, yet they deal with the same subject. Which one came first? Does anyone care now?

Both publishers claimed to be the first to have books dealing with what is now loosely called aquaculture. But for me —when I got these two books I was probably 18 or 19 having bought them in 1959 or 1960— they were absolutely thrilling. I was into skin diving and had devoured whatever diving/adventure books that were available, such as *Diving to Adventure* by Hans Haas, *The silent World* by Jacques Yves Cousteau, *The Blue World* by Folco Quilici, and other related books like *The Con Tiki Expedition* by Thor Heyerdahl and *Shallow Water Diving and Spearfishing* by Hilbert Schenk and Henry Kendall, (a technical book which we used as a 'bible' to help us with our diving) to find science fiction novels that dramatically dealt with the future of the Sea and mankind's attempts to live in and under it was a real thrill. What more alien environment could you have that was so readily accessible?

No doubt a lot of other stuff on this theme was extrapolated and published in science fiction stories around that time but at the moment (almost 60 years later) it eludes me. Looking more at *City Under the Sea* Kenneth Bulmer coined the term aquiculture which he used a few times throughout this book, so whether he was trying to be different or whether the term aquaculture had actually been thought of to describe fish farming and other associated stuff I'm not sure. I suspect the term had not been used at that point and Bulmer was original in coming up with it. I do think he read Cousteau who definitely called his scuba divers menfish and dreamed of them being able to breathe underwater without the use of scuba or hookah or any other system that supplied compressed air. Bulmer's descriptions of diving procedures and decompression and other deep diving activities seem accurate and I suspect he actually did some diving and had experience of it. The story was quite an adventure, very pulpy and melodramatic, and bits of it seemed too fantastic to be possible, turning humans into water breathing menfish —and using them a working slaves never able to go back on the land again— borders on being science fantasy, but to the 17 year old person that I was at the time it seemed to be one of the most exciting books I had read to that point. I could relate to it because I too was a skindiver just beginning to dabble with the use of scuba.

Clarke on the other hand was a very good diver and had already spent months exploring the Great Barrier Reef and even wrote a book about it before he wrote *The Deep Range*. His underwater descriptions and extrapolated use of equipment was cutting edge at the time, but whale herding…? That wouldn't be accepted today, yet 54 years ago… I can't imagine that even then it would have been an acceptable idea. The general hunting of whales has only recently been stopped —except for a few countries that claim to need it for scientific research or worse still as an ethnic and cultural activity— so it is possible that hunting still occurred to a limited degree when he wrote the book and simply extrapolated the idea of hunting whales into herding them as a source of food and whatever else they could supply.

What both books had in common was the idea of the time that the oceans could be exploited for man's benefit, and that development of the ocean realm was equally as possible as development and exploration of space. Both books had a central character that came back to earth from space and ended up one way or another living on, in, or under the ocean. Both books demonstrated through their plots the possibilities of fish farming, whale herding, and general control of the ocean's resources. I think however, Clark's was the better book overall.

Most science fiction around the middle of the last century, fifty to sixty years ago, was written by young men some of whom were not much out of adolescence and if they weren't writing wish fulfilment stories for themselves they were writing for an audience which basically comprised teenage boys or those who were in their early 20s; boys who were mechanically or scientifically minded or who yearned for adventure. These books were often simplistic in theme and relied mostly on action, adventure, solving scientific puzzles, space travel, alien contact, and other themes that required no emotional depth or characterization but in which an individual triumphed against all odds. There was plenty of excitement, descriptions of how things worked, and thrills a minute. It was little wonder that science fiction became ghettoized and was looked down upon by those people who claimed to write and read literature. The few quality SF novels written by famous mainstream authors at that time were not marketed as SF (and still aren't). As a consequence they had larger audiences and the readers of these books never thought twice about what they were reading. They frowned upon SF but happily exclaimed how wonderful the books by George Orwell, Aldous Huxley were, even though *Brave New World* and *1984* were clearly SF. They didn't even mind H.G. Wells, or Jules Verne, both of whom probably established the parameters that every other SF writer used in subsequent stories. But the kind of SF that people like me read… that was something they discarded out of hand. Well, as far as I was concerned it was their loss, not mine.

Gigging around town

In the meantime I still gigged around various nightclubs, in some places just sitting in with the resident band, in others, doing the floor show. My sister Zara had a job at nights in the chorus of the girls at the Tivoli theatre. These were scantily clad girls who posed in elegant phalanxes across the stage, sometimes even performing group choreography in between the various acts. The Tivoli was a variety theatre which was basically a modern extension of Vaudeville. The shows there had that not quite sleazy feeling of early vaudeville but were much more modern and tasteful. They had lead acts like Winifred Atwell, who was always popular and her shows were invariable packed out. Albert La Guerre borrowed my bongoes to do one of her shows because there was some calypso involved, and he didn't own any bongoes. Nat King Cole's brother Ike also performed there.

Harry Belafonte (performing to a packed Palais Theatre on St Kilda Esplanade) was all the rage with his interpretations of calypso from Jamaica and the Bahamas, and many local singers performed his songs. I played bongoes for Kamahl at one show not long after and he sang calypso amongst his more romantic songs. I didn't mind Calypso, it had lots of percussion, but I didn't think it had the depth that Haitian and Cuban music had; perhaps because it was sung in English. Its origins were vaguely similar to Haitian and Cuban in that it came about as an amalgamation of African and the colonial power's culture and language via the slave trade, but somehow English seemed wrong compared to the more romantic Spanish and French.

On the Jazz side Dave Brubeck had an enormous hit with his piece Take Five in 1959 and that filtered across into the local groups who all played it in some form or another. I remember doing a floor show at an elegant club in Toorak Road called The Embers Nightclub, and Garry Hyde was the drummer there with his group. Garry's father Billy Hyde also did floorshows there. The singer that night was Johnny Summers, who did shows at Birdland. I went to The Embers because Johnny asked me to come and sit in. I knew the guys in the band because they also played at other venues around town, so they didn't mind one extra sitting in.

This night everyone wanted to play Take Five, because it was the latest hit. Gary said to me before they started 'You can do a solo in this, okay?' I agreed. I had heard the piece but never actually played it. Most musicians found it difficult because the count was in 5. Each bar had 5 instead of the customary 4 quarter notes hence the notation of 5/4, so they found it difficult. It was usually broken into 2 groups —one of 3 followed by one of 2, which made it easier to count. The piano played a repeated phrase made up of that 3 and 2 structure. The first solo was the trumpet before the saxophone came in, then it was my turn…

I think Garry was trying to embarrass me thinking that I would come unstuck and muck up the piece, and that they would have some fun ribbing me afterwards. He forgot that I grew up with Greek heritage and we often listened and danced to music that was in odd time structures compared to what Anglo Australians were used to, and with the piano repeating the one bar 5 beat phrase, similar to a montuno guajeo in Cuban music, all I had to do was lock the melody of the phrase in my mind and play around based on that structure. It was easy and I think I did a good solo without getting lost, much to the surprise of Garry, who later told me he was impressed. Brubeck went on to introduce his progressive jazz with odd time structures in 7/4 and 9/8 to a wide audience, but often his music sounded almost like classical music and the improvisations at first seemed contrived or mechanical. It wasn't easy to swing in rhythms that had odd time structures, and I think one of the problems initially with jazz musicians was that they tried to count rather than simply feel the structure. Once they got beyond counting they became more comfortable with playing in those time signatures, and these days music is often infused with odd time structures that everyone seems to find perfectly natural.

Zara rehearsing in one of the costumes used in our floorshows.

I also did some gigs around town with my sister Zara. We had some musical arrangements of popular songs that Australians were familiar with written for small groups and between us we choreographed some routines that fitted to the music and to a drum solo that was meant to appear improvised but was written down and learnt, so it could be repeated exactly each time we did it. This way it fitted the dance, and the musicians of whatever group we may have performed with could also follow it on paper as we did it; that way they didn't get lost and knew exactly when to come back in for the finale. The whole thing only went for about five minutes and we were usually part of a floorshow that included other singers. We did these gigs at hotel lounge bars where people stayed for dinner and could also drink with their meals, so it was more like a cabaret setting than a nightclub.

Then West Side Story came to Melbourne and Zara got a job in the chorus line with that fabulous production and that was the end of our cabaret shows.

The 6 o'clock swill

1962 in the state of Victoria was one of the last years of the 6 o'clock swill. That was, for those who don't remember or simply have no idea, the frantic rush to buy and down as many drinks as possible in the last 15 minutes or so before the pub (or bar) officially had to close and stop selling drinks. People would crowd with raucous joy or noisy desperation against the bar and buy four or five or even six beers, stack them in front of them, or precariously carry them supported in both hands to a nearby table, after which they would scull them one after the other before they were all ejected from the pub by 10 minutes after 6 p.m. They would stagger out into the street drunk, because coming straight from work to their favourite watering hole, without having had anything to eat, their main object was to drink as much as possible before closing time, and this inevitably resulted in drunks outside in the street jostling and often fighting each other, and more often than not, drunken abuse at home. It was not uncommon that these drunks, having filled extended guts with litres of liquid, would be forced to relieve themselves in side streets, alleyways, or people's front gardens as they struggled to walk back to their parked cars. Streets surrounding the more popular pubs stank of stale piss, which even solid downpours of rain failed to wash away.

My recollections of the 6 o'clock swill are of Williamstown, which has more pubs in it than any other suburban area in Melbourne; 26 the last time I was there. There were more than 100 back in its heyday, when Williamstown was the main port of entry for new arrivals (in the 1800s) who headed for the goldfields of Ballarat and Bendigo. The myriad pubs were their first stop after disembarking from the sailing clippers. Later, when the dockyards with the shipbuilding, wool packers, and other heavy industries, such as railway maintenance, were the mainstay of workers in the suburb (new arrivals having been shifted to

Port Melbourne across Hobson's Bay), the number of pubs slowly came down to 26. Even so, it seemed that there was a pub on just about every corner in Williamstown. Anyone attempting a 'pub crawl' never made it all the way around: 26 are too many to get through even if you only take one drink at each venue.

Not very nice, but Victoria was famous for its 6 o'clock swill: rather like the action of a bunch of huge fat pigs jostling each other to get at food dispensed in a trough.

This also explained why many hotels in the city proper had restaurants and dining rooms where drinks could be served with dinner, and drinkers from the bar could migrate to the dining room where they could continue if they ordered something to eat. These customers were often entertained with a floorshow. Even though these places also had to close by a specific time after which they were not allowed to serve drinks, usually by 10 p.m., they were very popular, and many ¬talented performers gained experience working in those floorshows. The same performers would then go on to the night clubs that opened later, where the same diners who wanted to continue drinking would smuggle spirits in under their jacket or in a flask in their back pockets so they could put some oomph into the soft drinks and coffees ordered at the night clubs.

Zara and I performed our little floor show in some of the hotel venues, but she never went on to the night clubs, where often I went to play conga drums into the early hours of the morning. That was far too late for her.

I don't know how I managed, but on Thursdays, Fridays, and Saturdays I would be at Birdland playing congas and performing as an accompanist to whoever was actually doing the floorshow. I would get home at 3 or 4 in the morning, sleep a couple of hours, and then go to work at the dry cleaner, driving, picking up, and delivering clothes between the factory and the various agencies scattered across the triangle between Sunshine, Footscray, and Williamstown.

The sound of different drums

The floorshows at Birdland were always a lot of fun, with exotic dancers: strippers (or girls who wore very little) dancing with snakes or some other prop designed to titillate or thrill the customers. There were singers like Johnny Summers, a great singer who died too young before his potential could be realised, Inez Amaya, who later called herself Beryl Sellers (she was married to the house drummer Roger Sellers), and regular performances by the comedy duo Crocker and Clarke. They used their performances at Birdland to work on their act, which was constantly evolving. The outstanding one in this duo was Barry Crocker, who went on the have an amazing solo career. Musicians or singers and even dancers often turned up after their shows had finished, and on many occasions were induced by the band to do an impromptu performance. You never knew what was going to happen, so it was always an exciting place to go late at night.

JoJo Smith as he looked the first night I saw him at Birdland.

It was on one of these nights that a young dancer who was a lead dancer with West Side Story's company in Melbourne turned up and asked if he could sit in and play congas. He was from New York, and had a charisma that made everyone turn and look at him the moment he walked in the door. It wasn't just his clothes, or the way he walked, or his self-confidence, although they were obviously part of it. There was something indefinable that compelled those around to look at him; especially the women, of whom he always had someone accompanying him. There were two with him that night, dancers from the West Side Story cast.

Why is it dancers never stop dancing? Do they always need to be the centre of attraction? My sister at the drop of a hat would break into a dance at whatever party she found herself. Being good at it, she quickly ended up surrounded by an audience encouraging her to continue. These girls were hardly into the place when they started dancing with this young man. Their impromptu floorshow had everyone staring at them in rapture while the band of which I was a part felt compelled to play as best we could. I can't remember what we played, other than it was Latin orientated so the congas fitted in. But with those superb dancers performing we played tighter and more precisely than we had ever played. It was just one of those things that happen sometimes; everything comes together exactly as it should and the result is outstanding.

The applause lifted the roof off. Even the band members stood up to applaud the dancers. As soon as they stopped dancing the young man came over to me and introduced himself.

'I'm JoJo Smith.'

We shook hands. That was an unusual name.

'Do you mind if I play your congas?'

'Be my guest,' I invited him as I moved aside. I had been sitting on the bandstand with the -congas on the dance floor. The other musicians of course had chairs or stools to sit on, so they towered above me on the bandstand.

'Stay there.' He said. 'You play tumbao and I'll improvise.' He sat beside me with the higher pitched drum between his legs. 'It's been awhile,' he added.

Tumbao is a base drum pattern around which other drums in a group either play counterpoint or improvise or do both. JoJo counted one two, one two three four fairly rapidly, and I started dead on the next count of one, which wasn't stated. There were only two drums, so he didn't play counterpoint but launched straight into an impressive solo that wove phrases and patterns around the tones and slaps of the tumbao. He tapped his foot on the floor (on one and three) so I had a good metronome to help keep time, because if I listened too closely to what he was doing I could lose the beat, but the tapping foot kept me on time. He looked at me as we played, and when his playing reached a crescendo he nodded once and said 'four', which meant four more bars, which I subconsciously counted. When we reached the end of the four bars we both hit one note on the first beat of the next bar and simultaneously stopped. The band members on the stage behind us stood up and cheered and clapped, and the applause from the audience in the club was overpowering.

JoJo leaned over and gave me a hug and a slap on the back. 'Thanks for that. I haven't played in a long time and I needed to get that out.'

What could I say? The guy was a fantastic player. After that the boss of the club fawned all over him and gave him a great table, shooing a couple of other people out of the way.

Events like that happened often enough to make Birdland the premier night club in Melbourne at that time.

That was a Friday night. When I got there Saturday night, two extra conga drums were next to mine. I hadn't seen before. They had scratches and scuff marks on them so they had obviously been well used, as well as having travelled a lot. Drums only get scratched and marked if they've been in and out of vans and dragged about from venue to venue. I tapped each one, discovering they had a very good sound with cleaner tones that sounded more melodic than my heavier drums. They were also made of lighter wood than mine so they required less effort to transport. I knew immediately that these drums belonged to JoJo. And sure enough he turned up around midnight accompanied by a different dancer, and he played all four drums in another impromptu floorshow that sent the place wild.

'You've got to teach me how to do that,' I said afterwards.

'Me too,' George said. He hadn't been there the night before and this was the first time he had seen and heard JoJo play.

George was the other conga drummer I shared Saturday nights with. He wasn't there on Fridays, but each alternate Saturday he played with the band. On the Saturday he wasn't there he played with an Italian orchestra over in Carlton. I usually did all the floorshows and would then play with the band until closing time. George always left about midnight because he had an early start in the jewellery business he ran.

'You have to learn to isolate one hand from the other,' JoJo explained. 'While one hand plays the base pattern or tumbao the other is free to improvise or play a counter pattern to the other one.'

He demonstrated by playing a few repetitions of tumbao with one hand on the lowest pitched drum. By cutting the rhythm in half, only the four main notes are played with the one hand. 'It's called rumba abierta, or tumbao abierta,' he said, while continuing to play it with the right hand.

'Then we add the tones of the Repicador or the second or third drum.' He started playing on a higher-pitched drum with his left hand while maintaining the lower-pitched right hand drum rhythm unchanged. The counterpoint rhythm on the higher drum went across two repetitions of the tumbao to produce what sounded like two drummers playing.

'And now we vary it by adding tones from the other drums.' He said this while continuing to play both patterns simultaneously. With both hands he started bringing in odd tones from the two other drums, one on his left side and the other on his right, so he used both the right and the left hand to do this while maintaining the two basic patterns he had started with. If you closed your eyes and simply listened it sounded a little like two or perhaps three people playing, instead of one single person. When played very fast it was amazing.

JoJo explained that the various drums in a group are given names depending on their role in the group. In Cuban rumba groups the base drum is called tumbao; the others are called segundo, tres-golpes, and quinto, repicador. The repicador is usually the quinto, which is called that because it is five tones higher in pitch than the base drum or tumbao. Repica is the Spanish exhortation to improvise using the quinto or another higher pitched drum in the group. The names given the drums vary in each country where similar types of conga drums are used in groups. Conga is the English name given to the Cuban drums, which generically are called tumbadores. This was probably because they were first seen played in the streets during carnival with large groups of people dancing in lines and singing in unison. The dance was the conga, which in Cuba is known as a comparsa. Conga is most likely an African name, but it was one the English-speaking people latched onto. There was a time in the 1940s when the conga was a dance craze across the USA. There are many names and structured groups that relate back to

Africa, with various infusions of Spanish, French, Portuguese, or English melody or singing styles throughout the Caribbean and the continent of South America. More than enough books on the subject are available for anyone interested in delving into the history of African-influenced music in the New World.

What JoJo was doing was something we had never seen before. We made arrangements to meet at Birdland during the week early in the afternoon for some conga drum lessons with him. George and I arranged time off from work to do this.

We also played and practiced a lot in my backyard which inadvertantly entertained some of our neighbours who just loved watching us over the back fence.

George and myself with JoJo – our first lesson at Birdland in St Kilda, where we learnt the various parts that make up traditional rumba, and how they fit together to make a rythmic and melodic whole around which the quinto or highest pitched drum can improvise. The parts are generally called tumbao, segundo, tres golpes, repicador, although different names can be found in different places for the same rythms which are locked together by the clave or an extended stick pattern based on the clave. By understanding each part we could then hear the whole as a melodic structure rather than as a group of rythms. Once we understood the melodic structure we also learnt you could improvise within that melodic structure providing it was consistant and didn't get too far away from the overal melody expressed by the differen tones of each drum. What didn't change was the stick pattern since that held it together.

George and JoJo practicing two part playing in my backyard.

It didn't take long for me to pick up the way of playing that allowed isolation of one hand from another. George, though, struggled to get it, and eventually he switched back to his old way of playing, which was fine because he was a good solid player. When the three of us played together, George often played tumbao and I played segundo or counterpoint. JoJo of course improvised on the drum nominated as repicador.

If we played bembe, which is a combination of 6/8 rhythms in which the order of the drums is reversed, being based on bata drumming (religious drumming in both Nigeria and in Cuba, and more recently elsewhere, such as in the USA and Puerto Rico); the highest pitched drum played a simple rhythm, counterpointed by the two drums of lower pitch, with a fourth drum, the biggest and lowest in pitch doing the improvisation.

Sometimes we would spend Sunday afternoons at my place practising and recording what we played so we could listen back and hear our mistakes. A few times Albert La Guerre joined us, and he and JoJo made some wonderful recordings. On other occasions Albert, with another friend from Katherine Dunham days, Antonio Rodriguez, a dancer, would come and play drums and sing in my front bedroom. We even got Mum and my sister Zara to sing some choruses for Albert's Haitian songs, which I recorded. I used an Akai reel-to-reel tape machine. Some years later I transferred these taped tracks to cassette and finally after losing them for many years, found them again in a box of old home movies, so I digitised them and made a CD. The quality is not good, but it is something that can never be repeated and so for me they are invaluable — a priceless reminder of a past that is now so distant it seems to have belonged to someone else.

Antonio Rodriguez seen here at Birdland. c1960

In the meantime I saw West Side Story — it was much better than I expected. Fifty years later we all know the story, but back then it was astonishing. It resonated on many levels with people in this country (as it did in the USA) because all of us had experienced to varying degrees the problems involving integration into a stable society of immigrant newcomers with different cultural biases: the fears that jobs would be taken and that our women would be violated resonated on both sides of the cultural barriers. That the story depicted was an updating of Shakespeare's Romeo and Juliet was well known, but its translation into the concrete jungle of New York suburbs, with Shakespeare's rival feuding families becoming American and Puerto Rican gangs, was outstanding, setting new benchmarks in modern dancing and athleticism. The use of music to represent feelings of the the rival gangs was for me fantastic, as is the montage that crosscuts back and forth between the two gangs as they prepare for the rumble (a big fight between the two gangs), while Maria and Tony are anxiously determined to see each other later that night. That the whole thing ends tragically is a foregone conclusion, but audiences watching that performance on stage were on tenterhooks waiting to see how it all unfolded.

The astonishing choreography was by Jerome Robbins and the unforgettable music was by Leonard Bernstein. Stephen Sondheim created the lyrics for such wonderful songs as Maria, I Feel Pretty, Tonight, I Want to Be in America (America), and others.

This show changed the genre of musical ¬theatre, stepping way outside of the previous lighthearted froth-and-bubble escapism of almost every other musical before it, bringing to audiences an awareness of cultural themes, racial integration, immigrants' desires to improve the lot of themselves and their families, and the feelings of locals who, though stable for years, suddenly felt threatened at every level by these new people coming into their neighbourhood: themes that resonated with most people in every country where the show performed.

That these new people would enrich their society, with new music, new ideas, and new foods never entered people's minds at that stage. All they could perceive was the imagined threat. West Side Story emphasised it all, while presenting a classic but tragic love story and thoroughly entertaining people with its beauty and exuberance. Almost everyone who saw it went back to see the show more than once. Only much later did its deeper impact become apparent.

Not long after the show's Broadway run a musical film of it was made, with George Chakiris and Natalie Wood. For me, though, the best part was played by Rita Moreno, who played the ever-excitable character Anita. George Chakiris was forgettable and never did much after that film, but the others, including Russ Tamblyn, who played the leader of the Jets (the American gang), went on to have outstanding film careers. The filmed version won 10 Academy Awards.

I also saw the film when it came out, but didn't think it had the same ambience as the live show, though technically it was more spectacular. Also, I met many of the people involved in the show as it was presented in Melbourne, went backstage, watched rehearsals, and saw the show many times from both in front and from behind the stage.

Cal Tjader later bought out an album with his inimitable jazz and Latin jazz styling of West Side Story's wonderful music, which was for a long time one of my favourite recordings, probably because it featured two of my favourite drummers, Mongo Santamaria on congas and Willie Bobo on timbales. They worked with Cal Tjader for a number of years before going on to create their own groups or bands, which in their individual ways set trends in combining jazz, popular music, and light rock with Cuban musical genres.

Floor shows with JoJo

Looking tired as we went into the fourth show for the night, this time at Birdland.

When West Side Story finished its season in Melbourne some of the cast stayed on. JoJo was one of them. He organised to do a series of floorshows in and around some night clubs as well as appearing on the Federal Hotel Circuit, which included the Savoy Plaza, the Menzies, and the Federal. We started at the Savoy Plaza. When our ten- minute show finished we quickly packed the drums into my yellow van and drove around to the Menzies Hotel for our second show. Again we would pack up and move on to the next hotel, after which it was close to midnight; we headed off to Birdland, where we did the show again. We did this Thursday, Friday, and Saturday nights. The routine was straightforward, a mixture of JoJo dancing, playing drums, and dancing. I didn't get paid for this, but did it for the fun of it, for the experience of working in front of a live audience, and for the practice of playing drums with different band combinations. In most places there were groups of four, or sometimes five. It was rarely a trio, which would have made it harder.

We started with a song everyone knew, one that was a major hit at the time, 'Hit the Road Jack' by Ray Charles. While I sat and accompanied the house band with one conga drum, JoJo came in with a cool strut and did this funky dance to the first chorus and the verse, then at the end of the second chorus he would take off his jacket and fling it to the bandstand as the musicians segued into a fast mambo guaracha called 'Mama Guela'. This was a song Latin dancers in New York went wild over. It was a huge hit for Tito Rodriguez and his orchestra during the times he and Tito Puente competed and ruled over the dance floor at the Palladium Ballroom in New York. When 'Mama Guela' started I switched to two congas while JoJo went into a fairly fast streetwise salsa routine. Then he would grab the third conga drum and, swirling it around as he danced, he worked his way over to sit next to me and commence a solo as the band behind faded away, apart from the drummer who continued to play his version of a cowbell pattern for mambo. As JoJo soloed I switched from the mambo guaracha pattern to a guaguanco on the two drums. Once this was established JoJo left his drum next to me so I could incorporate it into the pattern and play on the three drums. The drummer from the band behind would fall silent so JoJo only had the conga drums to dance to. His dance this time was very Afro-Cuban in style, as if he were possessed by a spirit. He danced and gyrated as if in ecstasy, then just as we reached a crescendo he would collapse onto the floor, the band would come in with a drawn-out drum roll overlaid by a screeching trumpet, and the lights would go off. That was it. When the lights came on JoJo would be gone, waiting for me behind the bandstand.

As the applause died down we packed up and headed for the next venue, where we repeated the show again.

We did the floorshows for a couple of months, after which JoJo moved to Sydney and finally returned to New York.

A year or so later I read a good review in Time magazine about him performing with his drums in New York. That was the last any of us ever heard of him.

JoJo Smith soloing on quinto
during a floor show at Birdland.

A fantastic time for readers of science fiction

The late fifties and early sixties was a fantastic time for young readers of science fiction. Many novels covered adventures in space, intergalactic travel, and time travel with all its many paradoxes. I couldn't get enough of them. But this was also the time of the Cold War with the Russians and the Americans trying to outdo each other with detonations of ever bigger and bigger bombs. Even the French joined in with their experiments on Mururoa atoll in the South Pacific. Britain, not to be outdone, detonated its atomic bombs in Australia. It was inevitable as the world drew closer to total destruction and atomic war that the major writers of science fiction concocted disaster ¬stories extrapolating many possible consequences from this ridiculous and insane international concept of Mutually Assured Destruction (MAD).

In retrospect it seems that most of the stories I read during the late fifties and into the sixties were disaster stories: disasters brought about by nuclear war or armed conflict using biological weapons, or in keeping with the times, psychedelic drug-influenced chaos and destruction in Europe (see the stories from New Worlds and Impulse magazines during 1967 and 1968 by Brian Aldiss that later made up his mind-boggling 1969 novel *Barefoot in the Head*), as well as disasters brought on by massive overpopulation (*Stand on Zanzibar* by John Brunner in 1968 being one of the best examples, which he followed up with other ramifications of overpopulation and pollution in *The Sheep Look Up* and *The Jagged Orbit*). Degradation of the environment through some kind of rapid climate change or constant pollution and attempts by humans to change things were other common themes, and gradually the boys' own adventures of Arthur C. Clarke and writers of his ilk faded into the background as the world-encompassing disaster stories took over.

So what's new? These themes permeate SF (science fiction, science fantasy, and speculative fiction) more so today than way back then. These days they are often crossed with horror, murder mystery, technological thrillers, and so on, but many of those novels stand up today as examples of well-thought-out reactions to possible worldwide calamities. Of course there was a lot of rubbish written then, just as there is today, but many of the better books were more engrossing than today's novels, which are too easily forgotten once you have read them. Today there is a sameness to them that makes each one blend into the other, repeating themes and possibilities that have already been considered many times before. At least in the fifties and sixties those themes were new and frighteningly possible.

Earth Abides (1950) was one of the best of the disaster novels. A virus is spread rapidly around the world as a result of air travel (more likely to happen today than it would have then, when air travel was relatively new). Most of the population are killed, with only a few survivors left to start again. This is possibly the only novel of this type that is upbeat: positive rather than negative. It should be more widely available so readers of today can see how well a disaster story can be written. Wilson Tucker's *The Long Loud Silence,* though well written and engrossing, is very downbeat by comparison, with its implied theme of cannibalism adding a morbid touch of reality.

Make Room! Make Room! by Harry Harrison (1966) is another story of overpopulation and its frightening consequences. Some years later it was made into a reasonable movie with Charlton Heston in the lead and renamed *Soylent Green*. I think the most notable scene in this film was when Edward G. Robinson (who should have been the star), while dying, watches a HD video presentation of how beautiful the Earth once was so he can die while remembering something nice. It was the last film this highly respected actor made, because he actually died two weeks after filming that scene. He knew he was dying when he filmed it, which adds much poignancy to the scene. This is such a bleak film that I doubt if anyone would be game enough to remake it.

Other novels from the same era include *The Death of Grass* by John Christopher, who wrote many disaster novels, using a different premise for each, and extrapolating each into a worldwide catastrophe seen from a British viewpoint. It was 10 years or so later turned into a low-budget film, starring and directed by Cornel Wilde, called *No Blade of Grass*. The film is basically a motorcycle gang film, and the themes of the novel are mostly ignored, other than the part about everybody starving to death because there is no wheat, rice, corn, oats, or barley or any other grain related to grass that humans use as a staple. Cattle and sheep die, horses die, as well as any other ruminant that eats some kind of grass.

You can imagine what is left for the remnants of society to eat!

John Wyndham's *The Day of The Triffids* is an outstanding book that deals with many themes, including the oil crisis, illegal genetic modifications of plants, and the Cold War with satellites battling it out in near space which turns most of the population blind. The triffids — the genetically modified plants — escape, preying on the newly blind humans. It was a creepy and frightening story for a fifteen-year-old to read. Although it published in 1951 but I probably didn't read it until 1955. It was made into an atrociously bad film starring Howard Keel, who was better known for musicals such as Annie Get your Gun and Seven Brides for Seven Brothers. He was at the end of his career and way out of depth in a dramatic role. It could have been a bad script, bad direction, or bad acting in general, but whatever it was, it finished him off. As far as I can recall he never appeared in a film again. (Recently another much better realisation of *The Day of The Triffids* has been made as a mini TV series.)

John Wyndham wrote a series of well-written disaster novels, such as *The Kraken Wakes* in 1953, *The Chrysalids* (about mutants and the effects of widespread radiation, also a common theme of many mainstream as well as SF authors), and *The Midwich Cuckoos* in 1957, a scary but subtle alien invasion story where all the women in a village are impregnated and give birth within hours of each other nine months later to normal looking but increasingly strange children. I read that just after coming back from Darwin in late 1958. It was later made into an excellent film called *Village of The Damned*. (The remake years later with Christopher Reeve was not much good.)

And there was J. G. Ballard, one of New Worlds' New Wave writers, who, along with Brian Aldiss and others, helped define a new way of seeing the world and writing about it. Ballard's triptych of novels *The Drowned World* (1963), *The Burning World*, aka *The Drought* (1964), and *The Crystal World* (1966) set new standards in literary quality. These books, especially *The Drowned World*, crossed over into the mainstream and garnered a wide readership. I was particularly fond of *The Drowned World*. Overheating of the world is caused by continuous solar flares heating the planet until the ice caps melt and flood the rest of the world. As usual with a Ballard story the main concern is with the lead character as he negotiates a continually degrading environment. In this case a warming world is becoming more and more tropical, with areas along the equator already uninhabitable as jungles grow massive and ancient reptiles start to make a comeback. Kerans, the lead character, is part of a team surveying the gradual destruction of old cities. The survey turns out to be useless because the water levels continue rising. When other members of the team are ready to retreat to the polar regions Kerans does not want to go but wants to travel further into the ever-increasing jungles in search of ... who knows what? This is echoed in a much later book, *The Day of Creation,* in which his lead character follows an ever-increasing and broadening river into the jungles in central Africa in search of its origins. This is more a fantasy than science fiction.

Ballard was not that concerned with the science but with the gradual deterioration of character in situations that show environments decaying and falling apart (see also his *Memoirs of the Space Age* and *The Day of Forever*). His mini stories that made up *The Atrocity Exhibition* stand as the ultimate condensations of epic disasters in a format that set new standards for experimental modern fiction.

I just loved those stories. Obviously they weren't to everyone's taste. He later abandoned that approach and again became more conventional, yet still unequalled in literary value, as he continued to map the world as we know it in various states of decay and self-destruction almost always brought on by ever increasing numbers of humans unable to deal with the complexity of the world around them (see *High Rise, Crash,* and *Concrete Island*). The fact that as a boy Ballard lived in Shanghai, where he was born, and witnessed the destruction of this city by the Japanese and was interned in prison camp until rescued by Allied forces, no doubt influenced his obsession with disintegrating societies and ways of coping with them.

Ballard, like Aldiss, remains for me as one of the great British writers in the latter half of the twentieth century. He should be more appreciated than he is.

In my room...

I had thrown out the fruit boxes that held my books and built proper shelves, which enabled me to store my records and tapes, many more books and magazines, my turntable, tape player, amplifier, and speakers, as well as the conga drums and bongos that took up floor space. (I hadn't added timbales yet.) There was not a lot of room for the bed, or space to move around in. Still, I was happy. It was my room, my own personal space and I could while away the hours reading or listening to music while practising conga and bongo patterns, which must have driven Mum and Dad nuts as they tried to watch TV in the lounge room.

British publications

Most of the books I read were British publications. It was difficult to get American books in Australia at that time. The few I did get were paperbacks in the Ballantine range of themed anthologies that Merv Binns was able to import for McGill's Newsagency, where he worked. I missed out on many American writers simply because English editions of their books were not published. Some, however, found their way into English book publication.

T. V. Boardman was a publisher of a regular series of hardcover books all sporting a lovely emblem of a rocket ship passing by Saturn with the words Science Fiction written underneath. When you saw that emblem on the spine you knew it would be a good story. Boardman published A. E. Van Vogt's *Slan* and *The Weapon Shops of Isher*, and many others, such as *Children of the Atom* by Wilmar H. Shiras. The artist who illustrated their distinctive covers was Pagram. All his (or her) covers had a brooding dark look with lots of green and grey that made these books stand out on the shelf from all the others displayed there.

T.V. Boardman Publisher's emblam

Weidenfeld & Nicholson Publisher's emblam

Weidenfeld and Nicholson also published science fiction regularly. It too had an emblem — neutrons spinning around an invisible centre, presumably representing a stylised atom — with the words Science above it and Fiction below. It published the British edition of Clifford D. ¬Simak's *City*, which was not a novel but a collection of shorter stories linked together to form a more-or-less continuous narrative which could be loosely called a novel. Though it was copyrighted in 1952 it was first published in England in 1954, and I bought my copy from McGill's in Elizabeth Street, Melbourne, sometime in 1955. I was impressed, and immediately searched for more of Simak's work. Over the years he built up a reputation for producing gentle stories that were beautifully written and almost nostalgic in ¬nature, with many stories using a country or pastoral setting rather than the darker urban setting used by many others. City tells of Earth abandoned by humans and robots, leaving the planet to domestic dogs, which become the dominant species. The stories in this book are those told by the dogs to each other as they recount history as legendary tales of their predecessors, the humans and their robots.

Victor Gollancz was another stalwart of British SF publishing. Their covers were atrocious and unattractive, but at least they stood out as unique on the shelves of the shops that carried them: bright yellow with red and black or blue text. Gollancz published English editions of American authors such as Theodore Sturgeon, Robert Sheckley, and many others. I still have my copy of *More Than Human* by Theodore Sturgeon, which cost me 15 shillings and sixpence back in 1954. It was published in 1953 in America, but the Gollancz edition arrived in Australia only towards the end of 1954. I read it early in 1955. It had a slightly different cover to the standard Gollancz design: some decorative squiggles and a blurb that stated, '*Six minds come together and form a composite human being. Prophetic? — possibly. Unputdownable? — surely*'.

Who could resist that? I couldn't, and it was unputdownable: a brilliant story by a master writer who dealt not with hard science but with the condition of the mind and its emotions and all those popular (at that time) concepts of para- normal phenomena, such as telekinesis, levitation, human gestalt, and the idea that we shouldn't dismiss those who appear less fortunate than normal, who could well be mental giants so far beyond us that we wouldn't be able to comprehend them.

Sturgeon wrote many novellas and only a few novels. He wrote lots of short stories. Although I was heading away from reading short works that often left me disappointed because they didn't go anywhere, I made an exception for Sturgeon (as well as Bradbury) and bought whatever collections of his stories I could find. The earlier Sturgeon were harder SF, what Sturgeon sometimes called the 'Macho Sturgeon', but later he wrote beautiful sensitive stories that resonated in my mind long after I had read them. Two that I will never forget are *'The Man Who Lost the Sea'* and *'When You Care, When you Love'*. The latter is a portion of a novel about cloning that would have been a great success had it ever been finished. It never was. The former, however, as much as Sturgeon sweated over it and didn't think it would be any good, went on to be possibly the best short story he ever wrote; and which was collected in that year's (1959) Martha Foley Award Anthology as one of the best short stories for the year, with all the finest mainstream American stories. There was nothing macho about these. Most of them were highly developed and deeply emotional: 'soft SF' if you need a category.

He also ventured into areas no other science fiction writer of the time was willing to go, areas that dealt with sexuality and psychosis and what could be called abnormal behaviour, and for a young reader like I was this was very different reading material (see *Some of Your Blood* and *Venus Plus X*). No matter what the subject matter, he always made it seem sympathetic. If there were others writing similar stuff at that time, I don't believe there was anyone better at it than he was.

Something I recently discovered and find most astonishing is that Sturgeon never or hardly ever revised what he had written. Usually he sent off a first draft as soon as it was written. How he must have sweated and agonised over the typewriter as he poured himself onto those pages. How much better could he have been had he revised his first drafts? Perhaps we would have lost the rawness of his work, the strength of the emotion that poured out of him. He should have been as famous as his contemporary mainstream authors, but he stayed writing science fiction, apart from a few Westerns and one atrocious film tie-in. To the rest of the world today Sturgeon is almost forgotten.

The magazines I bought were mostly British, with the occasional American one thrown in. I didn't like Astounding, which later morphed into Analog, but I did sometimes read Galaxy and Worlds of If. The stories in the themed anthologies from Ballantine Books were mostly American. Even so, there was something about the 'British voice' that I preferred rather than the more jingoistic American sound. People raved about Robert Heinlein but I didn't like him, and read a few of his stories and novels if nothing else was available. I never read much of his later work. I didn't like the fact that he and many other American writers saw the future as American.

But there were exceptions. Authors like Clifford D. Simak and Chad Oliver were highly respected and enjoyed a wide readership, not because they were American but simply because they were good writers and wrote very beautiful novels. Chad Oliver was a professor of Anthropology at the University of Texas in Austin. All his stories had an anthropological base, and dealt with first human contact with aliens on strange and very different yet similar worlds to Earth. Frederick Pohl said of Chad Oliver: '*Other science fiction writers have invented more "alien" aliens than these for us to make contact with. Few, though, have been as able as Oliver to convince us that this is the way first contact is going to be.*'

I loved Chad Oliver stories, but unfortunately he was not as prolific as other writers. I read all I could get my hands on: *Mists of Dawn* (1952), *The Winds of Time* (1957), and *Unearthly Neighbours* (1960), a Ballantine original paperback.

I preferred novels, as well as the serials in the magazines, which I found more attractive than the shorter works. The first serial I ever read in a magazine was *The Time Masters* by Wilson Tucker, which was serialised in New Worlds and beautifully illustrated by Virgil Finlay.

The magazines were illustrated with some wonderful black-and-white drawings, sketches, and images. These were usually done on scraper board, which made them look more like etchings, and technically more difficult to produce than pen-and-ink drawings, which also were often very good but had a very different look to them. The serials were later published as books; for instance, Dune, serialised first in Analog magazine, but the accompanying John Schoenherr illustrations were not used in the book version.

Most of the book versions had attractive and inviting cover illustrations — the American ones, anyway. The British Gollanz editions had plain yellow covers with black and red text on them (ugly as hell, but it was the content that was important). An exception was *Dune*, which appeared in 1965 with a black cover with silver white text and a couple of white squiggles across the middle representing sand dunes, a dramatic change from the usual yellow jacket.

Years later I had this book signed and dedicated to me by Frank Herbert himself when he visited Australia and attended a book signing at Space Age Books. I remember him telling me over dinner that his favourite book was the least popular novel he wrote, a mainstream novel called *Soul Catcher*. This in my view was the best book he wrote. It was billed as his first 'major' novel, whatever that meant.

What on earth was Dune, if not a 'major' novel?

I guess the publishers wanted to distinguish *Soul Catcher* as a mainstream novel. Much of the book has similar themes to Herbert's SF novels, and he uses similar methods of telling his story as he did in his SF novels. *Soul Catcher* deals with death and retribution and the clash of cultures that occurred between the native Americans and those who now occupy their land, but on a personal level between the protagonist and his captured victim. It could very well have taken place with humans and aliens on a different world around a different star, but Herbert didn't want that. I think he wanted to show the same clash of culture, the same inevitability of the result, and what more emotive way to do it than set it there in his own back yard, his own country?

Can you believe it?

I managed to read almost every science fiction, or vaguely science fiction, book that was published and available in Australia until the mid 1960s. After that it was harder to keep up, but I made a valiant effort. After 1975 I became much more selective, because it was simply impossible to read everything.

Books like *The Death of Iron*, by S. S. Held in 1952, I would have avoided if it had been published later than 1964. The premise is silly: something which was never actually specified or even scientifically plausible affects iron, turning it soft and rubbery, which means that buildings collapse because the iron reinforcing basically dissolves. Anything made from iron or steel becomes like melting rubber or soft plasticine. The cover shows a half-dissolved steam locomotive slowly collapsing over twisted railway lines, which reminds me of Salvador Dali's melting watches. Everyone returns to the Stone Age: implements made of chipped rock and bone needles being used to repair clothes. It was an awful story that I read with ever decreasing enthusiasm. I don't know why I remember it now, except for its name. Its only redeeming feature was its demonstration of how impossible it would be for modern people to revert to a Stone Age culture. There were lots of stories like that which are best forgotten. This one was published between T*he Day of the Triffids* and *The Kraken Wakes*, and most SF fans would have quickly forgotten it, whereas they never forget the John Wyndham books which are continuously reprinted.

Some Books you can't read

There are some books you never can read, or at least, if started never can finish. Two of these are the *Lord of the Rings* trilogy, and *20,000 Leagues under the Sea*. I tried to read them on a number of occasions, but I did not even want to start *Lord of The Rings*. I had a look at it once in a bookshop. After a few minutes I put it back on the shelf. I was never into that kind of fantasy, and the more people insisted that I should read it — *'It's a classic'; 'You have to read it' or 'It should be on every fan's bookshelf'* — the more I refused even to think about reading it. Years later my wife Monica bought a copy for me as a Christmas present and I was under an obligation to make an attempt to read it. I was in my late sixties, too late in my view to start reading *Lord of The Rings*. You have to read this book as a teenager or at the very least when you are in your early twenties. I managed to get through the first 50 pages and found it turgid and unreadable. I have never gone back to it since. It even put me off wanting to see the three films that were so extraordinarily popular and won so many Academy Awards. My son read the book, and borrowed and later bought the three films on DVD, and reckons they are fantastic. Exactly! — but not my cup of tea. I did watch some bits of the films here and there (hard to avoid in a small house when someone else is watching them and has the volume up rather loud), but not any one complete. They looked spectacular and I could see why they were so popular, but they simply didn't interest me enough to make the effort to watch them.

Jules Verne's *20,000 Leagues under the Sea* is another. This is a major book and has some very interesting things in it. I was a keen snorkeller and skin diver as a teenager, having read Hans Haas and Jacques Yves Cousteau, and was experimenting with underwater photography.

The edition I had was a hardcover with lots of illustrations. It has never been out of print in one form or another since Jules Verne wrote it in 1870. It was an instant success. Everyone knows the story of Captain Nemo, both demonic and sympathetic at the same time, taking revenge for what he perceives as society's wrongdoings, and his incredible submarine Nautilus, supposedly run on 'electricity' generated by some unknown, at that time, power source.

The first American nuclear submarine was named Nautilus perhaps to acknowledge that Jules Verne, although he never named his power source, came up with the idea that later generations called atomic power.

This book at first is enthralling, but too much of it is repetitious and boring. I started to skip pages in search of the more interesting or exciting bits. I never actually finished reading the book, although I kept my copy for years.

Before I could finish it the Walt Disney film of it appeared in colour and Cinemascope, and I rushed off to see it. It starred the wonderful James Mason as Captain Nemo, and with equal billing as Ned was Kirk Douglas. An outstanding character played by Peter Lorre and teamed with Kirk Douglas made an unlikely comedy duo that stole the limelight.

The underwater gear looked good: equipment you could imagine cexisting in 1870 and functioning in the way the modern aqualung works: almost a cross between an aqualung and the old fashioned helmet diving suit. The submarine is beautiful in a steampunk metal fish way. It absolutely suits the book's descriptions of the Nautilus, made of iron plates riveted together, able to power through the sea with unbelievable speed.

It was one of the better films of the 1950s, and still looks good even today. This film captures the grand adventure presented in the book, with superb underwater photography and a sense of wonder at the gothic magnificence of the submarine. The battle with the giant squid seems now to be rather tacky and artificial.

However, the film did win an Academy Award for special effects among others, and stands out as a major science fiction film along with *This Island Earth, Forbidden Planet, The War of the Worlds, When Worlds Collide, The Day the Earth Stood Still, Invasion of the Body Snatchers,* and *The Creature from the Black Lagoon.*

A later film, *Voyage to the Bottom of the Sea* (1961) was a ridiculous load of rubbish written and scripted by Irwin Allen which was later rewritten as a novel by Theodore Sturgeon, who must have been desperate for money to take this one on.

Almost a disaster at Cape Schanck

'We should dive at Cape Schanck,' George said one Saturday night at Birdland.

'What's it like?' I had to ask. I had not at that stage been there. Situated along the coast ¬between the Mornington Peninsula and Westernport Bay near Phillip Island, which I had been to, it is a spectacular spot with a series of low cliffs dropping down into the ocean with a similar terrain underwater: tall outcrops (called bommies by divers) that continue as ever-deepening rocky reefs until they are so deep they no longer affect the surface. These bommies are like volcanic plugs from which the softer material has been eroded away leaving the hard interior jutting up like jagged chimneys. The sea swirls around them as each wave comes in and sucks back around them as it retreats. There are currents and eddies that drag huge kelp fronds down into deeper water before pushing them back up against the rocks. The bommies are surrounded by a huge variety of fish that feed on the seaweed and on each other. In the nooks and crannies, holes and small caves, there are crayfish.

'It's a great spot for crayfish, but it's fairly deep. Not many people dive there, so there are lots of crayfish.'

I could see why not many wanted to dive there when we got there the next morning. Standing on the cliff and looking down I saw the water smashing onto and flowing over the tops of the bommies before retreating and sucking back around them. It was dangerous, no question about that. The waves roared and thumped onto the rocks and sucked back with deep gurgling sounds that sent a shiver up my spine. Or was that just the cold wind blowing off the Southern Ocean up over the clifftops?

We had decided to make a day of it as a group. George had his wife Margaret with him, and with me were my brothers and sisters, Phillip, Zara, and Christine, and Zara's fiancé Fred, who was keen on skindiving and couldn't wait to get into the water. We trooped off down the goat path of a dirt track that wound down first on the inside of the cliff, where a small safe bay without waves was located. The girls went for swim there but didn't stay in long because the water was icy. (It was early summer and the ocean still retained its winter temperature.) We boys, however, worked our way around the bottom of the cliff to the ocean side where the big waves from Bass Strait hammered a series of flat rock ledges.

We quickly suited up in our wetsuits and worked our way across slippery rocks to the edge of a gully. When the waves came in, the water slipped over the top of these flat ledges leaving them slimy and slippery with a fine sheen of green seaweed and sea grapes that burst and squished under foot as we stepped on them. When the wave sucked out, the water level in the gully dropped two to three feet. You could see the black surface swirling as the water sucked out. The dark brown kelp quivered as the water rapidly flowed over it. Beyond about three metres the water was deeper and clearer, with no kelp to obscure the view of the gully sides.

Fred was excited and fiddled with his lead belt. George had a hessian bag, which had a long orange cord tied to it as well as to his lead belt. He sat on the edge of the rock ledge and slipped on his flippers (swim fins), spat into his mask, rinsed it out with seawater, and splashed some cold water onto his face to cool it before putting on the mask and gripping the snorkel with a firm bite. He waited a moment for the next wave to roll in up the gully. When the water level came up to the edge of the shelf he was sitting on, he slipped into the water. Almost instantly he was sucked out as the wave retreated. Within a couple of seconds he was halfway along the gully and already diving down.

'That's how it's done,' I told Fred. 'Watch the waves. Every so often a bigger one comes in and floods over the edge. You sit there like George did, and then you step into it. The wave will suck you out, no problem. You'll go right over the top of the kelp so you won't notice it.'

'Not a problem,' Fred said. He sat down on the ledge where George had sat.

'You sure about this?'

He nodded affirmatively. He had the snorkel stuck in his mouth and couldn't speak.

'When you are ready to come back in, you have to sit at the opening to the gully and watch the waves. They're not all big enough to come up to the top of the ledge. Wait until a big wave comes along and ride that one in. Swim with it and grab the rocks when you get to the ledge. The water will suck back out and when it has gone you can climb out before the next big wave comes in. If you are not out then it will suck you back out.'

'Okay, I've got it.' He pulled the snorkel out so he could reply. 'You don't have to tell me again.'

'All right, I'll see you out there.' I stepped into a wave as it surged up the gully. Within a second it sucked me out and I swam along with it until I was just outside the gully opening. Further out, the waves surged over a huge bommie with greedy sucking sounds. There was no sign of George. But he was a powerful swimmer and an experienced free diver so I didn't worry about him. I turned to watch Fred as he slipped into the water. He joined me a moment later with thumbs up to indicate he had no problem in getting in.

We spent a few minutes diving along the edge of the rock wall marvelling at the fish life when Fred indicated he wanted to go back. He didn't like the strong currents swirling around the space between the gully opening and the nearby ¬bommie. Back on the surface and treading water he told me he was going back in.

'Remember to wait for a big wave to carry you up onto the ledge.'

He nodded and then started to swim back towards the gully opening. I could see Zara and Christine standing on the beach above the rock ledge watching us. One of them waved. Fred waved back as he waited for a big wave.

When we first went in I think the tide must have been out. It was turning and starting to move back in. You could feel the waves were stronger and the currents had more power.

I drifted towards the bommie and could see way down George swimming along the side near the bottom. It must have been at least sixty feet deep. He was a long way down. The water was exceptionally clear, as cold ocean water usually is. There was no sand or silt to reduce visibility. I tried to dive down to George but it was too far down. I hovered there a moment until I ran out of breath and had to surface. George came up beside me.

'This is a paradise,' he said as pulled out his snorkel. 'I've got half a dozen already.'

He held the hessian bag open a bit so I could see the crayfish huddled together, legs twitching and feelers waving. 'A couple more should do it.'

I watched as he dived down again. His method was to tease a crayfish out of its hiding place by putting something there to attract it. That something was usually a clam or a mussel that he smashed with the hilt of his diving knife. Scraping up the flesh, he would use this to attract a crayfish out of its lair. They hated being out in the open. If George blocked their way back to their hiding place they would look for somewhere else to hide. He held open the hessian bag which I suppose to them looked like a cave, a safe place to hide so they would shoot into it and stay there. He didn't even bother grabbing them.

When he came back up for a breath I told him I was heading back.

He nodded, gave me a thumbs up and went down again.

I swam back to the gully, waited for a big surge and rode the wave in. It came up higher over the rock ledge than before so the tide was definitely coming in. I swam up onto the top of the ledge and grabbed hold of a jutting rock. The water sucked away behind me and I stood up to see Zara and Christine gesticulating wildly and pointing towards another inlet. There was a fair bit of wind gusting so I couldn't hear what they were yelling about over that and the sound of the waves smashing and sucking at the rocks. I stood up and unlatched my leaden belt, tossing it up higher onto the dry rocks. I took off my flippers. While looking around, I realised I couldn't see Fred anywhere.

Shit! Now I knew what Zara and Christine were agitated about.

I tossed my flippers up where the lead belt was and looked about for Fred.

There he was in a different gully. I ran across towards it and got there just as Fred was being sucked out again, tumbling over the rocks and looking dangerously close to being tangled up in the massive kelp fronds.

He looked up when he cleared the rocks and saw me standing by the edge.

He was whiter than I had ever seen him.

He tried swimming in again but the wave wasn't big enough. He only got half way up onto the more slippery rocks before being sucked back out again, only to be tumbled over by the next wave coming in.

'Swim out a bit further and wait for a big one,' I yelled at him. He didn't seem to hear me, and started swimming in with the next wave.

I ran back and grabbed a spear gun that we had brought but hadn't taken into the water. Back by the ledge I stepped down into the opening and wedged myself between some rocks and the edge of the ledge. Holding the gun by the spear point I reached out towards Fred.

He saw me. As he swam in this third or fourth time he grabbed the handle of the gun and hung on with a fierce grip. I pulled him towards me as the wave sucked back past him and he scrabbled across the slippery with desperate speed. I stepped back up onto the ledge and continued pulling him up until he was well out of the water, and quite safe.

Once again I was reminded that a spear gun had more uses than simply being used to kill fish. We were lucky that George had decided to bring a spear gun in case there were no crayfish. The trip wouldn't have been wasted, because he would have shot a meal of fresh fish. But with the crayfish there was no need for that.

Within five minutes Fred was out of his wetsuit and soaking up some sunshine and chatting happily about what a spectacular dive spot it was. The fact that he could have drowned was already forgotten.

George came in shortly with his hessian bag full of crayfish. We went back to my place in Yarraville and Mum soon filled with boiling water the gigantic pot she kept for such occasions. She cooked the crayfish, while we sat in the yard drinking beer and recounting the events of the trip.

'You saved my life,' Fred said afterwards. 'I don't know how much water I swallowed.'

'You should have waited for the bigger wave like I told you,' I said, and went back inside to get another can of beer and to see how the crayfish were doing. Mum had already made a huge Greek salad with heaps of feta cheese and kalamata olives. Half the crayfish were hot, bright red, and steaming in a pile on the kitchen table while the rest were still cooking.

It had been a perfect day.

Waves smashing over bommies close to the base of the cliff producing whirlpools of water at the entrance to a gully which could easily suck an inexperienced swimmer out into very deep water.

Road Rage

There were a lot of days like that.

Sometimes they ended well. Other times there was a bit of drama, such as the time when we were coming back from Barwon Heads after another successful day of catching crayfish.

Geelong Road was full of traffic with everybody cutting in and out in a rush to get back to Melbourne. A guy cut George off. This pissed him off, so he sped up and passed the guy, got in front, and slammed on his brakes, forcing the guy to almost crash into us.

George leapt out. When the other man got out of his car. George was yelling at him, telling him that he had cut him off and why the fuck did he do that. The guy protested and George started hitting him.

Unfortunately for George he had forgotten to do up the button on his jeans and his pants started to fall down.

Traffic backed up behind us. Car horns honked and tooted. George kept trying to hit the other guy with one hand while holding up his pants. He didn't have on any underwear, otherwise he wouldn't have bothered. Meanwhile the man's wife and kids had gotten out of the car and were screaming at George to stop hitting the man. George's wife Margaret had also gotten out of our car and was hitting George on the head with an umbrella to make him stop. I just sat in the car and watched it all unfold. I don't know where Zara and Fred were. They were most likely several cars back wondering what the hell the hold-up was about.

Eventually George let the man go and still holding up his pants with his left hand he got back into the car. Margaret barely had time to get in the back seat before George slammed the gear in and we shot off along Geelong Road way ahead of the mob of backed-up cars. All the way he kept berating Margaret for hitting him on the head with the umbrella.

'You should have helped me,' he told her. 'You should have hit him instead of me.'

'What? With his family watching you beat up their husband and father?'

And so it went all the way back until both of them fell silent and refused to say anything to each other.

With George on the rocks at Bermagui in NSW.
Getting in and out of the water is similar to Cape Schanck but less dangerous.

– *Ephemeron* –

Bermagui

George was a wild man. As a boy he survived the Second World War in Hungary, ran away to Switzerland where he somehow got himself adopted and learnt how to be a watchmaker, qualifying by the age of thirteen, and in the process managed to acquire his second language, German. He then went to Canada and worked in the mining industry. There he learnt to speak English. After an accident in winter when he fell down a frozen tailings dump — so he said; it was most likely the result of a fight — landing at the bottom unconscious, his scalp froze by the time the other workers climbed down to rescue him. He lost all his hair and was bald after that. In the early 1950s he ended up in New York, where he discovered the Palladium Dance Hall and the big bands of Tito Puente, Tito Rodriguez, and others. He fell in love with the salsa music they played. After a couple of years, he left for Australia, where he had an aunt and uncle living in Elwood, a suburb of Melbourne. He opened a gold and silver chain jewellery manufacturing plant in collaboration with them using special knitting machinery he imported from Italy. (He had to sneak out of his hotel room in Rome in the middle of the night without paying his bill because he spent all his money on buying and getting those knitting machines ready for export to Australia.) He discovered Birdland in St Kilda and started playing conga drums there, and that's where I met him.

He had already been in Melbourne for two or three years when we met. He had married his girlfriend Margaret. We knocked around playing drums and skindiving at weekends for a couple of years before he sold his chain knitting business and moved to Sydney, where he eventually opened a watch repair shop somewhere near Redfern. He also started creating handmade jewellery, concentrating on expensive custom made pieces. He moved this business to a luxury hotel foyer in Kings Cross.

Stopping for a break on the way. We drove up in two Volkswagons, each stuffed with camping and diving gear. As seen here where we stopped for a break the road was unpaved, and this was Highway One, The Princes Highway. It was an unpaved corrugated mess from Lake's Entrance to Eden, about 180 kilometres, and was possibly the worst stretch of road along the coastal route at that time.

Below: Eden as seen from the road leading down into the town.

That first year after he moved up to Sydney we decided to drive up to Bermagui for a skindiving holiday over Easter long weekend. George and another friend drove down from Sydney and joined us. This may have been 1962. Bermagui is a great fishing town. Its pub's walls have displays of lots of photos of famous people who went big game fishing out of Bermagui. In one large photo standing next to the scales where his catch was strung up and weighed was the author Zane Gray. I had read some of his western novels so I knew who he was. Until my first trip to Bermagui I had no idea he was a keen big game fisherman.

Arriving late at night after the long drive from Melbourne we set up a huge tent and promptly went to sleep.

My brother Phillip took this shot of us before we settled down to sleep. In front is George, Zara and Christine, while kneeling behind are myself, Vince, and Fred. George and Vince stayed in another tent.

Huddled outside the tent for early morning decision on where to dive.

Early in the morning we found George and his mate and we all went diving in a small bay not far from the camp site. The tide was out and we clambered down over the rocks and used the method of waiting for a big wave to wash up onto the rocks then, stepping into it, to be carried out into deeper water. Coming back we used the same method: wait for the bigger wave and have it carry us back up onto the rocks, where we would grab hold and hang on until the wave receded. The next several waves were always smaller so we had time to clamber higher up.

The underwater terrain here consisted of huge rounded boulders scattered from the rocky edge across a sandy bottom. There were gullies and narrow splits between the boulders. You could see the water sucking back and forth through them — the sand swirled and made small eddies as the swells above came in and out. There was some kelp, but nowhere near the amount we were used to in the southern waters around Port Phillip Bay. There was also plenty of plankton scattered throughout. Light sparkled off some of it from time to time, giving a slight haziness. The water was also warmer than we expected. There was a warm current that drifted down the coast from the more subtropical areas to the north, which obviously kept the temperature higher than we were used to. There were few fish, and those we saw were very shy and quickly disappeared. I suspected that because it was a spot easily accessible, many other divers, spearfishermen, and rock fishermen had been here and the fish were shy and difficult to find.

It was a lovely sunny morning as we sorted out our gear on the beach near the jagged channels.

A series of jagged rocky channels which lead to a sandy beach where we did some diving and swimming the day after we arrived.

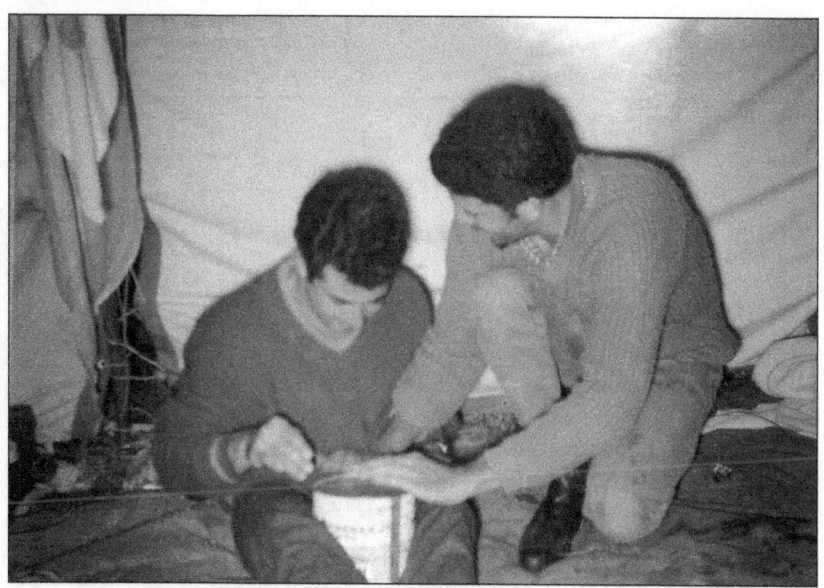

Showing Vince how to play a conga drum using a tin can as a substitute.

Half dressed, (left) and ready to go into the water. (right) We wore thermal cell underwear and jumpers for warmth and to prevent the rubber dry suit from pinching when under pressure.

My sister Christine, myself kneeling, Fred, Vince, and my brother Phillip with some of the fish Fred and Vince shot.

The boys had these new compressed-air spear guns and the damn things didn't work properly. I had my 16 mm Bolex in an underwater housing, and I remember filming Fred as he swam over a gigantic stingray. He looked down, and for some reason he pointed the spear gun down also. The spear slid out and fell point first on top of the stingray. It wasn't supposed to do that! The stingray flicked its tail up and the poison barb must have been two feet long. At the same instant it flapped its giant wings and took off like a rocket, disappearing within a heartbeat into the hazy blue distance of deeper water. Fred stared at me ashen faced. The sting had missed him by only a few inches. I gave him a thumbs-up sign and pointed to the camera indicating I had shot this on film. We would laugh about this later once the film was processed and we could watch it on screen. He retrieved his spear and swam off in the direction the stingray had gone, through a gully into deeper water.

If anyone could find some fish to shoot, George would. He came back after Fred and Phillip and I had been out of the water for some time. He had some fish he had speared which we later had for dinner, but his mate who came in perhaps ten minutes after George had trouble getting out of the water and had to climb up the short cliff face on the other side because the tide was in and waves were smashing on the rocks where we first entered.

The next day was bright and sunny. We drove out of town south along the coast road until we found a beautiful beach about two miles out of town. A couple of pyramid-shaped rocks made a tiny island about half a mile off the beach. Another friend of George's had arrived with a small aluminium dinghy. They climbed into it with all their gear and headed out towards the jagged islets offshore. Fred went with them, so there were four of them in the dinghy: George, the owner of the dinghy, the friend who had come down with him from Sydney, and Fred.

I stayed on the beach with the girls and Phillip, and filmed the group as they headed off towards the tiny island. The beach was clean with rich white sand. We settled down to wait for the others to finish with their diving. There was a gentle breeze and not a cloud in the sky.

About two hours later I noticed the boys were in the dinghy and starting back.

'What's that?' Zara asked. She was looking south, where the beach stretched in an almost straight line for several miles.

There seemed to be a patch of boiling white water just off the beach. It looked like a fountain bursting out of the water.

I had never seen anything like that before. It was coming towards us.

Suddenly sand started to whip up around our feet, and the white water rushed towards where we were on the beach. A ferocious wind blasted us with fine sand particles that stung all over like vicious mosquito bites.

'Those guys are going to cop it if they don't get back in time,' I said.

The water in front of us started to whip up violently. White caps formed, and foam was ripped off by the ever-increasing wind. It looked as if the wind were trying to suck the water up out of the sea.

The dinghy was halfway back to the beach when the squall hit. It vanished in a swirl of white crashing waves and blasting wind.

I had the camera running and I hoped that some of this could be captured. There was absolutely nothing we could do.

The wind seemed to swing around the tiny island offshore. The worst of the churning white water followed it out to sea. There was a dark spot, which must have been the dinghy bouncing along with the white water. Then it was too far out to see. Someone was standing on the island and waving to us. A moment later George floundered in the choppy waves crashing onto the beach and stood up. He staggered towards us.

'Fred's on the island,' he called as he ran up the beach. 'The other two are with the dinghy.'

'At the rate they're going they'll be in New Zealand soon.'

'We'll have to go back to town and see if we can get one of the fishing trawlers to go out and rescue them. Last I saw they were clinging to the upturned dinghy.'

George grabbed a pair of jeans as he said this, quickly pulling them on over his wet trunks. He and Phillip raced up to one of the cars and took off in a cloud of wind-swirled dust.

By the time they had disappeared, the wind started to die down and the waves calmed. The beach soon gave the appearance that nothing had happened, that the sudden ferocious squall had never passed by. And as far as I could see out to sea nothing was there. The squall had completely dissipated.

We packed our gear and waited. About half an hour later a fishing trawler motored up to the small island offshore and we saw Fred clamber on board. It then headed out to sea in the direction the squall had gone. We headed back into town and down to the wharf to wait for the trawler to come back.

It came back a couple of hours later. Everyone had been rescued. They even had the dinghy on board, but it was minus its outboard motor. When it flipped over everything on board had gone to the bottom including the motor. The dinghy didn't sink because it had flotation panels built in to prevent that from happening. The boys had hung on, and were lucky the waves hadn't washed them away. They were suffering a bit from hypothermia but a few whiskeys at the pub soon fixed that. They would certainly have a story to tell when they got home.

Those were the days!

With my sister Zara and below the group minus Fred who took the picture in front of our campsite.

A kindred soul

Next to the dry-cleaning shop in Douglas Parade, Williamstown was a plant nursery. It had a display of subtropical and tropical plants in our shop window, where the warmth and steam in the atmosphere from the pressing machines created an ideal micro-climate for these plants. Dad had run some extra steam pipes through the nursery glasshouse, which was located at the rear of their premises and close to our boiler. These pipes supplied enough warmth to raise the ambient temperature in the glasshouse a few degrees, which kept any winter chill away from the propagated plants growing there. The nursery owner appreciated that, and always maintained a good-looking display in our window.

The chap who looked after the display was an Englishman called Walter Shaw.

'Call me Wally,' he said when he introduced himself, and we always did, although most others called him Walt.

He and his wife and son were 'ten pound Poms', having migrated to Australia under that program whereby they contributed ten pounds per person and the government paid for their trip over and billeted them in a hostel until they found work and accommodation. Wally had stayed in the hostel in Kororoit Creek Road, where it bordered on North Altona. Terrible accommodation, so I was told, and it got worse later on when the Mobil Oil refinery increased its storage capacity and built huge holding tanks that went right up to a few hundred metres from the hostel. Perhaps this is what encouraged people to find somewhere better to live. Eventually that hostel was mothballed. Years later it was rebuilt in the same location in spite of many protests that it was unhealthy, being so close to the storage facility of the refinery. It was used to house Vietnamese boat people refugees.

Almost immediately after arriving at the hostel Wally got a job in the control room of the Mobil Oil refinery across the road. He monitored the flow from the processing to storage in the holding tanks. Since this was shift work, he also looked for work during the days. He worked for the nursery next door, where his job was maintaining the plants the nursery leased to businesses in Melbourne's city centre, banks, head offices of large corporations, and so on. The nursery supplied plants, maintained them, and rotated them so the ones beginning to look haggard could be rehabilitated.

Wally was about fifteen years older than me: a bit scrawny, which I assumed was because he grew up in England during the harsh years leading up to the Second World War. Towards the end of the war he had been conscripted. Once he had finished his basic training, he was sent with a small unit to Germany, where he participated in the reconstruction the allied forces were doing immediately after the war ended. He spent two years there, and learned to speak German.

One day I went into the nursery and found Wally in the office reading a book. There was no one else there. As it was the middle of the afternoon it was very quiet. There was hardly anyone in the street, no customers in the nursery, and we'd finished work for the day and the pressers had gone home. The nursery always smelt fresh, almost like being out in the bush, very different from the white spirit and other chemical smells that pervaded the atmosphere in the dry-cleaning factory. It was a science fiction book that Wally was reading. That immediately made him a kindred soul. I knew there were lots of people who read SF books — especially as some sold very well, far more than could have been bought by true fans — but I had never met any SF readers other than Merv Binns and one or two people encountered at the SF section of the counter in McGill's Newsagency. Wally was the first outsider: the first reader of SF that I had met who was not a fan. He was also the first person with whom I spent time talking about science fiction and books.

Suddenly we became great friends. We discussed books and authors, what we had read, and discovered we liked similar types of stories. Mostly they were adventure, escapist, and space opera. Although he was English, he was fonder of American SF than I was. We started lending each other books, which we discussed at great length, and eventually we talked about writing our own book. I had always wanted to write, but didn't think I had enough ability. I had a typewriter and had started writing a murder mystery set in a nightclub where girls danced semi-naked in cages suspended from the ceiling — typical juvenile bullshit. Wally, it turned out, had published several stories in British magazines, stories about smuggling stuff from England to Europe or vice versa, but he hadn't done anything else since coming to Australia. He was too busy working two jobs and paying off a mortgage on a house in Altona to find time for writing. With another baby on the way there would be even less time, so any ambitions towards further writing he had shelved.

Out of place

I always felt out of place working at the dry cleaning factory. It was not something I really wanted to do, but rather it was something I fell into because it was part of the family activities. I had grown up initially in the residence at the back of the shop (until I was seven and we moved to Yarraville West). Later I worked part time in the shop and learnt the ropes of how the whole process worked; so too did my two sisters and my brother Phillip. It seemed natural or inevitable that I would be, that we all would be, working there full time.

I didn't have to like it. I was interested in books and writing, in art and painting, and in Afro-Cuban music and its various permutations in different parts of the world. Zara and Christine were interested in dancing and show business. Phillip, out of the four of us, was the only one really happy working at the dry cleaner. Working in the dry cleaning business allowed us to have money to devote to our other interests. I guess we were lucky in that respect.

I never imagined for one second that I would be a dry cleaner on and off over the next forty years. But who at any given moment can imagine what his or her future will be?

An impulse

The Age's Green Pages is its weekly section dealing with entertainment, containing a TV and radio guide, lists of theatre shows in town, showbiz gossip, and much else. One day I saw a picture of the most beautiful woman I had ever seen. The name under the photo said Ynez Amaya, a suitably exotic name. She was performing in a TV broadcast at the ABC studios in Elwood. I knew those studios because I had appeared there in a dance show with Zara and the girls from her dance school. On an impulse I decided to go over to the studios and watch her performance.

I was of course hoping to meet her. God only knows what I would say to her. Being young I never gave that a thought. I simply went over and walked into the studios as if I had every right to be there. No one questioned me. One of the security men near the main entrance to the studios nodded and said 'Hi. You're back again.' He remembered me from the dance show we did a few months back. I smiled at him and asked him how he was and walked by without waiting for an answer.

Ynez Amaya had recently come over from South Africa, which explained her exotic appearance. She was one of these people of mixed racial heritage blended in such a way as to produce a stunningly beautiful person.

In the same studio where we had performed the dance routine, she was standing by the piano and going over her movements within the allowed space. Two huge cameras shifted to position themselves for a long shot and a close-up shot. A number of people were in the studio: the floor manager, camera operators, a man holding a padded mike above the singer's head high enough to be out of camera shot, as well as the musicians, and a jazz trio of whom only the piano player seemed familiar. I had eyes only for Ynez. There were a number of other people in the studio as well as a small audience. The recording or broadcast had not yet begun, so I slipped quietly in through the door and stood near the back of the studio close to the audience.

A sign flashed indicating the broadcast was about to begin.

Someone standing in front of the audience said, 'Quiet please.'

The floor manager held up his right hand, fist closed. Everyone watched him. He was wearing earphones and obviously listening. 'Ten seconds,' he announced and started counting backwards. When he got to five he fell silent, but opened his fist finger by finger starting with his thumb to indicate the last five seconds.

I saw the piano player mouthing the count: one – two – one two three just loud enough for the trio and the singer to hear, but no one else. They began at the instant the floor manager finished his silent five-count. I was unfamiliar with the song but it was beautifully sung in a modern jazz style, and the playing of the trio was quietly understated to enhance and not take any attention away from the singer.

All too soon it was over. The audience clapped, and the band members stood up smiling with obvious pleasure at a fine performance. Cameras moved around, and before I could take more than a tentative step towards the band, the singer and the trio vanished. The floor manager was waving his arms above his head. Through a glass partition in an adjoining studio another performance was underway as part of the live broadcast, and in the studio where I was standing cameras were being repositioned and someone else was getting ready for another performance. I slipped out of the studio into the corridor.

It was empty. Not knowing what else to do, I headed back to the front entrance. I felt relieved that I hadn't been able to approach the singer, because in that instant I realised I had no idea what I would have said to her, other than something that may have made me look like a dickhead. Outside and walking towards my van in the car park I saw her with the piano player getting into a car. They drove past me and quickly disappeared down the narrow street outside the studio.

About a month later I was sitting on a Saturday night at the table reserved for the band at Birdland when someone sat beside me. I was watching George play with the band while a couple of bad dancers gyrated around the small dance floor almost in time to the music. Those lessons and various impromptu playing sessions we had had with JoJo had improved his playing. It was much better than when I had first met him. The playing was cleaner, and more precise.

'The band sounds good, doesn't it?' the girl who had sat at the table beside me said.

'They really are good,' I agreed, turning towards her, adding 'probably the best in Melbourne at the moment', and almost fell off my chair when I saw who it was beside me.

'Ynez,' I blurted. 'Ynez Amaya?'

'The name is Beryl,' she said. 'That Ynez name was something the ABC dreamed up because it made me sound more exotic.'

'Well, for a jazz singer Beryl is probably a more appropriate name.'

'Thanks.'

She smiled, and up close like that I was stunned at how radiant she appeared. She was even more beautiful than I had imagined from the distant view I had seen at the studios in Elwood. Suddenly I was lost for words. I had no idea what else to say. But then the band finished and George joined us. 'Hello, Beryl,' he said as he sat down. She nodded at him, and by then the rest of the band was also sitting at the table for their break. The others all greeted her cheerfully. She knew everyone even though I had never seen her at Birdland before. Roger, the band's drummer, gave her a peck on the cheek and sat beside her on the other side. She seemed overly familiar with him. They must be a couple, was my immediate thought, and for some strange reason I felt relieved.

Roger and I got on really well together as players. He was an excellent jazz drummer, but he had also learned some authentic cowbell patterns for Cuban-based music from JoJo and from some records JoJo had lent him to study. He had mastered the patterns and sounded like an authentic Latin drummer when we played together. It gave a whole different ambience to the music and to the band.

Roger leaned across in front of Beryl and was about to introduce us when she told him we had just met, so instead he said, 'John is going to do the floorshow with us.' She immediately looked at me with a different expression in her eyes. Maybe it was curiosity, Perhaps she had been wondering what I was doing sitting at the band's table. Maybe it was acceptance because suddenly I was one of them and not an outsider.

George stood up. 'I've got to go,' he said. He never stayed for the floorshow.

Everyone was drinking a soft drink with a shot of brandy in it. Quickly they downed their drinks as the lights on the bandstand dimmed and the area of the dance floor brightened. The other people crowding the tables in the club dropped their volume a little in anticipation of the show. The band members stood up and quietly made their way towards the bandstand. I followed along behind and sat behind the conga drums at the edge of the dance floor.

Johnny Summers, a brilliant singer from New Zealand, came out and acted as MC. He got the audience warmed with a joke or two and sang the popular hit of the day, 'Moon River'. We did it as a bolero, slow and romantic, and a warm sensuous voice. I imagined half the women in the audience sitting in the dark swooning as he sang.

Next was the ever-popular almost naked exotic dancer (who was actually born in Russia, but grew up in Australia) with her two pythons. Fortunately this time they behaved themselves and slithered towards the audience instead of my congas. I smiled as I heard the frantic scrambling from the darkened tables as people tried to get away from the snakes, only to have them pulled back by the dancer before anything serious happened.

Crocker and Clarke weren't there that particular night. Johnny announced Beryl and she stepped into the spotlight. She sang two songs; a standard slow jazz ballad that required soft brushes payed on the snare drum, which she followed with the familiar up-tempo version of 'I've

Got Rhythm' in which I played. We had not rehearsed it, but we had all played this so many times in so many different ways that it didn't matter. We swung into it. At an appropriate moment Chuck, the pianist, indicated that Roger should do a sixteen-bar solo, which he did beautifully. Chuck nodded to me just as Roger was concluding and I did another sixteen bars of conga solo. I took some of Roger's phrases and expanded on them before Beryl came back in for the final coda and the number was over. It went very smoothly and the audience responded with sustained applause. Johnny came back into the limelight and sang another popular hit and then the show was over.

'Nice solo,' Roger commented as we made our way back to the table reserved for us.

'Thanks. You too.'

'I mean it. You played a lot better than you've ever done before.'

I didn't tell him I felt it was Beryl who had inspired me that night. I could see her studying me with a quizzical look. I think she suspected, but wasn't going to say anything, certainly not to Roger.

Over the next few months we chatted together while the band played. We became close and I was sure I was in love with her. I had not felt like this about anyone else before. In fact I thought I had fallen in love with her when I first saw her photo in the Green Pages. She reciprocated my feelings, and for a while she too was in love with me.

Unfortunately there was no way we could take it any further because she was married to Roger. We cuddled and kissed in the dark at the back of the club but it never came to anything more than that. Our relationship remained platonic. It could be no other way. People thought we were having an affair and we didn't disabuse them of that idea. We simply never spoke about it. I took Beryl as my partner to my sister's wedding to Fred. It was the first wedding in our family and it was a massive affair as befits a traditional Greek wedding.

I discovered Beryl was interested in science fiction stories and I had found one by Ray Bradbury that I thought was profound. I took the paperback with me and read this story to her at the back of the club one night and no one noticed us at all. I can't remember which story it was. Bradbury was a genius with words, and could take an idea that had little substance and write a beautifully poetic story around it that was so moving it could almost bring tears to your eyes.

Stories by Ray Bradbury turned up in the most unexpected publications. He was one of the few who had crossed into the mainstream without compromising what he wrote, and was known to a very much wider audience than some other well-known authors within science fiction circles. One of his stories, 'The Fruit at the Bottom of the Bowl', was printed in Australian Women's Weekly when it was a weekly magazine. It must have confused regular readers expecting a story about fruit salad including a recipe. It was a story about obsessive behaviour and murder and how a compulsive habit brought the protagonist undone.

After a year Beryl told me one night that I was in love with the idea of being in love with her and not really in love with her. That took me by surprise. Maybe she was annoyed that I hadn't taken our relationship further, or perhaps realised I didn't have the courage to pursue it beyond what it was, knowing that she was married to Roger. Maybe she actually loved me at one point and was disappointed I didn't fully reciprocate. I really did love her — I was sure of that — but perhaps it later devolved into the idea of being in love with her rather than actually being in love.

It was a strange relationship, which Roger knew all about. That he wasn't too concerned meant that they had obviously spoken about it and he knew exactly what the situation was between us. When she became pregnant with Roger's baby we drifted further apart. We remained friends, but the particular intimacy that we had experienced over the previous year when I had been truly infatuated with her was gone. As her pregnancy evolved she stopped singing at the club and I rarely saw her again.

I heard much later that she had split up with Roger and had moved back to living with her parents. I wondered if it had been my fault that the split-up had occurred; a delayed reaction to our platonic affair. I wasn't going to find out, because the band members changed and I lost interest in playing at Birdland because the music changed. The ambience degenerated into a seedier, grimier feeling, and it seemed as if the owners no longer cared about how the place looked.

Music was changing too; the Beatles and the Rolling Stones had appeared on the scene, and hundreds of would-be copycats gigged around town mostly in pubs rather than nightclubs. Birdland could no longer compete with newer venues that promoted rock and roll bands.

Everything was changing

It was time to move on.

Looking across to the city (Melbourne) from Nelson Place while still dreaming of travelling around the world in a yacht.

— *Ephemeron* —

At loose ends...

I often found myself down on The Strand or in Nelson Place at Williamstown where watching yachts bobbing at their moorings in Hobson's Bay somehow made me feel less lonely. I also enjoyed watching the huge passenger liners come in and moor across the harbour at Port Melbourne. It seemed as if a new one arrived —and departed — every week. You could hear the foghorn bellow of the ship's siren as it left the port, and often drifting across the water was the sound of thousands of people yelling and calling goodbye to their loved ones as they embarked on an adventure to the old world. At night these massive liners departing were a spectacular sight, with thousands of lights from the decks and countless portholes brightening the darkness and glistening in reflections bounced off the waves across Hobson's Bay. I would watch as they diminished in size, the glow of the lights shrinking and finally disappearing the further the ship travelled down the channel towards the distant Heads of Port Phillip Bay.

Williamstown is a peninsula that juts out into Port Phillip Bay near the mouth of the Yarra River, and it forms a small protected bay, which is Hobson's Bay. Historically it was the harbour where the tall sailing ships came when they arrived. It was the location of the original settlement of Melbourne, but because there was no fresh water available the town was shifted up the Yarra river to a location near Dight's Falls, where the tidal rise and ebb of the river came up against a rocky barrier. On the other side, fresh water was available for the growing settlement.

Still, all the ships arriving came into the piers at Williamstown, and Williamstown was where immigrants and new settlers disembarked and stayed before heading for the nearby goldfields or into the growing city of Melbourne. Dockyards were built (The Alfred Graving Dock) using convict slave labour. This dry and wet dock serviced the hundreds of tall ships that came in every year. Every street corner near the piers and docks and boat repair businesses had a pub on it. At one point there were more than one hundred in the city of Williamstown, but now that number is greatly reduced. Even so, Williamstown has more pubs than any other suburb in greater Melbourne, and each has its loyal customers.

I would watch the liners come in up the channel and head across to Port Melbourne. The arriving and departing foghorn bellows often brought to mind Bradbury's story '*The Foghorn*', which was filmed as *The Beast from 20,000 Fathoms*. This very short story, first published in 1952, dealt with a lovesick marine dinosaur (a pliosaur perhaps? Bradbury was rather vague with his description, other than to say it had a neck about 70 feet long, and that it rose up out of the sea and wrapped around the light house.) It believed the sound of the fog horn was a long lost mate calling. It emerged from the sea one foggy night only to create mayhem and destruction instead of finding love. Bradbury could make any silly idea beautiful and compelling to read.

The film was a typical disaster film, with the monster created by Ray Harryhausen and his stop-motion model animation. More than anything, the movie monster looked like a dinosaur, not something that would have lived in the sea, which seemed incongruous. A pliosaur would not have been able to come on land and smash up a city, as it did in the film, so a dinosaur it had to be. This made the film ridiculous even though it was popular. It took the world by storm and unleashed a series of even worse films from many countries about dinosaur-like monsters, created by the effects of radiation or other such ideas, destroying major cities. Godzilla from Japan became the enduring and most popular one. Maybe I was lonely too, which is why that film and that Bradbury story kept popping into my head every time I heard a big ship's siren echo across the water.

I watched the yachts sailing on weekends. I would walk along the piers and into the yacht clubs and look at the most beautiful boats moored there. I even joined the Hobson's Bay Yacht Club, with the idea of one day buying a yacht and sailing around the world. I started buying yachting magazines to read about the adventures of all those long-distance sailors and the exotic places they visited, such as the islands of the Caribbean, Tahiti, Fiji, the Greek Islands in the Mediterranean, and the South Pacific Islands closer to home, even sailing boats up the rivers and canals of Europe. You could practically go anywhere in a good yacht.

The catch was I simply couldn't afford to buy one, let alone pay for the maintenance of one. For a while I thought I should have stayed in Darwin; driving a dry cleaning van to pick up and deliver clothes was not something I imagined I would be doing forever, but at least it was better than being inside a dry cleaning factory all day working the machines for cleaning or the presses for the finishing.

There were lots of musicians out of work too. The jazz clubs disappeared and the few big balls weren't enough to earn decent living. There were not enough variety shows, ballets, or other theatrical work to employ all the musos who were out there looking for something. I managed a couple of small recording gigs, but after that it all dried up. No one wanted anything else but rock and roll. If you couldn't switch to rock and roll, you were out of a job. I was lucky, because we had a family business to fall back on. My sister Zara, when she wasn't dancing or working as a showgirl at the Tivoli, worked at the factory. Christine too. If I had anything on and needed to rehearse, I could always get a few hours off to do that.

For a while my good friend Brian and I would go down to the Williamstown front beach and swim from the lifesavers' club across to the dressing sheds and the fishing clubs at the other end, then run back along the sand. We went through a winter and into the following summer doing this every day, then for some reason which escapes me now we stopped. He got tied up with his advertising and just didn't have the time, I suspect. Once you stop, though, you never go back to it.

My brother-in-law Fred stopped driving buses and took up abalone diving, and I would go out with him on his boat to take photos and shoot film of him in action. Apart from that, we dived at various locations around the Victorian coast, and ventured several times as far north as Bermagui in New South Wales. We would drive there usually at night so we would have all day for diving and snorkelling, but the drive was gruelling once you left Lakes Entrance. The highway, if you could call it that, was a gravel road that twisted and wound through the foothills on the coast side of the Dividing Range between Lakes Entrance and Eden on the NSW border. It was hard driving, bone shaking, with constant gear changes to prevent skidding on corrugated gravel. But the diving was fabulous once you got there. We also tried water skiing on some of Victoria's inland lakes but I preferred to stay in the boat rather than climb on a pair of skis to be dragged across a choppy lake. Falling off skis and hitting the water at high speed was not my idea of fun.

Not much luck with girls

Apart from the platonic relationship with Beryl I hadn't had much luck with girls.

My only two dates ended in disasters, the first being when I was 17 and trying to impress a girl I met while we camped at Portarlington on the Bellarine Peninsula I was trying to back Dad's car out and up onto the gravel road through the camp, when instead of going back I shot forward and smashed a hole in the neighbour's caravan. Dad's car's gear shift was a column shift. The position of reverse was up and forward while first gear was forward. I accidentally put it into first instead of reverse, and while looking back through the rear window to watch out for traffic I released the clutch and the damned car shot forward instead of backwards and smashed into the caravan before I could even get my foot off the accelerator pedal. The engine stalled and the caravan shook like it was in an earthquake while I sat there stunned. Needless to say, the girl sitting beside me quickly got out of the car and I never saw her again.

During my other unfortunate date, I invited a Russian girl from high school to go out to a Russian club. I drank too much vodka and was determined to show that I could do a Cossack dance with the best of them. I managed the dance, but got too drunk to take the girl home so she went in a taxi. For a week after that dance my legs were so painfully stiff I could hardly walk.

I was kind of shy, having spent a lot of time reading books and not chasing girls. My friend Brian had no such qualms, and it seemed he had a different girlfriend every week. I don't know to this day what impulse made me go over to the ABC studios in Elwood to see Inez Amaya (Beryl) but the impulses one's mind generates are often incomprehensible If it hadn't been for the fact that she was at Birdland I would never have spoken to her or have had the chance to meet her. However, that hadn't worked out in the long run.

Diving into some good books

Feeling lonely but unable to articulate it, my answer, as always, was to dive into some good books.

This was the year I read *A Canticle for Leibowitz* by Walter Miller (1959) and *A Case of Conscience* by James Blish (1958), both fantastic books by very good authors writing in top form. I would put these books on a par with anything written by mainstream authors of both literary and genre novels. Although both of these books were published in the last two years of the 1950s, I didn't see either of them until sometime in 1963. Perhaps it took that long for them to reach Australia. That these two books didn't get the recognition they deserved was because they were characterised as Science Fiction. Yet my hardcover copy of *A Canticle for Leibowitz* doesn't have any mention of SF or Science Fiction on the dust jacket or inside. Weidenfeld & Nicolson simply marketed it as 'A Novel by Walter Miller'.

Kingsley Amis chose the American edition as his novel of the year, and said in the Observer: '*This book goes as far as any I have read to justify the claim that science fiction has become a mature vehicle for the expression of certain important themes which ordinary fiction cannot well accommodate. It is a serious (not earnest), imaginative (not fantastic), religious (not religiose) novel.*'

This was one of the best books I ever read, and I can't recommend it highly enough to anyone looking for a serious and insightful reading experience. I am about to re-read it, and I am sure it will hold up as well today as it did 50 years ago.

So too was *A Case of Conscience* by James Blish, which I am also about to re-read. This is a powerful novel that examines the problems and conflicts raised by a man of the cloth who struggles to reconcile the teachings of his faith with the teachings of science as he becomes part of an expedition to a world similar to Earth, but populated by intelligent reptilian beings who have no concept of religion or of original sin, and who live their lives governed by pure reason. It was first serialized in *If Worlds of Science Fiction* magazine, but I did not see that publication until years later. I read it as a paperback novel.

1963 was also the year that *Dune World* by Frank Herbert appeared in *Analog*, I believe, although I didn't see it until it was published as a Gollancz hardcover in 1965. Who would have or could have thought that it would be so popular and successful that fans wouldn't let Herbert write much of anything else? The saga became six books, and after Herbert died his son Brian, in collaboration with Kevin J Anderson, went on to write another 12 books in a now never-ending saga of trilogy after trilogy. No doubt there will be more, but I won't be reading them. I lost interest in *Dune* by the time I got to the fourth book, *The God Emperor of Dune*.

1963 was about the time I couldn't keep up with everything being published as science fiction. There was simply too much of it. Up until at least 1960 I had managed to read everything available as novels or collections of short stories as well as some of the popular magazines, and for a while there I could remember all the plots and story-lines of each book. I can't now. My brain over the last 50 years has devoured too many books, and similarities of plots get confused and become indistinguishable. Even recent stuff I thought was very good is hard to remember and indistinguishable from fragments of earlier books that continue to impinge upon my consciousness.

I did of course read more Heinlein, even though I was not fond of him. His stories were everywhere, since he was so prolific. Many adhered to a timeline into the future that he designated as future history, so there was a consistency in background detail that gave them a kind of reality. Asimov did the same with his stories of the *Foundation* and the future history it presided over (written and published in the early 1940s, but which I didn't see until the mid 1950s).

I do remember *The Puppet Masters* as being one of Heinlein's better early stories. It was made many years later into a suitably creepy film. One author I must have read but whose stories I can only recall from much later was Jack Vance. It's odd how an author like him could be bypassed in my mind when I would certainly have read *The Dying Earth* (1950) and *Big Planet* (1952). I must have dismissed *The Dying Earth* as a fantasy, which meant I would not remember it, since I didn't really like fantasy, and *Big Planet* must have been so badly written it guaranteed I wouldn't remember it. I did re-read *The Dying Earth* in the 1970s after coming across some of Jack Vance's later books, but still can't remember much about it. So too for *Dust of Far Suns,* which was originally *Sail 25* in its magazine publication, but was renamed and used as the lead story in a collection by Daw Books in 1964. *The Languages of Pao* was another of Vance's science fantasies that I remember enjoying, but of which I can no longer recall any details. Perhaps I will have to read this one again, along with most of the other later books Vance wrote.

Phillip K. Dick I must also have read, although not too many spring to mind from that early period. There were of course his many short stories, which I read and forgot and then remembered again when re-reading them in later collections. There were also some novels that I read in the late '50s and early '60s that I have subsequently forgotten. Books like *The Man who Japed, The Cosmic Puppets, The Game Players of Titan, Time out of Joint,* and *Solar Lottery* spring to mind, but without much detail, and so these will go on a pile for possible re-reading. To be honest, I didn't really discover Phillip K Dick or Jack Vance in any significant way until after I came back from Europe at the end of 1965. And only then I remembered that I had read much of their early output without being aware of them.

I think the last major science fiction novel I read in 1963 was *Stranger in a Strange Land* (1961) by Robert Heinlein. This was a book that generated a cult for hippies and university students, with its portrayal of free love and religion as seen through the eyes of a Martian born human. However popular this book was, it wasn't one of Heinlein's best. It just happened to appear at a time when the ideas espoused in it were also being adopted by the younger generation on a broad scale across the USA, and so became the unofficial Bible of the free spirits of the time. I also came across a 'speculative novel', *Messiah* by Gore Vidal, about a religious prophet who generated a huge following and who ended up taking over the whole country. This was a much better book than Heinlein's.

Gore Vidal is famous for other mainstream novels, historical and political as well as controversial, but his only science fiction or speculative novel seems to be forgotten and is never listed anywhere. So too was his murder mystery on a patrol boat in the last days of the Second World War, *Williwaw,* which was published only a few months after the end of that war. Though not specifically a war story, it can be classified as such, and thus beats Norman Mailer's claim to have written the very first Second World War novel *The Naked and The Dead* (1948).

Williwaw, though enjoyable and readable, is not a patch on *The Naked and The Dead*, which stands today as a great classic war novel. It is still one of my all-time favourite novels. It certainly wasn't science fiction, but it could very well have been, because for me the world depicted by Mailer was so far from any reality I had experienced or could understand that it might as well have been set on an alien world.

The only other two war novels I read about this time that I remember were *The Cruel Sea* (published in 1951) by Nicholas Monserrat, which was made into a documentary style war film by a British film company, and *The Caine Mutiny* by Herman Wouk, which was also made into a brilliant film starring Humphrey Bogart — possibly his best performance as an actor, certainly on a par with his performance in *The African Queen*.

Nicholas Monserrat also wrote a creepy novella about an alien found frozen in ice thousands of years old, presumably at the North Pole. The alien was thawed out and all sorts of havoc ensued. It sounded to me like *Who Goes There?*, which of course became the Howard Hawks film *The Thing from another World*. I can't remember the name of the Monserrat story but I do believe it was originally published in the late '30s or early '40s, which would have made it contemporary to John W Campbell's story that became the famous movie. The copy I saw was a small hardcover re-issue after that film had become popular, which means I would have read it around 1960.

The early sixties was a time when science fiction fans as well as many other people held great dreams for the future. The space race was in its infancy, with the Americans and the Russians trying to outdo each other with constant spectacular launches into space. The Russians had the first man in orbit (Yuri Gagarin). They'd sent up a dog (Laika), which had died in space, in the second Sputnik in November 1957, while the Americans could only counter by sending up unmanned sub-orbital flights.

The Russians had powered ahead, with Sputniks getting bigger and better. They even sent more dogs into space, but this time they managed to bring them back to Earth, while the best the Americans could do (in 1961) was to counter by sending a chimpanzee up in a capsule, again only in a sub orbital flight.

Once more the Russians beat the Americans by sending Yuri Gagarin into orbit (April 12 1961). By the end of that frantic year America finally managed a manned suborbital flight with Alan Shepard.

In February 1962 America finally made it into space with a manned capsule (containing John Glenn). It orbited four times in just under five hours.

I devoured all this with ever growing excitement. Humans were taking their first faltering steps towards the conquering of space. I had been reading about this for years and finally it was all starting to come true.

Again the Russians trumped the Americans by sending a woman into space. Valentina Tereshkova went into orbit (June 16) and made 42 orbits over two days and passed close enough to another Russian satellite, containing another cosmonaut, that they could each see the other's capsule.

The Americans couldn't compete, and it appeared as if they were losing the space race, so they took a step sideways. They sent an atomic submarine under the Arctic Ice Cap for the first time; a magnificent feat in its own right, which upset and frightened the Russians, who became even more paranoid about the security of their homeland. This American achievement was certainly not as visible or as spectacular as a rocket launched into space, but it started concurrently another much more deadly race which was to see who had domination of the seas. Atomic submarines from each nation started patrolling the other's coastal seas, and they all had missiles with atomic warheads aimed at each other's major cities. It came to a head in 1962. We almost had an atomic war when the Russians wanted to install atomic missiles in Cuba aimed at nearby America.

Frank Herbert published a wonderful novel called *Under Pressure* around this time. It told of the crew of an American atomic submarine towing underwater barges and stealing oil from deposits under the Arctic ice in territory that belonged to USSR. There was a saboteur on board and the confrontation between the Russians in similar atomic submarines trying to stop the Americans, and the threat of what the saboteur would do, made a taut psychological drama that was a very much an up-to-the-minute reflection of what was happening in the real world. It was one of Herbert's better books before he got lost in the Dune saga.

Perhaps to divert attention away from the Cuban missile crisis, President Kennedy announced that America was determined to send a man to the moon within the decade. Once again the space race was on. Everyone started dreaming about moon bases and voyages to Mars, hotels in space and giant passenger liners plying the currents of space (to pinch a title from Isaac Asimov) to travel between far solar systems and their myriad planets teaming with strange and bewildering life forms.

It would all be happening soon ... we wished ... we hoped ... in the not too distant future, but it was not to be. As Arthur C. Clarke wrote, *'The Future is not the way we remember it,'* or something like that, and he was right.

What we dreamed about happening never happened, and the future that we presently live in is certainly not what we wanted.

Although we have no choice but to accept it for what it is, we can still dream, and science fiction and speculative fiction can help us do this, as it did before and will always do.

Sitting in the backyard thinking about going to Europe in October or November 1963.

An Innocent Afloat

A surprise announcement

I came home one day and announced that I had bought a ticket to go on the Chandris Line's RHMS Ellinis to England and Europe. In 1964 the Ellinis was one of three Greek passenger ships that took passengers to Europe, where they disembarked either in Piraeus (Greece) or Southampton (England). I would be getting off in Southampton, since that was its second last stop after Lisbon (Portugal) before finishing in Greece, where it would take on immigrants bound for Australia.

The Ellinis's sister-ships, the smaller Patris and the much larger Australis, also did the same. Several years later they stopped using the Patris and introduced a larger ship again, the Britanis. These were basically secondhand ships that had been built after the First World War, and used for other purposes before being taken over by Chandris Lines, which converted them to single-class passenger ships to bring migrants from Europe to Australia. Taking passengers to Europe for holidays with 'round the world cruising' was the company's cream: its bread and butter were the migrants brought to Australia. For example, the Australis, on which I returned from Europe, was originally a luxury passenger ship sailing between Europe and North America, then used as a troop carrying ship during World War II, after which it was acquired by Chandris Lines. Sadly, as the ship aged it became too expensive to rebuild the engines, and maintain the propeller shafts and other major repairs (18 million pounds the estimated cost) so they sold it for scrap. In the process of towing it around Africa to the Indian subcontinent, where it was to be broken up, it mysteriously ran aground off a group of Spanish islands where it was abandoned. What's left of it still sits there on the rocks offshore.

There were also two Italian ships that took passengers to Europe (via Southampton or Italy) and in turn brought back loads if immigrants. Four years later, when I was in Acapulco, my sister Christine and her friend Yvonne stopped for a day on their way to Europe on one of those Italian ships. I had been there for almost a year then, and could show them all the best places to visit.

It must be remembered that these passenger ships were nothing like the cruise ships of today, which are bigger and carry many more passengers and are more like miniature cities than those refurbished one-class liners. There are even giant ships today where people can buy apartments and live in them on a permanent basis, only renting them out when they want to spend some time ashore. These giant ships are always cruising around the world. They are floating cities. They contain parks and gardens, malls with innumerable shops, private and public accommodation with unprecedented views, clubs and bars, restaurants and coffee shops; everything you would find in a small city centre. They are perhaps the first step in the development of floating cities of the future; cities whose inhabitants will not have to go ashore if they don't want to, and who will have no need to worry about rising oceans resulting from the warming of the Earth. But the closest you got to them in the

1960s were the luxurious P&O liners, priced beyond what people like me could afford. Chandris Lines and its one-class passenger ships were affordable, and did give the impression of a degree of luxury, so all on board could pretend that the ships were better than they actually were.

Air travel to Europe was ferociously expensive, so going by ship was the only way. It cost me $600 or thereabouts for the trip (which included all meals, accommodation, and entertainment) to go across the Pacific, stopping at Auckland, Tahiti, Panama, then through the canal to Colon, to the island of Aruba (Dutch Antilles), on to Fort De France on Martinique, the French island famous for its massive volcano Mont Pele, over to Lisbon in Portugal, and finally to Southampton, where most of the passengers would be getting off. Only a few would go on to Greece and the port of Piraeus, where the ship terminated its voyage.

I thought the price was very reasonable. It was a one-way ticket that I bought. I didn't mention that, and hoped Mum and Dad wouldn't notice. I didn't want to be constrained by a specific date to return to Australia. I was even thinking at that time that maybe if things went well I wouldn't return, at least in the foreseeable future. I wanted to be free to see what would happen in Europe, and that would determine how long I stayed in any country. I didn't know what I wanted to do, but only that I needed the time to discover this and that would ultimately determine how long I would stay.

They were sitting around the kitchen table and staring at me, Mum and Dad. Christine was in the other room watching TV with young Paul. Zara, married to Fred, wasn't there because they had their own house now in North Altona.

'What do you mean?' Mum asked. 'You're going to Europe?'

I pushed the ship's ticket across to her.

'Have a look at it, at all the places it's going to stop at on the way.'

'You can't go to Europe.'

'Why not? Everyone else is doing it.' Just about everyone my age was going, had been, or was returning from a pilgrimage to Europe — usually to England, the 'Mother Country', unless of course they had European parentage, which meant probably Greece or Italy, with smaller numbers heading for France or Germany or Holland. It was almost a rite of passage for those in their twenties.

'But what about the business? Who is going to do the driving, the pick-up and deliveries?'

'Phillip will.'

'He's in Alice Springs.'

'Write him a letter and ask him to come back. There's plenty of time. I'm not leaving until April 4th. It's only the end of January now.'

'You're leaving on your birthday?'

'Yeah ... Don't you think that's a great time to start something different, something new?'

Mum just shook her head.

Dad finally said, 'It's all right. Nothing will change. Phillip will come back and do the driving. Everything else will be the same, you'll see.' He said this to Mum.

No doubt he was recalling his own moments when he told his parents first that he was going to America with his older brother George. He was only 13 or so at the time. Much later again, when he was in his late twenties or early thirties, he told his parents he was going to Australia, knowing then that he would never see them again. That must have been hard. But I knew he understood that this was something I had to do, though for different reasons. His reasons had been economic, and the desire to better himself, to make life better for his family, whereas mine were ... well I wasn't exactly sure what mine were. They were vague and unformed, mixed with the desire to see if I could be independent of the family, to discover myself, or to assuage the empty feeling I had, and the belief that I wasn't achieving anything by staying at home doing what I was doing. This would be more like an adventure, and not something that was necessary in order to survive. Having spent almost a year in Darwin, I was impatient to do something like that again, only on a grander scale. It was five years since then, and I hadn't

Chandris Lines rhms Ellinis – from their publicity pamphlet.

had a holiday other than a number of weekend diving trips to various locations around the coast, and I felt it was time to do something different. Going to Europe would certainly be different.

Dad looked at me from the other side of the table. 'Do it,' he said with a smile. He stood up and left the kitchen without saying anything else.

'Well,' Mum said after a long moment of silence. 'I suppose I'd better start organising what you will take with you.'

Typical... She was a great organizer. It was her way of coping with the unexpected, or with something she didn't like but inevitably had to accept. She had done the same thing when she was a young girl, but not by her own choice. Her stepmother had basically forced her and her older sister Betty to leave home at a young age. She was only 13 at the time, about the same age as Dad when he went to America. They both managed, and they knew that I would too. Besides, I was older than they had been, already 23, and the world was a much better place to go out into than it had been back in the 1920s. Whether I took any notice of what she planned was irrelevant. What it meant was that she had already accepted the idea that I was going to leave for a voyage to Europe and that it was all okay.

The S.S.Australis

The Sea Around Us

Wandering into bookshops around town was always a pastime I enjoyed immensely (even today). In Collins bookshop at the top end of Bourke Street, I discovered a lovely book with an attractive cover. It showed a three-masted sailing ship at the top, and in a circle all the way round were delightful illustrations of sea creatures. In the centre of the circle was the title: *The Sea Around Us,* by Rachel L Carson. Since it was a popular science book and about the sea I couldn't resist buying it. It only cost 15 shillings and six pence ($1.55 in today's terms). It had no illustrations. A book like that today would be full of technical drawings, and photos both colour and black and white, but this book was entirely text, and so beautifully written and easy to understand that I just couldn't put it down. It was better than any of the science fiction books I had read up to that time.

This little book took the world by storm when it first appeared in the early 1950s. The edition I had was published in 1953, although I didn't see it until early 1960. The New York Herald Tribune described this little book as *'the book, not only of the year, but of the decade.'* It won the National Book Award 1952 for the 'most distinguished work of non-fiction in 1951 (USA)'.

And what was it about? It was about the Sea, its formation and history, and how life developed in it and evolved to fill every part of it from the abyssal depths to the bright sunny areas just below the surface, about how it enveloped the continents and affected life on those lands, how it affected human endeavours over millennia, and ultimately how much we as a species, and all life on this planet, depends on the sea — a truly wonderful book.

There are probably some things in it that are now outdated, because over the last 60 years marine sciences have discovered much more than was known then, but nevertheless what is in that book is still very relevant and is still beautiful to read. It is, in my opinion, one of the best and most accessible popular science books ever written.

A fire in the kitchen

After coming back from Darwin, one of the first things I did was to paint our garage doors with a huge picture of termite mounds and Pandanus palms partly obscured by tufts of fast growing grass, something I also included in the big mural for the Department of Agriculture that I painted in Darwin. Like that one, it was done with house paint, but being on the garage door it was exposed to the rain and wind and the sun which soon caused the paint to flake and peel off. But while it lasted I thought it looked pretty good.

Antonio Rodriguez and Albert LaGuerre, who shared part of an old heritage-listed house just off St Kilda Road near the junction, were friends of mine, and I often went there to play drums. Antonio was principally a dancer, but he played conga drums (called Atabaques in Brazil) in the Brazilian style, while Albert played Haitian style. I was studying how to play Cuban style, yet there was enough in common between us to allow us to play quite well together. Albert was the master drummer here. I still have some tape recordings from these sessions, but no longer have a machine capable of playing them.

Also sharing a studio at the back of this house was a young artist called Asher Bilou. He was experimenting with abstract art in many different forms, which included sculpture.

I remember being impressed by one huge sphere-like construction made entirely of hundreds of thousands of watch movements, from the tiniest bits to quite large watch movements. All of these individual bits and pieces of watches of various sizes were soldered or welded together to make a sculpture that moved. All of the watch movements functioned each with its own time and ticking sound. In my imagination it was a time machine, but it didn't work. No matter where you looked some part of it was moving and ticking telling its own time. All the different sounds from the movements blended together to make an unearthly whisper that seemed to penetrate right into your mind.

Asher went on to become quite famous, and has many paintings in galleries around Australia and overseas, but at that time he was relatively unknown. I loved the way he blended glue and paint together, sometimes selectively burning the glue-paint mixture to create unexpected textures, and then used this thick mixture to build up surface features on the canvas and boards he painted.

Antonio also was experimenting with wood carving, and he too used glue and paint mixtures applied and simultaneously burnt onto the wood sculpture to create a unique texture on his carvings. They were very successful at later exhibitions.

In the meantime I was experimenting in doing something similar. At first I simply applied rubber-based glue to pre-painted board surface, then would laboriously paint the splashed glue afterwards. This was far too time consuming, so I progressed to mixing artist's oil paint and spirit-based cellulose glue — Tarzan's Grip — together. I applied this mixture to the surface of the pre-painted board, and would then set fire to it. It would burn furiously, and I had to blow it out rather quickly or there'd be nothing left. Doing this repeatedly, small sections at a time, I could build all kinds of uniquely textured surfaces. Sometimes I would then hand-paint sections of it when it appeared too burnt, or I would have to paint over the parts in between the mixture where the underlying background paint had been scorched.

Gluing things like pieces of papier-mâché or sections of cardboard egg cups to Masonite boards and painting over them and eventually burning glue and paint mixtures and touching them up afterwards produced a series of fairly interesting paintings, which were a lot of fun to create. Art should be fun, shouldn't it? It can be serious, but some people take it too seriously. Shouldn't there be some enjoyment in the creative process, or why bother doing it?

I loved it. I even got my prospective brother-in-law to help with one larger picture, which I later gave to him as a present. He was also helping me the night I almost burnt down the kitchen.

I had made a huge frame about two metres long by one and a half high. It was a large piece of Masonite, with a wooden frame to support it. I had sealed and undercoated it. When it was dry I laid it down flat on the table in the kitchen. Mum and Dad were watching TV in the lounge room, so I shut the door to the passage and thus isolated the kitchen from the rest of the house. With great abandon I spread a rubber based glue over various parts of the board. Fred was also watching this act of creation. The rubber-based glue, some of which was mixed with raw colour, was for the background texture. Once I had burnt this to develop the texture I would then apply oil-based paint mixed with transparent Tarzan's Grip, bought in half-pint tins, to complete the textural and colour development of the painting. I had a rough idea of what I was trying to achieve and of what the painting might look like when it was finished, but there was no control over how it bubbled and textured when it was burning, and that was what made each painting individual and unrepeatable. You never really knew how it would look until it was finished.

I should have realised that the smell in the kitchen was quite strong, like the smell of petrol or white spirit in an enclosed space, but then I was used to that kind of smell at the dry cleaning factory and didn't think about it.

I looked at Fred.

'Are you ready?'

He nodded and passed me a box of matches.

'Let's see what happens,' I said as I lit match. 'I've never done a painting this big, before so it should be quite interesting.'

I reached over and touched the match to one corner and immediately the glue and paint started bubbling. Above the bubbles there seemed to be an open space and above that some green coloured flames. I quickly blew it out to see how the texture was. When the bubbles settled, there didn't seem to be much texture, so I decided I would let the next bit burn a little longer before blowing it out. A little wisp of dark smoke drifted up towards the ceiling. It was an old house and we had a 10 foot high ceiling in the kitchen.

I lit another match, and moved to a different spot along one side of the frame and touched the burning match to the glue. It started to burn nicely. Black smoke rose up.

'Shouldn't you blow it out?' Fred suggested.

'Just a bit longer,' I mumbled as I leaned in closer to see how the mixture was bubbling.

It was bubbling nicely so I leaned over and blew on it to put it out before moving on to light another patch. The flames didn't go out, but shot across to another part and ignited that. Suddenly there was loud swoosh and flames shot across the whole surface.

'Shit,' Fred yelled. He humped back.

I pulled my head back. I was sure my hair was singed. It felt like it. My eyes were watering but I didn't want to wipe them in case I rubbed oily soot into them.

Black smoke enveloped us and rose to the ceiling like huge cumulous clouds.

'Get some water,' I yelled at Fred.

I grabbed the edge of the painting to drag it off the table without thinking about how I was going to get it outside through the door into the back yard. It was too hot to grab as the burning surface came right to the edge of the frame. I could hear the tap running as Fred filled something with water to throw over the flames. I couldn't see him because now the smoke was all the way from the ceiling down to chest height.

Swirling and black, it was greasy, horrible smoke that smelled of burning car tyres. It roiled and rolled down the walls. I could see the smoke above the painting glowing red with the flames roaring up.

I dropped to the floor and crawled to the door that opened into the back yard. Outside Mum always had a hose connected to a tap over a gully trap and I turned this on and raced back inside to spray the painting with water. With the flames doused I took the hose back outside and turned it off.

'Let's get this outside,' I said to Fred.

He grabbed one end, and with me on the other we turned the painting sideways and I backed across the wet slippery floor towards the door. Out in the yard we threw the painting on the lawn. Because parts were still glowing and possibly likely to burst into flames again I gave it a thorough hosing. After that we went back into the kitchen, turned on the exhaust fan and opened all the louvre windows above the sink and beside the door to the back yard. There was a large mop in the laundry so I went in there and got that. While the smoke started to clear I mopped up the water on the floor.

Within a few minutes the smoke had cleared enough to see through it, but it was still like looking through a dense fog.

'Well, that was fun,' Fred said, just as the door to the passage opened and Dad stood there with a look of astonishment.

'What the hell happened here?'

Before we could think of a sensible explanation he bent over so that his head was below the layer of smoke still filling the top half of the kitchen. In this bent-over position he made his way across and into the laundry, obviously on his way to the toilet.

Mum had replaced him in the doorway from the passage.

'Did you set the kitchen on fire?' she asked as she stared at the heavy smoke slowly dissipating. It didn't seem to faze her at all. But then she was always like that, calm and collected, no matter what the disaster.

'It's all right. It's fine,' I mumbled shamefaced. 'Fred and I will clean it up.'

'You can have that on your own,' Fred said with grin and pushed past Mum to go and see what was on TV.

'I'll leave it to you then,' Mum said, and she closed the door so the foul smell wouldn't get into the rest of the house.

Dad reappeared closing the laundry door behind him.

'It's a good thing the kitchen needs to be repainted isn't it?'

This time he wasn't bent over, as the worst of the smoke had cleared. There was still a layer clinging to the ceiling. This seemed to be twisting and writhing as if reluctant to be sucked away by the exhaust fan above the stove.

Dad disappeared into the passage, closing the door behind to leave me alone contemplating the mess I had made. I think that if we hadn't had such a high ceiling in the kitchen the damage would have been much worse, and most likely the ceiling would have been set on fire as well. I was lucky that all I had to do was clean up the greasy residue left by the smoke.

It took me almost two hours to clean the bench tops and the cupboards above them and to get rid of the greasy soot that penetrated in through the closed doors. I had to clean the window slats as well, and mop the floor again. I didn't bother with the ceiling, as we didn't have a ladder handy. I cleaned that the next day. Even so, the burnt rubber smell lingered for several days, until finally I had to repaint the kitchen to cover the smoke stains.

I decided after that effort that painting abstract art wasn't something I would continue doing and so I never attempted another painting in that way again, with only one exception: one for the Art Show at Aussicon (1975). Someone bought it and shipped it to America. It was meant to illustrate a novel by Poul Anderson called *Firetime*, and it was abstract in the style I had developed in the early 1960s. That was the second painting I ever sold. All the others were given away or left at home.

The disappearance of memory

It's odd how things you think you will never forget you do, and years later you curse yourself for not writing stuff down or for not taking photos that would later help you remember. When I was 23 just going on 24, I thought my memories of the first big trip, the first trip overseas on a huge passenger liner, would stay in my mind forever. I had never done anything like that before. I had been on lots of small and not so small trips away, but nothing that would take five weeks to reach the initial destination.

I imagined it to be like a trip in a hyper-space passenger ship: you leave earth orbit and head out-system for a few days, and when you are clear of the gravitational effects of the major planets the ship drops into hyper-space and you are off to another star system, and weeks later you get there. Your whole world is enclosed in that tiny space, and after a while it seems huge enough that the rest of the world diminishes so much in size and concept that it almost ceases to exist. Only the world of the ship is real while it is there all around you.

I didn't take a still camera. I decided it was one less thing to worry about. I would buy postcards and send them back home. Why take photos when everywhere you went someone would have already taken better shots than mine, available as postcards? Every place has postcards; even the smallest and most backward place has them. However, I did take my Bolex movie camera and 10 rolls of 16 mm film. I would buy film as I needed it and perhaps I could put together a short documentary.

Could I find work as a drummer somewhere in Europe? I took the drums with me. Unlike piano players, who can always find a piano wherever they go, conga drums were not ubiquitous in the 1960s. Unfortunately they took up space. My solution was to have them double up as suitcases, so whatever clothes I needed I stuffed inside the drums. They were heavy being made of wood and metal, but manageable.

So what happened to the memories I thought I would never forget?

I suspect that over many years they became buried in my subconscious mind, or worse still, vanished as they were overwritten by later information.

I cannot remember how I reached Station Pier in Port Melbourne, where the RHMS Ellinis was to depart, but I suspect my friend Brian Mealy took me there. It would have been early enough to take my drums on board, find my cabin way down below the promenade deck, about two thirds along the length of the ship on C deck, to stash them in there and select one of the four beds as my own, by leaving a drum/suitcase on top of it. The cabin was tiny, like a small cave. Apart from the four bunks, two on each side, there was a tiny table and a mirror, which gave the impression the cabin was bigger than it was. There was some storage space for clothes and personal items. Only one chair faced the small table. For showers and toilet facilities we used a communal bathroom just along the corridor. The cabin was right on the centreline of the ship, so there was very little movement from side to side or even up and down. Being inside, we had no porthole to let light in. The only light was artificial, so I decided I would spend as little time as possible in there; it would be someplace to sleep, and nothing else.

There were lounges, and libraries, and a cinema way down in the bowels of the ship near the bow, cocktail bars on various levels, shops, a swimming pool, a ball room, two large dining rooms, and heaps of other stuff on board, so there really was no need to spend time in the cabin. These ships were the latest cross between passenger ships and cruise ships as we know them today. Before the airlines took over the job of transporting people around the world, the only efficient method was by passenger ship.

Having got everything stowed away, I stood with Brian on the promenade deck and watched luggage being loaded through a huge doorway in the side of the ship lower than the lowest passenger deck. Crates of fresh fruit and vegetables went on board, sides of lamb and beef from a freezer truck, and all kinds of cardboard boxes with who knows what? There were lighter vessels on the seaward side of the ship with huge hoses, giant umbilical cords connected to the bowels of our ship throbbing as fuel was pumped through them. These were small sea-going tankers, the equivalent of the tanker trucks that deliver fuel to service stations.

It was a fantastic feeling to be standing there watching all the activity as the ship was prepared for the voyage ahead, not being at work, not having to even think about going to work. I was free for the moment, and full of anticipation for the coming voyage and whatever it might lead to.

And the bar exploded

I had just taken a sip from my second glass of beer when the bar exploded. Something flew past my head and smashed to bits against the side concrete wall. There was yelling and screaming and people jumped up, knocking chairs over as they did so.

'What the ...?'

'Sit still,' I told the young bloke sitting next to me. He was one of the others staying in my cabin. I had gone back down to unpack a few things and met him there. Together we went back up on deck for a while before deciding to go over to the bar where a large partly enclosed beer garden was a popular drinking hole for crews from the passenger liners that came and went regularly from Station Pier. It was within a short walking distance from the pier and was often the first port of call for crewmen and sailors.

We were sitting at a large table in the middle of the beer garden, a partly covered lounge with a few people from the ship, cabin staff, passengers and friends there to see them off. One of the cabin staff was a young and beautiful girl with a gorgeous smile. She was flirting with one of the friends of a passenger. At least that is what it seemed to me. She shifted over and sat on this man's lap. She planted a kiss on his cheek and suddenly the mood around our table went black. The guy sitting on the other side of the girl's empty chair stood up, flinging his chair away to make space. It crashed into the back of someone sitting at the table beside us.

'Hey ...' the man yelled as he too stood up and turned, pissed off that someone or something had thumped him in the back and made him spill his beer.

The guy grabbed the young girl and dragged her off the other man's lap. 'You keep your hands off her,' he snarled at the other man.

'Get your hands off me.' The girl yelled and pulled her arm away from the guy's grip.

The man who had been hit in the back with the chair threw a punch which connected with the guy who had grabbed the girl by the arm. He staggered back and fell against our table. The table shifted and several glasses of beer fell over. I grabbed mine just before it would have fallen.

'Leave him alone, you bastard,' the girl yelled.

In that instant several crewman or cabin staff stood up together. They converged on the man who had thrown the punch at one of their own. He wasn't one of them. They knocked him down, but before any of them could do more than try to kick him —there wasn't much space between the tables — all his mates stood up and turned on the crewmen.

And that was it. Instantaneously bottles and glasses flew everywhere. People yelled and screamed. Some fell over. Others ran off holding noses spurting blood. A jug flew past my head, trailing a stream of frothing beer. I took a sip of my drink and looked around. It was exactly like one of those bar fights in old cowboy movies. Everyone was trying to hit, push, or punch whoever happened in that moment to be in front of them. There were people outside gleefully looking in, enjoying the spectacle. In the distance I heard a police siren, so someone, probably the bar manager, had called the cops.

'It's time we left,' I said.

My cabin mate just nodded.

We stood up slowly and pretending to be invisible, quietly made our way towards the side wall, then moved along it until we came to a gate. Then we were outside looking in.

'I can't believe we never got hit,' my mate said as he watched the melee inside.

'That's why I told you to sit still. If we didn't move we wouldn't be a target.'

'But we had to move when we got up to leave.'

'It didn't matter then. Everyone was busy with someone else, and as long as we didn't get in their way they wouldn't see us let alone try to hit us.'

Suddenly the siren wailing became very loud, then cut off with a high squawk as a police van rolled into the side street next to the beer garden. Four officers leapt out.

'It's time we got back to the ship,' I suggested.

We walked away leaving the yelling and fighting and the glasses and jugs being smashed behind us.

Underway at last

The ship left around seven that evening, and there wasn't a large crowd to see it off. There were only a couple of hundred passengers on board. The other sixteen hundred or so would embark in Sydney. There were few streamers thrown, no whistles blown, and none of the excitement I would have expected at the ship's departure. It was an anti-climax. All that happened later, when we departed from Sydney. A small group of people stood along Station Pier and waved as the tugs manoeuvred the Ellinis out into open water, allowing her to turn and face the direction of the channel to the Port Phillip Heads.

I stood by the stern and watched the water churn furiously as the huge propellers beneath started to turn. It frothed and splashed and sea gulls flittered above it, searching for food scraps. Their white flapping wings created a stroboscopic affect as they passed through beams of light from the ship. Slowly the Ellinis moved away from the pier and the whirling sand and mud churned up by the propellers dissipated. Station Pier and the nearby shoreline slowly diminished in size as we moved out into the channel. Very soon there was nothing to see other than distant lights along the shoreline as twilight turned into night.

The ship's siren vibrated my bones as it blasted a farewell note. The deck hummed beneath my feet, but there was no other obvious suggestion of movement. We were still in calm waters until we left Port Phillip Bay. Once through the Heads things would no doubt be different.

— *Ephemeron* —

'Did you bring sea-sick tablets?' my cabin mate asked.

I looked at him, surprised to think that he would need such tablets. I had been on lots of boats of various sizes, from large fishing trawlers to small runabouts, and had never thought about getting sea-sick.

'Are you feeling sea-sick?'

'No, not yet. But what about when we get out through the Heads?'

'This is a big ship. You probably won't notice much movement. I read in the brochure that it has stabilisers installed to minimise sideways movement, to make it smooth.'

'I guess we'll find out soon enough, won't we?'

Supper was served once the ship was through the Heads and into Bass Strait. Since there were only a couple of hundred passengers, supper was nothing elaborate, but there was plenty of it: huge vats of tea and coffee with cups and saucers stacked beside them, piles of biscuits both sweet and dry, stacks of cakes, trays of sandwiches cut into small triangles, platters of cheese with every type of cheese available in Europe there for the sampling, freshly baked bread rolls that smelled superb, and bowls of fresh apples, oranges, bananas, and pears, all there for us to help ourselves. Supper, as well as morning tea and afternoon tea, although served in the main dining room, was not subject to the usual seating arrangements. Passengers could wander in and help themselves at any time during the period set aside. The main meals were subject to three sittings of about 450 people each time, three times a day. This was obviously an enormous amount of work for the dining room and kitchen staff. Once the passengers in Sydney came on board we would all be told which sitting was ours, and those three sittings would be strictly adhered to.

It turned out that there was almost half the number of crew and staff as there were passengers, which meant once we left Sydney there would be some two thousand people on board. The Ellinis, which catered for 1800 passengers plus crew, was a big ship, but not quite as big as her sister ship the Australis, which could carry 2300 passengers. These two ships were nowhere near the size of the P&O passenger liners that regularly came to Sydney and Melbourne, but they were somewhat larger than the two Italian ships, which also took Australians to Europe and brought back migrants.

The cruise along Bass Strait was smooth with a gentle up-and-down movement that could be felt only near the bow or the stern; amidships it was hardly noticeable. There was no sideways rolling, since the wind and sea were behind us.

'See, you don't need those tablets at all,' I told my cabin mate. 'If you'd been out there in a fishing boat you'd be bouncing all over the place, but this ship is so big any movement is going to be slow and easy; no problem at all to adjust to.'

'I took one anyway, just in case,' he said, almost as if he was embarrassed to admit it.

'At least it will make you sleep well.'

A few moments later he left to go back to the cabin to sleep after making sure to remind me to wake him up when we were entering Sydney Harbour. He didn't want to miss that, and neither did I. I had never entered Sydney Harbour on a ship before. But I wasn't tired enough to go to bed. I was still excited by the fact that I was on such a big ship.

From the promenade deck the sea was black. The sky was clear and glittered with billions of stars, most of which couldn't be seen from Melbourne, no matter how clear the sky was. But out here at sea there was no ambient light to obscure the sky by reflecting off microscopic particles in suspension, so you could see everything.

The ship's wake stretched behind with pale white phosphorescence as the churned water disturbed tiny creatures, dinoflagellates like *Noctiluca miliaris*, whose presence was only visible by the luminescence their bodies gave off when disturbed by the ship's movement through the water.

The sound of the waves sloshing along the side of the ship was quiet and soothing and was always there, along with a deep hum that denoted somewhere hidden in the bowels of the ship huge turbines generated electric power to run the lights, refrigerators, the water desalination plant, and any other things that needed electric power. There was also a deeper, barely audible rumble that came from the huge engines that controlled the propellers. This was not noticeable on the promenade deck, but was clearly audible down below where my cabin was located. I found it disturbing at first, trying to sleep with that barely audible sound and the faint vibration that could always be felt in the floor when you stood barefoot, but after a day or so it became reassuring and comforting. It receded into the subconscious, and I was hardly aware of it until it stopped when the ship berthed.

A very brief history

I always thought the *Ellinis* (which translates as 'Greek Lady') was a new ship.

It only seemed that way because it had been completely refurbished the year before. It had been converted from a luxury liner into a one-class liner with perhaps more cabins. Chandris Lines had bought the liner, which was originally called the Lurline, and built for the Matson Line, a US company that used it as a cruise ship travelling from San Francisco to Los Angeles and on to Hawaii. The Lurline's maiden voyage had taken her to Sydney in 1933. She was also used as a troop ship from 1942 until 1946, after which she returned to cruising, before being sold to Chandris Lines in 1963 and was refitted as the Ellinis.

She was decommissioned in 1986, with equipment removed to be kept as spare parts for use in the Britanis, and then sold for scrap to a Taiwanese company. Every ship belonging to Chandris had been a different ship belonging to a different company. Once aeroplanes took over the job of importing migrants, the shipping lines switched to cruising holidays, Many of them stopped coming to Australia because it wasn't profitable any more.

Culture shock

Culture shock is defined as the feeling of anxiety and confusion experienced when suddenly encountering an unusual or unfamiliar environment. The word shock has the wrong connotation, as it implies something frightening. The word surprise would be more adequate. Coming from an environment where pubs and bars were forced to close by law at 6 p.m. to finding the bars on the ship serving drinks well after that time was a pleasant surprise. Not only were they serving drinks, the prices were less than half of what we had to pay onshore. Being a ship at sea, it was not subject to local taxes, import duties, luxury levies, and so on. Once the Ellinis left the harbour and was technically at sea, everything on board was sold without any imposts whatsoever.

Did this encourage passengers to drink more? Certainly. For the price paid in a pub in Melbourne, and presumably Sydney and elsewhere in Australia, on board the Ellinis you could buy four drinks. So of course people drank more. But was it necessarily because booze was cheaper? I don't think so. I think it was because first, we were on holiday and not at work, so had more free time available — all day and night — and second, because we were having a good time, free from any worries we might have had onshore. We were having a party. Having a drink to relax and loosen inhibitions is what one does at a party. It seemed even more appropriate on board a ship cruising across the Pacific Ocean.

So the first intimation of cultural shock was that sense of being in an endless party on a floating city where for successive days and weeks there was nothing around us other than endless vistas of profoundly deep, very dark blue ocean beneath an unlimited sky. The feeling of being the only people alive in the whole world pervaded us and heightened the sense of excitement felt by each passenger, which was broken only momentarily when the ship arrived at a port where we stayed usually for 24 hours before returning to that vast endless ocean.

That first night, as we headed around Wilson's Promontory well inside the islands of the Furneaux Group, the largest of which was Flinders Island, I kept my back to the bright ship's lights so my eyes could adjust to the darkness beyond, and peering over the side rail along the promenade deck I looked for the smaller islands, such as Curtis Island and others, that were the bane of early sailors. Nothing more than large rocks that jutted up above the waves, they were often invisible to early sailing ships attempting to go through the Strait on their way to Sydney and the colony of New South Wales. Hundreds of shipwrecks in Bass Strait are a testament to the danger these tiny islands presented, but ships' captains would rather take a risk and go through Bass Strait instead of taking added weeks of worse weather encountered by going around the bottom of Tasmania.

I couldn't see anything. No searchlights or navigation lights to indicate where these many small islands were, only stars and a rising moon reflected off unbroken swells that remained black except where the moonlight glistened. It was a bit scary, but I trusted the navigators and the crew of the ship, who had been through this area literally hundreds of times without mishaps. Finally deciding there was really nothing to see, I went down to my cabin, climbed into my bunk, and was asleep before I knew it.

Culture shock for some came at the first dinner served while we were on our way north to Sydney. A couple of lovely old ladies shared the same dinner table as me. They looked with wide eyes at everything served to them by the waiters. I suspect they had never been exposed to Greek or other Southern European dishes. This was confirmed after the first entrée. It was rich with tomatoes and oregano as well as paprika, with a hint of lime, and tasted delicious. The meat was tender and absolutely white once you bit into it. It melted in your mouth.

'What did you think of that?' I asked the ladies who had tentatively tasted it at first, but then, deciding they liked it, they gobbled it down rather quickly.

'That was fabulous,' someone else at the table commented. 'Best I've ever tasted.'

'It was nice,' one of the ladies spoke hesitantly, while the other asked, 'What was it? I've never had anything like that before'

'Octopodia,' I told them with a Greek accent, 'in a piquant sweet paprika sauce.'

'Paprika I know ...' One said.

They looked at each other and smiled.

The waiter then arrived with a big tray stacked with plates and began serving the main course, which was roasted lamb with fetta and olives, baked potatoes and carrots with a selection of green vegetables steamed, with melted butter on top. The moment the main course had been served the ladies looked at me again, waiting for me to tell them what they had just eaten.

'Octopus, Greek style, served hot instead of cold as in a salad.'

'Oh yuck,' one said.

'I feel sick,' the other one added.

'Why? You just ate it and said it was delicious. You obviously enjoyed it'

'But we didn't know what it was,' they both said simultaneously.

There were a lot of people in Australia in the 1960s who had never eaten anything other than the British-style foods they were accustomed to. Some had by this time started to experience Italian food, especially in the way of coffee drinking, because espressos and cappuccinos sold in lots of small coffee shops were becoming popular. But this by no means stretched to food other than bastardised spaghetti or macaroni dishes. Few true Australians ventured into the Greek or Italian quarters of the city (Melbourne) to try other cuisines. Their first experience of food that was different was when, like these two old ladies, they boarded a ship like the Ellinis to travel to Europe and England.

'Should it make a difference, knowing what it was?'

'Well, of course.'

'That's cultural prejudice. It's okay if you don't know what it is, to eat it, but if you know ... suddenly it's horrible. This is a Greek ship, and you'd better get used to the food because there are a lot of Greek Australians travelling on board and a lot of Greek food is going to be served.'

'On second thought it wasn't too bad was it?' one said to the other, and she nodded reluctantly in agreement.

Once those ladies got over the initial shock of knowing what it was they were eating they decided it was better not to know. If it tasted good, they would eat it, and enjoy it. So, like many other passengers, they gradually overcame their previously held ideas of what food should taste like, and learnt to embrace new things, new tastes, and new sensations.

In Sydney, moored at a pier beside the Harbour Bridge, I didn't go ashore because I had been to Sydney many times and didn't think there was any point in doing it again. I watched the ship being loaded with luggage, this time from the back of a barge. It was on the side of the ship away from the pier where the passengers were streaming aboard. As the workers on the barge threw suitcases, bags, and boxes into the open hatch a suitcase fell off the barge and into the water. It was quickly fished out by someone using a long handled fish hook to drag it back to the side of the barge, but not before it had started to sink, where it was retrieved and thrown through the hatch into the ship. There was probably a lot of water damage to whatever was inside. I'd hate to be the person who owned that bag at the end of the voyage. I imagined most of the contents would be mouldy and totally ruined after five or six weeks of being wet.

All day passengers and their friends and relatives streamed aboard. Their excitement was palpable. Lots of laughter and kids running around ... The bars were full of people sharing their last moments with drinks. The volume of chatter was ear splitting. I was happy to avoid this, and stayed up on the promenade deck sitting in one of the deck chairs. I enjoyed watching the ferries that cross Sydney Harbour coming and going from nearby Circular Quay. Almost 1600 people boarded in Sydney, so the ship would really be jumping when we left later that afternoon.

Bass Strait and the Tasman Sea are notorious for sudden squalls and vicious storms that brew and explode unexpectedly. Many a yacht in the Sydney-to-Hobart Yacht Race can attest to this. During the night a storm had been developing in the Tasman Sea while we travelled north to Sydney. The Ellinis kept just ahead of it, so we didn't notice any adverse movement in the ship other than the usual barely perceptible side-to-side roll.

The Ellinis was quite large — 24,000 tonnes, 624 feet long by 79 feet wide, and capable of achieving 20 knots — but while we had been in Sydney taking on passengers the storm in the Tasman Sea had continued to evolve into something resembling a medium-sized hurricane. It had moved slowly up the coast and was sitting just outside Sydney Heads.

With the Ellinis loaded to capacity with 1800 passengers and probably as many crew, we headed up the Harbour towards Sydney Heads. As we got closer the ferocity of what waited for us outside became apparent. Powerful winds lashed the upper and promenade decks with stinging sea spray that kept all but the hardiest inside. The ship's bow dived into the massive swells while forcing its way through Sydney Heads. The ship rose and fell with the sickening feel of a fast lift dropping out from under you, before suddenly rising up again to push your stomach back up into your throat. Not very pleasant, but this was also combined with a side roll that even the stabilizers couldn't prevent, although they no doubt lessened its extremes.

The Ellinis rolled and heaved like a sick whale unable to dive but having to keep coming up for air. Each time the bow dived into a swell, masses of spume sprayed up over it high enough to engulf the whole fore deck area. No one was out there. I presume most of the passengers were in their cabins trying to unpack or sitting in lounges terrified that the whole voyage was going to be like this.

I was on the promenade deck, from where I could see a small pilot boat running alongside of us. A ladder had been dropped down the side and the pilot on board who had taken us out of the harbour to the

Heads was standing by the rail at the top of the ladder, waiting for the pilot boat to get close enough so he could scramble down and leave us. His job was done once the Ellinis reached the Heads and was about to head out to sea.

Normally the pilot boat would run right next to the hull and the pilot would simply climb down the ladder and step aboard. Then the pilot boat would move away and head back to port. This time, however, it couldn't get close enough. The swells were so huge it rose up 20 or 30 feet, sometimes scraping ominously against the side of the Ellinis. The Ellinis would heave away as it rolled to one side, suddenly leaving a huge gap between the pilot boat and itself, and then as it dived down and rolled back the pilot boat would pull away so as not to be crushed by the descending mass of the much bigger ship. At one point there was a moment of calm when both the pilot boat and the Ellinis moved in unison. It seemed stable. The pilot started to scramble down the ladder. He was halfway down when a large trough opened up and the pilot boat was sucked away from the side of the Ellinis, creating a wide gap with the pilot dangling half way down the ladder.

He must have realised that if the next swell made the pilot boat swing back in against the side of the Ellinis he would be crushed between them. As the trough started to fill with the next big swell, he scrambled back up the ladder to be dragged back on board the Ellinis by the several crewmen who were waiting at the top.

The pilot boat pulled away, turned and went back through the Heads. The Ellinis ploughed into the storm, rolling and bucking like a small dinghy in a fierce chop. The pilot stayed on board until our first stop, which was Auckland, New Zealand, from where he flew back to Sydney.

That evening as we rode and pushed through the storm with the ship rolling and heaving no one other than a few hardy souls turned up for dinner. Where were all of those people who came on in Sydney? The dining room was empty. It was hard to keep anything on the table. Waiters scurried feverishly about trying sometimes unsuccessfully to prevent stacks of plates and cups and saucers from sliding off the tables. There was a loud crash somewhere in the kitchen, followed by a lot of yelling and swearing in Greek.

I doubt that anybody slept that night as the Ellinis drove through the storm at close to 20 knots. The captain wanted to get through it as quickly as possible. He slowed the ship in the morning when the sea was calmer. The storm, still raging, was way behind us. Even then, very few people turned up for breakfast. It wasn't until later that afternoon., when the sea was calmer, although still choppy, and the movement of the ship had abated to its usual gentleness, suddenly a thousand or more people appeared. The dining room that night was full, the musicians later in the lounge started playing, people danced, and the bars were busy. Everything was back to normal and everyone had finally gotten their sea legs.

Two days later, as we arrived in Auckland, the storm outside of Sydney was long forgotten as everyone was doing their best to enjoy the holiday, making new friends and partying day and night.

Coming in to Auckland by sea is magnificent. The harbour here is I think as fine as Sydney Harbour and just as beautiful. There seemed to be millions of yachts, and there were ferry boats coming and going to locations around the harbour as well as many inhabited islands within the harbour. The sun was shining and everything sparkled as light bounced off it.

I had got to know the guys in my cabin, and we decided we would rent a car and drive to Rotorua to see the bubbling mud and the volcanic springs. There was nothing like that in Australia. We invited a few others, and in the end we rented two cars for the trip.

It turned out to be a longer drive than we expected and we didn't really get to see Auckland at all.

This fenced off section was almost like a river of foul mud.

Bubbling hot mud: This looks like it could be at the bottom of the ocean but it wasn't. It was a lake of mud bubbling and spluttering, and spewing foul gas. The smell of sulphur filled the air. It made your eyes water and breathing was hard. Each time a bubble of sulphurous gas burst into the air with a sound like a wet fart, a crater would form, but almost immediately it would dissolve back into the gooey substrate and another would explode nearby. It never stopped.

It was hard to tell whether the mud buried the plants as it flowed and expanded or whether the plants grew close because of the nourishment supplied by the bubbling mud. The whole area smelled of sulphur, even the town of Rotarua was periodically enveloped by the sulphurous gas that constantly rose from the lake beside the town. The mud pools were a little way out of town. In these pictures the white fuzzy areas are gas rising out of the mud.

However, Auckland looked much the same as the bigger cities in Australia; they drive on the same side of the road as us, and the people speak the same language except for a few mangled vowels.

The smaller towns we drove through seemed very British, in appearance, much more so than similar small towns in Australia. At Rotorua we saw bubbling mud pools, smelt sulphurous steam, saw Maori dancers and singers perform, tried paddling or bathing in a foul-smelling hot pool, which we were told was good for our health, but I had to wonder about that as the pool we waded into was full of green slime and felt weirdly furry under-foot. None of us felt much like immersing ourselves in the water as we had to sit down on the slimy bottom.

By the time we drove back to Auckland it was very late, too late for dinner on board the ship. There was as always plenty of supper, though, served in many different lounges as well as the dining room, so we didn't go hungry.

I slept well that night, and when I got up for breakfast in the morning we were already at sea, having left Auckland way behind.

Ahead was a week of traversing gradually increasingly tropical weather as we headed for Tahiti, our next port of call.

Part of the band

The ship had a well-stocked library, but I found nothing that I felt compelled to read. This was the first time on a holiday that I did not take a book, or bought books on the way to read. Being on a big passenger ship was different from any other holiday I had ever taken, so I had no desire to sit down to read. I did play drums, though. I introduced myself to the band members, and they were happy for me to bring up a couple of congas to play. The drummer in the group had a set of bongos, which he lent to me. He asked me to teach him how to play them and I was happy to oblige. I played congas and bongos with the band every night. Many passengers actually thought I was part of the band rather than simply another passenger like themselves. It was good practice for me, keeping my hands and fingers hard and my arm muscles toned and flexible for playing. As with any physical activity, if you don't continue practising you soon lose the ability to perform. It's hard to regain that edge again.

During the day I did what everyone else did: hung around swimming and sunbaking by the pool, played an occasional game of quoits or deck tennis, sat in a deck chair, watched the endless ocean, had mindless conversations around the cocktail bars and buffets, ate too much food, went to late-night parties, and often slept in late enough to miss breakfast. It was all very relaxing, since there really wasn't much else to do. It didn't take long before everyone more or less knew everyone else, if not by name, then by facial recognition.

Years later, in the most unexpected places, people came up to me to tell me they remembered me from the Ellinis. They always mentioned that they remembered me because I played with the band. Often I didn't remember them. If it did, it was because the face seemed familiar. I doubt if I would remember any of them now, almost 60 years later.

One face I do remember, though, was that of a Greek girl who seemed reluctant to mix with the rowdy mob who made up the bulk of the passengers who came on in Sydney. I thought at first she had come aboard in Sydney, but she had actually boarded in Melbourne, and was seasick during the short run up the coast to Sydney. It wasn't that she was very beautiful, but there was something about her that attracted all the guys. Everyone made a pass at her, but she just smiled and was nice and polite. She refused all advances other than those that were simply friendly. Her sense of inner beauty made her appear serene, even saintly.

She went to the church services on board on Sundays — Greek Orthodox services, but a non-denominational service was performed on Sundays as well. Although she seemed devout she didn't give the impression of being very religious. I did not go to these services, simply because I am not religious, and don't like the trappings the various churches use to entice people into following their beliefs, but I did get the impression she found some solace there.

It was odd was she was getting off in England, not going on to Greece as most of the other Greek passengers were going to do.

I found out later that she had fallen in love with an English photographer. In the two years she stayed in London they had a wonderful life together. They came to Australia, but shortly after she died of leukaemia. On the ship, she knew she had leukaemia, and had only had a short time to live unless she could be cured by specialist treatment in London. It also explained her quiet reserve; why she did not want to form any sort of relationship with fellow travellers. She didn't want people to be disappointed or sad because she was going to die, so did not allow herself to become close to anyone. But there is no denying love when it happens, and I'm glad she did have those two years with her photographer friend.

A letter to Wally

I do remember writing a letter to my friend and science fiction fan Walter (Wally) Shaw, who worked part time at the nursery next door to the dry cleaner, in which I suggested we should write a story about floating cities in a future world where the population had grown so huge that there was no room left for city expansion plus space to grow food, so that the only place where mankind could expand into were the oceans. These huge floating cities could hold millions of people and would be so large that no bad weather or cyclonic storms could affect them. They could have airports and harbours just like any shoreside city. They would have parks and gardens and all the amenities one expects in a normal city. And if you were born and lived somewhere inside these cities, you might never be aware that they were floating, unless of course you went to the edge and saw the ocean beyond. I could not have imagined then that something like this would be in its infancy today, with serious marine architects designing such floating cities as possible solutions to housing people in today's warming world with its slowly rising ocean levels and coastal cities that may one day disappear beneath the waves.

I bought a stamp and posted the letter in the mailbox on board the ship. Presumably the mail was sent by the ship's post office staff at each port of call. I also sent postcards from the ship back home to Mum and Dad. Mum kept these for many years in a box at home, but eventually they disappeared, along with much else, when we did a big clean up.

I probably thought at the time 'What do I want to keep all this stuff for?' and tossed them out with other rubbish. Now I regret it, because it would have been nice to see what I wrote way back then — my actual thoughts in 1964.

Fragments from my Life – with Science Fiction

A Toast to the good life, drinking Tahitian beer at a waterfront cafe.

The view from the cafe along the coast of the nearby island of Moorea

A typical Tahitian beauty at kerbside cafe.

Tahiti – once a paradise on Earth

I think the captain of the Ellinis always adjusted her cruising speed so we would arrive at each port early in the morning. In that way we would have all day to explore as well as most of the night for dining and partying before having to be back on board for departure the next morning.

The sun was just illuminating the sky and the waves with a faint splash of warm colour when I raced up from C deck to the promenade deck to watch us arrive at Tahiti.

Tahiti! The place that those early European sailors, French and English, thought was paradise on Earth. And it must have been for those who manned the ships that rounded Cape Horn and survived its ferocious storms to find themselves negotiating the narrow opening through the surrounding reef where they could anchor in calm clear tropical waters, where a thousand species of fish unknown to them could be seen as clearly as if the water they swam in didn't exist; and smelling the air with its scent of frangipani and other tropical flowers, and listening to the trade winds ruffle the fronds of coconut palms overhanging the lagoon along the shore. Seeing the rugged rainforest-covered volcanic mountain that made up the bulk of the island, and half-naked women running along the beach towards where they were mooring their ship would surely have convinced them that they were arriving at a place that was as close to heaven as they were ever likely to get. It was no wonder many of them never wanted to leave this place where beautiful women with skin the colour of golden honey and sparkling brown eyes bestowed sexual favours upon them because they were different from their own men, and where some sailors went 'native' with local wives and refused to come back on board when their ship was due to depart. Captain Cook had to force several of his men at gunpoint to return.

It was the place Gaughin fell in love with and for which left his job in a bank in Paris, his wife and family, moving to Tahiti to live like a native and paint gorgeous pictures that everyone all over the world has seen, so they all know an idealised version of Tahiti, whether they have been there or not.

In 1964 you still had to arrive in Tahiti by ship or boat. There was no airport. It wouldn't be constructed for several more years. The narrow channel had been dredged to accommodate large liners like Ellinis, but it seemed certain that we would scrape the sides of the ship with the coral walls that made up the edge of the channel. The water against the side of the ship seemed jet black, but it was so clear I could see the jagged edges of the reef that had been cut away to allow large ships to enter the channel through the reef. Those closest to the surface were bleached white, but deeper down the dead coral edges faded into greenish grey until they became almost invisible shadows near the bottom.

Suddenly the gap in the reef was behind us. The sun was higher and the mountain behind the town of Papeete glowed with all shades of green as the sun illuminated its slopes. The air no longer smelt only of salt, but there were hints of mouldy rotting vegetable matter mixed with indefinable sweet scents from flowers. It was the kind of smell I associated with all tropical places no matter where you find them. Across the sea, only about 12 miles away, was the unbelievable volcanic mountain that made the island of Moorea so beautiful. It was on this island that the musical South Pacific was filmed. It was in these waters around Tahiti, Moorea and the nearby Marquesas, that Marlon Brando would film his version of Mutiny on the Bounty. And we all know now that he ended up marrying his co-star and moving to live on an island in the Marquesas. I'm sure everyone on board the ship had seen other films that depicted life in the South Pacific, especially with Tahiti as a backdrop, so there was no cultural shock on landing and spending time ashore.

We were greeted by a dance troupe of gorgeous girls with a group of solidly muscled drummers playing, singing, and dancing as the passengers came down the gangplank. The girls wore long grass skirts, and leis of flowers covered their breasts. Each one had a flower in her hair. The grass swished and swirled with the manic movement of their hips as they kept time with an ear-shattering barrage of drum logs pounded with sticks. I found the rhythms fascinating, quite different to what I was accustomed to hearing and playing. But before I could get off the ship they had finished their little show and departed.

There were some formalities requiring passports to be stamped, after which we were free to go ashore. The first thing I did was to wander along the road that ran around the harbour. There were cafés and restaurants all along the foreshore, with tables and chairs outside on wide footpaths. I sat at a table at a small café and admired a lovely Tahitian girl at the table next to mine. The place looked a bit scruffy, but it seemed to be popular with the locals. There was no one from the ship here. The menu had ham sandwiches listed (sandwich de jambon) so I ordered a café au lait and a ham sandwich.

Cultural shock isn't something sudden, so that you walk into a place and it is so unexpectedly different that you are stunned; it's more the accumulation of small things that are different that add up over time to change your perception of what is expected. In my mind a sandwich was made from two slices of bread buttered lightly and filled with whatever you want, such as ham and lettuce. What I received was a huge long chunk of what we would now call French bread stick, with no butter and with thick slices of ham in it. No lettuce or any other condiments such as mustard; just the bread stick and the ham. It was the same in France, as I later found out while staying in Paris. The coffee was better than expected, but the sandwich ... At least the bread stick was freshly baked and it had a lovely crumbly crust with a soft texture inside, making it possibly the best piece of bread roll I had tasted.

Papeete extended from the foreshore, where yachts and fishing boats were moored, back away and up into the towering hills inland. It was a moribund ramshackle village with few buildings more than two storeys high, with washed-out and often flaking pastel-coloured paint, and with winding streets full of barefoot happy people going about their business. Many of these people were heading towards the waterfront, where at least a thousand potential customers were disembarking from the Ellinis. I saw some loaded with flower leis, or similar shell necklaces. Several had strings of fish dangling from lines strung over their shoulders. I would have expected them to be heading away from the waterfront, not towards it. Who among the sightseeing passengers would be buying fresh fish? Unless of course they were hoping to sell them to the kitchen staff on board the Ellinis. This must have been the case, because in the two days after leaving Tahiti we had some wonderful lunches and dinners with beautiful tropical fish that I had never heard of or tasted before, mahi-mahi being one particularly fine example.

Many yachts were moored right in front of the most popular café bar, the Vaima Bar. At one stage it had been a dream to own a yacht and sail around the world, stopping at places like Tahiti. And I must admit I felt tinges of jealousy at the sight of these yachts and the suntanned people lazing on the decks with cups of coffee as they contemplated the morning. The yachts looked well kept, as if they had been here for a while. None of them had that weather-beaten look they took on after spending a long time at sea. I guess, as my brother-in-law's friend said to me before I left, 'Once you get to Tahiti, you never want to leave.' He went there on a surfing trip a few years earlier, fell in love with the place, and never wanted to leave. He married a lovely Tahitian lass, who it turned out had been Marlon Brando's choice as a girlfriend before he started filming Mutiny on the Bounty, but when she fell for an Australian he left her for someone else, who became his co-star in the film. Eventually Fred's friend had to return to Melbourne with his wife and children because he was needed as part of the business that ran the Moonee Ponds to Williamstown bus route. For a moment, as I looked around at the sheer beauty of Tahiti, I wondered why he did that, and then had to ask myself: would I do that after I had been in Europe? Would I come home to work again in the dry cleaning business? I wasn't planning to, but then one never knows how circumstances can change.

The only disruptive sight to the quiet native village atmosphere of Tahiti was the sheer bulk of the Ellinis towering high above the water. It was moored beside a new wharf constructed in deeper water to accommodate such huge ships.

Suddenly one of the guys from my cabin was standing next to me. 'You should check that out,' he said as he pointed towards one of the bars over the road from the boat moorings. 'Men and women use the same toilets.'

I gave him an odd look.

'It's true. The women line up waiting to use a cubicle, and while they wait they get to check out the guys who are standing there and pissing against the other wall.'

'And you want me to check that out?'

'None of the women from the ship are game to use it, so only Tahitian women are in there.'

'It's a bit early in the morning for me to be going over to look at a toilet. But I suppose if you are bursting and there is no other place nearby, then you'd have to use it' — and to hell with the possibility of a line of women looking at you.

It was the talk of the day, with every bloke I encountered from the ship telling me I should have a look, or asking if I'd been there yet. It wasn't something I was interested in doing, although later than night, when we were in the bar drinking beer, pernod, and other spirits, partying with great gusto, there came a time when you simply had to go to the toilet, and that was the only one. So I went and pissed against the wall with the other blokes while a long line of Tahitian ladies admired or joked about which one of us had the biggest tackle. They may have been prostitutes, because often they would lean on your shoulder while you were taking a piss so they could have a good look. If they liked what they saw, they propositioned you. Quite often a guy having a piss would leave the 'amenity' with the lady who had leaned on his shoulder. There were rooms upstairs. To my great relief, no lady leaned on my shoulder while I was taking a piss, and so I was not propositioned. I returned to the bar and ordered another drink.

Earlier that day I discovered a man on the waterfront renting chunky bicycles with a small petrol motor on the back. Each bicycle featured a gear that rolled against the wheel so that when you hopped on and pedalled fast, it ignited a spark plug that started the motor. You could then stop pedalling and the small spluttering motor would turn the back wheel for you. This was the first time I'd ever seen one of these.

It seemed every second person in Papeete was riding around on these motor-driven bikes. A chaotic flow of them meandered along every street, dodging other vehicles as well as pedestrians. There must have

Along the road around the island, palm trees and lush undergrowth.

been some road rules, but I couldn't figure out what they could have been, so I joined the throng, sitting nervously on my rented motorised bike. It wasn't long before I was out of town and in open country on a road that paralleled the beach and the lagoon surrounding the island.

I travelled a good distance around the island along this coast road until I came to a place where something large was being constructed. Tractors were grading coral rock, flattening out quite a broad area and pushing stuff towards the shallow water to extend parts of it into the lagoon. A row of coconut palms had been knocked down, and had been pushed haphazardly to one side of the construction area. They looked as if a cyclone had ripped them up and scattered them like matchsticks against the side of the rainforest that extended back towards the volcano near the spine of the island. It could only be an airport they were building. The air was full of diesel fumes and the roar of heavy machinery. Just wait until the planes started landing ... civilisation was arriving!

This devastation spoilt my impression of Tahiti. I turned around and went back to Papeete, where I returned the motorised bike and had lunch at a nearby café. I spent the rest of the day in and around the waterfront area enjoying the relaxed feel of the place.

The Ellinis in Tahiti Towers over the low set buildings of Papeete. It was enormous compared to anything else in the harbour.

These two images courtesy of Wolfram Dallwitz who also travelled on the Ellinis

Relaxing and wondering if I should stay longer.

After a happy night at the bar where virtually everyone eventually had the need to check out Tahiti's famous unisex toilet, we finally found ourselves wandering back, in some cases staggering back, to board the Ellinis.

When we woke up the next morning the ship was steaming out through the opening in the reef, with Moorea on our starboard side. It wasn't long before both islands were gone, nothing more than a pile of cumulous clouds towering into the sky way behind us marking their location as we headed north and east towards the isthmus of Panama.

A glimpse of Moorea as we sailed past on our way to Panama.

Lazing in deck chairs

Ten days of lazing around in deck chairs by the swimming pool, eating loads of great food, drinking too much perhaps, chasing girls, or girls flirting with the eligible boys, dancing and continuing the endless party at night; those were the days that are hard to remember because they all blurred one into another.

We did not encounter even a slight storm as we crossed the wide expanse between the Friendly Islands and the coast of Central America. Once we left the Trade Winds zone the air was still, and the sea for miles in all directions was smooth and glassy. The sky above, without a single cloud anywhere, was so bright it was hard to look at. The sea itself reflected that extreme brightness across its glass smooth surface, which apart from the wake created by the ship was absolutely unmarked. Not even a flying fish jumped out of the water. Apparently these deep areas of the ocean are like deserts. There are hardly any fish here during the day. At night it was different. Things came up from deep down, and often you could see flashing and sparkling lights flit through the water as something or other chased something else in an unrelenting hunt for sustenance.

There was no breeze other than what we created as the ship moved forward. These were the famous Doldrums, where sailing ships were often stuck for long periods of time without a wind to move them. Sailors hated these glassy hot seas and tried to avoid this zone at all costs, but if you were going from south to north or the other way it was unavoidable. Big ships like Ellinis simply powered through this zone without any problems at all.

There was a silly ceremony when we crossed the Equator. Someone was dressed as King Neptune. His minions, dressed to resemble sea nymphs, tossed everybody into the swimming pool but I stayed away from that.

I spent most of those 10 days working on my suntan. Back then nobody had any inkling about skin cancer or the damage the sun could do to your skin, and everyone wanted to be bronzed evenly all over. At night I played drums with the band. The music was very commercial dance music, such as 'Tea for Two Cha Cha', 'I talk to the Trees Cha Cha', 'Mambo #5', as well as romantic songs played with a Latin feel, such as the slow rhumba. Very un-Latin, commercial pap, but it was what people wanted. It kept me practising, and maintained the hardness in my fingers and hands.

Gunfire in the streets

Panama City gave me a big cultural shock. It was the first city I had ever been to where people openly shot at each other with guns. We had been warned not to leave the Canal Zone to go to Panama City because there were impending elections, and members of the various political parties were often seen shooting at each other or violently fighting whenever they met during the course of their political activities. I thought this could not be real, so took a bus into the city. Some crew members from the Ellinis were on that bus. I figured that if they could go into the city, so could I.

There was no escaping the tropical feel to the city, even though it was a lot more modern than Papeete. It was hot and humid and whenever you stood in the sun you could feel it burning into you. This was a big city with wide boulevards, lots of buses, and traffic that seemed to tear along the roads without any concern for other vehicles or for pedestrians trying to cross streets. They wove in and out and dodged each other in a neverending chaotic flow. It was noisy too, with every driver in every vehicle honking the horn continuously and yelling at each other.

I had hardly been in town longer than 15 minutes when there was a scuffle across the street from where I stood eating a fabulous orange and chocolate ice cream I had bought from a street vendor. A small group was sticking signs on the broad columns of a large building. I couldn't see what the signs said, but hardly had this group finished sticking them up when a long dark car screeched to a stop. Someone leaned out of the window and started shooting a pistol at the people putting up the signs. The people scattered, dropping spare signs and a bucket of water-based glue. They ran behind the columns or skittered away along the footpath. Other pedestrians too, ran away in a frantic dance to escape the spray of bullets.

As I watched, two men jumped out of the car and started ripping off the posters the other group had just put up. One of them gesticulated towards the bucket left in the gutter and the other grabbed it. Within minutes they had put up their own posters, jumped back into their car, and driven off with loads of loud horn honking and yells as they leaned out of their car and fired the odd pistol into the air.

I could hardly believe it. It was something straight out of an American gangster movie. I suddenly realised my ice cream had started to melt and was dribbling down my hand.

'Happens all the time,' the vendor said to me in American-accented English. 'You watch. It won't be long before the first group comes back and replaces the posters the others tore down.'

And he was right. Ten minutes later they were back again to tear down their rival's posters to replace them with their own. I left then, just in case the guys in the black car came back and started shooting. Who knows where those bullets might go?

What I loved about Panama City was that everywhere I went there was the sound of tropical music: the real stuff, not the watered-down pap we played on the ship. Every shop I passed had music blaring through its front door. By tropical music I mean Cuban music. That's what it was called then — *música tropical*. Mambos, guarachas, and pachangas assailed my ears as I passed and I had to pause at each shop to listen. Pachangas played by Charanga bands were very popular in the early sixties, with their violins and flutes replacing the heavy sound of brass instruments.

I felt like dancing as I moved along the street, and a sudden revelation struck me. If everyone driving seemingly so chaotically in the streets listening to tropical music pouring out of their car radios felt like dancing, then that probably explained the chaotic movement of their vehicles and why they suffered far fewer crashes than I would have expected. They drove in time with the music they listened to. I did not get into a bus or a taxi without a radio playing *música tropical*.

Later that day I bumped into some of the crew members. They told me they were going to a night club and I was welcome to come along. It was one of those seedy places where there was a show that had something to do with a woman having sex with a donkey. Unable to imagine how that was possible I agreed to go with them, but the memory of that night is a blur. I drank too much alcohol, breathed in too much secondary smoke, which made me as sick as a dog, and remembered absolutely nothing about the floor show that I supposedly saw. All I remember was staggering out of the taxi on the wharf and weaving up the gangplank onto the deck, where I promptly sat in a deck chair to wait for the sun to rise and the ship to head into the first lock of the Panama Canal. I didn't want to miss that.

Unfortunately I fell asleep. When I woke up, the Ellinis was long through the famous canal, having bypassed the city of Colon, and was heading out into the bright sparkling Caribbean Sea.

What I missed while sleeping in a deck chair...
The Ellinis entering the first lock on its journey through the Panama Canal.
These two images courtesy of Wolfram Dallwitz.

I also missed traversing the lake in the centre of the canal zone before the ships begin to go through the next set of locks leading to the Caribbean Sea.

Netherlands Antilles

Curacao was our next stop. The largest of the Netherlands Antilles islands, it is a small low flat island only a short distance off the coast of Venezuela. The ship came into what seemed like short wide canal in the middle of the town of Willemstadt, which I assumed was the capital. The Ellinis dwarfed the myriad small fishing and pleasure craft moored along the waterfront. The passengers poured off the ship in droves and headed through winding, spotlessly clean streets lined with brightly painted stone buildings. Many walked, but there were loads of taxis waiting to take passengers into the main part of town.

I took a taxi and sat in the front so I could shoot some movie film through the window as we drove along. I remember the street being very narrow with hardly any sun shining down — it was early — and with the sides of the buildings very close to the both sides of the taxi. It seemed like the driver went very fast, but that was only because the sides of the buildings were so close that they could have ripped off the vehicle's side mirrors if the driver wasn't careful. Suddenly we burst out into a central plaza, a huge open space that seemed to extend beyond sight. It was filled with light and hundreds of people wandering about dressed in colourful clothes. All the buildings that surrounded the plaza seemed out of place, too European for the tropics, but that was compensated for by the bright pastel colours in which they were painted, and the very colourful clothes the local people wore. Passengers from the Ellinis looked drab by comparison.

In the heart of Willemstadt with its quaint Dutch architecture painted in bright colours that seemed out of place in the tropics.

Fresh fruit and vegetables from Venezuela brought across in luggers and sold in sltalls alongside the wharf.

I left the taxi beside an ice cream vendor, from whom I bought a fantastic orange-and-mango-flavoured double scoop. It was the best ice cream I had ever tasted. I wandered about shooting some film of the general activity, finally concentrating on a small group of musicians who were playing Venezuelan music and singing in Spanish. The group consisted of two guitarists, one with a regular guitar while the other had a bass guitar (again, something I hadn't seen before), an accordion, a metal scraper, and a drum like a small tambora, which was slung over one shoulder and played with one bare hand and one stick. I wished I had some way of recording them. I think they played *Joropo* because it was in 6/4 time. They had come over from Venezuela, which is less than 20 miles away, knowing that they would be able to make some money entertaining tourists from the cruise ship. Everyone would have known that the ship was arriving.

From the talk I overheard on the ship Curacao was famous for two things, its casino and a place called Happy Valley some distance out of town. Because the Netherlands Antilles major industry was processing oil, which they did on nearby Aruba, there were plenty of workers, foreign and local, who spent lots of money. Happy Valley was a township that was a huge brothel, with bars to entertain the visitors and shop fronts where the lovely ladies could show off their wares and demonstrate what they had for sale. It was legal, just as doing this was legal in the Dutch capital, so there was nothing seedy or sleazy about the place. It was clean and above board, a great place to have some fun, even if you weren't interested in the basic occupation of the place.

Half the ship's passengers were there, having a wonderful time in the bars and dance clubs if they weren't occupied elsewhere in the town. The other half went to the casino. I went to the casino with a couple of friends from the ship, but they wouldn't let us in because we weren't dressed appropriately. You had to wear a lounge suit, at the very least. I didn't have a suit. The glimpse they allowed me through the front showed me that everyone inside was dressed in evening clothes — black dinner suits and bow ties, and the women in elegant gowns. It looked like something I had seen in a James Bond movie: very expensive. Definitely not my style. We turned around and took a taxi back to Happy Valley, where no one cared whether you wore a suit or not.

Martinique and a hint of Africa

Once again I don't remember leaving port; only sailing across a sparkling brilliant crystal sea with small choppy waves that made no impression on the ship. It was rock steady as we cruised along and there was always a warm fresh breeze: the famous trade winds? A couple of days later, a faint smudge against the rising sun on the horizon ahead gradually grew into a rugged jungle-covered mountainous island.

This was Martinique, one of the windward series of islands in the Eastern Caribbean, famous for the eruption of Mont Pele, which devastated one half of the island a long time ago. Of the inhabitants who lived in a small town near the foot of the volcano only one survived; a prisoner locked in solitary confinement in a cell underground. The pyroclastic flow from the erupting volcano killed everyone else who remained in the town. Those who tried to escape by running into the sea were cooked as the sea boiled.

Mont Pele isn't the only quiescent volcano on this magnificent island, but it is the highest, at 1379 metres.

Martinique is also famous for being the birthplace of Napoleon's Josephine. It was originally discovered by Columbus (Cristobal Colon) in 1493, but no Spanish group could settle there because of the fierce Carib Indians who slaughtered anyone who tried, at least until the French arrived in 1635. They brought in slaves from West Africa to start growing sugar cane and bananas. They also make very nice rum, which of course we all sampled once we got ashore. These days the island is an Overseas French Department, which has its own government.

My first glimpse was of the brilliant spires and dome of a huge cathedral that stood proud above a forest of trees and palms. The sun glistened off the whiteness of it. I found out later it was an exact copy of the Sacré Coeur Cathedral in Paris. Behind it I could see the base of a towering mountain, the top of which was obscured by a layer of greyish early morning cloud.

Fishermen launched dozens of lifeboat-sized craft and motored across to the ship. The crew opened a wide door several decks down and dropped a kind of pontoon landing platform so passengers could walk down a short gangway to the landing platform, transfer to a fishing boat, and be ferried across to the short pier jutting out from the the town which came right down to the water's edge. Young boys gesticulated and called out in French for us to throw coins into the water so they could dive for them.

Going ashore and wandering up the street towards the centre of the town of Port au Prince, I could not stop thinking how African the place looked. I had never been to Africa, but I had seen a documentary about Guinea and the troubadour musicians. Everyone I saw was of African descent, children of those whose grandparents had once been slaves bought across from West Africa to work the cane fields. I hardly saw anyone who was unmixed European; they were all mixed, African, and European in varying degrees, all friendly with gorgeous smiles whenever they stopped and spoke to us.

The market in the middle of town.

Note in the picture top left the woman in the centre covering her face with a hat because she saw me shooting film. Also in the background someone from the ship is standing on a bin looking down to take a picture.

A market place was filled with stalls selling all kinds of weird and wonderful local produce and hundreds of people dressed in brilliant colours who stood out under the tropical sun. I couldn't wait to start shooting some film.

As unobtrusively as possible, I took my camera out from its bag slung over my shoulder and started filming. I was well aware that some people don't like to be filmed or have their photos taken. I was a bit nervous at first, but no one bothered me. With a telephoto lens I didn't need to get too close to anyone in particular. I wandered about, and people actually smiled at me. Strangely enough, they didn't try to sell me anything. I was obviously a tourist from the recently arrived ship and tourists rarely bought fresh produce in local markets.

It was hot and humid, but I could feel the continuous warm breeze that fluttered the tree tops and made the air smell sweet as it blew across the market stalls, evaporating any sweat so you didn't realise that it was hot. This market place looked exactly like any number of market places I had seen in numerous adventure films about Africa. I was sure it would look great when I saw the film projected; but of course there would be no sound. I regretted not being able to record the ambient sound of the place, as this would have added so much character to the film.

Back in town later that afternoon, I found a record shop and bought two EPs of local music (to use on a soundtrack for the film I had shot), and discovered an LP by Tito Puente called Dance Mania.

It was a recent release being played when I went in, and it just blew me away. I had to have it. I also bought a small portable record player so I could play it on board the ship, and with my new-found treasures I made my way back to the ship.

That recording was by far the best recording Tito Puente ever made, and he made hundreds of LPs over his entire career as a band leader and musician. It was already a bestseller in 1964, and it has remained a bestseller (*always in the top 10 Latin LPs*) from the time it was released until today, almost 60 years later. There was an excitement about it, a freshness, something intangible that has rarely been captured in other similar recordings, and that is still apparent whenever you listen to it.

It makes you want to get up and dance. It is irresistible.

It is my favourite big (Tropical Latin) band recording of all time.

The best selling Tito Puente album of all time.

Europe at last – but what an entrance...

After another week at sea we finally approached our first European port.

We came around Cabo Espichel, a smudgy dark shape off in the distance. Not long after we entered one of the widest and most beautiful entrances to a large harbour that I had ever seen. There was a feeling of excitement mingled with anticipation in everyone who crowded on the decks to watch us enter this ancient harbour, from where, over 500 years ago, Portuguese sailors and explorers left in their tiny wooden caravels to discover a way around Africa, or the way across to South America.

The Portuguese were the first Europeans to visit China and Japan, the first to establish overseas colonies in Brazil, India, and Africa. Yet at the time we arrived in Lisboa (Lisbon), Portugal was one of the poorest countries in Europe, when once it had been the richest and most influential. I wondered if the massive earthquake and the subsequent tsunami that wiped Lisbon off the map in 1755 had anything to do with the country's subsequent downfall. Lisbon, of course, has been rebuilt, yet it looks like a very old and ancient place, while at the same time being modern and bustling.

I had never seen any place like this before. Tahiti and Panama were not so different from my expectations, but this was Europe, the place from where civilisation, if you want to call it that, spread around the world, to absorb or destroy many ancient cultures.

It was late afternoon when we finally berthed, and it was starting to get dark by the time we could clear customs and go ashore.

As in Panama City the air was filled with music, but unfamiliar music. There was joy, but also a hint of sadness within the music. I just loved the minor tonality and the huskiness of the singers. The streets were jammed with cars, everyone honking horns and gesticulating at each other. It was like permanent road rage, yet happy rather than angry and frustrated. Many of the cars driven were convertibles with the tops down, and music blared from all of them.

It was early summer, and the air was warm, the breeze pleasant. I was with a group of people from the Elinis. We wandered happily along a wide footpath that was composed of swirling mosaic designs— a work of art in itself! And the people thronging along it took no notice of it. It was just somewhere you walked along. But what I found extraordinary was that Lisbon was like this everywhere: little works of art in the most unexpected places, plazas and footpaths filled with gorgeous mosaic patterns that only revealed themselves sporadically when the press of people lessened for a moment.

Tables and chairs outside of cafes and restaurants in all the main streets were filled with people enjoying evening meals or drinking coffees with the port wine for which Portugal is famous. There was nothing like this in Melbourne then, in 1964. It was unheard of, probably not even thought of, unseen. You couldn't take a drink out of any premises after 6 p.m., no one was allowed to sell alcoholic drinks unless at a licensed restaurant, and there were very few of those, yet here in Lisbon in the middle of the evening, probably about 9 p.m. I sat down at an outdoor table with two of the girls from the ship and we ordered a coffee and a cognac to sip with it. I could have done this any time of the day or night, something you could never do in Melbourne. It was the simplicity of the situation that shocked us all, and made us realise how backward and straitlaced we were in Australia.

Almost 2000 people from the ship spread out into Lisbon that night. It was obvious we were tourists from the way we dressed, but more so from the way we looked so intently at everything, the old buildings, the strange cable car that seemed to go from the top of some buildings up the side of a jutting hill, the brilliantly lit ancient fortress perched on top of a nearby hill, the thousands of outdoor tables and chairs filled with people enjoying the early summer evening with glasses of wine or cognac and coffees, snacking on tiny plates filled with tasty morsels of food (which I later found out were similar to the tapas served in the bars of Seville).

While we were seated sipping our cognac a car pulled up to the curb right next to us. The driver leaned out and, obviously taken by the girls, asked if they wanted to take a drive around the city. The car was a convertible, a big American one, so there was plenty of room for the three of us. The girls were reluctant at first to get into the car, but he seemed so honest, and genuine in his desire to show off his beloved Lisbon, that they finally acquiesced as long as I came along with them. He was happy with that, and we all piled into the car.

He took off with a roar and chorus of car horns honking as he cut into the flow of traffic. He took us everywhere. He was so proud of his city he was happy to show it off and explain in hesitant English about the history and the relevance of everything we saw. We finished the night in a wonderful club where he insisted on paying for us and where for the first time I heard genuine *Fado* music. This is the music of Portugal. This is the music that expresses all desires of life and the sadness of love lost and won again combined in a form that makes you shiver to listen to it even when you don't understand the words. Our guide told me the woman singing was the most famous Fado singer in Portugal. I presume now that she must have been Amalia Rodrigues.

Finally, as the sun started to come up for a new day, our guide dropped us off at the pier where the Ellinis waited for her passengers to return, and thanked us for letting him show us his beautiful city. We were quite sad to see him drive off, and slowly, as if reluctant to leave this incredible city, we walked back up into the ship.

Last days on board Ellinis

Those last few days that it took to get to England, for me at least, lacked excitement or anticipation. I wasn't looking forward to getting off in England. I would rather have gotten off in Lisbon, stayed there for a while before moving on into other parts of Europe, but it was not to be. Unfortunately I never did return to Portugal.

But that's the way things go ... never what you expect.

'Get a move on.'

The feeling I had — gut churning anticipation — as I watched the activity involved with docking such a huge liner as Ellinis at Southampton was odd and unexpected. I was both excited to have arrived at the end of a long sea voyage, yet at the same time was reluctant to leave the familiarity of the Ship. The thought of going out into a world that seemed quite alien to me was unnerving. With my three drums in their canvas carry bags beside me, I stayed transfixed by the rail along the promenade deck unable to proceed further, watching what was happening below.

Finally I had no choice. A ship's officer tapped me on the shoulder and when I turned to see who it was he told bluntly to 'Get a move on.' He pointed towards the nearest gangplank leading into the terminal building. It was time to disembark.

There was utter chaos everywhere. Ship's officers directed passengers towards various gangplanks. The huge area where we all went to collect luggage was a madhouse of people gesticulating and voices raised, calling for missing children or friends, demanding to know where their luggage was, and through this melee I managed to drag my three drums stuffed with clothing as well as the odd things I had bought en-route until I found myself sitting in a bus along with others from the ship. I don't remember having gone through customs but I must have; everyone had to.

Even then I thought travelling was about the journey and not so much about the destination. You had to go somewhere when you travelled or else you weren't actually travelling. The problem was after spending so much time on a voyage the ship becomes like a home, its nooks and hiding places, its restaurants and bars, dining rooms and recreation areas all become so familiar the very thought of leaving them and venturing out into the unknown suddenly becomes frightening. I wasn't the only one who didn't want to get off the ship.

Although I had become so used the ship's environment and was comfortable with it and didn't want to leave, at the same time I couldn't wait to venture out into the unknown to discover what new things there were to see and to experience. The trap with big ships is that they can become too comfortable. Travelling on them doesn't seem like travelling at all (until you arrive at some exotic port for a 24 hour stopover), but more like you are living in a small and very comfortable (but enclosed) town or village. Everything you may need and want is there. And then suddenly you have to leave it all behind…

It was a good thing the disembarkation was so chaotic. It gave no one time to think about leaving until after they were ashore, and by then it was too late.

I found myself along with many familiar faces from the Ellinis on a large tourist bus which was heading towards London. These busses went straight to Earl's Court.

Travelling to London through the English countryside was surprisingly bright. The sun was shining and everything looked so green and fresh. I had expected rain or cloudy weather with light drizzle, but to have sunshine and a bright fresh smell to the air, the smell of plants growing, was truly delightful. I'm sure helped a lot of those who were reluctant to leave the ship readjust to being on land again.

The Ellinis was fast becoming a shadowy memory as I stared through the bus window at the rolling English countryside. It was springtime in England, the first week in May, and after five weeks at sea with nothing but the most incredibly vast Ocean surrounding us it really was fantastic to be on land no matter how it looked. Until you take a long voyage at sea you simply can't comprehend how huge the ocean is, how the land by comparison is such a small part of the planet. This is a water world and it beats me why everyone calls it Earth, or Terra as they do in SF stories.

This was the end of my sea journey and the start of the overland travel. My destination at this point was Stuttgart in Germany, where my brother in law Fred came from, where his parents lived in a small town called Backnang and they were expecting me.

The bus dropped us off late in the afternoon in Earle's Court several of us stood around not knowing where to go or what to do. I found a phone booth and made a call to Fred's mum and dad. I told them I didn't know when I would get to Stuttgart but would call from the central train station once I had arrived. I was happy Fred's mum spoke good English. She had been born and lived in America until she was a young woman. She had married there and Fred was born there. Coming back to Germany to visit relatives in the late 1930s they were unable to leave as the Second World War began. After the War was over they stayed in Germany, in Backnang, and never went back to America.

A couple of Aussies who had been there for some time told us about a nightclub where newcomers hung out and that we should go there. They pointed out its location only a couple of buildings down from where we had been left, so not long after that I found myself in this nightclub. Perhaps the club owners had spotters on the street who guided newcomers to them, because as soon as I went inside I discovered lots of people from the Ellinis dancing and drinking with abandon.

Another cultural shock; nobody in England, so it seemed, wanted cold beer. The beer they served me was quite warm. Warm beer tastes bloody horrible, and I could barely drink it. I saw the shock on the faces of a few people who had ordered a beer about the same time as I did when they tried that first sip, but somehow we managed to drink it. After the first couple it didn't seem to matter.

The dance floor was crowded with people dancing something they called Ska. I had never heard it before but it sounded like Calypso mixed with Rock and Roll, and it didn't sound too bad. It just wasn't the kind of music I liked. The dance was uninspiring though: couples simply stood on a spot facing each other and jerked their hands up and down from their stomach in time with the simple beat bashed out by a drum kit. They shook their heads in unison. It looked like they were trying to climb an invisible rope ladder.

There were so many Australians in Earle's Court that you could have thought you were still in Australia in a place like St Kilda. The only difference however was the architecture. It wasn't Australian at all. The air smelt different too, but that was something indefinable, and there were a lot more people in the streets than in Australian cities. Today our major cities are jam packed with people, population levels having jumped more than double in some cases. Sydney and Melbourne are both massive cities now, with Brisbane, Adelaide, and Perth rapidly catching up. But London was the first 'mega' city I had been to and was impressed by the sheer numbers of people in the streets at all hours.

An offer I couldn't refuse

Sometimes it is a good thing to talk about where you want to go. I talked to a couple of people from the Ellinis at this night club, one of whom, it turned out, had arranged to buy a small station wagon in which they were going to use to drive across Europe. They offered me a lift to Stuttgart, a city they had planned to drive through on their journey across Europe and down to Turkey. Before they left Australia they had arranged for a vehicle to be waiting for them the moment they arrived in London. I hadn't at that stage considered how I was going to get to Germany but their offer out of the blue bowled me over. I immediately accepted.

I left my three bags (drums) and my portable record player at this nightclub. Apparently lots of new Australian arrivals left baggage there until they found somewhere to live. I don't know where I spent the night. Perhaps I stayed up all night because the very next morning I was met in front of the nightclub and once my stuff was loaded into the station wagon the four of us took off and headed back through the rolling bright green countryside to Dover to take the ferry over to Calais in France. There was luggage piled on top of a roof rack and my drums in their bags in the back. Over the drums and in between them were all kinds of small bags with things the people in the car would like to use without having to unpack other bags. Everything was wedged in so tight nothing moved no matter how the vehicle twisted or turned.

Sleeping while travelling

I caught up with some sleep on the ferry as it crossed the English Channel. What was there to see other than the grey choppy windswept water?

Sleeping while travelling (usually at night on a train or at a train station while waiting for a night train) avoided having to pay for accommodation. I wouldn't do that now, preferring more comfortable and safer places to sleep, but back in 1964, young, and with limited funds available, I didn't have much option while travelling. Looking back I don't think times then were anywhere near as dangerous as they are today.

Passport stamps

There was a slight delay while our passports were checked and stamped at our insistence. We wanted the stamps in our passports as a record of travel, because in most places officials had already stopped doing that. They always checked, but never bothered to stamp them. This time they had to look for a stamp pad as well as the required stamp. They were annoyed because it slowed them down checking other passengers from the ferry.

Once we had the passports stamped the officials barely glanced through the windows of the vehicle before they sent us on our way.

The only problem was getting used to driving on the wrong side of the road. There were a couple of near misses until the driver got used to being on the right instead of the left side of the road. This was more likely to happen on country roads with little traffic where inadvertently we would drift to the other side, the side we considered to be correct. In towns and villages it was less likely since we followed what the other vehicles were doing.

— Ephemeron —

Twenty years after the War

1964 was just on twenty years after the War in Europe ended and the driver wanted to go to one of the beaches where the allied troops landed when they crossed the channel to push the German army back. His father had been in the later part of this landing. He insisted we drive along the coast from Calais to Oostende in Belgium. Perhaps his father had been amongst the troops who came ashore there.

The beaches at Oostende were still barricaded with giant bunkers and pillboxes, and for miles along the beach as far as we could see in both directions concrete pylons jutted up at obtuse angles. Barbed wire had once stretched between and over these pillars in multiple layers forming an almost impenetrable barrier to the allied troops landing on the beach.

In the pillboxes and bunkers were enormous cannons used to sink ships and landing barges, and rusting machine guns used to mow down the troops attempting to land on this beach. It was hard to imagine that all the beaches along the English Channel facing towards England were similarly covered and barricaded. I couldn't imagine how anyone got through this, yet they did, and at great loss, and still they managed to push the Germans back.

The sun shone and sparkled on the choppy waves and wind gusts blew small eddies of sand around the bleached concrete pylons along the beach. The concrete of the pillboxes and bunkers were decaying and crumbling as wind, salt spray, and rain weathered them. Perhaps in another twenty years there would be little to show an enormous invasion had occurred here, unless of course sections of this barricade could be preserved for future generations.

Leaving Oostende behind, we followed back roads through country towns and villages. I liked that because there was only local traffic instead of masses of fast moving vehicles tearing along super-wide freeways. We saw countryside which you wouldn't see from a freeway and could stop anywhere we felt like if we wanted to look at something.

You couldn't do that on a freeway; you had to keep moving at whatever speed the rest of the vehicles were doing, and that was frightening when they were all driving on the wrong side of the road as far as we were concerned.

All I remember of Rotterdam was the vast port with massive ships lined up row after row at wharves festooned with colossal cranes; very industrial, and the impression that came into my mind was Victorian Futuristic, which today would probably be called Steampunk. That word and the ideas it conjures didn't exist then, and no doubt the port has since been modernized and wouldn't look like that now.

We passed through Rotterdam surrounded and accompanied by massive trucks and busses until we finally could get onto some country roads that would lead us towards Amsterdam.

Now here was a beautiful city of lovely quaint buildings lining streets and canals. It was colourful and very busy with people on bicycles, pedestrians thronging narrow streets, and lots of tourists. There were barges slowly moving along the canals; fancy barges with big windows lining both sides through which many faces peered up at the buildings they passed. There were also lots of smaller boats traversing the canals, so many it seemed there was more traffic on the water than there was in the streets if you discounted pedestrians and bicycle riders. Lovely garden beds had tulips growing in them.

We didn't stay very long but we did stay long enough to walk along the street where the women selling themselves displayed themselves in shop windows for all to see and appreciate. Each shop window was set up like a small lounge room and the woman either sat reclining provocatively or moved around seductively. Most of the women in the windows that we saw as we walked along were very beautiful. If anyone stopped to look in she would immediately try to entice that person inside either with gestures or a more enticing display. Some windows had curtains drawn and we presumed someone had been induced to go in and the curtains were drawn for both privacy and to let potential clients know this person behind this window was occupied.

Nothing like this ever existed in Australia. Nothing so blatant… yet it was tasteful and elegant, like fashion displays in windows of major department stores, except here the store dummies were real women who moved around and interacted with those passing by who paused to look in. That many people strolling along this street didn't even glance at the windows hinted at a level of acceptance, which indicated to me that this was a normal and ordinary part of the shopping precinct. We were quite stunned when we realized this.

Wow, Europe certainly was different.

We drove between endless fields of tulips, crossed many tiny canals used for irrigation, and it never once crossed our minds that we were actually below sea level, that if the famous dykes had not been built to hold the North Sea back a vast portion of this country simply wouldn't exist. I didn't see any of the iconic windmills that appear on postcards.

Eventually we found ourselves driving along roads that followed the course of the Rhine River, and very soon we left Holland behind and were in Germany. Dusseldorf was the first city we came to and we basically drove right through it. Koln (Cologne) was where the driver wanted to stop. He had a friend living there who had invited us to stay overnight in his apartment.

The apartment building dissected two main streets and was triangular shaped. The apartment was on the third floor and was quite large. The front windows curved around the front of the building (which was like the prow of a ship) and we could look along the length of the two streets the building dissected. We slept on the floor and drank lots of coffee with beautiful Danish pastries early the next morning before taking a walk to see the cathedral nearby which many considered to be one of the biggest and most beautiful in Europe but which I found to be quite monstrous. I didn't like Gothic architecture. I felt it was ridiculously ornate as well as ugly. But since Cologne was a river port and the largest city in the Westphalia district of Germany it seemed appropriate. Looking up at the twisting distorted spires made me dizzy. And the thought that it took generations of stonemasons several hundred years to build, (like most other cathedrals in Europe and England) left me cold.

What I couldn't quite get my head around was that so much of what we saw was so old. The cathedrals took hundreds of years to build and that was hundreds of years ago. We had yet to celebrate out bi-centenary and here I was looking at a building that took longer to build than our whole (European) history had occupied to that point in time. We had driven through villages and small towns that had existed almost unchanged for hundreds if not as much as a thousand years. Even the bigger cities we passed through, though much rebuilt to fix war damage, still looked ancient compared to any of our towns and cities in Australia. It was quite something to confront. What made many buildings look even older was the patina of dirt, grime and dust that had been absorbed into the bricks and stones and old concrete they were constructed from. If these were cleaned the cities would sparkle.

Eventually we made our way back to the apartment, said goodbye and thanked our host, and were once again following the river upstream. It was still a massive river here and there were many seagoing cargo ships docked or anchored near loading bays and wharves.

I hadn't realised the importance of river systems and canals to the European economy. Every major city is situated along a navigable river. Until roads were built after motor vehicles became prominent, all commerce and travel in and around Europe took place on rivers, and canals which intersected them, joining rivers, cities and countries together. It still does to great extent, although these days I imagine there are more tourists on the rivers and canals than there are cargo and other commercial boats, barges and ships.

We spent the night in Manheim sleeping in the station wagon parked in a rest spot beside the river. It rained during the night and we woke to a grey morning with everything around us dripping with water. The inside of the station wagon had fogged up and water droplets clung to the ceiling and dripped onto our faces. The sloshing of barges pushing their way along the river was muffled by the density of drizzling rain. We looked across the river's expanse to lines of smudged factories that belched thick black smoke into the air. I remember lots of huge trucks splashed past us on the road beside where we were parked. Tired, full of aches and pains from sleeping uncomfortably, we stood by the station wagon and stretched before hopping back in to drive off and leave this depressing city behind. We also left the Rhine River behind as we headed towards Stuttgart on the Neckar River with its wine growing areas.

Stuttgart was the home of Volkswagon and this world famous manufacturer employed many people from the surrounding villages and towns who swelled the population of the city to well over a million each working day. That's a massive amount of people who commuted into and out of Stuttgart every working day; mostly by train and the central railway station was an incredible edifice in the heart of the city.

This was where they left me. They helped me unload my drum bags and waited while I called Fred's parents on the phone. Fred's father was coming to get me, but it would take about forty minutes because Backnang where they lived was a regional country town to the north of Stuttgart about 30 minutes by train, and the drive in from there could take a while depending on the traffic.

At long last, someone from Australia

I watched the guys drive off and disappear into the traffic thundering past the front of the railway station, and then walked into the main concourse where I stacked my drums against a wall between two coffee bars. We had arranged to meet inside rather than out in front of the station, but I had no idea what he looked like. It had never occurred to me to get a photo from Fred. I would have to look for someone who was obviously looking for someone, namely me. Did he know what I looked like? I don't think Fred or I had thought of sending them a photo of me either.

There were thousands of people swarming through the concourse heading towards a plethora of platforms, and half of them looked as if they were looking for someone. Coffee bars and sausage bars were crowded with people grabbing quick snacks, a beer, or a coffee while they waited for a train or before departing the station for work in the city. I went to a money changing office inside an information centre and got some Deutschemarks so I too could get something to eat while I waited. I bought a bratwurst on a roll which was delicious, and a coffee. I sipped it slowly as I searched for someone who could have been looking for me.

People came in waves through the concourse; those leaving trains that had just arrived pushing their way through those heading towards the very same trains to depart. It seemed trains arrived and departed every few seconds. I had never seen a station as busy as this before. There were hardly any moments when there weren't crowds surging one way or the other through the concourse. After about an hour I decided what I had to look for was someone who was relatively stationary (no pun intended) amongst all the movement, someone like myself who wasn't going anywhere. It wasn't long after that when I saw a short stocky bald headed man who seemed to be looking anxiously at faces in the crowded concourse. It had to be Fred's dad.

'Excuse me, Mister Glasbrenner?' I asked tentatively.

'Yes,' his face lit up with a smile. 'You must be John.'

I nodded happily.

We shook hands.

'At long last, someone from Australia.'

I knew what he meant. Fred had left Germany with two mates riding bicycles sometime in 1954, their intention to ride all the way to Australia for the Olympic Games in Melbourne in 1956. They got there, and how they did it is an incredible story in itself, and though Fred corresponded with his parents and phoned them regularly, they had not seen him since the day he left and now it was the middle of May 1964. In that time he had been a bus driver and was now an abalone diver, and he had married my sister, so I was family by marriage, and they were so happy to have someone who could tell them all the things they wanted to know about their son and his adventures.

Fred's Dad and Mum in Backnang. 1965.

– *Ephemeron* –

A postcard of Backnang in the 1960s

They gave me Fred's old room and I didn't stop talking for two days, in between morning tea, lunch, afternoon tea, and dinner. All the people in the building from the two floors above came to morning and afternoon teas, bringing cakes to share and wanting to hear all about Australia and Fred's life there. Living directly above was one of Fred's mates who had accompanied him to Australia on their bikes. He was married to Fred's cousin. He had returned after only a few years in Australia and now worked as a top salesman for Mercedes Benz. The other mate was somewhere in Africa working as an engineer.

Walking down the street to the shopping centre everyone I passed nodded and smiled and wished me good morning or afternoon whatever the time was, and quite a few actually thought I was Fred who after nine or so years had returned. The fact that I was tanned brown — from sunbaking on the ship for 5 weeks through the tropics — and had black hair only convinced them that Australia was as hot as they all imagined it to be. They thought Fred's blonde hair had been burnt black by the sun. And because I was staying with the Glasbrenners they automatically assumed I must be Fred. It was only when I spoke English, which many of them couldn't understand that it occurred to them that I was not Fred but somebody else.

They were also convinced I had brought the warm weather with me. Germany, along with the rest of Europe was experiencing a much warmer than usual beginning to summer, and as the days drifted towards summertime it got hotter and hotter.

By my standards it seemed quite normal. It was like the summer temperatures we often get in Melbourne. I never realised how unusual it was for Southern Germany to be that hot.

London too, I saw on the TV news, was extraordinarily hot with traffic jams leading out of the city miles in length as millions of people tried to head for coastal towns and rocky beaches where they could get some relief from the heat.

If it was that hot today everyone would be running around talking about global warming and climate change, but back in 1964 no one thought about such matters. It was just weather – and sometimes it was worse than other times – just as it always had been, and probably always will be.

And what was I doing during this hot period? I sat outside in the back yard, stripped to the waist, and wrote a long letter to my friend

Wally in Melbourne. I had been into Stuttgart to a foreign language bookshop and found a copy of a book called Silent Spring, by Rachel Carson. This was a phenomenal book that dealt with the dire consequences of what humans were doing to the world and its animals and insects and birds and fish with our overuse of chlorinated hydrocarbon insecticides and pesticides like DDT, Dieldrin, and other chemicals similar to Agent Orange that was later unleashed upon Vietnam, and how we were disrupting and poisoning the food chain ultimately affecting the top predators and ourselves.

It was not alarmist propaganda but a logical and reasoned assessment of what we had been doing and were continuing to do to ourselves and our planet by a renowned scientist whose findings were so catastrophic she had to write about it to warn the World.

'The control of Nature' she believed was a concept full of arrogance, relating to our early beginnings where nature was considered to be at the service of man as part of a 'Stone Age science' and mentality we still have today. That we have armed ourselves with such devastating chemical weapons to apply against nature and the environment can only result in the destruction of Earth itself.

Though the book was a sensation in its time, in the long run no one took much notice and the world continued on its destructive course with results becoming more apparent every day. If we don't change the way we think as a species, then eventually we will be doomed.

This book affected me on a deep level and I just had to write to Wally and tell him about it. It was a long (over 5000 words) letter, and during the process of writing this I came up with the idea that we should write a novel about a devastated world where humans had retreated to the oceans where they lived in underwater habitats because the earth's surface had been destroyed and poisoned so much it was uninhabitable. It never occurred to me that the ocean environment would be equally as poisoned as the land it surrounded, but we tossed the idea around for a while and when I got home we actually started writing it. It wasn't very good, though we enjoyed the writing together, consuming far too many flagons of wine in the process.

The book was never published. It was awful.

But we had fun writing it and that was the main thing.

The excitement of Science Fiction

What got me into reading science fiction at a fairly young age were two things: adventure/ excitement, and imaginative ideas.

The adventure/excitement covered travel to exotic places and worlds where danger threatened the protagonists at every turn or step they took. This was also why I liked cowboy stories and murder mysteries. They were so far removed from my life as a growing boy in suburban Melbourne that they might as well have been on some other planet or in an alternative parallel universe. But science fiction took over simply because it was more exotic and different. The stories could take place on Earth, under the oceans or in Space on a space ship, on newly discovered worlds in weird and wonderful star systems throughout the galaxy and so on. This aspect probably fuelled my subconscious desire to travel around my own country (Australia), and eventually to other countries, and to experiment with new sports like skin diving and scuba diving. How more alien can you get than some of the life that exists beneath the sea's surface?

The other aspect involved the sense of wonder engendered by fascinating ideas, like time travel and its paradoxes, alien or exobiology, other worldly anthropology, generation ships and time dilation, First contact, and the list goes on. There were also the technological extrapolations that were fascinating like moving sidewalks, air cars, videophones, space ships, unbelievable future cities, possible catastrophes and apocalypses of all kinds extrapolated from obvious trends, intelligent artificial beings whether mobile or otherwise, living spaceships, faster than light travel…

At first I didn't care whether the story was well written; I didn't read it for that. I enjoyed the sense of wonder engendered. I wanted the escapism it gave. I wanted to immerse myself in another world that at my age I could never have envisioned. That someone else had imagined it was a wonder in itself. I thrived on the stuff. I had no idea whether the science was accurate or not: it didn't matter. It was the escapism that enthralled me, and the wonderful ideas like flying cars and spaceships going to other planets that were very different from the one I lived on.

The fact that someone could write a whole novel about the effects of a simple idea like a device to remove all particles of dust from the atmosphere so women would never have to vacuum the house again, and the dire consequences this development produced was to me mind boggling. That was a novel from either Volstead Gridban or Vargo Statten — publishing house names for a prolific pulp writer or a team of them who produced new novels every day. These books were distributed through newsagents alongside the Carter Brown and Mike Hammer series and innumerable westerns. They never appeared in bookshops which should have clued me in to how awful they really were. But I didn't care; I enjoyed every one I could get my hands on…

It was a few years later, when I started to reach 16 or 17 that I found these books shallow and empty and started to look for stories with more character development than those that simply extrapolated an idea into infinity. It was people that made stories, not ideas. It was how people's lives were affected by the events or extrapolated scientific developments within the story that actually made the story interesting, not the stuff in the background.

Some of these pulp novels probably still exist today and are reprinted as 'classics' because they were memorable by being so ridiculously bad they were inadvertently funny, or they were written well enough around a single idea to be good.

Surely someone capable of writing hundreds of books or thousands of short stories over a lifetime could occasionally produce something memorable that would outlast them, and most of the writers I liked as a teenager and a young adult did do that. *The Songs of distant Earth* by Arthur C Clarke, which he wrote late in his life is one that springs to mind. This was the most emotionally memorable book he ever wrote as far as I am concerned, a result of his answer to the realities of galactic space flight compared to the fantasy of it depicted in Star Wars and other SF Films. *Nightfall* by Isaac Asimov was a brilliant early short story which he could never better no matter what else he wrote, and he was very prolific. Robert Silverberg, John Brunner, Gordon R. Dixon, Poul Anderson, Frederic Pohl, Ray Bradbury, are all writers who began their careers in the golden age of pulp fiction, before movies and later TV stole readers away, who managed to produce some brilliant stories amongst the dross they pumped out, but no matter how pulpy or wooden their stories were they were better writers than those whose names were hidden behind a publishing house name. Many of their stories will endure and remain memorable long into the future.

Their generation, compared to the early pulp writers publishing before the Second World War or immediately just after it, could be compared to Wally and me. Wally experienced the war in Britain as a teenager and as a young man went to Germany in the Army and took a small part in the reconstruction of Germany after the War. He would have been fifteen years older than me. I was born in 1940 and was just 5 when the Second World War finished.

When we got together to write our novel Wally's ideas of how things worked were Victorian, like something out of Jules Verne, whereas mine (I liked to think) were more modern. A simple example of this was his idea for shifting the underwater habitats was to have propellers push them through the water in the same way a submarine or a ship worked.

I said that was ridiculous. 'Have you ever seen the way an octopus moves?' I asked him when we were half way through a flagon of wine one night.

He just shook his head. He had never been underwater, had never even considered skindiving. He could swim, and often went to the beach in summer, but he had never looked at life under the sea. He wanted airlocks in the habitats so people could go in or out; again like a submarine, or more like a space ship which would require an airlock to be used when entering or exiting a ship in a vacuum.

'When an octopus hunts it drifts across the bottom using its arms to help it glide and creep along. It remains upright and bulbous, almost globular in shape, but flaccid. Its legs are very sensitive and can sniff out small prey which it will grab and hold tight with the suckers on the legs. If something frightens it, it lifts off the bottom and suddenly shoots away like a rocket.' I told him. And I emphasized the following. 'It changes shape. Its body becomes elongated like a spear and its legs trail behind. Actually this is the front because octopus and squid and cuttlefish swim backwards. It sucks in water and spurts it out to propel it along at an incredible speed. It uses jet propulsion. It doesn't use fins, which would be on a toadfish or a boxfish be like propellers on a submarine.'

'How does it see where it's going if it swims backwards?'

'No idea. It must have some way of sensing objects so it can shoot around them. It changes colour and patterns almost instantaneously to match the background it is swimming past, so it becomes very hard to see. Arthur C Clark suggested giant squid use these rapid colour changes as a form of communication.'

'I don't know,' Wally mumbled, still thinking about shape changing. 'How can you get metal to change shape?'

'It is in the future. Why can't we have metal capable of changing shape at higher speeds but return to the original shape when it slows down? Why can't metal remember the shape it is supposed to have, and always be able to return to that shape? The spaces inside the habitat could elongate without losing integrity. It would take some getting used to but we don't have to make the change too radical. The habitat could change just enough to be a bit more streamlined so it could move quicker though the water. The octopus' changed shape doesn't affect its internal organs. They remain the same only more elongated. They quickly revert to the original shape when it settles back in a safe spot.'

I could see him thinking about that. His eyes glazed over a bit, or was that the effect of the wine we had been drinking?

'We can invent anything that's plausible, so why not? I read a story which may have been written by Kenneth Bulmer, and he had submarines in the river near New York that cruised slowly, but when they went out into the ocean and wanted to make more speed they became streamlined, changing shape so they could cut through the water faster and more smoothly. Why can't we do the same?'

'I don't remember reading that story. I suppose it could work. How would that affect the airlocks though?'

'You don't have airlocks. I presume you want those on the side?'

'Well you couldn't have them on the top...'

'Forget airlocks. You have a hole in the bottom. If you keep the atmosphere inside the same as the water outside a hole in the bottom is all you need. To anyone inside it would be like a swimming pool or a hole in the ice if you lived near the North Pole and the arctic sea. People cut holes in the ice to go fishing. The water doesn't well up and over it does it? The same in the habitat, a hole in the bottom will stay just that. Something you can jump into or climb out of. Imagine it like an arsehole in the habitat. When the habitat changes shape to move somewhere else the opening in the bottom also changes shape. It may iris closed to allow smoother movement through the water but when the habitat resettles it opens again as before. Using water propelled out through orifices all around the perimeter the habitat could drift along the bottom, grazing so the speak, but it could also move faster across open ocean like an octopus does using jet propulsion with water drawn in from the forward section and expelled through the rear.'

'Haven't you read about Jacque Cousteau's Conshelf-2 Habitat? It was thirty feet underwater in the Red Sea. Divers lived and worked in it for a month entering and exiting the habitat through a hole in the bottom. However because the air pressure inside was the same as the water outside, which was why the habitat didn't flood, when the divers wanted to come back to the surface they had to decompress and purge their bodies of accumulated nitrogen which could bubble out of their bloodstream causing the bends.'

Our discussions went on along those lines for many months as we constructed our huge novel and drank heaps of wine. But in hindsight, it was too narrow in approach; like many other novels up to that point in time where the authors took a single idea and extrapolated that into the future. Sometimes the idea would be extrapolated to extremes and the result just wasn't believable. The world is far more complex than we can imagine and we should have extrapolated many trends and ideas forward simultaneously, not just the one.

Apart from that our science was bad so the whole idea inevitably became preposterous. Of course we didn't think that at the time. We thought we had some good ideas and that they would be interesting to readers. We wrote alternate chapters and exchanged them for reworking so the overall result would be a mixture of the two. It just didn't work. Individually our ideas were too different, and our styles of writing were also too different. We just couldn't blend them together in a way that was readable over the hundreds of pages we did. That the end result was an unreadable epic which no one would publish inevitably didn't matter. We had lots of fun in the process and any disappointments were quickly forgotten.

We eventually did write a short story together where we used a valuable piezoelectric crystal to solve a difficult problem which was published in a magazine called Rats. It paid us $20 each for the story.

What killed science fiction for modern readers is that reality caught up and surpassed early imagination. We live in a world that has everything and more than what was imagined in many stories we read as teenagers. We live in a science fiction world. A world where science fiction extrapolated ideas and gadgets that in time became real because the scientists who grew up reading science fiction thought it would be cool to have stuff like that, so they invented it for real. It isn't like what we wanted or imagined but it is what we've got.

Single idea extrapolations don't work anymore. Modern writers like Peter F Hamilton, Alastair Reynolds, Ian M Banks, Kim Stanley Robinson and David Brin have shown how complex a future can be when they extrapolate many present trends into the near and far future. Their latest books are truly awesome and have that sense of wonder that attracted me as a young teenager to the genre in the first place. Grand Space Opera! There's nothing like it, really. These writers give hope that good science fiction isn't a thing of the past, but that it can still be fresh, exciting and relevant.

Happily for me there has been a revival of the Grand Space Opera with stories set in far futures with incredible plots in vast universes that open endless possibilities. The writing in these novels is good, sometimes even superb, and characters human and non-human are developed who are completely believable. These are books about people, living beings, and not books about things. These show that science fiction hasn't died or become nothing more than contemporary thrillers with a bit of science background thrown in. It is a genre that continues to evolve, that continues to stay ahead of present day reality, and perhaps even suggests ways in which present day reality can follow. Unfortunately some of the books are so long, so big and heavy, you can hardly pick them up or hold them while you read them.

That 5000 word letter was written with me sitting in the Glasbrenner's backyard at small coffee table. The sun was shining and since I had already obtained a good tan while on board Ellinis as we travelled through the tropics, it didn't bother me to sit out there for a few hours while writing this letter. The temperature would have been in the low 30s which was quite pleasant, and for me the sun didn't have the intensity it has in Australia, but for those in Southern Germany it was extraordinarily hot. The Glasbrenners stayed inside where it was slightly cooler but more humid so they still felt the heat as stifling. They couldn't understand how I could sit out there all afternoon in the sun. About 5pm when the sun had dropped and the temperature actually cooled a bit I came back inside. I had finished my letter.

'How can you sit out there in that heat?' they asked me with a hint of astonishment underlying the question. They looked at me as if I was bordering on being crazy.

'It wasn't so hot,' I replied. 'In fact it is starting to get a bit cooler, so I thought I'd better come inside.'

They stared at me struggling to understand what I had said.

'It gets a lot hotter than that in Melbourne.' I added for emphasis.

'It never gets this hot in Backnang,' Fred's Mum said. 'Never ever…'

'Maybe the climate is changing…' I suggested. Even back then some SF stories had been based upon themes relating to climate change. *The Drowned World* by JG Ballard was a classic example of that. It wasn't only post or near apocalyptic but the whole premise behind the story was climate change brought about by our sun's instability and increasing heat had melted the ice caps and rising seas flooded the world rendering the tropics uninhabitable. The world's population was in retreat towards the cooler Polar Regions, except for one or two crazy ones who wanted to go further into the hot regions to see what was happening. That the book dealt with characters and how their lives were affected rather than the mechanics of climate change makes this a classic; one of the few books from that time which is still being reprinted 50 years later.

It was in fact an extraordinarily hot spring and summer in Europe that year (1964), much hotter than had been experienced for as far back as people could remember. Subsequent years were more or less back to normal with no extremes. (*That is until this new century where climate change is finally becoming apparent with extreme summer and winter fluctuations.*)

I went back to London for a couple of days to visit my Aunt Maria who took a flat for the summer somewhere near Hyde Park while her husband, my Uncle Bill was somewhere in North Africa working as usual for the United Nations Food and Agricultural department.

Hyde park was full of people who for whatever reasons couldn't leave London and so they searched for somewhere cooler and it seemed Hyde Park was the place to be.

Many of the younger people stripped down to their underwear to lay around on the grass for sunbathing or hopped in and out of the various public fountains, much to the consternation of the local Bobbies who kept trying to get them out of the water and to put some more clothes on.

It seemed a half-hearted effort though; it was simply too hot for them to care. They probably felt like doing the same thing, but of course they couldn't. I had a lovely afternoon tea with my aunt, wandered around Hyde Park for a bit, had a quick look at the guards outside the Royal Palace, and decided I didn't find London all that enticing. I went back to Germany for the rest of the summer.

Hard hands

Well, I thought I had hard hands from playing conga and bongo drums for a long time, but I soon found otherwise. Some of Fred's school mates heard that I played drums and were fascinated to see how conga drums would fit into their rock group so they invited me to play one night with them. They had this gig at what could be called a pub. They were a heavily amplified rock band. Well, fitting in with them was no problem. The problem was they were amplified and I wasn't. I sat to one side of the band near the drummer and when they started I just couldn't hear myself play against the sheer volume they put out.

They had huge speakers on each side of the stage in stacks like giant boxes piled on top of each other. Several other smaller speakers were placed along the front of the small stage so the band members could hear themselves, but my drums weren't miked. I knew what I was playing but couldn't hear it. Whether the audience could hear it was also hard to discern. They were more into ecstatic dancing than listening. They pounded their feet, contorted their bodies like marionettes manipulated by a mad man, and were totally lost in the waves of wailing sound that enveloped them. Even my ears ached and I wasn't out in front of those enormous speakers either side of us.

I played as hard and loud as I could, and within the first fifteen minutes I could feel my hands blistering. The blisters soon split and the drum skins became slick with the exudation which quickly turned into blood. When our set was over my hands were a mess.

I told these guys I wouldn't do it again. It was an interesting experiment and the congas did fit with the band. It turned out the audience of dancers loved it and wanted more, but I simply couldn't play with my hands almost stripped of skin and exuding blood. That was it as far as I was concerned... no more playing in rock bands unless I was as amplified as the rest of them.

It took a couple of weeks for my hands to heal properly.

Down, but not out, in Paris, London, and Seville.

Ernest Hemmingway was born the same year as my father, 1898. He died in 1961 having committed suicide with his own shotgun. Distraught at being unable to write anymore, unable to finish the last few sentences of his final novel, he took his shotgun, loaded it and placed both barrels into his mouth and pulled both triggers.

He had tried several times before that but was thwarted each time. Even on his way to the Mayo clinic, where he was to undergo psychiatric treatment for severe depression and his tendency to suicide, he had tried to throw himself out of the plane taking him there. But eventually back home in Ketchum he succeeded, and the world was poorer for the loss of his great talent.

Hemingway was one of the authors we had to study in my English literature class at University High School in my last year there. The book chosen was *For Whom the Bell Tolls*, which I managed to read all the way through. At the time I thought it was heavy-going, but there were parts of it that really grabbed me. However I much preferred his collections of short stories as they were so beautifully crafted, with no words wasted, that it was a joy to read them.

At that time, around 1961, I bought a copy of his most famous book, *The Old Man and The Sea*, which was the book that nailed him the Nobel Prize for literature. It was my favourite of all his books. It was a beautifully illustrated edition by two artists who both used scraper board illustrations that although very different from each other, managed to capture the essence of the character and the story. They were commissioned for separate editions but the publishers thought they both were so excellent and so interesting in their various styles they were both included in this edition. It is a book I still treasure and have read several times over the years. It was the most popular book Hemingway ever wrote. Perhaps its simplicity was what made it so good and popular. Basically it was about an old fisherman who after months of bad luck rows one day out into the Gulf Stream (where Hemmingway often fished for marlin) and catches the biggest marlin he has ever seen. He fights it for several days while the giant fish drags his skiff further out into the Gulf Stream. When finally the fish gives up, the old man ties it to the side of his skiff because it is far too big to haul on board, and rows back to his village. In the meantime the fish is attacked by a shark which he fights off, then another and another, until finally there is a feeding frenzy and many sharks devour the whole fish. By the time the old man gets home there is nothing left tied to his boat but a bony head, attached to the skeleton with only the tail-fin still intact.

The film version starring Spencer Tracey as the old fisherman wasn't a patch on the book even though Hemmingway helped work the script and acted as an adviser. The film was shot in Cuba and in the Pacific off the coast of Peru. Hemingway caught several marlins but because it was too early or too late in the day the Technicolor film couldn't get good results so the fish shots seen in the film were shot in a tank with a sponge-rubber fish. His only comment on seeing the finished film was *'Spencer Tracy looked like a fat, very rich actor playing a fisherman'*.

He wasn't happy about any of the films made from his books except for *The Killers* (1947) which starred Burt Lancaster and Ava Gardner. A later version of this same story starred Lee Marvin and Ronald Reagan. Burt Lancaster and Lee Marvin went on to become, if not great actors, certainly well-known and popular ones. As we all know Ronald Reagan went into politics and eventually became President of the United States of America.

Just before I went to Europe I had been reading Hemmingway's book about the time he spent in Paris in the 1920s. I think it was called *A Moveable Feast*, and although I knew Paris would be very different from those wild bohemian days, and many of the people mentioned in that book were either long gone or had moved away, I still thought Paris was the city every artist, no matter what the art, wanted to go to.

I was no different. I wasn't really anything; not an artist, not a writer, not a musician, but a kind of amalgam of all three — at least all those things interested me enough to make me have some small proficiency at them. Depending on where I was and what was happening around me, one or the other would dominate, and at this moment what dominated was playing conga drums. I had to go to Paris because I knew I would find a great variety of good musicians and bands there and would have some opportunities to play and get better at it.

There was not much chance of me doing anything like that in Backnang.

What can I say about Paris that hasn't already been said a million times by more people than I can possibly imagine?

It's a beautiful city, a superb city, an elegant city with unbelievably beautiful gardens and tree lined boulevards, multicultural, artistic, hedonistic, dynamic, trend-setting, wonderfully aged like fine wine, full of history at every turn, very French – the epitome of French, and in one word – unique.

It may not be as much like that now: most cities have modernized, evolved to such a degree that in many of them there is hardly anything left that gave each major city its uniqueness. In appearance they have become homogenised.

I am remembering what I saw at the end of 1964, half a century ago, and memory being what it is, all I have left are impressions.

Walking along a tree shaded street on the left bank of the Seine hundreds of stalls selling books and postcards demanded my attention. There were lots of bookshops here too and I browsed happily in search of anything interesting and found elegant photographic postcards that were black and white, not colour, but very artistic. I bought heaps and scribbled impressions on the backs of them in preparation to sending them home. There were books in a profusion of many languages. There weren't that many in English but there were some in dingy green covers. Two were by Henry Miller who was known as a pornographic novelist living in Paris. *Tropic of Cancer* and *Tropic of Capricorn* stood out as being examples of biographical fiction that showed no limits in what it portrayed. These were banned in every English speaking country at that time so I bought copies. Over time as laws and morals became more open, these books would become available in countries where they were once banned, but having them in my hands in Paris in 1964 was exciting. I also found three incomprehensible novels by William Burroughs whose books were also banned everywhere else but were famous for being SF written under the influence of mind bending drugs. *The Naked Lunch, The Soft Machine,* and *Nova Express* were all there in green covers. They were the ugliest looking books, but anything published in a green cover was usually something banned in most countries so they sold well to foreign tourists.

Something else I found as a massive paperback was John Dos Passos' epic trilogy of novels called *U.S.A*. This I couldn't wait to read. I had heard so much about it.

Dos Passos created a much copied style, writing of lives in parallel, interspersed with newsreel type information as impressionistic info dumps, and biographies of famous people to build up an enormous series of images of the whole of the USA in simultaneous development and turmoil.

The only author to my mind who mastered Dos Passos style of writing was John Brunner who's finest work should include *Stand on Zanzibar, The Sheep look Up,* and *The Jagged Orbit*, a loose trilogy of novels dealing prophetically with terrorism, pollution, population explosion, food shortages, climate change, and all those things that worry us today. *Stand on Zanzibar* was clearly the best of these and owes its style to that pioneered by John Dos Passos.

John Brunner was prolific and churned out a few 'pot-boilers' but he also wrote some memorable and extraordinarily good stuff and he should be remembered more than he is.

Standing on an ancient bridge over the Seine I watched barges slowly travelling along the river, lovers relaxing along the pathways beside it, and in the distance I couldn't miss seeing the Eiffel Tower reaching for the sky above the city. I also saw the monstrous brooding bulk of the famous Notre Dame Cathedral on its island (Ile de la cité which is where the original settlement that became Paris began) in the river and couldn't help thinking of the hunchback that inhabited its secret passages and rooms from the film The Hunchback of Notre Dame. I didn't like the look of it and never visited it. This massive cathedral was commenced in 1163 but wasn't finished until the 14th century, hundreds of years later. You have to give credit where it is due; the people who built these things had certainly been dedicated. It took many generations to build, which is something I could never understand. Why would they dedicate their lives and those of generations to come to build such a thing?

I did go to the Louvre mainly to see the famous Mona Lisa, which it turned out was a disappointment. I had the impression it would be a larger than life painting, but it was tiny, and from the distance it could be viewed it seemed as small as a postage stamp. It was also covered by glass which kept the space it occupied absolutely climate controlled. There were other paintings that I thought were much better than that little portrait, but then that was only my opinion.

Streets were busy with people from all around the world, people from French colonial provinces, locals going about their business, and tourists like me gawking at everything in sight. Cars and chunky dark green busses drove seemingly chaotically along the streets, filling every bit of space on the roadway leaving no room for anyone trying to cross. If you drove, finding a parking space was almost impossible. There were cars jammed into the smallest of spaces and many in narrow streets were parked with the side wheels up on the footpath.

What fascinated me as I walked along the streets were fat tubelike towers two to three metres tall every few hundred metres. These fat tubes were covered with posters plastered one on top of the other advertising concerts, shows, theatre events, bands playing, lectures at the nearby Sorbonne University, anything and everything that was happening in the area where the particular tower was located.

I suspected that the towers were air vents to allow air to escape the underground tunnels where Paris' famous Metro ran. The trains pushed the air in front of them compressing it and it had to go somewhere, hence the vents. It was always draughty going down the escalators into the underground stations so air pushed out of the vents was replaced by air being sucked in through the entrances to the stations.

A poster advertising a Cuban band called Los Matecocos, caught my attention. They were playing nearby that same evening as I stood there and looked at the picture. I had found a record shop earlier and browsing through the albums (12 inch vinyl records) the photograph of a group on the cover of one in the vast section devoted to Cuban music had caught my eye. It was an album by Los Matecocos and I listened to it, pretending that I was interested in buying it. They sounded great and when I saw the poster advertising them I just had to go and see them live, in the flesh, to see if they sounded as good live as they did on the recording.

— *Ephemeron* —

This was the same picture used to advertize the group that I saw on the round concrete air vent. The record above was their best selling album. They had many others but this was the best.

They were playing in a small hall on the second floor of a building that looked like an old warehouse. I could hear them as I walked up the steps. It was such a great sound I got goose bumps, and the flute, that was brilliant. I just loved the Cuban flute. It was a simple wooden flute with two less keys than the classical flute, but it had a far more penetrating sound than its classical counterpart. It cut through the heavy sounding congas and timbales with ease and floated above the rhythm that enticed the listener to get up on the dance floor and start moving. This guy was good. I found out later that he, Clemente Lozano, was the brother of the famous Rolando Lozano who played flute with Mongo Santamaria in America. I had copies of his Pachanga and Charanga records at home.

There were eight of them in the band and when there was a break I approached the leader Pancho Cataneo and asked if I could sit in for a number or two on congas. He spoke English (as well as French and of course Spanish). I doubt if I would do that now, but back then when it came to playing congas I was young and fearless and would ask anyone if I could sit it and play. I think he only agreed because he thought it unusual for an English speaking person to play Cuban music. He wanted to hear what I could do.

I jumped up on the stage when the band regrouped for the next set and the conga drummer stood aside and played guiro (gourd scraper) allowing me to play his congas. Pancho said they would play *Cachita* a well-known and popular medium tempo rumba. I knew it, and I knew the breaks, having listened to it many times on records at home. We flew into it and it sailed along at a good pace. People danced but I didn't take much notice of them. I focussed on how this group played and made a few slight changes to the well-known breaks. I wasn't exactly sure of their break so I simply stopped and waited for the two bars before coming back in again when they all started after the break. I saw Pancho nodding and smiling. He touched his right ear briefly and winked as if to say, 'that's good, you listen…' As soon as Cachita was over, the conga drummer came back and stood behind the higher pitched drum.

I heard Pancho announce a '*potpouri* (a medley) *de comparsas*' and instantly the timbales player began the fast bell pattern. The band's conga drummer nodded to me and I came in on the lower drum with the expected base tumbao (called abierto) typical of the congas played in the streets of Santiago or Havana during Carnival. He played counterpoint and improvised a bit while the trumpets blasted out the melody followed by Pancho leading the choruses for several very popular congas or comparsas, *La Chambelona, Mirala Que Linda Viene, Siento un Bombo, Tumbando Caña,* and *Los Dandis*.

The conga had been popular around the world for quite some time, but it was traditionally played in Carnivals throughout Cuba and because it had the ability to get large crowds dancing and marching in unison it was used by political parties to motivate people. Certain congas became associated with either the liberal parties or the conservative parties, and many of the songs had satirical or political conotations behind them. The watered down bastardization played in European and American dance floors of the 30s and 40s which consisted of simply lines of people moving in a one- two- three- kick pattern was absolute rubbish compared to the real thing.

— Ephemeron —

What we played was an approximation also, but it was closer to the real thing than anything I had heard other than on records of folkloric music. With two congas, timbales and two trumpets alternating with sung choruses we sounded pretty good. It finished with Clemente taking a Chinese gourd flute, which sounds weird to me but is traditionally used during comparsas, to lead us into the finale. The whole building pounded to the dancers on the floor who almost went berserk.

My hands were still tender from the blistering they had taken in Germany, but I felt really good.

'What are you doing next Friday?' Pancho asked me.

'Nothing yet,' I said.

'Good. I have a recording happening at the Bel Air Studios and I would like you to play congas for me.'

Stunned, I didn't know what to say. I didn't even have them with me, having only come to Paris by train to see what it was like.

'I want a bigger band sound for this recording.'

'What about…?' I indicated the conga player.

'He'll play bongo. You play conga. I have Alberto Beltran singing lead and playing Tambora.'

I had some early Seeco records at home with Alberto Beltran playing and singing merengue, as well as bolero. I hadn't heard of him for years though. I explained that I would have to go back to Germany to collect my drums.

Europe is quite small so a train from Paris to Stuttgart really doesn't take very long. I could be there and back with my drums in two days.

He gave me his address, and the address of the studio which it turned out was in a side street off the Champs Elysees just before the famous L'arc de Triomphe. But before I left I would have to find someplace to stay, which I did. It was a small hotel with rooms that overlooked a nice little courtyard. I booked a room there for a month, and then went and caught the train back to Stuttgart where I would get off to take the local to Backnang.

Coming back to Paris I settled in. I called Pancho and he invited me to his flat where I met his wife and children as well as Alberto who was staying there until the recording was done. We went over the music they were to record and it was straight forward; several boleros, a couple of merenges, two cha chas and a guaracha. It was a reasonable mix focussing predominantly on what Alberto was best at.

As it turned out I was lucky to meet Pancho Cataneo. He led the most popular Cuban conjunto in Paris and often made work for out-of-favour musicians or forgotten musicians, or tried unknowns to see how he could develop his band. He told me his timbale drummer was leaving after a huge annual ball the record company was organizing in a few weeks so he would need a new timbale player. Could I play timbales? Of course I told him, even though I really couldn't. He knew that so he showed me how to get certain rim shots by dropping both sticks onto the taut skin and controlling the bounce with last bounce hitting the rim. He also gave me several LPs they had previously recorded and suggested I learn the breaks and arrangements for the songs so I could fit in. I had three weeks to learn them. But in the meantime we had this recording to do at the Bel Air Studios.

I went to the studio via the metro, dragging two drums down the stairs to the station, pushing onto the crowded carriage with little regard for the passengers who glared at me. I got off at the station nearest the street where the studios were located and got there dead on 9am which was when they wanted to start recording.

It was the first time I had ever been inside a recording studio and I found it disconcerting in the way we were set up. I thought we would play as we did on a stage, altogether beside each other, but not here. Alberto was in a glassed off booth with its own microphone. The bass player was in another booth. The piano player was in the middle of the studio about 3 metres in front of us the percussion section, with me on congas, the band's resident conguero on bongos, and beside me the timbale player and his drums. Clemente and his flute were in another booth and four (instead of two) trumpet players were seated in a half booth across the other side of the studio.

Everyone was individually miked and everyone had to wear massive earphones so they could hear what the rest were doing. I like to be able to hear myself to gauge the volume I need to play at but with these earphones I couldn't do that. If I didn't wear them I wouldn't hear what people in the various sound booths were doing, so I finally compromised and wore them so that my right ear was covered and my left partially uncovered so I could hear myself as well as all the others. That worked fine and we started recording. The first song was the guaracha and we actually recorded it three times before Pancho was satisfied. The merengues were next and they were done with one take each.

Alberto played Tambora while he sang the merengues. The Tambora is a tubelike double headed drum. One head is played using a stick while the other is played with an open hand. Very nice drumming, and the first time I had ever seen a real merengue drum being played. I got him to show me the basic rhythm pattern because it was so different to the corrupted version I had known on the conga. Similarly the boleros only took one rehearsal before each recording. The Cha chas we did several times each. And that was it, all done, and it took about five hours with a short break for lunch.

After the musicians left, Pancho stayed in the studio to go over the recordings which were done on multi-channel tape to ensure the right balance was mixed for the master from which the actual record would be made.

Two days later I heard a soft disc copy of the recording which Pancho had in the flat and to me it sounded good. Everybody liked it. However, it would be at least three months before it was to be released into the shops.

I never saw the record released, since by then I had left Paris, and that one time in Pancho's flat was the only time I ever heard it.

Wandering around Paris

I didn't do too many gigs but there were rehearsals to attend so I could familiarize myself with the band before the big night of the Bel Air Ball. I had a great time playing and learning timbale breaks as well as just wandering about this magnificent city.

I watched literally hundreds of would-be artists in the square in front of the Sacré-Coeur Cathedral painting at their easels. The Sacré-Coeur with its beautiful white basilica was built on top of the Artist's hill at Montmartre in the late 19th century so this is a beautifully bright and cheerful modern cathedral. Some of the artists were great while others were amateurish or simply awful. Tourists abounded, and they happily spent money buying paintings directly from artists. In fact, because it was summer there were artists everywhere: along the banks of the Seine and in the Tuilleries gardens they were furiously painting and sketching, mostly in styles that imitated already famous artists, but there were some genuine originals.

The nearby coffee shops had tables and chairs that spilled over onto footpaths, something rarely seen in Australia in 1964. Both inside and outside tables were always full. The summer weather encouraged outdoor activities and taking a sandwich and a coffee was no exception. I found a coffee shop not far from where I was staying on the Left Bank that was full of students and would be artists of all kinds, poets, musicians, writers, from many different countries. Sometimes buskers would perform for loose change before waiters who feared they might lose a tip shooed them away.

There was one guy, an American hippie, whom I met and talked with who always ordered black tea into which he would put a big spoonful of butter. When I asked him about it he said that this was what tea was like in Tibet. He had read somewhere that they made tea with Yak Butter. He carried a dog-eared battered copy of the Tibetan Book of the Dead with him everywhere he went. 'I'm going to Tibet one day', he told me earnestly. I suppose drinking tea with butter in it was his way of preparing himself. I doubt if he knew what he would be getting into if he actually went to Tibet.

'And what are you doing?' he asked.

'I'm writing a book about an insane killer who murders people at random because he feels like it's a fun thing to do, to see other people suffer, to see how many different ways he can devise to kill them.'

'Wow.' He sat back and stared at me.

I had written something like that based around a nightclub I called The Birdcage which was vaguely like the place where I had played drums in Melbourne, and scrapped it when it got rejected. It was a terrible book and I had no qualms in tossing it in a rubbish bin.

'That's profound,' he said at long last.

He thought I was serious, but I was having him on. So I just smiled in a way I thought was enigmatic.

After that whenever I came into the coffee shop and he was there he treated me with a lot of respect. I even heard him on another occasion when he was unaware that I was behind him, telling someone about the book I was supposedly writing, telling them how good it was, how authentic and weird. He said it with such conviction I almost believed it myself.

I wonder if Hemmingway and his literary friends found the same thing back in the twenties. How much of what they said to each other was no more than bullshit to impress casual listeners. But then some of them went on to prove they weren't bullshitting because they wrote the books and lived the life they talked about.

The night of the ball was fantastic. Many people wore masks and the women had elaborate dresses that screamed, I'm ready to party. There would have been a thousand people in that huge hall. A magnificent dinner had been served during which a small group had played relaxing non-descript music. After that the dance started. There were six groups, all of whom recorded with the Bel Air record company. They were the featured bands. A French Rock group were up first and they sounded a bit like the Beatles. Everyone wanted to sound like the Beatles, which obviously said something for the quality of their music and their particular sound, but not all the imitators were successful. This group wasn't. Perhaps it was because they sang in French rather than English, but I suspected it was because they were too derivative, too slavish in trying to copy something they could never really do. The vast dance floor looked bigger than it was because so few people got up to dance. I could see the disappointment on the faces of the group members but they played their set with a fair degree of enthusiasm which at least showed they had a professional attitude.

Next up were the Brazilians. There were ten in the group three of whom were female dancers. They wore incredible costumes as they would for Carnival in Rio where the Samba schools paraded in competition to each other. They hit the floor with a fast Batucada and in no time, encouraged by the three scantily clad female dancers almost everyone got up to dance. There is something about pounding drums that makes people want to dance. Whether they are good at it or not, dancing to pounding drums is irresistible. Once everyone was on the dance floor the group played a selection of Samba, Bossa Nova, and Choros that were very melodic as well as rhythmic; they were a good group.

We followed them almost without a break. As soon as they moved off stage we started moving on. Congas and timbales were on stands and were easy to carry and place centre stage. The other members carried their own instruments. I helped the piano player, the only lady in our group (who incidentally wasn't Cuban or Mexican, but came from Poland) bring out her electric piano which was also on a stand. Within a minute everyone was miked or plugged in and we were ready to start. The only thing I didn't like much was that we had to wear these crazy frilly shirts, but I suppose that went with the carnival atmosphere of the Gala Ball.

We started with a *Bomba*, a Puerto Rican song called *Barrio de San Anton*. The Bomba is a catchy rhythm with its main accent on one (the first beat of the bar) that is easy to dance to. We followed this with *Emilio Dolores*, an up-tempo *rumba* that the Los Matecocos had made popular in Paris among Cuban exiles. After that we dropped the tempo and played a couple of medium to slow *cha chas*, so dancers could get their breath back, *a son montuno*, one *bolero* to encourage the romantics on the dance floor, and then finished the set with a medium *guaracha* and our potpourri of up-tempo *congas* or *comparsas*. Then we were done.

I couldn't help notice that no one left the dance floor when the Brazilians were playing or when we played.

After our set we joined the other musicians at the bar for some drinks while another band got onstage for its set. I drank more than I should have. I was happy because the Brazilian group and the Los Matecocos were the highlights of the night. They were the company's two top groups as far as record sales were concerned and it was the advertising of those two bands that had attracted the large crowd to the ball. I'm sure the Bel Air record company was happy with the result.

Unfortunately that was the last big event for Latin bands in France. Rock was taking over here just as it was everywhere else. I had the job as a Timbalero, but there weren't too many gigs happening. A couple of private parties were all Pancho could arrange.

'I've been talking to my booking agent,' he told me over coffee in his flat one afternoon, 'and I've accepted a job for six months in Bamako. Are you interested in going there?'

Of course I was interested but where the hell was Bamako?

'You wouldn't be paid in Dolares Americano. Payment would be Malien Franks.'

So it was in the Republic of Mali. North Africa. Somewhere near Senegal and Guinea.

'What does that mean?'

'Since you can't spend Malien Franks anywhere else; no one wants them, and you can't exchange them for any other useful money, you will have to spend them in Mali.'

'That's fine by me. I get paid to go there…'
'And you get accommodation at the hotel we would be playing at.'
'I'm in. I'd be happy to spend whatever money I earned over there. I'd love to go to Africa, especially West Africa. A lot of Cuban music originated from that area.'
'…which is why Cuban bands are so popular there. They just love our music… love what we've done with what we inherited from them.' Pancho completed what I was thinking.

But I could see he was concerned. It was by no means fully organized yet, though in principle we had the job waiting for us.

'What is the problem though?'
'Apart from Clemente, no one else wants to go. As far as they are concerned they'll be working for nothing, for six months and unable to send any money to support their families. We've been there before and the Matecocos are very popular in Bamako, but the guys don't want to go back again because of the money thing.'
'So what are you going to do?'
'I might have to get a different band together, with you, Clemente, and me for a start…just hang around and we'll see what happens.'

A gig at the Eiffel Tower

Nothing happened.
We waited and waited and the weather slowly changed from late summer to autumn into the start of winter.

I found a small jazz club in a basement where a lot of Americans hung out. There was a group of musicians there from New Orleans playing bluesy jazz that was good basic stuff and I asked the leader who played a soprano saxophone if I could join in with my congas and he was okay with that. It was a popular club and often well-known visiting American jazz musicians would drop by, sit in and play a couple of numbers. It kind of reminded me of the old 'Birdland' where I used to play in St Kilda. It had a good vibe to it. There were many American jazz musos in Paris, most of whom had left America to escape the ramifications of segregation or the low esteem given to people of African descent. The French loved jazz and regarded it as an art form so these musical refugees were welcome in Paris. The guy leading this group with whom I played was called Pony (I think) Poindexter, and he was the first person I had ever heard playing Soprano sax. It was a lovely instrument. They were easy to play with, rhythmically quite simple — everything accented on two and four in a straight four count bar — nothing in six/eight or three/four, or complex like guaguanco or other fundamental Cuban rhythm groupings. There was just enough hint of Latinism in their playing of blues to enable the congas to fit as if they belonged there.

(*A couple of years after I returned from Europe I found a 12 inch LP by Poindexter called Gumbo at a record shop in Melbourne. I bought it and found it to be good to listen to a few times as it brought back memories of playing with them but in the end it wasn't all that remarkable. I don't know what happened to it; it kind of disappeared. And I never ever saw another record by him…*)

I played with them for a few days and one night some important people came in and the group was hired for a gig at the Eiffel Tower. Even though I wasn't a part of the group and wasn't being paid they asked: 'Do you want to come along, be a part of the group for the night?' How could I say no to that invitation?

We all know the Eiffel Tower was designed and constructed by Gustave Eiffel for the Paris Exposition in 1889 to demonstrate the ability of iron's strength in large constructions, and what a magnificent example the tower was and still is. What is less remembered is that Gustave also designed and built the interior structure of the Statue of Liberty, a gift from France to the USA.

There are several levels in the Eiffel Tower and on the second level about a third of the way up the tower is a reception centre. This centre was hired by LBJ's (Lyndon Baines Johnson) political party to hold a reception to raise funds for his coming election as President of the USA. He had succeeded President Kennedy after the assassination but had yet to be elected in his own right. It was a huge function with the American Ambassador, embassy officials and every American who was of any importance in France as well as many expatriates and visiting tourists. LBJ may or may not have been there, I didn't know what he looked like. I stayed in the background with the other musicians and no one took any notice of us. At these functions musicians are generally invisible, only there to produce a background ambiance in case people stop talking. No body stopped talking at this function. There were obviously too many potential politicians there. Speeches were made to exuberant applause, lots of champagne and wine and spirits were consumed, and no doubt much money was raised or pledged while the band played and we nevertheless had a wonderful time.

That was the only time I had been up or in the Eiffel Tower. I had walked around the base of it and stared up at its dizzying height, almost 1000 feet, or 300 metres, and marvelled at the intricacy of its structure as seen from below, but only that once was I ever inside it.

What I enjoyed about Paris was travelling about the city and its environs on green painted busses so I could see what the city looked like. I hated travelling anywhere on the Metro unless there was no other way to get where I had to go. It was passing by on a bus that I found Les Halles market where you could buy anything and everything you could imagine in the way of fresh food. This was the first place where I had ever seen such an abundance of different sea foods that I never knew could be eaten. Again this was a huge rusty old iron constructed building that no doubt had seen better days. Was it designed by Gustave? I don't know. Unfortunately it was demolished in 1971 so no one now will ever discover it again.

The bus to Chatelet, the kind of bus I took whenever I went anywhere too far to walk. It had a kind of platform at the rear where you could stand for a better view of wherever you went. I prefered standing there than going inside where it was usually crowded

A crowded street in Paris c1965

Three great movies

Not far from where I was staying was a small movie theatre and sometimes I would while away a bit of time seeing a movie. It was a theatre that showed foreign films, what I suppose back home in Australia would be called an art cinema, only the foreign films it showed here were mostly in English, with French subtitles.

Of all the films I saw there three stand out in my memory for various reasons. The first one I can't remember the name. It was a documentary made up of black and white still shots taken in Cuba before, during, and not long after the Cuban revolution. Some of the shots were sequences and the filmmakers had animated them to fit with the music on the soundtrack. It was a brilliant film and the music soundtrack featured some of the best Cuban music ever recorded to that time. It was narrated in Spanish, which I didn't understand at that stage, with French subtitles, which I couldn't read, but I sat there entranced watching the images and listening to the music. I saw this film several times because it had a long run and there were many expatriate Cubans at each session I attended. Some came out of that theatre crying as the music and photos brought back memories of the homeland they had been forced to leave only five years earlier. I knew that like my father and his friends, they would never stop talking about where they came from, would never forget; it was what made them who they were.

Another film was a black and white movie from Elia Kazan. It was based on the true story of his Uncle who had been forced to leave Turkey as a young man. He was part of the Greek diaspora, of those Greeks who had lived for years in places like Turkey and Armenia who were forced to leave or be killed. Everything was taken from them and millions were ejected from this part of the world. Greece couldn't take them, so they migrated one way or another to other countries in Europe seeking refuge. In the case of Kazan's uncle he managed to find his way to America. It was his dream destination, as it was for millions of other refugees. This film, *America America*, brought tears to my eyes as so much of it was similar to what my own father had experienced. Although he and his compatriots had left twenty or thirty years earlier than the events in this film, they would have had similar experiences. This was the first time I was able to understand something of what my father would have gone through.

I saw many films there but the only other one I can remember was an epic western, *The Magnificent Seven*. I thought it was a recent release but it had been made three years earlier. Perhaps it took a few years to get released in France; films often took a long time to be seen in other countries especially in Australia where they were often two years or more after their original release in the USA.

I loved this film and saw it several times. It had everything going for it, likeable characters who were rugged individuals, even the bad guy, played by Eli Wallach was a likeable person. Yul Brynner was the star, but he was surrounded by young guns who had made names for themselves in TV shows prior to this film so their faces were familiar. Steve McQueen, Charles Bronson, and James Coburn, were outstanding. This film made them famous and started their big screen careers.

Robert Vaughn was a sleazy character as was Brad Dexter and neither of them amounted to much afterwards, although Robert Vaughn managed to reprise his role in a Science Fiction version of this film a couple of years later. As for Horst Buchholz, he over-acted and was rather silly.

Even then Mexico fascinated me. It was just so different, exotic in a subdued way, but their attitude towards life, no matter how hard, was always so positive. I guess it was the positiveness, the joy of being alive that I found attractive.

I didn't know until years later that this film was almost the same as Kurosawa's Seven Samurai, the story of villagers terrorized periodically by bandits, but who are too poor to hire anyone to help them. They give all they have to a Ronin, a masterless Samurai for help. He hires six others mostly with promises rather than anything real to assist and they save the village. In the process a few of them are killed, and of course it would have to be the ones the audience liked the most and didn't want to see killed.

Almost down and out

I was getting low on money and was forced to look for a cheaper hotel. I couldn't afford to buy winter clothes so Pancho lent me an overcoat to wear.

I found a low dive that inside was like being in a cave. The passage leading deep inside had a stale smell like disinfectant covering up a mixture of vomit and piss that had been cleaned up but the smell lingered since there was little ventilation. I was dubious about staying there, but I did want to hang on as long as possible in case Pancho got a band together for the trip to Africa. The cheapest room was somewhere in the bowels of this dark dungeon and it was a small room with no windows. When I shut the door it was pitch-black and there was no way I could tell what time it was. My sleep patterns as a result became erratic. Strangely enough it was quiet without much noise at any time, so there was nothing to give me a hint as to what time of day it was. It was cosy enough to induce me to sleep more than I needed. What else could you do when the weather outside was so cold and miserable?

Once I got up I would lock the room with what few possessions I had and head out to drink coffee, and eat some cheap meals at diners that basically served students. This was the Quartier Latin, the district where historically students resided because it was cheap and close the colleges and the Sorbonne University. I would stay out all day. When the weather turned sleety and freezing I was glad I had the overcoat to keep me warm. I would often pass down and out people huddled in doorways to keep out of the wind. One guy seemed to hang around quite a lot. Sometimes he spread newspapers taken from a rubbish bin over a grate where warm air came up from underground. Periodically the police would round up these vagabonds and take them somewhere for the night. This guy always came back, always claimed the same grating where warm air came up from underground.

Inside my favourite café it was quite warm, too warm to wear an overcoat. People left the coats and jackets on hooks along the wall beside the front entrance, so I did the same. I never thought much about it. I simply did what everyone else did. I had been doing this while reading a book I had found in the street stalls written by George Orwell of 1984 and Animal Farm fame. It was about the time he was a destitute bum in Paris and London before the Spanish civil war. He had been a policeman in Burma but in 1927 he came back to Europe and it was really tough then during the Great Depression. The decade of the 1960s was not a depression. Twenty years or so after the 2nd World War and everything was developing with rebuilding of infrastructure and businesses and life in general. There was work available. But somehow it seemed appropriate that I should immerse myself in Down and Out in Paris and London while I was myself running out of money and living in a place that I thought harboured destitute people. There will always be destitute people about no matter how good things are. I did have some money in the bank in Melbourne, but I didn't want to access that just yet. I had only been in Europe eight months, and I wanted to see if I could actually make a go of it without falling back on savings, which wouldn't last very long anyway.

You could sit for hours in a café or a coffee shop and sip coffee, occasionally ordering a replacement when the waiter started staring at you too much. Coffee didn't cost much, so you could afford to have several spread out over a few hours. Everyone lingered because it was so cold outside and no one wanted to go back out there, but the food in this café, though very good, was too expensive for me.

Whenever I was hungry and I had to go to one of the student diners that reminded me of the food section at an airport. You formed a queue and wandered along a set of Bain Marie keeping food hot, selected what you wanted and then paid for it at the cash register further along. The cheapest meat on offer was horse meat, and I must admit I did eat it sometimes. At the time I didn't realize it was horsemeat or I probably wouldn't have eaten it, being like most of us, subject to the cultural preferences of the place we grew up in: no one eats horse meat in Australia. Tables and benches were long and everyone sat crowded together to eat their meals. It was cheap and cheerful.

After several coffees and with waiters suggesting I should leave because they wanted the table space for diners to use, I took the hint and got up to leave. When I got to the door I couldn't see my overcoat. I searched beneath several coats that were piled up on top of each other completely covering the hooks. A couple of guys watched me perhaps fearful that I was trying to steal something. One of them stood up and stared menacingly at me. I shrugged and spread my arms as if to say it's not there. The coat wasn't there. Someone had either taken it by mistake or deliberately stolen it.

There was no other coat there that even looked vaguely like it, so I had to conclude it had been stolen. Fuck! What was I going to say to Pancho?

I stared out through the glass door of the café and saw rain being ripped along the street by what would be a very cold gusty wind. The canvas cover that hardly protected the empty outdoor area flapped and rippled as if having a fit. Food forgotten, I slipped out the door and ran along the footpath, blown along by the wind. Fortunately this section of the street had a number of short verandas overhanging the footpath so I didn't get too wet. I buzzed the doorbell and Pancho let me in.

I hadn't seen him for a few days and there were boxes packed and stacked on his dining room table.

'We're going to Spain,' he said the moment I walked in. 'I've got a job singing with a band in Barcelona.'

'So Africa is off?'

'I make a little in royalties from the songs I've composed but that's not enough to live on or to pay the rent here. This was a good job offered to me by a friend. I couldn't say no.'

I understood. 'When are you leaving?'

'Tomorrow.'

Pancho's wife came in, took one look at me and said, 'You're wet. Come into the bathroom and dry off.'

'Thanks, but I have to tell you that someone stole the overcoat, while I was in the coffee shop. When I went to leave about half an hour ago it wasn't there.'

'Don't worry about it,' Pancho said.

'I'll replace it as soon as I ...'

'I've got other coats. It's all right.'

'You'll need another jacket or something,' his wife said. She disappeared and shortly came back with an old woollen jacket like a short duffel coat. 'We were going to leave it here because there is no more room in the suitcases. You might as well have it.'

I didn't know what to say.

'Come on, let's get you dried off.'

I stayed about half an hour there.

I didn't want to stay any longer because they were busy and I also felt bad about the overcoat. The longer I stayed the worse I felt. Finally after Pancho gave me an address in Barcelona where to contact him I wished them all the best and took my leave.

I had been in Paris for five months. And that was long enough I finally decided. I would head across to London and see if I could get some work. At least I would be able to work there.

The next morning I headed for the Metro which would take me to the main station where I could catch a train to Calais and then the ferry across the English Channel, to connect with another train to London. Carrying my two drums stuffed with whatever I had, I saw that bum who hung around near my hole of a hotel curled up in a miserable heap in a doorway. He was wearing the coat that Pancho had lent me. It was the only thing on him that looked reasonably clean.

'You bastard,' I mumbled, and was about to put the drums down and take the coat off him, but he looked so pathetic, a grimy figure shivering in the doorway. Was he shivering with the cold or was he cringing with aprehension because he thought I might do something horrible to him for having stolen my coat?

He looked at me and he knew that I knew he had stolen my coat.

But then I thought 'what the hell was I going to do with that coat now anyway?'

'You need the coat more than I do,' I said in English which he probably didn't understand, 'Keep it.'

And I walked on by.

Finding my way in London

London was cold, with wet sleet lashing streets when I got there. I found a temporary place near Earle's Court, familiar because it was full of Aussies. I went to an employment agency and the first job I got was at the BBC studios stripping paint off sets that had be repainted for a new show in production. I had no idea what the show was. There were three of us doing this and we just did what we were told.

I would get up early in the morning make a coffee in the bed sitter I had rented for a week, go out and descend into the underground tunnels where trains ran all across and around London. They were always packed with passengers who ignored each other, often staring blankly through windows at dark walls flashing past in a blur, if they weren't reading a newspaper. If you weren't careful, staring at those blurred walls would put you to sleep. Those apparently somnambulant passengers always managed to wake up when they had to get off, to be replaced by others who immediately went into temporary hibernation for the duration of their journey. What a way to get around!

I hated the underground. You never knew where you were and if you came up somewhere the surrounds looked almost the same as those where you went down to catch the train. I could have travelled for an hour across London only to emerge in place that looked virtually the same as where I was before. I had no idea of how the city looked or how it changed from suburb to suburb, so after a couple of days using the Underground I started using the double decker busses to get around. They were much slower and often caught in traffic jams, but I did get to see the city and did get an idea of how enormous London was and how it was laid out. I could after a few days of surface travelling orient myself quite well.

My next job was as a kitchen hand in a popular restaurant in Notting Hill. It was only 4 hours a night and the wages were paltry but I didn't care. I got a free dinner, nothing expensive, but filling none the less. My main activity was preparing small salads, chopping onions, peeling potatoes, and slicing beef fillets into individual serves for one of the main courses. The beef was imported from Yugoslavia.

I could have this job as long as I wanted, so I was happy with that. If there was anything that had been prepared earlier left over at the end of the night, the staff could take it home rather than throw it out. As a consequence the girls who were waitresses and the kitchen staff always had something to take home to eat the next day.

I had started midweek, and as Friday came one of the girls who worked the front came back and told us she and her friends (who incidentally all lived in the same building, a couple of blocks away from the restaurant) were having a party on Saturday night after they finished. We were welcome to come along. I was happy to accept the invitation. I didn't know anyone else in London apart from those who worked in this restaurant, and going to a party would be infinitely better than spending the night in crappy bed sitter.

When we left the restaurant the night of the party, carrying our leftovers to be used for snacks at the party, we discovered the temperature had dropped and it was gently snowing. I had never been in a place where it snowed and it was a beautiful sight. The street and all the cars parked in it were covered with a light dusting that looked like icing sugar. The streetlights were haloed with rainbow rims, but the weird thing for me was the silence. Notting Hill was normally quite noisy, even at night; being an extroverted suburb with may Caribbean island inhabitants. This night what sound there was seemed distant and heavily muffled. Even our footsteps as we walked along couldn't be heard. Snowflakes drifted down in slow motion and there was not a breath of wind. By the time we reached the boarding house where the girls lived everything was covered completely by a layer of fine snow at least two centimetres thick.

All the houses in this street were old three and four story Victorian residences that had been converted into boarding houses. Rooms were rented out as bed-sitters and each room, just like the place I was staying in, had a small wash basin or sink, a few chairs, a table, a lounge chair, and a couple of standard beds. Bathrooms and toilets were at the end of the hall on each floor. There were three floors in this building. Each room had a heater but you had to feed shilling coins into a meter to get electricity to make it work. Except for one single room, most of the rooms on the first and second floors were shared with two girls in each.

Some of the rooms were larger than others and it was in one of the larger shared rooms that the party was held.

It was well under way when we arrived a bit before midnight and quite noisy. The noise didn't matter since everyone in the building plus boy friends were at the party. Only girls rented rooms in this building and none of them were Australian. They were Irish, Scottish, and English girls from other parts outside of London, all working at low paid jobs, all trying to make a life for themselves.

The food we brought plus some unfinished bottles of wine from the restaurant were put on the table in the kitchen area to be shared with all the other stuff already there. There was cold beer in the fridge (thank God!) and plenty of wine and spirits. The latest rock music filled the room making everyone talk loud to be heard over it. Some couples were dancing, but most stood or sat around, with a drink in one hand chatting to each other. The lighting was dim so there were dark areas where a few couples were cuddled together.

By two in the morning we were all in pairs in various states of inebriation, kissing, cuddling, and generally trying to be seductive. I had drank just enough alcohol for my inhibitions to have disappeared and when the Irish girl wrapped around me suggested we go into her room, the one next door to this one, I didn't think twice about it.

We slipped out into a very cold corridor and she unlocked her door which was only a few feet along the passage from the other room. Inside her room we could still hear the party but it was muffled. The room however was quite cold.

'Ah shit,' she said once inside. 'I forgot to put money into the meter.'

You had to pay for electricity and for gas as you used it. Each system was metered separately for each bed-sitter room and you had to feed shillings into it so you could switch on the power or the gas. If you weren't in the room no power was consumed. If you were there, you needed to feed the meter in order to have power supplied. One shilling gave approximately one hour. The owners of the building emptied the meters when they got their overall service bills. And I have no doubt that they made a tidy profit on the consumption as well.

'I've got some coins,' I said. I found several shillings and fed them into the meter, and almost immediately the three bar electric heater came on throwing a dim glow through the room. It would take a while to warm up though.

Shortly after that we found ourselves wrapped in a doona on a big couch, continuing on from where we left off and in our semi drunken state we found ourselves having intercourse before we quite knew what was happening. It was all over too quick, even though it didn't seem too bad.

'I need a toilet break' she said.

'Yeah, me too.'

We found the toilet down the hall, used it, and quickly went back to the room.

'You should stay tonight; it's too late to go home now.'

It must have been about 4 am, and going out into the snow covered streets to find my way to the underground station to get a train back to Earle's Court was the last thing on my mind. We quickly snuggled into her bed and pulled the doona up over us. Just before falling asleep I heard some muffled laughter as the door opened, and then the other girl who stayed in this bed-sitter shushed her partner, whispering 'Don't make so much noise.' The two of them climbed into her bed on the other side of the room and I heard nothing after that since I fell asleep.

I woke in the morning with an erection and it didn't take much to convince my partner to have sex again. This time it lasted much longer but we had to be quiet about it so not to wake up the other couple in the other bed.

She was up and wearing a dressing gown when the other couple started to wake up. I was still covered by the doona. The room was quite cold. The heater had gone off during the night, since the electricity had cut off.

'I've got to take a shower and get ready for work,' she told me. She didn't work at the restaurant but in an office near the underground station. 'Will you come back tonight?'

What a crazy question. Of course I would come back. What red-blooded male wouldn't?

'Good. Boil the kettle and we'll have a cup of tea when I come back from my shower.'

She nudged her friend in the other bed and told her to wake up. She also had to go to work unlike the indolent males who had occupied their beds for the night.

I got up, got dressed, and put the kettle on. We shared a cup of tea and some toast with the other couple. I had to put some more coins in the meter for the power to boil the kettle and make the toast. Putting coins into a meter for electricity took a bit of getting used to at first, but after a while I thought nothing of it. It was the way things were done. You simply had to make sure you had lots of coins for the various meters.

'Lock the door behind you,' she called when she left.

After that I had a shower down the hall, and when I came back the other couple were leaving. I made sure the door was shut and left to go back to my place for a change of clothes. I went out and found the way to Buckingham Palace to watch the changing of the guard, so I could say I had seen it, not for any other reason. I watched barges along the Thames, listened to Big Ben chiming the hour and went to the museum of natural history.

At work that night I was ribbed by the waitress who lived in the room where the party had been. 'You did alright for yourself,' she teased.

I just nodded to acknowledge her statement.

'…You coming back tonight for seconds?'

'Of course, who wouldn't?'

'All you men are the same,' she laughed as she grabbed an order to take out to the tables. 'That's all you think about.'

'I don't suppose you mind either,' I said.

'I'm not telling…' she said before disappearing through the flapping door leaving me to continue chopping onions.

A few seconds later she was back to collect another order. 'Make sure you wash your hands properly after those onions,' she said with a chuckle. 'I wouldn't want you to put onion juice in places it shouldn't go.'

I stayed there for three weeks, going back each night after work at the restaurant.

I had collected my stuff from where I originally stayed and took it to the flat where the girls were. I didn't have a key, but went back with the waitresses after work so there was no problem getting in. I would also bring back some offcuts of meat, potatoes, carrots, and any other fresh vegetables that may have been left over at the end of the evening cooking shift. This was my contribution to the girls so they always had stuff to cook for lunches or for the nights they weren't working.

I had no plans to move on or do anything specific, but simply went along with whatever was happening. Everywhere in London was like this as far as I could tell: parties all the time, people having sex with everyone and anyone. There was a sensation of freedom that pervaded the mind, with no parents to tell you what to do, inhibitions were quite loose.

One night I turned up but couldn't get into any of the rooms. It seemed that everyone was somewhere else. I sat in the hall on the top of the steps to the first floor and waited. It was cold there, and it got colder and colder the longer I waited. About two am the Scottish girl who lived in the small room by herself came back. She saw me there and smiled.

'Everyone went to a party. Didn't you know about it?'

'I had no idea. Are they coming back soon?'

'Probably not. It looked like one of those all-nighters to me.'

'You were there?'

'I was, but I didn't like the crowd.'

I wondered whether it was worth going somewhere to find a place to have a hot drink. It was too cold to sit on the steps in the hallway all night.

'Well, are you coming in or not?' the girl asked as she stood by her open door. 'It's too cold to stay out here.'

I jumped up and followed her into her room. It was small and cosy and most of it was occupied by the three quarter size bed. There was a big doona on top. Although the heater wasn't on, the room was warm compared to the hall outside.

'We can keep each other warm. But remember, no hanky-panky, all right?'

'That's fine by me.' I was tired, and she looked exhausted anyway.

After undressing down to our underwear we climbed into bed, and in no time it was as warm as toast under the huge doona. We both fell asleep before any thoughts about anything could cross our minds.

She was awake bright and early, and already dressed nudged me in the ribs.

'Come on, get up. I have to go to work and you can't stay here.'

'Sorry,' I mumbled and climbed out of bed. I quickly dressed and went down the hall to the toilet. When I got back she was gone, but I could hear the girls in the room I usually stayed in wandering about and talking. I knocked on the door and went in.

'Where were you all night?' my girlfriend asked. 'You weren't here when we got back and I was worried.'

Yeah, right…

'I thought you'd be waiting…'

'What time did you get back?'
'About three, or a bit after.'
'I found somewhere to sleep that was warm.' I said and left it at that.

She looked suspiciously at me for a moment, then blinked a couple of times as if to clear her eyes, and her head, and then said, 'I can't stop and chat, I've got to get ready for work.'

We were all in our early twenties, and seemed to have boundless energy. We had no problems with managing only a few hours of sleep each night in between working and partying, but this could only go on for so long.

About three weeks later she told me she had to go back to Ireland in a couple of days. I was a bit shocked. I had gotten used to our arrangement…took advantage of it, I suppose. She didn't give any reason for going, only that she had to.

When she left I decided I had had enough of London and promptly went back to Germany for a good rest.

A cognac drinking competition

There was more snow in Backnang than there had been in London, but somehow it didn't seem as cold. I had hardly been back two days when Theo who lived upstairs and had married Fred's cousin told me we were going to a special party that night. It was to be at a friend's house just out of town. Fred and Theo had both gone to school with this friend whose job was a stone cutter. He made tombstones for the local cemetery.

The stone cutter was happy to meet me and made me welcome with a beer thrust into my hand the moment I walked in the front door. I was introduced around and everyone was told I was *aus Astralien*, from Australia. It seemed everyone knew Fred, they had all gone to school with him. I should have been suspicious when they all talked about how good Australians were at drinking, but my limited understanding of German, or Swabish, a dialect which most of them spoke, along with their attempts at speaking English that was undecipherable, went over my head.

A glass of cognac was thrust into my hand and the host stood in front of me with a similar glass. *'Skål'* he said as he raised his glass of cognac and gulped the contents down.

Not wanting to be impolite I did the same. *'Skål,'* I said and gulped the cognac down, which I then followed with a sip of beer. It was pretty rough cognac.

Some people watching started joking and laughing.

Suddenly the host reached forward with more cognac in a bottle and filled my glass again. He also topped his up, raised it again and said *'Skål.'* He obviously expected me to do the same, so I did. We both drank at the same instant. Then he filled our glasses again. I suddenly realised something was up and looked around. Everyone was watching us without trying to be seen watching. It was quite funny.

Theo came over and told me to drink it. It was a competition.

'A competition about what?'

'It's a cognac drinking competition. I told them Australians were good drinkers. Now you have to prove it.'

'You are fucking insane,' I told him and quickly downed the cognac.

The host did the same and everyone watching cheered. They were all drinking and were quite boisterous. I had no choice as the host was overly enthusiastic and we were both being encouraged by the others there who thought it was all a great joke.

In no time a whole bottle of cognac was emptied and a refill was called for. By this time the host was almost falling over himself. I must admit I was not too steady either but I had learned how to drink in Darwin and had been to many parties over the years honing my skills. I was sure I could at least keep up with whatever the stone cutter was capable of consuming.

The rest of the guests had stopped doing whatever they were doing and had formed a circle around us to watch us downing glass after glass of cognac with each followed by a sip of cold beer.

We were almost half way through the second bottle when the host yelled something and his wife rushed in with a bucket into which he promptly vomited.

I backed away from the smell. Everyone was laughing and cheering. Theo clapped me on the back. 'You won,' he said. The host disappeared into another room and I could hear him retching. Guests stood around not knowing what to do next.

'The party is over,' Theo said. 'We should be going.'

I was okay with that. I didn't actually feel too bad… a bit dizzy perhaps, but still capable of walking without wobbling. I certainly couldn't have drunk any more anyway. One more glass and the host would have won. Theo called out to Ilse his wife (Fred's cousin) as he led me to the front door. The host's wife was nowhere around, so I didn't get to say goodbye.

Outside the temperature must have been ten below zero and the icy contrast from the hot interior of the house where people had shirt sleeves rolled up, was like being smashed in the head with a hammer. The snow on either side of the path from the front door to the street where the car was parked was at least a metre high. And suddenly I had to vomit. There was no way I could keep any of that rough cognac down. I leaned over and it sprayed out into the snow beside the footpath, instantly burning a hole through it all the way to the ground. I retched and coughed until there was nothing left inside to come out, and still I could feel my stomach heaving. When I had finished and we had walked to the car Ilse came out and joined us and we went home.

I drank heaps of water when we got back to the house in Backnang, vomited once again to clean out my stomach and went to sleep.

The next morning I woke refreshed and after breakfast Theo and Ilse took me to a nearby lake where there were picnic areas and a running track for joggers, and who should we see trying to jog around this frozen lake but our stone cutter host.

Apparently he went jogging here every morning no matter what. He looked terrible, pale and quite sick. When he saw us he stopped and greeted us cheerfully enough considering how hung over he was. He congratulated me for winning, said he couldn't understand how I could look so good after drinking so much, and finally admitted that Australians were very good drinkers.

It was nothing to be proud of, that's for sure. I think Theo wanted him to see how good I was just to rub it in, to make him feel bad about losing; that's probably the only reason he wanted to bring me to this particular lake the morning after.

'I think we should go back,' I told Theo who was surprised I didn't want to stay longer. 'It's too cold out here,' I added.

He nodded as if he understood and we left the stone cutter to his misery as he struggled to clear his system by staggering around a frozen lake sucking in air cold enough to bite holes in your lungs.

Theo and his wife Ilse heading home after the cognac drinking affair.

Having fun in the snow with a small sled sliding down a hill not far out of Backnang. Below is Fred's Dad with Fred's cousin's daughter about to slide down the hill. (Images from a 16mm movie January 1965).

Frolicking in the early snow in the street in front of the house in Im Benzwasen where I stayed. It was fun for a few days until the snow began to pile up and we had to shovel it out of the pathway to the house and from the footpath in front of the house. Once everything is covered with a metre of snow it stops being fun.

Trains and more trains and the smell of fresh bread

I read in my travel book *Europe on $10 a day* about *La Semana Santa* (the religious week) in Spain and how it was celebrated throughout the country with festivals (*Ferias*) just before the week of Easter, and with more festivals and bullfights immediately after. And that of all the *ferias* in Spain at this time the one in *Sevilla* was the biggest, the best; the one you had to be there for... This was what made me want to go there. That as well as having worked with the Los Matecocos for a short period gave me the desire to learn Spanish to improve my understanding of the music and culture. Going to Spain would help me with the language, or so I thought.

I found a book written of all people by Leslie Charteris, the creator of *The Saint* novels, on how to learn Spanish. He claimed to speak about 16 or 17 languages and had devised a simple system to quickly learn any European language. Since he loved Spanish he wrote the book about learning this language, but his method of studying, he claimed, could be applied to any language. He was actually Anglo Chinese so he probably spoke two languages from early childhood, and obviously had no trouble learning others.

Being halfway through February (1965) it was too cold in Germany for me anyway, and I hated shovelling snow off footpaths in front of the house, or walking down a street and suddenly having snow slide off a roof on top of you. As a contrast Southern Spain seemed like a good idea. It was already spring down there. It would be weeks at least before spring arrived in Germany after which there would be weeks of slush as the snow melted. Not something to look forward to, so I packed some clothes into two conga drums and went to Spain.

Europe is small and could easily fit into Australia a couple of times and there would still be room left over, but nevertheless it took, as far as I can remember, two or three days of non-stop travelling to get to Seville. I had taken the train to Stuttgart where I purchased a ticket to

Sevilla. (Seville) The train I had to take was the one going to Paris. But this time all I did was get off in Gar du Nord, transit over to Gare de l'est where I took the train to Madrid. This travelled all day south across France and over into Spain. It arrived in Madrid about ten pm at Estacion de Atocha, and to get to Seville I had to find my way to the other main station, Estacion de Las Delicias.

I got there by using the oldest and most dilapidated metro you could imagine. It rattled along dark tunnels sounding as though it would fall apart at any moment. It was packed with people out for the night and looking for a good time. Someone was kind enough to tell me when I got to the stop I needed for Estacion de Las Delicias, so I could go up for the train to Sevilla.

By this time I was exhausted from lugging my two drums around, constantly travelling, and not having time to find something proper to eat. I hadn't eaten anything since Stuttgart and there was no time between arriving in Madrid at one station before having to find the other where the train to Seville departed. I just made it. This was overnight to Seville so fortunately I could sleep without being woken up because there were no more borders to cross with customs officials wanting to examine papers and passports.

But when I arrived at 6am and exited the station the first thing that greeted me was the aroma of freshly baked bread and there was no way I could resist buying some. I was ravenous.

I came out of the station into a small plaza from which a number of narrow streets led the way into the older parts as well as the newer developments of the city. In one of the streets there were narrow footpaths no wider than half a metre on each side of the cobbled pavement. This was too narrow for a car and must have been for foot traffic or at least someone on a horse. Barred windows and deep-set doors lined both sides of the street.

In the middle of the street was a man wearing a baker's beret coming slowly towards me while pulling along a three wheeled hand cart from where the delicious smell of the fresh bread emanated. He called out, '*Pan Fresco, Pan Fresco,*' in a melodious voice that echoed along the street. Fresh Bread!

It was so early in the morning that the sun had hardly risen, and most of this little street was in shadow, yet the light coloured walls were beginning to glow with tinges of sunlight that I could see at the end of the street behind the bread vendor. I was hungry, having not eaten since the day before. The delicious aroma made me salivate.

A door opened and a woman peered out. She bought some bread which the vendor placed in a brown paper bag and passed to her. By the time he had finished dealing with her I had reached him and said in my textbook speaking slow Spanish '*Yo quiero comprar un pedazo de pan, por favor.*'

He smiled encouragingly at my lousy pronunciation, and opened the lid to expose heaps of short chunky firm-crusted bread loaves each of which had a light dusting of flour over them. To describe them today I would say they had the rustic appearance of *ciabatta* crossed with *pane di casa,* but I had no idea of those names then, and those are Italian, not Spanish. The aroma that wafted over me almost made me faint. It was fantastic.

I had changed some money while transiting in Madrid and could pay with a small note. He happily gave me change, and passed one short loaf with a piece of butcher's paper rolled around it. He then continued out into the plaza heading for the next narrow street where he quickly vanished. I could still hear his voice calling out, '*Pan Fresco…*'

I ripped into it with the desperation of a starving man.

It was the most delicious bread I had ever eaten. Nobody made bread like that back home! In fact it was claimed that no one anywhere in Europe made bread like they make in Spain. I won't dispute that ever; in my memory it was the best bread I had ever eaten.

La Feria de Sevilla

It was a month before the Feria began and already tourists were arriving in search of good accommodation. Once closer to the event hotel room prices would skyrocket because there were always more people in town than could be accommodated. I found a small hotel in an old part of town following the guide book I always carried with me, Europe on $10 a day.

I stayed a couple of days there until I found a small Pension in one of the winding little streets that were for foot traffic only. They had one room left, right on top of the roof and I took it. It was the only room on the roof and was like a small shed that had been converted into a bedroom. The only other stuff up here was a clothes line where the maids or the owners hung washing. I had an uninterrupted view across the twisted narrow streets of the oldest part of the city.

This was an ancient city, a city that had accommodated invaders from Morocco for centuries. It had been one of the main centres of the Muslim world in Spain. Many of the older buildings epitomized the style of construction found in Northern Africa. The pensión I stayed in was typical with a closed façade facing the street; barred windows protecting a barely visible (from the street outside) small courtyard in the centre of which grew an ancient orange tree. There were stone benches tiled in tiny mosaic patterns to sit on beside wrought iron tables painted brilliant white. Vines and creepers hung from the walls facing into the courtyard to shroud the windows of the ground floor where the reception was. The smell of Jasmine permeated the air with a delicate hint of its existence. I paid for a month and a half in advance so I wouldn't have to worry about accommodation.

Impressions: The tower of Gold, *Torre de Oro*, where the records of the *Conquistadores* are held, the place from which they left on their expeditions to the new world and returned with ships full of gold artworks that though irreplaceable and truly priceless, were melted down for the royal family and the nobles of the court in Madrid wasn't as big as I thought it would be, but it certainly looked 1000 years old…

A Cos lettuce I bought which was elegantly prepared for me into a salad with a dressing where oranges replaced lemons in the dressing… beautiful full bodied coffee, better than anything served to me in Germany or France…or was that because the ambiente of *Sevilla* was so much more interesting and exotic than other places I had been so far that it imbued the coffee with something in my mind to make it distinct?

Guitars…everywhere you went there were great flamenco guitarists playing in bars, clubs, streets, plazas always with a fascinated group around them clapping in time while some girls danced sexy rumbas or young guys with super exaggerated postures showing the profundity of their dance steps…and if you were lucky you could stumble into a bar and hear a renowned singer with serious guitarists singing the *Cante-jondo*, the deep song that more than anything else epitomizes the character of Flamenco. The husky broken voice would send shivers up your spine as the singer's emotion and feeling poured out sounding more Moorish than Spanish. My sister Zara would have been fascinated with this as she had also studied flamenco dancing and was good enough at one point to do floor shows with two flamenco guitarists at the Spanish club in Melbourne. She would have been enraptured with this profound singing and with the intense way the guitarists attacked their instruments. I kept expecting the guitar stings to snap with force of their playing. …there were also bad guitarists awkwardly strumming, wannabe flamenco guitarists, and students who were studying both classical and flamenco guitar.

You couldn't escape the music; it permeated the atmosphere and anyone and everyone was a musician of some kind. It was in the blood of the people here.

One night while sitting on the steps in front of an old building with a couple of Americans trying to impress several other drunk foreigners from the colder parts of Europe with their guitar playing, two immaculately dressed gentlemen strolled by.

It was some time after midnight and these gentlemen were discussing something quite animatedly when one of them turned and looked at us and in particular the guy playing the guitar. He said something to the other man and they both came over. 'May I borrow your guitar for a moment' he asked the guitar player in perfect but slightly accented English, 'I need to show my friend something.'

'Sure' the player said and offered his guitar.

The man sat down and tested each string, adjusted one because it was slightly off, and then said something to his friend in Spanish which I didn't understand.

He started to play a part of the *Concierto de Aranjuez*, and his playing was absolutely beautiful. It was the slow solo part in which the guitar is featured as the lead instrument.

Now here was someone who could really play! He made whatever we had heard earlier that night seem fumbling and amateurish. When he finished that slow piece he said something again in Spanish and then did something I had never heard before or since that moment. He took the same slow piece and played it as if it was interpreted by a flamenco guitarist. You could recognize the melodic construction of the slow movement from the concierto but it was as authentically flamenco as anything else that I had heard in *Sevilla*.

We sat there stunned. I'm sure if someone had taken a photo of us it would show eyes wide, mouths open and perhaps even tongues hanging out like you see in cartoons depicting absolute astonishment.

When he finished playing, he thanked the player for lending him the guitar, handed it back and stood up. He then strolled off chatting animatedly with his friend, leaving us staring after him still in shock over what we had seen and heard. Someone mentioned a bit later that he was a professor of Music at the University, or something like that.

Horses, beautifully groomed until they gleamed, ridden by immaculately dressed riders with sometimes a female companion sitting behind them side saddle, clopped along streets where no cars were allowed or which were too narrow for anything other than people walking… Masses of people thronging and flowing along the old narrow streets in the ancient heart of the city… A steady stream of heavily decorated wagons, often pulled by two horses and full of country folk, gypsies and farmers arriving for the party of the year *La Feria de Sevilla* and *La Semana Santa*. Hundreds of these wagons were constantly arriving for the two weeks prior to the commencement of festivities.

Camps were being set up around the outskirts of the city. Huge tents for parties and receptions grew along main boulevards and in city parks where businesses and barrios sponsored groups of dancers who day and night rehearsed the *Sevillianas* that were the region's most characteristic dance in preparation for competition during the festival. There were hundreds of small bars scattered throughout the city with a never ending selection of *tapas* to accompany the wine and beer sold. These tiny plates of food were served with each glass of wine so people didn't get too drunk. Yet even so a dedicated drinker would always manage to finish up drunk.

I had never seen or heard of *tapas* until arriving in Seville. (Now the whole world knows about them.) It seemed each bar had its own specialty and I managed along with other foreigners I met at this time to survive for almost the whole time in Seville without having to buy a meal at night. We simply went from bar to bar eating a wide variety of small plates with one morsel of food with each drink, which were as far as I can remember given free with each drink bought. …and during the day there was junk food like *churros*, which were a million times better than doughnuts, barbecued meats on skewers, *chorizos*, sausages spiced with hot sweet-chili, free food at popular pavilions, and always music and dancing, and parades of young men and women, boys and girls dressed in their finest clothes parading the streets and plazas on horseback. No doubt marriages were arranged and engagements sealed.

I even had a wine skin which I would hold up high and squirt red wine (*rioja*) into my mouth. Some people couldn't do this without spraying it all over themselves, especially when they were a bit drunk. The secret was to start close to the mouth then gradually move the skin bag away increasing the squeeze to maintain the steady stream of wine, and when you were finished, to turn the nozzle up and stop squeezing at the same time. This cut off the stream and sucked a bit of air back into the skin bag without losing a drop. Once you get the knack, you never lose it, but the first few attempts can be messy, with wine in your eyes, hair, all over the face and down the front of your shirt… but who cared? It was fun learning,

Any idea of learning Spanish vanished, simply because there were so many foreigners in town it was inevitable that I spent a lot of time drinking and partying with them and mostly talking in English. Being lazy, if I needed to ask for something in Spanish, there was always someone amongst us who was fluent enough to do it for me. We stayed up day and night catching a few hours of sleep at odd moments, sometimes in a park, or sometimes I went back to my room for a shower and a change of clothes as well as a short sleep.

I remember one night after a particularly boisterous party I found myself accompanying an American woman back to her boarding house. I thought in my drunken stupor that I was being gentlemanly but she obviously saw this as an invitation, or perhaps she had invited me and I misinterpreted her motives, after all we were all drunk or semi-sober as I preferred to think. The street was a side street and there were fewer people here than just around the corner in one of the bigger brighter streets.

The moment we got to the door she came on so strong it terrified me with its unexpectedness. She wrapped herself around me and slobbered wet drunken kisses all over my face. Her hands started wandering and I found nothing sexy at all about this sudden attack. I know other guys would have envied me this situation and taken advantage of it. I was as red-blooded as any of them, but I had never encountered a woman as ferociously desperate as this one. I had no idea what to do. I was not in the least aroused and in fact all I felt was revulsion.

I couldn't get away quick enough. I disentangled myself while she rummaged in her purse for her front door key. These little boarding houses and pensions always locked their barred front doors at night and residents were supplied with a key to let themselves in, She couldn't find her key and while she cursed and snarled with frustration I slipped away and walked off as fast as I could manage. I went back to my pension and took a long shower after which I slept away what was left of the night.

Perhaps subconsciously the reason I wanted to go to Sevilla was to see if the *Feria* was anything like what was depicted in the film *The Sun Also Rises* which was Errol Flynn's last appearance in a film. Ava Gardner, Tyrone Power and Mel Ferrar also starred in this film. I had seen this film at the Regent Cinema in Collins Street probably about 1960. I was fascinated by the running of the bulls through the streets of Pamplona, the scenes of the *Corrida*, the spectacular colour, the flamenco guitar background and the whole idea of an endless party.

The book I had not read, but it was Hemingway's first novel and had been adopted by the beat generation almost as if it were The Bible. Probably half of the foreigners in Spain during the early 1960s were trying to find something that never existed except in the mind of Hemingway as he depicted his story in his novel which may have been called *Fiesta* before it became known as *The Sun Also Rises*. But thinking back in hindsight it may well have been the catalyst that induced me to go to *Sevilla*. It never occurred to me to go to Pamplona.

Finally as the actual week of *Semana Santa* arrived the party seemed to quieten down. The drinking didn't stop, it simply became less boisterous. There were more people in town than seemed possible. The narrow streets were so crowded you could barely move along them, and then when the huge floats that represented each of the twelve districts of *Sevilla* started to make their way through the streets to the Great Cathedral where they would be blessed before returning to their particular church, it was a bone crunching exercise trying to go anywhere.

These giant floats were made of wood and were highly decorated, each one depicting in superb life-size detail one of The Stations of Christ as he carried the cross he was to be crucified upon through streets of Bethlehem. Many of them also had angelic but elaborate statues of The Virgin Mary, surrounded by hundreds of burning candles. Each float was borne aloft on the backs of fifty to one hundred men who lifted it up onto their shoulders and shuffled slowly along the street. They would perhaps get a hundred metres before having to lower it down for a rest or to change the person underneath who would carry it. There were literally hundreds of men willing to do this following along behind each giant float. Ahead of the float the procession was led by acolytes and *penitentes* wearing mostly white robes with long pointed caps, each carrying a very long burning candle. Following along immediately behind were more *penitentes* carrying crosses some of which were purely symbolic, and light weight, but there were some who carried very heavy crosses. Each float and those attending it were also surrounded by onlookers packed into the narrow streets who ran before, or followed after their favourite float. It would take all day for the float to travel from its district church along the winding streets to the plaza in front of the Great Cathedral of *Sevilla* — once a mosque before the reconquest of Spain by the Christians with its huge tower, the *Giralda*, a brilliant example of Moorish architecture, looming high above it, and from which the faithful were once called to prayer — where it could finally enter the massive cathedral to be blessed. And then there would be the same amount of time needed for the return journey to its original location where it would remain until the next year's *Semana Santa*.

A typical float depicting one of the 'Stations of The Cross'. All the sculptures are beautifully delineated and painted so they appear completely lifelike.

Detail from the same float showing the sculpture from a different angle.

One of the many narrow streets through which the penitentes and the floats travelled on their way to the cathedral. These penitentes are waiting for their float to enter the narrow street.

– *Ephemeron* –

Penitentes, each carrying a cross filled the narrow streets in front and behind each float.

Fragments from my Life – with Science Fiction

All day and on into the night for a whole week the floats slowly moved from their barrio to the cathedral in the centre of Sevilla and then returned after being blessed. At night they were festooned with lit candles burning bright.

What kept the float carriers going was faith, and heaps of red wine passed to them by many attendants who themselves were waiting their turn at carrying. There were no toilet breaks and if you had to piss you did it beneath the float where onlookers couldn't see you. Every time a float was put down for the men to rest or change places thin streams of piss trickled out from underneath the float.

It took the whole week for all the floats to travel their course, after which the town lit up with even more of a party atmosphere. Dance competitions took place everywhere and often the females provocatively flirted with their male partners to the great enjoyment of each other and the many people watching and applauding. This was the only opportunity young people had to meet and size each other up, as very little contact was allowed any other time.

The bull fights commenced with top matadors competing in the ring. I didn't want to see an actual bullfight for two reasons: I couldn't afford the tickets, and I didn't want to see how the bull was tortured to make it crazy as well as weak enough to allow the matador to kill it. It wasn't fair.

The bull always loses and the matador is glorified. If it was just the bull and the one man, without the others on horseback stabbing it with lances to cut muscles, opening a cut in the top of the neck for the matador's sword, making it bleed with its furious heart pumping half its blood out onto the hot sand, then I might have gone to see it. But when it is made easy for the matador giving him time to show off with his cape, then the contest is uneven. The only good thing is that sometimes the bull gets the matador who is taken off to hospital, but even then the bull is summarily shot and dragged out of the ring.

This was definitely not something I wanted to see.

The party fizzled out and the tourists all departed leaving the mess created over the three weeks for the locals to clean up. The street when my pension was located had layers of wax covering it which had to be scraped up with men using flat shovels. I have no idea what they did with all the wax recovered. It went into containers and was taken away. It probably got melted down and purified to reuse for more candles. It hardly seems like something they would throw away.

I never used my drums; there was nowhere I could have fitted in with them, no music that they could have blended with, at least not in *Sevilla*, so I decided to send them back to Germany where they could stay with the rest of my stuff at Fred's parent's house. Shipping them by train used up most of what money I had left so I figured I would head down to the coast to Malaga then hitchhike or take local busses on short hops along the coast north to France and on into Germany.

The weather was good and hitchhiking didn't have the bad reputation it garnered some years later.

Along the Mediterranean coast

I had only walked a short distance along the highway out of Sevilla when a blue dilapidated van pulled up and the driver offered me a lift.

'*A donde vas?*'

I Shrugged to say I don't know. '*Torremolinos,*' I said, not really caring. This was a tourist resort a bit south of *Malaga*.

The driver pushed the door open saying '*Yo voy a Malaga.*'

''*ta bien…*' I said, which was about the limit of my Spanish apart from *Gracias* thank you, good morning, afternoon, evening, and bits like that. Still with a few broken words of English from him and an equal amount of broken Spanish from me, and lots of gesturing, we managed to entertain ourselves on the long winding road that after crossing a broad plain worked its way through mountains to emerge finally after two hundred or so kilometres into the outskirts of Malaga.

'*Buena suerte,*' were his final words as he drove off and left me near the middle of the city.

I didn't stay in Malaga very long. Just long enough to get lunch and find a bus depot where busses left to go up or down the coast to nearby towns. I took a bus which travelled along the coast to Almeria. It was fairly mountainous as the Sierra Nevada Mountains ran parallel to the coast and in amongst the twisting and winding I caught many a glimpse of sparkling blue seas and clear skies, the occasional partly enclosed bay where there were always several small fishing boats moored beside golden sand. The water was clear enough to through to the reefs underneath.

I changed busses at a place called Motril and caught another one that went inland to Granada. I was familiar with the song since it had been popular for years and thought since it wasn't that far inland I should see it.

As it got darker into twilight glimpses the land dimmed until only shadowy shapes could be made out. The occasional lights in the hills probably belonged to farmer's cottages. The bus wound back up through mountains and hills finally approaching a long rising plain. Far in the distance ahead I could see a glow. Was that Granada?

As we got closer I saw the shape of turrets and balustrades that made up the Al Hambra, the fortified castle city the Moors built on top of a rise ahead of us. This was a palace and a fortress combined and had been built by the Moorish kings who founded the city in 1235, so it had been there perched high on a ridge of the Sierra Nevadas for centuries. It was one of thousands of castles built during medieval times all across the Iberian Peninsula. This castle had filled with refugees fleeing the taking of Spain by the Christians. There they retained some independence until 1492 when after an eight year siege King Ferdinand and Queen Isabel conquered the city and took it from the Moors.

The bus arrived as twilight deepened into the edge of darkness. Stone walls were lit with spotlights, flocks of swallows or little birds like that swirled about above the light, the smell of oranges filled the air. The sounds of a thousand conversations assailed me as I got off the bus beside the central plaza. Tables and chairs were set in front of eateries and cafes all around the plaza and they were filled with people happily chatting and drinking coffee, beer, wine while at the same time watching the parade before them. Young men and women marched and strolled around the perimeter of the plaza, talking and joking. Sometimes people watching from the side tables would call out something and there would be a round of laughter. It was the evening paseo, the only chance many young people had to fraternize with members of the other sex. Some young couples were closely followed by a grim matronly woman or an older man, obviously keeping an eye on them so there would be no mischief. Many others were freer with their interactions. The shuffling of feet on the cobbles, the spontaneous bursts of soft laughter, the happy voices filled everyone watching with quiet sense of joy.

I sat outside in front of a café and had something to eat and drank a fine black coffee with a small glass of cognac. It was a lovely night.

At least it seemed that way until I tried to find a place to spend the night. Everything was full. There were no vacancies anywhere because it was still close to the end of the *Semana Santa* and the *Feria de Sevilla*, which meant much of the overflow from there, finished up here where they had also had their own festivities. I wandered around until after 11 pm and as the city centre quietened I decided I would have to sleep out somewhere since finding a room had proved to be impossible.

I picked up a broadsheet newspaper and somewhere near the outskirts I found a long hedge beside the road. I climbed over it and on the side invisible from the road I laid out some newspaper on the ground to have something to sleep on without getting dirty. I remember Mum telling once that newspapers made good insulation, and since Granada was inland and high up on a mountain ridge it would get very cold later on. The rest of the newspaper I covered myself with and used my backpack as a pillow. It was rough and uncomfortable but before it got too cold I fell asleep, so I didn't notice how cold it actually got.

I woke up shivering as the sun lightened the sky, but soon warmed as the sun got higher. I had barely bugun to walk along the road when I managed to hitch a ride with one of the many vehicles leaving the city. They had to be going to Motril because there was nothing else between Granada and the Coast except for some tiny villages that the vehicle I was in roared right through without even slowing down.

I found another ride to Almeria which was an hour's drive firstly along the coast for half the way after which we went through the mountains which came right down to the coast. I had something to eat in Almeria then decided to take a bus to Murcia which was a large town inland and almost a whole day's travelling. I remember nothing of Murcia but from there I went to Cartagena, a picturesque little city on a bay within a peninsula (*Cabo de Palos*) that jutted out into the sea. Lots of fishing boats here and there were little fishing villages all along the coast from Cartagena to Alicante.

I hitched various rides from village to village and remember sitting on a pale sandy beach where some fishermen were grilling fresh sardines they had just caught. They invited me to join them and we wolfed down the delicious tiny crisp and crunchy fish with great gusto, accompanied by chunks of homemade bread dipped in the hot frying oil and some wine, the ubiquitous *rioja*, (cheap red wine you could find everywhere). We laughed and talked to each other in languages none of us could understand, but we had a good time. It was one of the most memorable meals I had in Spain, sitting on the beach under a brilliant blue sky with salty air and fried fish cooking smells mingling together accompanied by the soft shushing of small waves splashing softly further down the beach.

Alicante was beautiful. There were wide footpaths and walkways covered with elaborate abstract mosaic patters of swirling colours that wound along the beachfront and towards the harbour where several Galleons lay at anchor. Behind them the nearby hills of a small peninsula split the water from the sky. These galleons were a tourist delight. I was told two of the ships had been featured in Movies about Wars between the British and the Spanish, and that they were slightly larger than life-size replicas because today's people were somewhat taller than those who lived in the fourteenth century. Rows of elegant palm trees highlighted the gardens that lay between the harbour and the city itself.

The next day once again in local busses I travelled along the coastal road arriving in Valencia in the afternoon. The sun was hot and dusty sand blew across the streets as I walked from the bust stop into town. It was quite a change from the greenery and the cool sea breezes of Alicante. This town looked as if it was in the middle of a desert even though it was right on the coast. The sea was choppy but the salt air didn't penetrate much beyond the foreshore. Walking into Valencia was like walking into a dust bowl. Sometimes a small whirlwind of dust would run along the street ahead of me before dissipating in a cross breeze and collapsing back down into dust on the road's surface.

I found a restaurant and sampled the food Valencia is famous for; paella. I must admit it was pretty good, as one would expect this being the regional dish, and there was plenty of it. What amazed me was how a rice dish could become the district's world famous contribution to Spanish cuisine when the surrounding land beyond the city looked and smelt like a desert. Where did they grow the rice? You needed swampy natural areas and irrigated rice paddies, none of which I could see coming into town or leaving it afterwards. There were just miles of drought stricken land with what appeared to be very marginal sandy soil.

Finally, and almost out of ready cash I found a truck driver willing to take me further north. They weren't allowed to pick up hitch hikers but he said he had to drive non-stop to Perpignan in France (just over the border with Spain) and needed someone to help keep him awake. We left in the afternoon and travelled all night arriving in Barcelona about

5 in the morning. He didn't stop anywhere in this city that I did want to see, but drove straight through, which meant I would have no chance of catching up with Pancho to see how he was doing. (In fact I never saw or heard from him again, which was rather sad.)

The weather had been deteriorating as we drove further north leaving the warm spring weather behind us. After we went through customs, no problems there, and straight on to Perpignan, it started to drizzle and got quite cold. Fortunately I still had the jacket given to me by Pancho's wife to wear. Somehow I found my way from Perpignan to Montpellier and from there to Lyon. Don't ask how because I can't remember. I slept on the station at Lyon while waiting for a train to take me to Geneva in Switzerland. It was cold and blustery and I was surprised to see the famous lake, which Geneva sits at one end of, with choppy waves and boats moored along a foreshore bouncing up and down vigorously. Spring hadn't arrived here and the last of the winter weather was making itself felt. I had only seen images of this lake exhibiting calmness and tranquillity. From Geneva it was only a short hop on another warm inviting train to Stuttgart and of course on to Backnang where I had somewhere to stay and a place to recover from the endless partying in Spain. It was the end of April, a month short of a year to the time I had first arrived in Backnang, and the weather was nothing like it had been the year before. It was still the end of winter and the weather was cold with drizzling rain. The streets were dirty and slippery with melted snow being washed away by the rain.

What made it even worse was that one of my beloved congas had been irreversibly damaged. My drums had arrived and I discovered that one of them had been split from top to bottom and was useless. It kind of spoilt the homecoming, but it taught me that you cannot leave valuable things to be transported with any sort of care. They get tossed around in transit and no one gives a damn what happens to them.

Theo took a photo of me holding the split drum. I don't know what happened to it after that. Perhaps they chopped it up after I left and used it in their slow combustion heater.

Once again, as soon as I could get some money from my account, I would move on.

My original plan had been to stay a lot longer in Europe playing congas and timbales with Latin groups which at one point had proliferated everywhere, and especially in Paris, but Rock and Roll, The Beatles and The Rolling Stones and the thousands of copycat bands killed that idea. Rock music had taken the world by storm and there simply wasn't a place for any other band playing any other kind of music. One of my congas was smashed and I gave away the other one so I wouldn't have to lug it around everywhere.

Looking at my smashed conga drum outside of the house in Im Benzwasen after returning to Backnang, Germany.

Thinking about returning to Australia, the idea of leaving Europe from Greece, where I would take the Ship from Piraeus, the home port of the Ellinis, began to fill my imagination.

And suddenly it was all I could think about. Would it be as beautiful as Dad always claimed? Would the light be different there? He always maintained it had a quality that existed nowhere else, that was unique to Greece. I always told him that those ideas were purely nostalgia for a place he left as a young man without ever returning, and which after 50 years had attained a mystic quality.

I would soon find out.

I would head to Greece, my father's homeland, where at the very least the weather would be better than the snow and slush in Germany.

A feeling of coming home

When you have been away for a very long time, living in an environment that is so different from what you grew up with, the feeling you get when you come back to the place or the country where you were born, is ineffable.

I remember my father telling me that when he went back after 50 years in Australia to the village in the country where he was born, which was at that time a part of Epirus in Northern Greece before a manmade border alienated it from Greece and the rest of the world, there were so many tears in his eyes he could barely see.

It had changed so much it was unrecognizable, yet there was something about it that made him feel he was home. Something in the air, in the light that illuminated the mountains that surround the village, a faint scent exuded from the ground; something in his blood that made a connection… he couldn't explain it. He simply stood there with tears in his eyes.

I felt exactly the same when I stepped off the bus that had taken me to Ioannina, the capital of Epirus in Northern Greece. Yet I had never been there.

I had this overwhelming feeling of having come home.

Perhaps it was that I had heard so many stories about this area it felt familiar. No one had ever described the place to me other than in the vaguest of terms, yet here I was standing in the street and staring out across a huge lake — with a surface so still it reflected the depth of the sky above, and where a small island in the middle that housed a mosque which had presided over an infamous part of the city's history seemed to float as if suspended in space — to the faded blue mountains on the far side that I knew extended over the border on into Albania, it seemed as if I had been here before. Was that Déjà vu?

It was hard to shake off that feeling while I stood there staring out across the lake.

The bus rapidly crowded with a new lot of people. They pushed and shoved each other to find a place to sit while they juggled bags and cases of various sizes. There was a lot of excited yelling and chatter which I couldn't understand, but it all seemed in good fun. With spurts of exhaust fumes and a loud roar of its engine the bus moved off and drove towards the road that went alongside part of an old stone wall that had been ramparts of a fort facing the lake.

Someone who had missed the bus, who perhaps had been too deeply involved in a game of backgammon in a *kafeneion* ran after it waving his arms in the air.

The bus didn't slow down or stop. It was on its way towards the mountains across the lake, through which it would laboriously wind its way to Thesaloniki, Greece's second largest city.

The man stopped in the middle of the road and his arms dropped to his side. He yelled a famous insult at the back of the rapidly diminishing bus that had something to do with the driver having a penis growing out of his forehead, and everyone around me laughed uproariously. He joined the laughing crowd and made his way with them back into a *kafeneion* to have another bitter black coffee, a glass of ouzo, and most likely another game of backgammon.

There would be another bus the next day, and with better luck next time he would catch it.

I didn't have that same feeling when I arrived in Athens the week before.

Unless you looked up at the Acropolis or one of the other temples located on ancient volcanic cores that jut up above the city, it looked like any other city elsewhere in Europe, except it seemed dustier and more polluted. There was a difference to the way the people moved about the city, the flow of traffic appeared more chaotic, and there were disruptions as some people still used horse-drawn wagons at times to deliver goods which caused bottlenecks with irate drivers creating a cacophony of yelled curses, expletives and blasting car horns.

It was certainly warmer. Having come from the end of winter in Germany it was nice to feel warm without having to put on layers of extra clothes.

Looking along a narrow street towards the Acropolis.

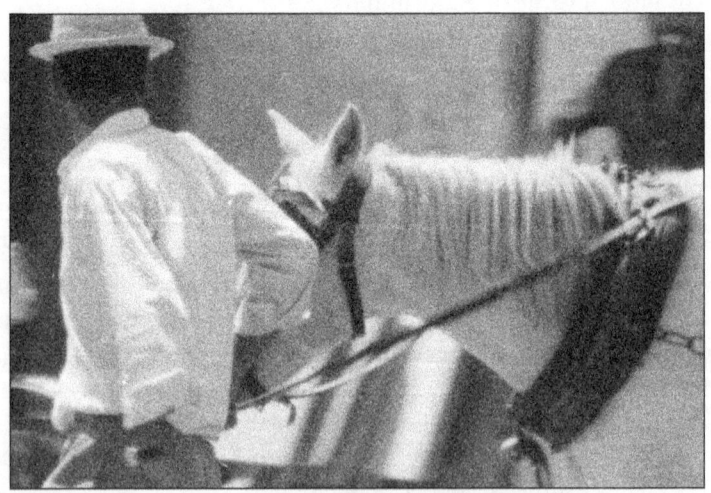

Leading a horse drawn wagon along a busy street in Athens.

Tourists at the Acropolis.

Delivering watermelons using a horse drawn wagon in Omonia Square.

An encounter on a train

With trains in Europe you have to make sure you get on the correct carriage listed as going to the destination you want, or you will find yourself somewhere most unexpected. Unlike Australia, if I got on a train going to Sydney it wouldn't matter where I got on or in which carriage I travelled; it was all going to the one destination. There were no side tracks to other cities. Even today a half a century later, the same still holds. In Europe however I had to be very sure I found the carriage that had a sign by its entrance that stated in several languages that this carriage was going to Athens. If I got on a different carriage I could end up in Bucharest, or Paris, or any of a dozen other major cities. Each time the train stopped at a major city carriages would be taken off and joined onto other trains going to different destinations, and new carriages from other parts of Europe would be added to the train I was still on. I didn't wonder how complex it was to manage all that but accepted it as the way it was. I simply had to make certain I got into the correct carriage and stayed there for the duration of the journey.

Knowing that I would be going through several countries before arriving in Greece I went to a customs agent at the train station in Stuttgart and had my suitcase examined and sealed with a statement that such had been done and it was not to be opened or checked until I claimed it at the customs department in Athens. Presumably it would go into a special luggage compartment (in the same carriage passengers to Greece used) and would only be taken out once the train had reached Athens. I had bought the suitcase to carry my clothes and a few souvenirs since I no longer had conga drums which I had previously used instead of a suitcase. That way I could travel light with a small backpack of essential items, and not have to worry about being checked and searched at every border crossing. They would of course still examine and stamp passports and verify that I had the correct papers to enter or transit through.

In the 1960s border officials were paranoid about checking passports and sometimes spent more time than necessary looking at the different stamps in my passport, and it seemed that it was always in the middle of the night when this would happen. The train would stop and customs officials would walk through the train carriage by carriage, compartment by compartment, checking everyone's passport or identity papers, permits, visas, even asking to look in bags if they thought you looked nervous, and sometimes you did because you had been asleep and were rudely awakened for this process to take place. Then after what seemed like hours the train started to move and just as passengers began to settle, to fall asleep, the train would stop again and another lot of officials wearing different uniforms would go through the same process. Sometimes this would take several hours if the train was very long, and especially when entering or exiting an Eastern Bloc country such as Yugoslavia. I had to go from one end of Yugoslavia (at that time a communist dictatorship under the control of Tito) to the other before entering the Macedonian province of Greece on my way to Athens. Everyone coming into Yugoslavia from a Western influenced European country was viewed with suspicion and all papers were carefully examined.

This business of checking papers and identities I found bewildering, annoying, and ultimately pointless. Why did they do this? In Australia we never had ID papers, and we could go anywhere we liked in the country without being asked for papers or having to give reasons for travelling. In Europe and especially in the Eastern Bloc countries under the communist banner you were constantly checked and harassed. No one could go anywhere without first having obtained some kind of permission and needing papers to prove it. It was their way of controlling people and their activities, but why did they need to know who everybody was and where they were going and for what purpose? It was beyond me and was in my view, the most insidious aspect of culture shock that I had encountered. George Orwell was right to forewarn people of its possible consequences in his great novel *1984*.

Because of unfamiliarity with the way of telling time here — everything was in a 24 hour cycle rather than twelve. Once 12 o'clock or mid-day arrived the time didn't revert back to 1 to 12 but continued on from 13 to 24 before going back to zero. — I didn't realize that the train trip from Stuttgart down to Athens would take almost 3 days rather than just overnight.

What was I thinking? I should have looked at a map, at the distance involved and it would have been obvious. Departure from Stuttgart was 1000 and arrival in Athens was 0830 which I assumed was the next day. I never occurred to me to look at the dates listed on the timetable.

It wasn't the next morning; it was 3 days later, which explained why some of the people in my second class carriage compartment had bags of food and drink with them, like they were going on a picnic. There was no food service on the train, at least not in second class, and it often didn't stop long enough at stations along the way for you to have time to go and buy something from a vendor on the platform. The first major stop for this semi-express train would be Zagreb and that wasn't until after midday the next day.

Until then you took your own food, or you went hungry.

They knew that, I didn't.

'I've written a film script,' the lovely young woman sitting across from me said. She looked very Greek but spoke with a very British accent. She had classical Greek features, the elegant straight nose, high cheekbones, almond eyes, long black hair, and she was slender and elegant like one imagines a priestess in an ancient temple may have looked…at least like the artwork I had seen on ancient Greek vases portrayed them.

I smiled to encourage her to keep talking. She was also the only person in the compartment who could speak English.

The others were a couple of immigrant workers, heavy set and weary looking as if they had been working for months without a rest, and two equally heavy set women wrapped up in shawls and heavy clothes who sat there in total silence. I presumed they were on their way back to Turkey or somewhere in Yugoslavia after having worked in Germany. There was another older man asleep by the door on my side of the compartment. I sat by the window. I had grabbed this seat because I was the first to enter the compartment after boarding the train in Stuttgart. The workers and their wives had come in next and they took the seats from the door leaving the one by the window vacant. The men chucked a couple of heavy bags up onto the rack above them and sat down hard enough to make the compartment feel as if it had driven over a bump even though it was still stationary.

The next in was the young woman, dressed in slacks and comfortable jumper and open jacket. I stood up and helped her to put her suitcase on the rack above and she thanked me. She took the window seat directly opposite. Then the old man wearing a fez came in and looked around for a moment before taking the corner seat by the sliding door opposite the workers and their wives. There was some space between me and the old man and I expected someone else would soon be in to take that but not long after the old man sat down the train began to move.

The movement was at first imperceptible. The only reason I noticed it was the platform outside the window seemed to be sliding slowly past. I blinked a couple of times to make sure I wasn't imagining it. There was a slight humming in the floor, a vibration so smooth it could barely be felt. I looked out the window again and the platform was moving past at quite a clip, so we were on our way. In moments we passed the end of the platform and exited the station, crossed many diverging train lines, and with barely a whisper slid past trains going the other way. Soon were out in a cold countryside that was still experiencing the end of winter, with bare trees and patches of snow still clinging to the ground. It was all so smooth it was hard to imagine anything had happened. Trains in Australia were rough, rattled, made lots of noise, and in general to me seemed much cruder than anything here in Germany.

Since the young woman and I were about the same age, (I was 24) and the other occupants were much older we eventually fell into conversation once the train had properly got under way.

'I'm going to Greece, to Athens to meet with a film producer. They said they were interested and wanted to see me and the script.'

'You're very lucky. That doesn't happen very often. What's the script about?'

'It's about this young woman who goes to Athens for a holiday and meets an exciting handsome man with whom she falls in love, almost at first sight. He literally sweeps her off her feet and they find themselves in a luxury hotel where they spend the night together. She wakes up happy and that's when the nightmare begins. The man beside her in the bed is dead, stabbed multiple times. The bed is covered with his blood. She has blood on her. She panics and leaps out of bed, showers to wash off the blood, gets dressed and leaves the hotel. She knows she didn't kill him. She had no reason to, she was in love. But who would believe her? Who would believe that while she slept blissfully someone came into the room and stabbed her lover to death, without her being aware of it? She has to find out who did this, who her lover really was, and why someone would want to kill him and lay the blame on her. But she doesn't know where to start, where to go; all she knows is she has to get out the hotel right away before the cleaning staff come to clean the room. Somewhere in Athens is a murderer and she intends to find him…'

'Wow that sounds pretty good. How does it end?'

'That's the trouble. I don't know. I haven't figured it out yet.'

'And yet the film producers asked you to come to Athens to consult with them?'

'That's right. They loved the idea but want me to come to Athens so I can get to know the city, and so I can work with them to finish the script.'

'That sounds a bit dicey to me.'

'Yeah I know. But I was bored in London, at least where I live, so I thought I'd take a chance. I mean, what's life worth if you don't take a chance sometimes, a chance to make a dream come true?'

I couldn't argue with that. 'I hope that works out. Have you been to Athens before?'

'I was born there but my parents moved to London when I was barely two years old. I have no idea what Athens or Greece is like. I only know what they remember, what they told me, and that is probably years out of date.'

'I know that feeling. My father was born in Northern Greece and went to America when he was 15 years old. That was in 1913. He was there for ten years before coming back, but couldn't find any work so he left with some friends for Australia and none of them have been back since. I know what he told me about Ioannina and Epirus and what it was like when he was a child. He was never in Athens except in passing before getting on a ship in Piraeus which brought him to Australia in 1924, so I have no idea about the place either.'

And so we chatted as the train sped through ever more mountainous country. We would later be passing through a tunnel under some of those mountains to go from Austria into Yugoslavia but that would be during the night. I realized after several hours that the journey would be a lot longer than I had thought. We had been travelling for quite a while and we still hadn't got to Yugoslavia. Obviously we weren't going to be in Athens the next morning. I was getting hungry, especially when the heavy-set workers and their wives pulled down a parcel from the rack above and unwrapped salami, chunky bread and foul smelling cheese which they proceeded to gulp down between sips of dark plum coloured wine.

I wondered when we would stop so I could buy something at a station, but the train didn't stop. In fact, except for the obligatory stamping of passports and checking of papers at the border with Yugoslavia the train wasn't going to stop until it arrived at Zagreb, well into Yugoslavia. After Zagreb it would go to Beograd and then Skopje before entering Greece to stop at Thesaloniki and finally Athens. There would be no stops in between these major stations. So it was a long haul from Vienna where we had stopped momentarily, where I could have had a chance to buy something to eat but didn't. No wonder these workers opposite me brought their food with them.

My script-writing friend had obviously known about the length of the journey and had brought some sandwiches and bottled water. She offered a sandwich to me which I gratefully accepted.

Entering darkness

When we emerged from the tunnel under the mountains it was dark and nothing could be seen until several hours later when the landscape flashing past appeared grey and bleak in the early morning. I saw what looked like abandoned farmlands with overgrown paddocks and dilapidated fences. Every hour or so we would cross a road and beside the flashing lights there was a guard standing there not far from a little guard-house as if to warn people in vehicles not to cross while a train was going through. I didn't see any cars or trucks though, so I guess we were still a long way from any major city. The guard never waved at the train, he stared at it as if it was something difficult to comprehend.

Was this the government's way of making sure everyone had a job, no matter how useless; making sure every railway crossing was manned? It seemed that in communist countries everyone worked for the government which in effect meant that no one worked much at all. Was that why everything looked so unattended like the overgrown farmlands and the odd dilapidated shacks we saw haphazardly scattered across the countryside?

It looked very cold outside with patches of snow or ice glistening in shaded places as the train sped by. I was glad it was warm inside the train.

Zagreb was a stop long enough for carriages to be re-arranged so some parts of the train would be going elsewhere while the carriage I was in was still going to Greece. It was also long enough for me to exchange some money to allow me to buy some food to take on the train.

Skopje was the same. Again the train was dismantled and reconstructed. Skopje was the city where one of Dad's employees came from. It was the major city in Macedonia. He was Macedonian Greek but he grew up in the part of Yugoslavia that bordered Greece and was primarily Greek speaking although he also spoke Serbian as well as the Macedonian dialect. At home he spoke Greek with Dad and English with everyone else. His province too had been taken from Greece to become part of Yugoslavia after the First World War in the same way Northern Epirus had been taken from Greece to become a part of the newly created Albania. There had been many changes to borders after the Turks had been ejected from this part of the world which they had occupied for over 400 years; minor wars, resettlement programs, shifting populations before borders were stabilized and then the 2nd World War where the same things happened all over again. Finally borders were established and had to this point become fixed, and for people in some countries travel was not easy to do if not impossible.

The station bustled with frantic activity and I noticed there were plenty of armed uniformed guards or official inspectors who were looking at the papers of everyone who got off the train. I would not get off the train here, even just for a walk along the station. It wasn't worth the hassle of being stopped and questioned in a language I couldn't understand.

The heavy-set workers who had been travelling in this compartment with their wives left here, I thought, to buy something on the station. They didn't come back and a guard with a rifle slung over his shoulder came in, looked around without saying anything. He had some papers in his hand which he glanced at before looking above where the workers had been sitting. He reached up and took down their luggage. He passed it to another armed guard in the passage outside the compartment. We sat silently and watched while the guards after a brief glance around the compartment took no notice of us. Five minutes after they had gone — there didn't seem to be anyone else getting on or off the train — it started to glide silently out of the station.

Once again we were on our way and would soon be crossing over into Greece.

Seeing the light

The mood in the train was different. I could feel it as I walked along the passageway from one end of the carriage to the other. There seemed to be more activity amongst passengers, more animation in their conversations, and quite a few smiles, which had not been apparent before while the train was still in Yugoslavia.

Looking out the windows it was obvious we were still in mountainous terrain but somehow the light shining on these mountains seemed to have a different quality; or was its luminosity a figment of my imagination?

Dad often spoke about the light in Greece and how it was different from anywhere else. I always assumed it was nostalgia penetrating his memories, making his recollection of childhood and youth somewhat surreal. But he could have been right; there was something about it that gave buoyancy to the air and a feeling of pleasant expectation. The landscape the train sliced through almost seemed familiar, even though I had never seen it before.

We had crossed the border from Yugoslavian Macedonia into Greek Macedonia, and after the obligatory passport stamping, ID papers and ticket checks, the train continued on its way towards *Athinai* or Athens.

The train made two brief stops and our compartment filled with passengers, this time all heading to Athens. I continued to chat with the young lady who wrote the film script as well as with the newcomers who couldn't speak English. She translated for us and the time rapidly passed. Since we had been in the carriage when the others got on in Greece they assumed that we were travelling together, that we were a couple. We weren't of course, we had simply become friends, as one often does on long trips with people you meet making the same journey.

We had one more night on the train and woke up to find suburban backyards flashing past the windows as the train travelled through outskirts of Athens. People quickly stood up and started to lift their luggage off the overhead racks, chatting excitedly.

Suddenly I was nervous. Travelling was always great, but arriving could sometimes be nerve-wracking, especially if you had nowhere to go or was uncertain about where you would be staying. I think my fellow traveller was equally as nervous now that the train was slowing down as it pulled into the main station. She also didn't know where she was going. She suggested that we should stick together until we found someplace, and I was happy with that since she could speak Greek while I couldn't.

I was right to have been nervous. When we went to collect our luggage from the section set aside for customs inspections there was nothing wrong with hers but mine was a mess. It had been opened somewhere in transit, and that could only have been in Yugoslavia, and it was obvious that everything had been taken out then rudely stuffed back in in such a way that it couldn't be properly closed. Whoever did it had tied a piece of thin rope around it, wrapping it several times around before tying a rough knot to hold it together.

Bastards! 'It was not supposed to be opened until it arrived here,' I told the customs official who handed it to me.

He shrugged. He couldn't have cared less. He said something in Greek which my friend immediately translated to 'Why don't you open it and see if anything is missing?'

He was being polite. What he really meant was to open it so he could see what it was that someone else had thought may have been in there. Well there was nothing in there other than clothes and some metal bits that belonged to my broken conga drum. I wanted to take the metal parts home to use on another drum I would have made.

He asked me what the metal parts were for, and I told him, 'the rim of a drum and the tuning bolts that connect it to the side'. He nodded at the translation and the demo I gave on how the parts connected together.

Maybe they had been detected with some device and that was why Yugoslavian customs had 'examined' the contents. Perhaps they thought I had a bomb hidden in my suitcase.

'Anything else missing?'

Taking another look I saw that at least half a dozen of my best shirts were not there.

These were expensive shirts I had bought, some at an exclusive men's wear shop in Kings Cross and others in a similar shop in Melbourne. I used to like good shirts that fitted well and were hand-made or tailor-made. I hardly ever bought cheap shirts from chain stores or even from department stores.

'Some shirts are missing,' I finally told him.

'Good clothes are hard to get in Yugoslavia. Customs people often go through people's luggage, especially if the suitcases look foreign and take clothes they can't buy in their own shops and stores. They don't have the money to buy them anyway, so they 'confiscate' what they can from foreigners passing through.' He shrugged again. 'That's life.'

When my new friend had finished translating this to me he added one more thing. 'We don't do that in Greece,' he said with a welcoming smile.

Yeah, I've heard that before…

You didn't do it because there was nothing left worth 'confiscating', I thought as I quickly stuffed my clothes back into the suitcase and had to use the rope to tie it together again because both locks had been broken.

A few moments later we were outside the station wondering where we would go. It was a lovely warm day and the city we faced seemed full of life and energy.

I watched the traffic passing by. While my friend made some phone calls from a public phone inside the main entrance to the station I found a money change booth and swapped some $US for Drachmas of which I ended up with a huge handful of seedy looking notes. Moments later she came over to me and said, 'All the hotels are full.'

She looked a bit lost. It had obviously not occurred to her that she wouldn't be able to find good hotel accommodation.

'Don't worry about it, we'll find somewhere.'

'How can you be so sure?'

'It's a big city. There are always places you can find, places tourists are unlikely to go to; you just have to know where to look. Why don't you grab a taxi over there?' There were several parked further down the road with drivers standing in a clump chatting and smoking. 'Tell the driver we want to go to a working class area close to the city and that we are looking for somewhere reasonable to stay. He'll know places or will have cousins or relatives who manage or own such a place.'

She did that, and in no time at all the taxi left us in front of a small hotel of four stories almost in the shadow of the Acropolis. There was a market across the road filled with buyers and sellers handling all kinds of second hand 'junk' interspersed with tiny Kafeneion (coffee shops) where people sat taking the time of day drinking small cups of rich black Turkish coffee while chatting with each other. Some played backgammon with severe intensity. The narrow street was packed with people on foot seemingly not in a hurry to go anywhere. Several men were unloading rolls of heavy wire from the back of a cart while the horse in front munched happily with its nose in a chaff bag. They carried the wire rolls into a shop where it appeared springs were being manufactured. A short stocky man approached us and offered to sell us hand-made clothes. He had a suitcase with wheels on it that he pulled along and as soon as he stopped in front of us he opened the case to show us his wares. We politely declined and went inside the hotel.

There was only one room left and it was on the top floor. The woman behind the reception desk took us up to see it and it was perfect as far as I was concerned. There was a view across the city looking away from the Acropolis. There was only one bed, a very large double bed which today would be called Queen-size, a small table by the window with two chairs, and a small wardrobe for clothes. It was clean, with its hand rendered plaster walls painted white. It glowed with pleasant warmth from the light coming in through the window.

Toilet and bathroom were down the passage and not part of the rooms on this floor. I told the woman I would take it for a month and offered to pay in advance in American dollars.

'There's only one bed,' my friend said.

'Is that a problem? It's big enough for the two of us.' I said this without realizing the complications that could occur.

She stared at me for as moment, her eyes unreadable before she turned and said something to the woman. A short discussion followed before the hotel woman left. She came back ten minutes later with what turned out to be a fold up bed. She unfolded it and placed it against the wall near the foot of the large bed and was about to make it when I told her to leave it, that we would do it. She quickly disappeared.

'What's that for?' I asked my.

'That's for you to sleep in.'

'I don't think so. I've booked this room for a month so I am sleeping in that bed.' I pointed to the big bed. 'If you want, you can sleep in the fold-up bed, or you can sleep in this one; it makes no difference to me.'

She stared at me for a while and the expression I held remained adamant. Eventually she said 'all right.'

I wasn't exactly sure what she had agreed to but I took it to mean both of us would use the larger bed. I immediately threw my battered suitcase onto the fold up bed and started to take stuff out so I could sort and fold things to make the contents neater. She disappeared to make some phone calls from the foyer downstairs. She came back after thirty minutes or so to tell me that she had an appointment the next morning with the producer who wanted to work on the script with her.

That night she was nervous about going to bed, but I just ignored her and after visiting the toilet I came back and hopped into bed, rolled to one side so my back was towards her and promptly went to sleep.

I woke briefly as I felt the bed move when she got in gingerly on the other side. How well she slept I don't know because I went back to sleep almost immediately and didn't wake up until the sun started shining through the window. She was already up and dressed and fiddling with her notebook and the folder that contained her script.

'What about breakfast?' I asked as I sat up.

'No time for that. I've got to go.'

'I hope it all works out,' I told her as she headed for the door.

'Thanks… See you later.'

Then she was gone.

Selling a suit

One item in my suitcase was a grey herringbone suit that I had brought with me and had never worn. I had packed it in case I needed to wear something formal, but an occasion to do that had not materialised so far. It was a winter suit of good quality and it seemed unlikely that I would be wearing it in Greece. I don't know why I bothered to bring it with me from Australia but in the 1960s everyone wore suits when they had to 'dress-up' for something. Since my best shirts had been stolen I figured I didn't need the suit any more. If I could get rid of it, that would be one less item to carry when travelling. I hated the idea of leaving it somewhere or of throwing it away when someone could make use of it or gain something from it. I decided to take it down and see if that clothes vendor would be interested in having it.

'How much do you want?' he asked me in broken English.

'I don't want anything,' I said. 'You can have it. Sell it, do what you want with it.'

'I do not accept charity. I buy and I sell. That is how I make a living. I will buy it from you.'

'Okay, I'll sell it to you then…'

'How much do you want?'

We were back to that. It was like reverse bargaining. 'Alright, give me ten dollars.'

'I will give you two hundred drachmas.'

That was ridiculously low for a suit of this quality, but what the hell. I was going to throw it away anyway. If it made him feel better to have bought it then I would accept whatever he offered.

'Deal.' We shook hands. He gave me the money which he carried in a belt around his waist and I handed the suit to him.

He went off with a big smile on his face probably believing he had conned me out of something valuable for very little money. Not 50 metres down the street he held the suit up to show someone who momentarily paused to look at him. He certainly wasn't wasting any time in reselling it. He looked back to see if I was watching and I waved to him. He nodded and smiled then moved further along the street holding the suit up to show people while he dragged his case of other wares behind.

Sometime after that I took my camera bag with the Bolex movie camera in it and started taking shots of the surrounding streets with the Parthenon and the Acropolis clearly seen as I looked along the narrow street. Eventually I found myself making the long walk up to have a close look at the Parthenon. It looked as if it had been blown up, as in fact it had when gunpowder stored there exploded.

The Parthenon was constructed in 438 BC dedicated to the Goddess Athena whose name was given to the capitol city surrounding it, and it can be seen from almost anywhere you go in the city. It towers above the city and it had remained complete for 2000 years before it was partially destroyed in 1687 when the Venetians besieged the city in an attempt to defeat the Turkish Empire which had ruled Greece since the fall of Constantinople around AD 1460. That they failed in this endeavour was a tragedy especially when something so magnificent was destroyed wantonly after two millennia. The Turks remained for another 200 years but the Parthenon was ruined. But what compounded this tragedy many years later was that people from countries that dominated the world during the 20th century stole parts of this monument (not to mention other great works of art) to display in their museums.

There was an old photographer with an ancient boxlike camera on a large tripod cajoling tourists into having their picture taken in front of the temple so I quite happily sat on a marble column that was lying down on the ground with the temple behind and got him to take one of me. It was grainy and contrasty and it was interesting the way he made it.

The photographer, in the white coat and hat, talking to a couple of tourists waiting for their photo to be ready.
Below: the photo he took of me in front of the Pathenon.

His first image was on paper and was a negative image. He developed this in buckets of chemicals he kept hidden under a black cloth. When this was done he set the negative photo on a stand fixed to the front of the camera lens and rephotographed that image. The result was a positive image which he then developed in the same way. This was the photo I got. It was (and still is) the only photo I have of me in Greece.

People seemed free to wander in and out and all around the site. I'm sure that now this would not be allowed, that visitors would be much more controlled to prevent accidental damage, wear and tear on the ancient stone, and to prevent minor theft as people try to break off a piece of stone for a souvenir. I shot some images across the city which was sprawled out but low level. A couple of hills also with ruined temples on them jutted up between the Acropolis and the hazy horizon some distance away.

In 1965 *Athinai* was a big as Melbourne, and as sprawled out as much too, covering approximately 1100 square kilometres. It had a population somewhere between two to three million people (probably a lot more now) which was about a quarter of the country's total.

Athens in 1965 seen from the top of the Acropolis was sprawled out as far as you could see with haze and dust obscuring its full extent.

Interestingly enough there are as many if not more Greeks living overseas in countries like Australia, and America than the total population in Greece itself. Melbourne in Australia for example, is the 2nd largest Greek city — bigger than Thesaloniki in regard to population.

But Athens was different. It had a history that went back for more than two and a half thousand years, older probably than any other established city in Europe.

2500 years ago Greece was the centre of the Western world, where the concept and practice of Democracy was born. It was where the greatest philosophers debated, where scientific thinking began, where drama was created and acted out in amphitheatres near the Acropolis, the country that gave birth to the Olympic Games. With the Parthenon standing on the Acropolis (the ancient high city) overlooking the sprawl that Athens has become, there is no other city like it in Europe., and in present times modern day pollution is creating acid rains (something barely thought about in 1965) that are rapidly consuming the ancient marble from which the great temple to Athena had been constructed.

My friend came back late in the afternoon full of excitement and told me she would stay one more night and would leave in the morning. She had arranged something with the producers who wanted her script. I did hope she wasn't being manipulated into doing something she really didn't want to do. Big cities like Athens were full of scumbags and scoundrels only too willing to con gullible people whose heads were full of dreams.

Again I wished her luck the next morning as she packed her bag, and that was the last I ever saw of her.

I hoped it all worked out the way she thought it would and that a successful film was made.

The smell of fresh roasting coffee

Athens bustled constantly with people and vehicles on the move from early in the morning. But everything slowed down though around two in the afternoon. It seemed that thousands of people sat in the plethora of kafeneion that surrounded the main plaza in the centre of the modern city. Waiters with tiny white aprons around their waists dodged between tables and ran across the wide street that surrounded the square with slow moving traffic, to deliver little cups of rich smelling black creamy coffee along with tall glasses of iced water placed on tiny trays which had a triangular wire handle above to make them easy to carry. I was amazed at their skill in dodging people, and tables, and cars, without spilling the water or losing a single drop of coffee. Every café had a large machine for roasting coffee beans just inside the front door or out on the footpath in front. There were paddles that revolved to turn the beans over constantly for a good even roasting. The paddles turning the coffee made soft swishing sounds as they rotated around the metre wide barrels of the machines and the smell, the delicious aroma of roasting coffee wafted up into the air with enough strength to make passers-by dizzy if they took too deep a breath.

Stitches in my head

Vouliagmeni is a beach not too far from Athens, a private beach owned by a resort and you had to pay a fee to go onto the beach. You never pay in Australia to go onto a beach. They are free for anyone to use or walk along, to swim at. Not even millionaires who build massive mansions of the foreshore can own the beach in front of their houses. Not so in other places apparently. Well, it had been a long time since I had been for a swim at a beach and someone had told me how good this beach was, so I went there.

It was disappointingly smaller than I expected being only a few hundred metres long with rocky headlands jutting into the sea at either end, and it was crowded with people from the resort nearby. I was reluctant to pay the fee but having come all the way from Athens I decided I might as well pay rather than turn around and go back, so I handed over the fee and went out onto the sand. Apparently the fee payed for facilities that were situated on this beach, dressing rooms, toilets, life-savers and a first aid station, so in a way it was a good thing that I had to pay, because I did something I had never done at home.

I was so excited to see a real beach after almost two years that I quickly got changed and ran straight down the sand towards the small waves that rolled softly in, and took a long shallow dive into the water. I should have waded out like everyone else did, waded out and then splashed around in the small waves. But I dived in and — whack! I saw stars and blacked out…

What the hell happened? I stood up and shook my head. There was blood running down my face and no matter how I tried to wash it off it kept flowing. I turned and staggered back towards the beach, and saw people running towards me. Someone wrapped a towel around my head to staunch the flow of blood and two people led me towards the first aid centre.

I had split my forehead open on a rock jutting up from the sand.

How many times had I silently castigated idiots who had dived off a pier or off steps into shallow water only for them to hit rocks or the bottom where the impact snapped their necks to leave them paralysed and in wheelchairs for the rest of their lives? It was something I would never do, but on the other hand I had dived into shallow waves on a beach many times without anything untoward happening. People do it all the time, splashing about in shallow water. It was just my luck that I happened to hit the only rock sticking up through the sand on this beach. Luckily I had hit it at an angle and had glanced off it rather than slamming directly into it.

The nurse on duty stapled the wound together after sprinkling some antiseptic powder on it. She bandaged my forehead and made me sit there for some time to see whether I had a concussion. She also told me in slow English that if there was any infection I should go straight to the hospital in Athens.

If this had happened on any other beach I would have been in real trouble, but fortunately paying to come onto this beach was what enabled me to have first aid treatment.

I went back to Athens, back to my hotel and lay down to rest, just as I had been told to do.

I had an awful headache and it seemed to be getting worse by the minute. I took some tablets the nurse had given me, some kind of pain killers and they made me drowsy. I fell asleep and didn't wake until the next morning.

In the morning I discovered my face was swollen and the forehead was numb. This was not good. I got dressed and went downstairs to find a taxi going by and asked the driver to take me to the Hospital.

In the emergency ward at the hospital I was eventually seen by a young doctor who spoke English and had studied in Australia. When he took off the bandage he told me the wound had become infected and he would apply a local anaesthetic and clean it. After doing that he stitched the wound and covered it with a clean dressing. He injected an antibiotic and gave me a small box of pills. 'Take one three times a day until they are all used up. If the infection returns, you come back here immediately. Is that clear? Come back in two days otherwise and I'll take the stitches out.'

Almost immediately it seemed, the swelling started to go down and the puffy look around my eyes diminished as I walked back towards Ommonia Square where I would have a coffee. I spent the rest of the day just sitting around doing nothing much while the dull throbbing in the head disappeared. I was lucky. All the damage I had two days later was a small scar and a slight indentation in the bone beneath it.

Once the stitches were removed and I could take the bandage off I went and booked my return passage. The first ship I could get was the Australis. It was bigger than the Ellinis and it was at that moment undergoing refurbishment. It was scheduled to depart from Piraeus in 9 weeks so I had some time to fill in. The Ellinis was pre booked and was full. These were the only two ships from Chandris Lines that were making the round trip to Australia from Greece at that time, so I immediately confirmed my booking (which included a 20 per cent discount for returning passengers).

Reading Kazantzakis

I found a bookshop that sold some books in English and bought an American paperback of *Report to Greco* by Nikos Kazantzakis. The only other two books of his in English were his continuation of *The Iliad* and *The Odyssey*, written as a tribute to Homer, and in the same epic poetical style. They were both huge books each being as long as the original it continued on from. I didn't buy them although I should have. I really wasn't into epic poetry at that stage of my life.

Report to Greco was a fantastic autobiographical work that illuminated the struggles and the desires that Kazantzakis had as he travelled through Greece and the Greek islands in search of himself and of God during the 1930s.

At one point he was for a long time ensconced in a monastery on a remote island living the ascetic life of a monk in the belief that this would bring him closer to God. Every morning he would get up at dawn and pray and look out over the surrounding sea. His descriptions of the sea and how it affected his mood for the day were different for each day as the sea was never the same twice. That he could find words to describe what he saw without ever repeating himself was for me quite incredible. Whoever the translator was, he or she must also have been a genius.

Like other famous writers of the early 20th century Kazantzakis toyed with the ideas and concepts of communism, even going so far as to travel to Russia and Italy and then later France. Most of the world in the 1930s was suffering a severe depression and it seemed that democracy as we knew it was collapsing while the success of countries that had adopted communism or fascism seemed to be developing rapidly. They were attractive models at the time with order and control. Many people were seduced by their ideals and went to those countries only to discover the dream was tainted and would inevitably lead to the standoff between East and West after 2nd World War.

Kazantzakis wrote his first two novels in French which were translated into German. The English version of *The Stone Gardens* was a translation from the German and not from the original French. (*When I had that book some years later I found it impossible to read and put it aside.*) Once he came back to Greece however, he never pursued communism and went on to write some beautiful work in Greek, of which his most Famous is *Zorba the Greek*.

I read *Report to Greco* after my forehead had healed and I would take a train to Piraeus then hop on a ferry which took a couple of hours to get to a nearby island. I would sit on the beach, sipping short black coffees and eating small servings of *dolmades*, olives, feta cheese, and *keftethis* (tiny meatballs made from minced lamb) and sometimes the almond sugar coated shortbread called *kourabiethis*. I did not like *baklava* because it was always dripping with honey and was sickly sweet.

Report to Greco was a long book and it took about a week for me to read it.

Wandering about Athens, I shot some movie film of people drinking coffee and other activities in Omonia Square, the largest square in the centre of Athens where many roads meet and cicle the vast open space. I also went and filmed the changing of the guards at the Palace where the soldiers wearing the ceremonial dress which vaguely resembled the tutus that ballerinas wore. Along with white tights and shoes with pompoms on them they also wore a cap with long hair cascading from one side of it and an ornamental cape over their backs. They marched rigidly in pairs or threes and ignored the many tourists crowding the path they marched along snapping pictures.

Trying to be unobtrusive while snapping a picture.

As far as the guards are concerned the tourists are invisible.

Someone in the crowd near me mumbled to his companion, 'They look silly.'

I turned towards him. 'What about the palace guards in London with their huge black hats? Don't you think they look silly too? What about the Swiss guards at the Vatican?'

He hadn't expected anyone to understand his American English and went red in the face.

'If you think the Greek guards look silly,' I went on, 'then all those other ones in other places must also look silly.'

He glared daggers at me.

'Each country has its own traditions and that's fine. If you criticise one group you criticise them all. Why not accept them for what they are and enjoy the spectacle?'

He didn't answer so I moved away from him while the guards continued with their ceremony.

The first American spacewalk

One moment in my wandering about the city I happened to pass the US Embassy and on prominent display was a breathtaking image of an astronaut tethered by a cable unwinding in graceful loops as the astronaut drifted away from the space capsule. It was in brilliant colour and the image was as sharp as a tack, not like the grey grainy image the Soviets had published in newspapers around the world only a couple of months previously. That image was claustrophobic and it looked as if the cosmonaut Alexei Leonov was being strangled by the cable that tethered him to his craft Voskhod 11. This had been a big boost for the Soviets who had again beaten the Americans to have had the first spacewalk which lasted 10 minutes. Not to be outdone the Americans three months later (June 3rd 1965) did their first spacewalk which lasted 21 minutes outside of Gemini 4 with Edwin White performing expansively and gracefully, recorded in gorgeous colour. Of course they had to have better images and a spacewalk that lasted twice as long, they were Americans weren't they? They were not going to be outdone at any cost, even though they were playing catch-up to the Russians.

This image proclaiming the first American Spacewalk got more publicity and generated more excitement than the previous record breaking Soviet effort. Of course they would go down in history as being the first, but it would be the Americans that were remembered rather than the Soviets. What does this say about the power of publicity?

It filled me with excitement because all of a sudden I was again thinking about humans in space and colonizing the Moon and Mars. I hadn't looked at a science fiction book during the time I had spent in Europe. For me it was such a different place from where I grew up that I might as well have been on another planet. It was exciting enough just being there.

I raced into the embassy and asked if it was possible to obtain a poster of that photo, and sure enough, the staff were happy to supply me with a magnificent large posted printed on both sides so if it was held up to the light it looked like a colour transparency. I took this home and mounted it between two sheets of glass and had it prominently displayed in my room.

The 1960s were years of world firsts, and the future that we unconsciously extrapolated from events and ideas promulgated over those 10 years, was bright and exciting, full of wondrous and magical possibilities. It seemed our imagination was unbounded and that anything was possible. Well, the future we imagined then is not the future we got, unfortunately. When the idea of colonizing space was abandoned, or rather forgotten and put off for some far future date, I was extremely disappointed. Sometime after that the poster of Edward White's mind boggling spacewalk disappeared. I have no recollection now of what happened to it, but it was probably put it aside with other stuff stored in the garage which would eventually have been thrown out to make room for more stuff to be stored.

The birthplace of Hellenic Culture

Epirus is considered by many to be the birthplace of Hellenic culture. It is the most mountainous area and is the home of the tallest mountain in Greece, Mount Olympus the home of the Gods.

Not 30 kilometres away from the capital Ioannina was the birthplace of Alexander the Great. The river Archeron which the ancients believed led to the underworld flows through Epirus. Dodona, the site of the oracle that the God Zeus consulted is only fifteen or so kilometres from Ioannina and is mentioned in the great epic poems of Homer.

I stood beside a high stone wall that surrounded the old city, the court of Ali Pasha, and the fortress built by the Turks who occupied this city for almost 500 years — they occupied Epirus for 480 years from 1431 to 1913 — and watched the bus depart.

Scattered along the wall were stalls where local farmers were selling produce, and the nearby kafeneion were noisy and crowded with people drinking 'Turkish' coffee and passing the time of day in lively conversation.

Dad once told me that the only good thing the Turks ever did was to introduce coffee brewing to Greece.

People strolled along the lakefront with barely a glance towards the island near its centre that was covered by a mosque dating back to the beginnings of the Turkish occupation. The Mosque is now a museum and a short boat ride takes you out there. The lake was infamous because the overlord Ali Pasha drowned concubines and lovers both male and female who had not satisfied him by binding their hands and feet and stuffing them into a large bag weighted with rocks after which his soldiers would throw the bag into the lake. They say the spirits of these dead concubines walk the surface of the lake at night, and few people are game enough to venture out there unless it is broad daylight.

In 1809 Lord Byron as a young poet visited this town and was fascinated by the opulence of the court of Ali Pasha. His first steps in Greece had been in Epirus and he fell in love with the wildness of the mountains and the rugged people inhabiting them. His poetry based on his experiences here helped make him famous. According to Aristotle, the part of Epirus where the border was forced upon the inhabitants is Threspotia, and it was here that the Greek race was born as well as its language.

My father was proud of this fact especially since he came from this very same area. The people here are lighter skinned, often with blue eyes and blondish hair. My father had bluish grey eyes and classical features. He lost his hair before I was born and I only ever saw greying light brown hair which he let grow on one side so he could brush it across his bald head; most of the time though he wore a hat which protected his head from the sun.

Dad's town found itself inside Albania when the Powers of the day delineated where the border line should be and he was forced to escape with some friends at night because no one was allowed to enter or leave the country. He had come back from America where he went in 1913, and had been home for only a couple of years when he decided to leave again because conditions were so difficult and there was no work for anyone. Unable to go back to America he opted for Australia. Unable to leave legitimately Dad and his friends sneaked out one night and made their way to the coast where they convinced a fisherman to smuggle them across to the island of Corfu (Kerkyra). There they managed to obtain Greek passports for the voyage to Australia. They refused even to consider an Albanian passport. 'We are not Albanian refugees. We have been Greeks for thousands of years, and suddenly we are told we are no longer Greek but are Albanian… Never,' Dad told them. 'I would rather die than be Albanian.' They were issued with Greek passports and they made their way to Athens and then Piraeus where they caught an Italian steamer (Re D'Italia which meant King of Italy but which Dad always called Red Italia) to Australia arriving on Boxing Day 1924 in Melbourne after months of constant sea sickness.

'*Yani…*' a voice called and I turned to see Spiro Lillis coming towards me. He was one of Dad's oldest friends, one of those who had escaped with Dad when the border between Albania and Greece became official and movement across it either way was prohibited. He came to Australia on the same dilapidated ship with Dad, and had worked and raised a family, but after 45 years in Australia he decided to retire in his homeland, so he sold up and went back to Greece, to Ioannina because it was the largest Epirotic city and the one nearest to Dervitzani where he and Dad were born and which was now just over the border in Albania.

He hardly looked a day older than the last time I had seen him, and that had been at least ten years earlier. Dad was the same; there was something about these guys from these mountains that when they got to certain age they never seemed to get older or change physically very much. They always looked the same, year after year.

We shook hands and he embraced me with a solid hug. He had known me since I was born. We had been to as many parties and name days at his house over the years as he had to ours. I had sent him a letter from Athens to say I would come for a visit and had given him the approximate arrival date and time.

He had been having a coffee with friends in the nearest kafeneion so he immediately took me there and ordered me a coffee and then introduced me to his friends, some of whom had found their way to America before Dad and Spiro had left and had done the same as him, retired, sold up, and returned to live in their homeland. They seemed happy enough but I got the feeling there was some underlying tension or perhaps it was disappointment. I don't know about the American Greeks but the ones like Spiro who had sold up and came back to retire and invest their savings so they could live off them discovered that having bought assets in Ioannina (or anywhere in Greece for that matter) if they decided they didn't want them, they could only sell them for local currency. Local currency, Drachmas, could not be exchanged for Australian or American dollars. No one outside of Greece wanted Drachmas. They were in effect worthless. The government was happy to exchange good currency for Drachmas, but simply wouldn't allow the reverse exchange.

After a few days there I understood the underlying tension was disappointment combined with frustration and resentment. In their minds while they had worked and lived in Australia for forty or more years were nostalgic memories of what the good things in life had been when they were children. They had constantly talked about this amongst themselves. Bad memories and difficult times were glossed over or hidden; only the good memories remained foremost in their minds. It was these good memories that drew them back, and the fact that their savings, or the money they got from liquidating the assets they had built up over their years in Australia could go a long way in Greece.

The discovery that Greece was not like they remembered it was forty or fifty years previously, and that it had changed radically over that time, was difficult to reconcile. What they also failed to realise is that over the time they had been away, almost a lifetime, they too had changed and were not anything like they were when they first arrived in Australia.

Spiro had liked it at first. He bought a small apartment block and leased out several units to generate some income. There was no reciprocal arrangement between Greece and Australia regarding pensions so although Spiro was eligible for an Australian age pension he could not obtain it while living in Greece. (*At least not until many years later when agreements had been fostered between the two countries and he came back for a visit to organize his pension. By then he had been there too long to envisage returning to Australia.*) He had to make what he had last for the rest of his life, which meant investing in something rather than simply spending it.

Too bad if he didn't like living where he was. He was trapped, and if he sold his property he would get a lot of money, none of which could be exchanged for a useful currency and none of which could be spent anywhere else but in Greece. The only place he wanted to live in Greece was Epirus. The rest of Greece was far too different for him. But Epirus was still provincial; perhaps too provincial, which had been attractive at first but he soon tired of what little it had to offer. He was not happy living here but he knew he would feel worse elsewhere in Greece so he stayed where he was.

I actually had a good time as all the old guys who had known me as a child wanted to show me around and tell me about their life. They were happy to have someone from Australia who would understand them and their reasons for their disappointment. It was fun at first but after a week or two the underlying depression these old timers unknowingly exhibited started to make me depressed as well, so I thought it better to move on.

I took the bus that goes from Ioannina to Thesaloniki (Salonica), a long winding trip through the most rugged mountains in Greece. It was a slow journey of seemingly endless twists and turns with the driver constantly changing up and down gears with much crunching noises from beneath the bus where the engine was located interspersed with spirited curses and swearing in Greek. Most of the passengers slept through this while I stared out the window at forested walls reaching up to an invisible sky or looked down very deep narrow clefts where water rippled and glistened at the bottom.

— *Ephemeron* —

It was late in the trip and close to Thesaloniki when the bus drove out onto a high plain where jagged peaks, old volcanic cores, jutted up into the sky. The tops of these peaks were often covered with monasteries where monks spent their days in contemplation. Their only access was some kind of pulley arrangement where they could be lowered down or hauled up in a basket like contraption. How they got up there centuries ago to build these monasteries was a mystery to me. They were built from the same stones that the peaks were composed of, and these would have to have been hauled up by hand in much the same contraptions the monks today use for access.

The main part of Thesaloniki facing the sea curved around a wide bay that had a sea wall built, I believe, by the Phoenicians. The space behind the wall had been filled in and the surface sealed to become road and pathway. There was no beach. City buildings came right up to the road and walkway. A wind blew in towards the city off the sea and waves splashed furiously against the sea wall as if in protest. Wet patches where spray flew over the walkway and road were something I had to negotiate as I walked along. There weren't too many people out walking so I guess it was the windy weather that was keeping them in.

The few people I spoke to in the hotel where I stayed a night were excited about the coming World's Fair which they were going to host in a few months' time but I wouldn't be in Greece by that time.

Thesalon*iki waterfront as it was 10 years earlier in 1955, photo courtesy of F. Glasbrenner.*

The next day I caught a bus going to Athens where I would spend the next three weeks while waiting for the departure of the Australis which was still being renovated or remodelled to convert it from the faded luxury liner it had once been as an American ship into a one class passenger shuttle to bring migrants to Australia.

(Chandris Lines never commissioned new ships, they always bought old liners from major shipping companies and remodelled or converted them to suit their present needs. The *Australis* had originally been the *American Star*.)

I went to Piraeus quite a lot and could see the ship in the shipyard which was closed off to the general public. It didn't look like it was anywhere near ready to set sail for Australia in three or four weeks' time.

I liked Piraeus because not only was it Greece's major shipping port and terminal for passenger liners, it was also a ferry terminal for the many smaller ships that travelled back and forth from a plethora of nearby islands; yet with all that it still maintained the atmosphere of a fishing port with trawlers and skiffs and smaller yachts, and all the sundry businesses to serve fishermen and travellers as well as assist with the maintenance of boats and ships of all sizes.

Barely three weeks later several tugboats, furiously churning water and puffing out huge black clouds of smoke, pulled and pushed the Australis from the shipyard across the harbour to position her beside a passenger wharf. Immediately dozens of workers precariously balanced in scaffolds hanging all along the length of the ship frantically scraped away rust and painted the sides a brilliant white, while cranes loaded on board what looked like stacks of panels and other building materials. She certainly didn't look ready to sail although I could see wisps of smoke coming from her blue funnels.

A few days later I was notified by letter that passengers could board in preparation for sailing in two days so I packed what I had with me in Athens and took the commuter train to Piraeus for the last time.

They were going to sail whether the ship was ready or not. They had a deadline to meet and about 2000 passengers in Australia waiting for this ship to take them to Europe. They were going to continue the modifications while at sea and by the time the Australis got to Australia she would be ready having doubled her carrying capacity.

The Australis, not quite ready for departure, photo courtesy of Wolfram Dallwitz.

The shambles of departure

The departure date was an absolute shambles. There were thousands of people everywhere and none of them knew what they were doing, where they were going or anything else. I managed to get on board and found my allocated cabin. No one else had been in there yet so I picked what I thought was the best bed and left my couple of bags on it to indicate possession, then I went back up to the top deck to watch the goings-on. There were several others who like me were returning after some time in Europe and I recognized one person who had been on the Ellinis with me 18 months before. We nodded briefly.

Passengers, the immigrants who were going to Australia filed on via a broad gangplank near the centre of the ship. Officers dressed immaculately in their white uniforms were explaining, becoming more harassed by the moment, where each arrival had to go. Stewards were taking them and showing them to their cabins. Meanwhile another gangplank nearer to the bow of the ship was occupied by a steady stream of workers coming and going. These were the people still making finishing touches to alterations to the living spaces on board. It seems that where luxury cabins had once been big and spacious, they were now being divided into smaller cabins that could pack in more people. Most of the heavy construction had been completed while the ship was in the dockyard nearby, but things like painting, wallpapering, laying of vinyl floors, and other finishing touches were still happening. My allocated cabin still smelt faintly of fresh paint, so I left the door open to allow it to air off after dumping my gear on my chosen bunk.

There was no lunch served but sandwiches and other small items were available in various locations around the ship, bars which would remain closed until the ship departed, and in shaded places on the upper decks and near the swimming pool were trestle tables laid out with food, tea and coffee, water and soft drinks. It looked makeshift, but was welcomed by all those who had settled in earlier and were wandering about watching the goings-on while waiting for departure.

Going back down to my cabin I found two other young men from a remote village had been allocated the other bunks. They looked a bit lost and couldn't speak any English. It was clear that they didn't know how to use the toilet facilities in the cabin and thought the shower recess was for shitting in since there was a pile of shit over the grate in the middle and some paper tossed aside in one corner. I tried to explain that this was for washing in, not shitting in, but they couldn't understand me. In the end I demonstrated how to use the adjacent toilet by dropping my pants and sitting down on it to show them. I then got them to pick up the shit and discarded toilet paper in the shower recess and indicated they should put it in the toilet. I showed them how to push the button to flush it. I went back and turned on the shower and left it on long enough to wash the residue down the grate. They still looked lost after that so I left them to ponder the wonders of modern plumbing and went back up on deck. They must have got the message because neither of them left any shit in the shower again although they still left piles of used toilet paper in the corner of the toilet recess.

Passengers were not allowed near the bow or in the area of the top deck. This was roped off and there were piles of old plaster board, planks of wood, imitation wood panelling, bits of furniture, strange tangles of wire and twisted plumbing pipes, huge empty paint tins and who knows what else haphazardly piled in heaps. It was explained that renovations were still continuing and that some parts so the ship would not be accessible until we were well out to sea and half way to Australia.

So to me what had seemed like thousands of people trying to board turned out to be a bit less than a thousand. Only half the ship was serviceable, but rather than sail an empty ship under renovation to Australia the company decided it would take a limited number to defray costs. The official maiden voyage would begin once the ship reached Australia and took on board some 2000 passengers bound for Europe. We were basically on a shakedown cruise during which they were racing against time to finish everything.

Departure was an anticlimax, nothing like what I had experienced on the Ellinis when she left Melbourne and then Sydney 18 months ago. There were no streamers no excitement, just a lot of worried poorly dressed people crowding the decks to watch the shore as the ship with the assistance of tugboats eased into deeper water. It was as if the ship was ashamed to be leaving in such a moribund state.

A dinner of sorts was served late that night and everyone felt disappointed with this. During the night the ship sailed out into the Sea of Crete and around this magnificent island of which we saw nothing.

We saw no islands at all and there are thousands of Greek islands. Half of Greece is made up of islands. We must have gone around the Dodecanese Islands around sunset but again we saw nothing but some lights in the darkening haze near the horizon which suggested a town on a nearby island. Much later that night we stopped beside a large dark mass which turned out to be the island of Cyprus. Lights along the shoreline indicated a big town but we were told we would only be here for an hour or two and no one was going ashore.

A number of Lebanese and French speaking passengers were ferried across to the ship. Most of them spoke English as well. Although we could barely see the island in the dark, we could smell it; a wonderful aroma of trees and grass and earth that tended to push aside the smell of sea and salt. I think there were about a hundred passengers ferried aboard before the ship sailed. Not long after the sun came up we arrived at Port Said where we joined a convoy of ships waiting to go through the Suez Canal.

Again, we were not allowed to go ashore and all we could do was peer at the sandy land and the outline of a distant city which was Port Said.

The air was oppressive, full of humidity, and the sea around appeared sluggish. A long line of ships of various sizes were anchored in the sea ahead of us and while we sat there sweltering more lined up behind us. The sky above was dirty and grey with the exhausts from the many ship's funnels as they waited with engines turning over for word to move into the canal.

There were problems with Egypt and with Israel (something to do with a brief war) which was why the Suez was being disputed and ships were being stopped from entering. Israel had control of the land, previously Egyptian, up to one side of the canal while Egypt controlled the other side. Eventually the convoy was allowed to enter and very slowly the ships began the tedious passage through the canal. We passed abandoned ships in the wider sections of the canal close to Port Suez. These ships had been stopped and they still had minimal crew on board to maintain them or they could have been taken for salvage. Slowly we made our way out into the Gulf of Suez and soon the ships ahead dispersed into the Red Sea. It seems we were lucky because not long after we exited the canal it was closed to all shipping and stayed that way for a long time.

Out next port of call was supposed to be Aden at the very tip of Yemen where the Gulf of Aden debouched into the Arabian Sea and eventually the Indian Ocean. This was a couple of days of slow cruising away.

Meanwhile the piles of rubbish on the foredeck grew bigger and more expansive with each hour at sea. There was some grumbling from returning passengers who thought they had been short-changed because this was not like the trip they had experienced on the way to Europe from Australia. The food wasn't good, there was no entertainment, but at least the bars were open and they could drown their sorrows at a very cheap price since drinks were tax and excise free.

I had two rolls of film left so I decided to shoot some sequences of the workmen piling the rubbish on the deck. There was nothing glamorous about this. It felt like being on a cargo boat but with lots of passengers.

Finally after much complaining from the hundred or so returning passengers the Captain organized a dance and miraculously found enough musicians to form a band to play for us. They had obviously been on board as part of the crew, but weren't supposed to start working until the ship reached Australia, but due to the number of complaints regarding the lack of suitable entertainment, which returning passengers expected, he convinced them to start early. The atmosphere seemed better after that first dance. Everyone had a few drinks, a nice dinner, and had danced the night away.

The next morning we were told that later that day we would be stopping at Djibouti instead of Aden. Apparently there was a civil war happening in Yemen and all boats had been advised to avoid stopping at Aden. Since the Australis needed to take on additional supplies we would have a 12 hour stop-over in Djibouti which was I think a part of Somalia at that time.

This was unexpected, and there was a lot of speculation about whether we should or could go ashore. We were advised not to go into the town of Djibouti as it was considered a dangerous place.

They should never tell people that because it only makes them want to go there more than ever, doesn't it?

The darkness that is Africa

It was sunset when docking procedures had been completed and after discussing whether to go into town or not with a couple of the Lebanese migrants who came aboard in Cyprus, I decided to share a taxi with them for a brief sojourn into the nearby town. There were dilapidated taxis coming and going from the dock where many passengers milled about uncertain as to whether they should go anywhere since it was rapidly getting darker.

We grabbed a taxi and one of the Lebanese guys spoke Arabic to the driver who was happy to take us. When we left the dock area there was no one to check passports, no customs officials, so we simply drove out onto the road into town. By this time it was dark and there was nothing to see. As we got closer to the town (also called Djibouti) flickering street lamps threw small cones of light onto the road which was barely paved and mostly dusty. These small patches of orange light were interspersed with much larger areas of blackness. Shadowy figures shuffled along through the darker areas as if trying to avoid the lighter patches.

The taxi driver was continuously speaking in Arabic, obviously extolling the virtues of his city and no doubt trying to convince the guys of the best places to go. As we got further into the central part of the city we encountered other taxis, trucks belching thick exhaust fumes, overcrowded busses with people hanging out of the doors, pedestrians who without looking wandered across the road or ran across unexpectedly while maniacally dodging in between the traffic. Our driver weaved in and out and all over the place while blasting his car horn. It appeared there were no traffic rules whatever. It was survival of the fastest, the one who could dodge the quickest to avoid being hit. Strangely enough, through this melee we never saw one accident.

We were deposited in front of a dubious looking bar in a part of town that seemed darker than it should be with nearby buildings much in need of repair and the few shops we could see had iron bars or metal screens in front of the windows. The taxi vanished in an instant.

This is not a good place, was what I thought the moment we were left on the footpath. The air in the street was heavy and humid — we were in the tropics — yet at the same time dry and dusty, which seemed an odd combination. There was a foul underlying odour which at first I couldn't identify but later thought it was the smell of shit… human shit? Dog shit? Other animal shit? There was also the scent of weird spice and food cooking somewhere on a grill or hotplate. Perhaps it was further down the street because I couldn't see anything where it could emanate from anywhere near us.

The people in the street looked warily at us. The taxi driver had dumped us and disappeared so quickly that to some passers-by it must have seemed that we suddenly appeared out of nowhere.

Are they sizing us up? I wondered, trying to figure out if it would be worth their while to assault us? This was the first time I had been in a place where everyone was African. We were the only Caucasians in the street and we obviously stood out. It was like we were on another planet. Everything was so different from what we were used to. The sound of the language people spoke, the clothes people wore, if they weren't flowing loose robes with splashes of colour, they were worn out hand-me-down mismatches of jeans and T shirts. Many people were barefoot. Others used sandals.

I nudged one of the guys to suggest we should get moving. 'We should look as if we know where we were going rather than standing here looking lost,' I said.

They grunted an agreement and we headed for the bar since we were right in front of it.

Inside it was the same. Though it was noisy and there was hardly any diminution of sound when we entered, everyone in the place turned to look at us and continued to stare at us the whole time we were in there. The two Lebanese guys bought beers for themselves and for me, ordering of course in Arabic. They told me the accent here was very different but they could understand the language. While we sat at a table and drank the beers more people came into the bar and stared at us. It was creepy, but it didn't seem to bother the two Lebanese guys. It bothered me though. No wonder we were told not to come into town. Eventually someone dressed in a fancy suit approached and spoke to the guys. He looked a bit like a dandy in his bright blue checked suit compared to the other men in the bar who all seemed scruffy.

'He wants to know if we want to go to a brothel. They have very good girls there.'

'I don't think that would be a good idea,' I said.

We all shook our heads while one of the guys said 'yeah right, I don't like that at all.' He turned and said something to the dandy, who smiled and nodded as he reluctantly backed away.

'I think it's time we went somewhere else' I suggested.

We finished out watery beers and stood up. Again as we walked towards the door everyone followed our movement. No one moved but the way they stared was upsetting. It was like they were a bunch of pack animals waiting for their prey to make a mistake so they could pounce upon it and tear it to pieces.

We wandered along the street looking into the shops that were open. I bought a couple of postcards to send home. We passed a dark side street and I heard a pack of dogs snarling and barking as they scrabbled over something unseen. Moving further along the street we paused in front of a small restaurant. A delicious smell emanated from it and we thought about having something to eat there, to try the local cuisine.

'It sure smells good,' I said. 'But I wonder how clean the kitchen is. Does anyone feel like a dose of diarrhoea?'

The two Lebanese guys laughed.

We decided that diarrhoea was definitely not something we wanted to take back to the ship.

'You know ever since we left the bar we have been followed' I said.

A small knot of men surreptitiously mumbling amongst themselves were standing about a hundred metres back along the footpath we had walked along. They were pretending to talk amongst themselves but they were all watching us.

'That's not a good sign is it?' one of the guys said.

The other one suggested we should go back to the ship immediately.

None of us could see any taxis in this street but the corner of a cross road was not too far ahead and that street seemed brighter so slowly we started walking towards it.

The group following kept pace stopping when we stopped and moving when we moved.

The moment we got around the corner we saw a taxi stand and there was a car stationed there. One of the guys immediately went to it and opened the rear door. The driver looked up and smiled as we piled into the back seat.

We told him to take us back to the docks where the ship was moored. He started to argue about the price when the guys dumped a pile of banknotes on the front seat next to him. He smiled expansively and scooped them up.

The group following us rounded the corner. They stopped when they saw us in the taxi. It looked like they were going to rush over and drag us out but the driver started the engine and took off with a screech of wheels, a blast of the car horn and the sound of brakes suddenly applied as we shot into a stream of traffic. I looked back to see the group wildly gesticulating and apparently making lots of noise, possibly screaming obscenities, maybe cursing the fact that they had hesitated and not acted sooner. Perhaps the reason we weren't attacked earlier was that there were three of us together and the two guys with me spoke Arabic which may have confused those we encountered long enough for us to be able to get away from them.

This taxi took us through a well-lit brighter part of the city where lots of clean looking shops were open and the many people there were much better dressed than those we saw in the dark part of town. The first driver had obviously dumped us in an area where he knew we would have been targets. I suspected he must have had some arrangement with the bar keeper or at the least with some of the bar's patrons.

All the way back we thought irrationally that we would be stopped, but even though we slowed down for a couple of makeshift roadblocks, the driver yelled something to the people manning the blockage and we were let through. Again there was no one to stop us going into the port area where the Australis was docked, no customs and no passport checks. Anyone could come and go without question, which is probably what made this place so dangerous.

These days this part of Africa is the home of pirates who attack and capture all manner of ships passing through the Gulf of Aden. They ransom the ships for millions of dollars and also the passengers for whatever they can get. The narrow passage between the Horn of Africa and the Arabian Peninsula is now patrolled by American, Australian and French warships to prevent piracy but it still goes on and ships are still captured and held for ransom. Pirate gangs rule the towns and cities which are all dangerous places, for visitors as well as those who have no choice but to live there. None of this was going on while we were there, but there was violence in the form of a civil war in Ethiopia and its province of Eritrea which borders Somalia and Djibouti, where there was also much civil unrest. It was a dangerous place then and unfortunately it is even worse now.

It was a relief to get back to the ship.

Onwards to Australia

The Australis departed at dawn. The ship's newsletter later that morning informed us that we would not stop in Bombay but would continue on to Fremantle in Australia.

The clean smell of the air at sea without a trace of the dust and rotten humidity of that part of Africa was uplifting. The Horn of Africa was only a smudge of greyish brown air low on the horizon behind us when I came up on deck later that morning. I was sure the rest of Africa must have been a lot better than where we had stopped, and for a moment wondered what The Republic of Chad would have been like. I was to go there with Los Matecocos but unfortunately not enough band members wanted to make the trip so it didn't happen. It was a disappointment for me, but if Chad had been anything like Somalia and Djibouti, then I was glad it had been cancelled and we never went.

The sun was shining and the sea sparkled. The swell was gentle and the colour of the water was no longer the greenish shade seen near the coast but was a dark almost-black blue which meant we were well into the Indian Ocean. Going towards the bow of the ship I found the workers who were doing the renovations had started to shovel the rubble from their work overboard. They threw over the old panels, the broken bits of wood, the wasted floor coverings, cracked plaster board, empty paint buckets, tangled wiring, twisted plumbing pipes, unused bags of cement, and whatever else they had accumulated on the foredeck since leaving Greece. I went back down to my cabin and got my Bolex camera to film this happening using the last roll of film left. It took a couple of hours for all the rubbish to be thrown overboard and the deck to be washed down and cleaned.

Meanwhile many of the passengers continued to complain that the food served was of poor quality. It was worse than what you could get at a local pub, or on a good day it was about equal to what was available at airport food dispensaries. It was nothing like the variety or quality we had on the voyage out. It seemed the crew and the ship's officers didn't care since individual paying passengers returning to Australia were of no importance. There were probably no more than a hundred of us. The shipping line was being paid by our government to ferry sponsored migrants to Australia, and these people wouldn't complain no matter what the quality of the food or the service of it was like. Apart from that, there was little in the way of entertainment, and worse still, sometimes the plumbing backed up and toilets and bathrooms smelled bad and were unhealthy places which no one wanted to visit, but unfortunately didn't have a choice. The crew kept promising all would be fine in a day or so but these promises never eventuated. They were delaying tactics to keep passengers quiet for the week it would take to cross the Indian Ocean. It was not a very happy voyage.

In the seven days it took to cross the ocean work continued on finishing the interior renovations and any more rubbish generated was enthusiastically tossed over the side. They were racing against time to get the ship finished and cleaned up to take on the huge number of passengers waiting in Melbourne. They finally got the plumbing fixed by the time the Australis docked at Fremantle.

The moment the Australis docked a lot of passengers contacted newspapers and TV stations and complained about the voyage and the conditions on board. By the time I managed to go ashore film crews were interviewing them. There were several groups of men with huge cameras resting on their shoulders or holding large padded microphones above their heads, as well as several reporters speaking at the cameras or talking to various clumps of passengers. I approached one of the crews from channel 9 and told them I had film of what the passengers were complaining about. They were very interested so I gave them the two rolls of film. (Each was four minutes long being a 100 foot 16 mm roll shot at 24 frames per second.) They also interviewed me and filmed me handing them the rolls of film.

It was on the news that night but I never saw any of it because once again the Australis was at sea travelling across the Great Australian Bight towards Melbourne where all of us, except for the Lebanese people from Cyprus who were going on to Sydney, were getting off.

There was a huge crowd waiting at Port Melbourne when we docked. Returning passengers disembarked first since all we had to do was to pass through customs and collect our luggage after which we were free to go.

Mum, Dad, My friend Brian who was virtually a member of the family, Christine and Verga with faces obscured and my very young brother Paul waiting for me to come down the gangplank at Port Melbourne.

The migrants would all have to be processed before they were allowed to come ashore and meet those waiting for them. I remembered what Dad had told me a number of times about how he felt when he first came to Australia, to this very same port back in 1924, and knew that the thousand or so migrants waiting to be processed must be feeling anxious and uncertain of their future, but all would no doubt be hoping that life here would be infinitely better than life had been wherever they had come from.

I felt happy to see Mum and Dad, my friend Brian, my older sister and young Paul waiting to greet me as I came down the long ramp from the customs lounge.

I wondered whether I would be able to settle back into life as it had been before, or whether I had changed while in Europe. I hadn't been away long enough to notice any obvious changes as we drove home, but nothing stays the same does it?

There is always change and we always have to adapt.

Home again

I had barely been home one day when the phone rang. The cheery voice on the other end said 'Hi John, it's Beryl.'

When I didn't respond immediately, too surprised to think of something to say — she was the last person I expected to ring me more or less the moment I got back — the empty low hiss on the phone line was broken once again with her voice, only this time she seemed hesitant.

'It's me, Beryl… from Birdland… I saw you on TV. Channel 9 news,' she said.

So that's how she knew I was back.

'That was broadcast while we were still at sea in the Great Australian Bight.' I said as I tried to gather my thoughts. 'I haven't seen it, but Mum told me it was a good report.'

'Yeah, that must have been one hell of a trip.'

'It had its moments.'

'I was just wondering how you were… if maybe we could get together and talk… You could tell me about Europe.'

That sounded reasonable. It suddenly occurred to me that something must have happened for her to be calling out of the blue like that and suggesting we should meet.

When I didn't say anything she said in a softer voice, 'Maybe this was a bad idea…'

'No it's fine; I'd love to get together with you. There's a lot to talk about.'

So we made a date. I would go over to her place the following night — because she had separated from Roger she was now living with her parents in Monash, somewhere near Dandenong and quite a drive from Yarraville — and after that we would decide whether to go out somewhere or just stay there and catch up on what had been happening since we'd last seen each other.

She introduced me to her mother who hovered about in the adjoining kitchen to the lounge room where we sat close together on a couch while ostensibly watching TV. Every time I looked sideways I could see her mum in the background doing something that wasn't making any noise so she could listen (I presumed) to what we were talking about.

Intimidated by the hovering presence I suggested we should meet in town in a couple of days, and she readily accepted. She clung to me at the front door, kissed me quite passionately (which startled me with its unexpectedness) and as she pulled away she whispered; 'Love me, love my child.'

I didn't say anything to that, but it certainly gave me something to think about. There had been kid's toys in the lounge room but I had not taken any notice of them. I had momentarily forgotten that she and Roger had a son, and that she most probably had custody of him which would explain why she was living at home with her parents. She would need their help to look after him while she was at work. He would be a bit over two years old so he was probably in bed and asleep when I had arrived at her parent's house.

She stood at the front door and watched as I got back into Dad's big blue Falcon. She waved as I drove off and I waved back.

After meeting in town we drove to my place. Mum and Dad were down at Portarlington where they had a holiday house which needed some maintenance; the usual stuff, grass cutting, dusting and cleaning inside since no one had been there during the winter, but it was spring now and they needed to get it ready for summer occupation.

I was wary of Beryl's intentions after that last enigmatic statement she had made the other night. I still liked her, but having just got home I had barely had time to settle down and think about what I wanted to do. I certainly wasn't prepared to get involved with anyone at that stage, at least not until I had some direction in life. Her unexpected contact had literally floored me. Her life had certainly changed dramatically from what it had previously been. Having a young child would do that, let alone separating from her husband.

We had a couple of drinks and listened to some music. I put on the disc of Los Matecocos that I had brought back from France. I explained to her that this was the band I had worked with for a couple of months. We danced a bit in the lounge room and perhaps our dancing suggested a degree of intimacy that wasn't really there, because suddenly she was all over me. It was like a jarring electric shock. To me her overwhelming approach suggested a feeling of desperation which stunned me.

Instinctively I pushed her away.

It wasn't so much the push but more my mental reaction that stopped us.

What was I getting myself into?

I was not ready for this kind of commitment. The thought of being involved with anyone had never entered my head and this was too sudden, too unexpected. The time spent in Europe had changed me without me consciously realizing it and I had grown away from what I once was. I was different now; definitely not the same person who had been infatuated with Beryl just over two years ago. But I couldn't articulate it. I didn't really know what to say.

There was an odd expression in her eyes; obviously she was disappointed with my reaction, perhaps even surprised. She gave me a sad smile as we stood apart for a moment, neither sure what to do next.

After a few minutes she suggested quietly that I take her home.

We have not seen or spoken to each other since then.

A notable year

I went back to working at Williamstown Dry Cleaners and quickly settled into the same old routines as before. It was as if nothing had changed, as if I had never been to Europe. Wally and I got together and discussed in more detail the story we wanted to write, that we had talked about in long letters while I had been away and we drank heaps of wine while writing. The end result was an unpublishable stack of pages, (over 500 of them in what we thought was a finished draft) that were absolutely awful to read when sober. Still we had fun writing it which I suppose is as good a reason as any to sit down and write.

That year however was notable because I bought a copy of a new book that caused a sensation amongst those who read it. It was *Dune*, by Frank Herbert.

Here was a book that I could not put down. I had to keep reading, totally immersed, turning page after page to see what was going to happen next. It was a magnificent sprawling epic full of intrigue and action, love and hate, set on an incredible desert world that supplied an essential ingredient needed to keep the Galactic Empire operating. Here was a galactic culture that had foresworn the use of machines and computers and relied on mental powers enhanced by a rare spice produced from the giant sandworms of Arrakis (Dune).

What I found great about this book was the meticulous way Frank Herbert had created his world of Dune, its desert ecology, the people who lived wild in the deserts and those who imposed their will on them in order to 'mine' the spice they so needed. The feuds between the families that controlled planets and star systems, the fight between the desert tribes and the controlling families, the coming of their messiah, the long term plans of those who worked deep behind the surface activities, the religions, the economics, the ecology and all the stuff that makes a world truly believable were all embedded into this story without being obvious info-dumps, as most lesser writers would have done it.

Herbert supplied an appendix detailing the history of Dune, its ecology in great detail, the religion of the desert tribes, and other background history. He even supplied a glossary of words and their meanings so we could understand the terminology used in the story, and maps of the planet Arrakis. For those who didn't like info-dumps this was wisely placed at the end of the book so it didn't interrupt the flow of the story.

The book became a huge seller, and if Frank Herbert's reputation had been obscure even though he had written some brilliant earlier work (*Dragon in the Sea* or *Under Pressure* to give an early novel both titles), everything he had done up to that point in time was eclipsed by *Dune*. (*Dune* won the Hugo and Nebula Awards and would go on to be regarded as the great SF novel for that decade.) It set such a high standard in quality and the complexity of the writing and research behind it that Frank Herbert himself had trouble equalling it.

The beauty of a great book is that it leaves much to your imagination and allows you to speculate endlessly about what might happen after the story ends. If there is a sequel it usually is a disappointment. I definitely felt this was the case with the two following books that completed what was then being called the *Dune trilogy*.

Dune became so popular with fans constantly clamouring for more of the same Frank Herbert unfortunately felt compelled to write a sequel which he did, a short volume called *Dune Messiah* published in 1971. It didn't sell near as well as *Dune*, and too many copies printed ended up in remainder bookshops, but nevertheless it was popular enough to suggest another book. This turned up in 1976 and was the rather turgid and less interesting *The Children of Dune*. It should have finished the 'trilogy'.

I felt *Dune* was complete in itself, with what it suggested of previous galactic history and what it promised for future galactic history. There was no need to write more.

In hindsight Frank was now saying that all along he had envisaged the Dune books as a trilogy. Perhaps he had to justify the years he had spent researching and creating his desert world. He was among other things a biologist and ecologist who had worked on schemes for reclaiming desert environments and knew a lot about it. He had done extensive research on undersea geology, jungle botany and anthropology, psychology, and navigation. He was the 20th century equivalent of the Victorian gentleman of science.

Many of his major works of writing involved an ecological theme. One that perhaps should have been as well-known as *Dune* was a novel, *The Green Brain*. It originally appeared as the novelette *Greenslaves* in Amazing Stories in 1965 —the same year as *Dune's* publication — and was later expanded into a brilliant novel. *The Green Brain* was published in 1968, long before any sequels to *Dune* appeared. It was a strangely brooding story set in a world ravaged by the overuse of insecticides (*Silent Spring* could possibly have inspired this as I'm sure it did many other author's extrapolations) and biological poisons, where finally the insects are starting to fight back. The whole point of the book was that we must live with them and they must live with us if the world as a whole is to survive. The solution is rather horrifying but inevitable in the context of this story. It takes place in the Amazon basin and if anyone is familiar with tropical climates or has been to the Amazon Basin they will immediately realize that Frank depicted this part of the world and the problems it suffers today with incredible accuracy. It was one of his best books, but sadly is almost forgotten today having been eclipsed by *Dune* and all the follow up books he was compelled by fans and publishers to write.

He published a non SF novel *Soul Catcher* in 1972 just after *Dune Messiah* appeared. It did well enough to go into a second printing as a hardcover but was ignored by the SF fans. It was also ignored on the whole by regular readers of mainstream fiction because they had already categorized Herbert as an SF writer. I think he wanted to prove he could write other stuff because quite possibly he could see himself getting locked into nothing but Dune books. In my view this was a better book than *Dune* and very different, yet at the same time it gave him the opportunity to have his characters living in harmony with a wilderness environment.

It was a revenge story in which a Native American student of anthropology, enraged by the rape and later suicide of his sister, kidnaps the young son of the Undersecretary of State and threatens to sacrifice him on behalf of all innocent American Indian children that had been murdered. This is a beautifully written story that examines the role of captor and captive and how they bond together and eventually depend upon each other.

I Spoke to Frank about this book when I met him in Melbourne at Space Age Books in 1981 and he told me he thought it was his best work. He was delighted that I also thought the same. What more can I say? He signed a copy of the book for me. The only other book I also got him to sign was my original Gollanz copy of *Dune*.

What is even sadder from my point of view is that even after he died there are seemingly endless trilogies supposedly based on notes he left behind detailing the galactic history that led to Dune, as well as future possible suggestions for what might happen after. These have been seized upon by fans that seem to want to read endlessly about Dune and beyond. How much of that really was left by Frank, and how much of that is invented or extrapolated by the writers tasked to continue the Dune Saga? I lost interest before Frank had completed the last two books (which have been on my shelf for years unread), let alone before his son Brian and his co-writer started continuing the saga.

The population Bomb was a book by Paul (and Anne) Ehrlich that hit bookshops in 1968.

It had gathered together pre-existing theories of possible catastrophes one of which was the Malthusian concept that population will overtake agriculture and food supply — unless controlled — resulting in massive famines, in Ehrlich's view theses famines and wars over food, producing massive camps of starving refugee would take place in the 1970s and 1980s. To stop this he advocated putting sterilizing drugs in water supplies, improved contraception, abortion and sex education. This caused outrage in the USA as well as many other countries which naturally turned his book into a best seller.

I thought this book was overly didactic and exaggerated. I had not seen any evidence of overpopulation, except perhaps in Paris and London which were big cities with millions of people in them. Perhaps it was worse in the large American cities; I had no idea. But at the very least his book got a lot of publicity and made massive numbers of people aware of the possibilities he predicted.

That his predictions never came true he claimed later was because he had warned people, but that his underlying premise still held for the future because the population was doubling every generation.

Rachel Carson whose book *Silent Spring* I had read in Europe but which had been published in 1962, 6 years earlier than Ehrlich's book, expounded similar ideas about how humans were destroying their environment and consequently their sources of food which could only have dire consequences in the future.

Many Science Fiction authors had also thought along similar lines and were producing new novels and stories about environmental hazards, overpopulation and how to control it. The post-apocalyptic scenario brought on by deliberate or accidental atomic war had run its course, and the new apocalypses for the 1960s and early 1970s were all about overpopulation or a world destroyed by human pollution and greenhouse warming.

So what's new today? One of the most telling comments from Professor Ehrlich is his recent statement that in 50 years we have turned the US from a country for people into a country for cars, and that we should spend the next 50 years reversing that.

But who listens to Professor Ehrlich?

Nobody, it seems, because we keep on doing the same things over and over, and will no doubt keep on doing them until the runaway greenhouse effect starts turning this beautiful planet into another one like Venus at which point people will certainly notice, but by then it will be too late to change it or stop it.

Not long after finishing *Dune*, I read *Make Room, Make Room* by Harry Harrison. It was the first novel I can recall reading about overpopulation, massive starvation, degradation of the human condition for all but the wealthiest, and it had a twist that for its time was frightening and unique. It also showed that no matter what the circumstances there will always be hope for a better future, and that some good people will always exist. Although it should have been a depressing book it was quite the opposite, leaving me feeling uplifted. This was, I felt at the time, Harry's best book. Much of the ideas in this book were duplicated by other authors and filmmakers over the next few years, but no one did it better than Harry Harrison.

A movie of this book, called Soylent Green, was made in 1973 starring Charlton Heston, Leigh Taylor Young, Chuck Connors and Edward G Robinson. It was a rather good film too, I thought when I saw it — A lot better than some of the other SF films of the previous decade which did nothing more than depict mutated monsters attacking humans and destroying cars and buildings ad infinitum. This film like several others from the 1970s, like Logan's Run, and Zero Population Growth, tried to deal with the consequences of overpopulation and shortage of food. Soylent Green did it better than most and therefore is worth another look if you come across it.

Music – noisier and ear shattering

One thing that had changed while I was away those 18 months was music. There were no longer any of the nightclubs I used to go to any more. They had either closed down or had changed to cater to a younger audience who wanted nothing but rock and roll groups that sounded like the Beetles or The Rolling Stones. Even groups that had started it like Bill Haley and the Comets, and others like that were passé. They weren't amplified enough or didn't use wailing screaming guitars. It seemed that the noisier and more ear-shattering the music was the better they liked it. Late night jazz clubs had vanished, and there was nowhere visiting musos other than rockers could play. I found it depressing.

I did manage a couple of recordings done in the studios at South Melbourne, but these recordings were to accompany a rock group or they were to make background crap to be piped into lifts and public spaces or in department stores where it was thought background music (derogatively called muzak) would enhance the workplace.

I even played for a Greek group on a 45 EP. I used a clay drum I had brought back with me from Egypt to create an Arabic sound in place of the tambourine like Turkish drums that should have been used but weren't because we didn't have any. The rhythm I played was the same afro sounding one based on the standard clave pattern which is common all down the East African coast. It sounds different when played on different types of drums but basically it fits into most kind of music that is in 4/4 or 4/8 patterns. It went well with the bouzoukis in the group.

Before we had gone into the Suez Canal, while the passenger ships were lined up in a long queue, some small boats had come alongside with vendors selling souvenirs and trinkets. I bought a simple clay drum with the skin head tied on with cord as a souvenir from one of them. I never thought that I would ever use it, but I did once, on that Greek recording, so in my mind that justified having bought it.

Les Ballets Africains

1965 was particularly notable for me as this was the year that the African Ballet (*Les Ballets Africains de la Republique de Guinea*) arrived in Melbourne as part of their tour of Australia. They were sponsored by David Hamilton McIlwraith who was known around the world as a choreographer and dancer using the name David Hamilton. Having sponsored this tour of the African Ballet he had been invited by the government of Guinea to sponsor a world tour.

Everywhere in the world these dancers were famous for their vigorous and athletic performances during which the girls always danced bare top. But not in backward Brisbane… it seemed the puritanical leaders of that State insisted the dancers wear bras. It was the joke of Australia, perhaps even the world and was widely reported in newspapers across the country.

The other thing David Hamilton did in 1965 was to build and operate a one million dollar theatre Restaurant in Russel Street underneath what had once been an art theatre. This was an astonishing theatre restaurant based on the famous Lido in Paris. He called it *The Lido* so everyone would know what it was like and my sister Zara was one of the chorus girl dancers employed there. My other sister Christine was also there as a showgirl or the Lido Goddesses as they called them. At

The cover of the programme issued for their performances around Australia autographed by Hamidou, one of the lead dancers and with a personal message from Italo Zambo to me.

that time showgirls who were nude or almost nude were not allowed to move much let alone dance. They simply posed or stood in strategic locations on the stage to create an exotic background. They were very popular with audiences. The dancers were free to move all over the stage as they were not nude, though they were scantily clad. It was a proper theatre with an orchestra in a pit below the level of the stage, between the stage and the audience which didn't sit in rows of seats as in a proper theatre but sat around tables where they were served a 4 course gourmet meal while they watched the show. It was extremely innovative for Melbourne in 1965. Needless to say initially it was very popular. Definitely a winner, it gave Melbourne an international aura that it had not had before.

The African Ballet was performing at the Comedy Theatre and the first day they arrived I went to the theatre and managed to get backstage where I wanted to talk to the drummers. These were spectacular performers and their drumming style, along with that of nearby Nigeria was what was taken to Cuba where it evolved into the kind of secular and religious drumming that I was interested in and had been playing. Most of the slaves taken to Cuba came from West Africa. This music was the basis of Cuban music, which was modified by Spanish and other European influences through syncretisation until it became what was known in the 1960s as Tropical Music. I simply had to see if I could play with them, offstage of course, because there was so much I wanted to learn.

I met the director of the company as well as the lead performers and invited them to come to my place (in Yarraville) on Sunday which was their day off, so we could share some food and talk about music, in other words a party.

Well they came, practically the whole company, 40 of them, and the girls cooked African food in the kitchen while Mum and Dad looked bemused, and the guys sat in groups and talked over coffee or tea, very few of them drank alcohol, and I got the drummers to show me some rhythm structures. I demonstrated to them how the Cuban guaguanco was put together with three drums and the stick pattern and they were fascinated because it was similar to some of the things they played. I also showed how it could be broken down into simpler parts that one drummer could play on three drums rather than having three drummers playing which was traditional. We had a great time and the next night when I watched a performance at the theatre I was delighted to hear the two lead drummers out of the group of six or so incorporating guaguanco into what they played.

What astonished me above all was the beautiful music played on a variety of instruments. One, like a primitive marimba (called a Balafon) was made from pieces of wood and had gourds underneath to echo and amplify the sound. And there were harps (Kora) utilizing a giant gourds as a sound boxes. They had at least eleven strings attached to a long wooden neck and produced the most exquisite sound when played and accompanied with singing. These were instruments never seen in

Playing congas with the lead drummer from the African Ballet at a private party. c.1965

Sharing a meal cooked by the ladies from the Ballet.

Italo Zambo *on the left playing what in Cuba was called a marimbula. It was a instrument using plucked metal tongs on a sounding box to produce base notes to accompany the guitar.*

Australia before, and the sophistication of the music played on them was unexpected enough to shatter anyone's idea that all Africans played were drums and that the music was primitive.

As for the drumming, it wasn't primitive at all. It was highly complex using several drummers to play rhythmic structures that were also melodic in nature, and these were overlaid with improvisation that accented the movements of the dancers who could dance to both the underlying structure as well as improvise within that structure. Every movement told a part of a story so there was nothing primitive about it. It was highly sophisticated. The music too, played on the other at-the-time strange instruments, had evolved over thousands of years into something as complex as Classical European music, but which retained

Acrobats and spectacular dancing apart from the music were the highlights of every performance. Italo Zambo is centre stage, wearing striped pants. Hamidou is behind him, the leading man in white baggy pants.

a freedom of improvisation that this European music didn't and couldn't have. They also used guitars and flutes which had been adopted from Western music culture which was unexpected. All in all Australia had never seen or heard anything like this before, and everybody was captivated.

There were many parties at my place with the ballet members, and as well they were invited to other parties and events most of which the lead drummer and the director insisted that I come along with them. I got to play drums with them at some of these parties so I was very happy. When the company started a regional tour of Victoria one of the ballet directors, Italo Zambo asked if his wife could stay behind because she was pregnant and was having some trouble and needed to rest. At our suggestion — that she should stay at our place where at least she knew someone rather than be by herself in a hotel room — he readily agreed. So for two weeks she stayed and my sister Christine was happy to be her companion during that time. If she had gone on tour she would have lost her baby. Staying with us saved her a lot of problems and possible discomfort. The baby was born not long after.

Forty years later when the company, with new dancers and musicians of course, arrived for a concert at the Gold Coast Arts Centre, I went to see them and was astonished to run into Italo in the foyer. He was the director of this company and although forty years older than that last time I had seen him, he had hardly changed. To me he still looked the same! He took me backstage and introduced me to the company as the second father of his son and explained that if it hadn't been for me suggesting his wife stay and rest at our place she would have lost her baby. It was in my eyes a great honour.

With the two artistic directors of the latest incarnation of Les ballets Africains, Italo Zambo and Hamidou Bangoura

40 years later, again with Italo Zambo, now director of Les Ballets Africains, on the Gold Coast in 2005.

Outside their Gold Coast hotel, one of the musicians demosntrating how to play the Kora – the beautiful West African Harp. c2005.

With Italo, Hamidou and the corps de ballet outside their Gold Coast hotel.

Tragedy at the beginnings of the Space Race

1965 became 1966 and things went back to being the same old boring stuff it had always been. The *Ballet Africains* had come and gone and the city of Melbourne seemed stifling to anyone with an artistic bent.

For me the only interesting events reported in newspapers that year and the one after were about the Russians and the Americans who were trying to outdo each other in their race into space. There was a lot of stuff about the war in Vietnam but that is not relevant here.

The first of the Apollo missions was sent up into orbit and it seemed as if whatever the Americans did the Russians outdid them in achieving something better or more spectacular.

There was the feeling the Americans were losing the space race.

Unmanned Apollo service modules were tested in space. These used the Saturn 1B rocket, the fore-runner to the giant Saturn 5.

And in January 1967 the first manned test of the Apollo command module became a disaster. Three astronauts, Gus Grissom, Ed White, and Roger Chaffee were making a countdown rehearsal when something went wrong.

As they climbed into the capsule they could smell something off. The radio wouldn't work at first but they fixed that. Sealed inside the capsule, a couple of hours later they frantically radioed mission control to report they were burning up. There was a fire inside.

The radio went dead.

The outside crew tried desperately to get the astronauts out but when they got the hatch open the smoke inside was impenetrable, the heat overwhelming.

It took only 4 minutes to open the hatch but it was too late. The three astronauts were dead.

This was a major setback and all flights and tests were cancelled until they could find out what had happened.

Meanwhile the Russians had forged ahead with a probe to the Moon.

Tropicana at The Lido

Once again at loose ends I was wondering what I should do because I was certainly sick of driving a dry cleaning van and working in the factory when my long-time friend Brian suggested we should go to Peru and become mural painters. He was very keen on the idea.

He was working as an artist for an advertising company and did lots of scraper board drawings of household goods that were advertised in newspapers and magazines. His stuff was very good, photographic in quality and it made me think of those classic artists who etched brilliantly realistic images of scenes and people before photography existed.

'The government sponsors mural painters in Peru,' Brian insisted with great enthusiasm. 'All you have to do is paint on the buildings.'

I was sure it wasn't like that — that if you were a foreigner you would not get sponsored by the Peruvian Government — but it was something to dream about. I knew Mexico City was famous for its mural artists and consequently it was easy to imagine Peru might also do something similar. I read about it somewhere, but couldn't remember where.

'Well, why not?' I agreed.

After that we talked about it for about 6 months which bored everyone else to tears but kept us excited with something to look forward to. However as the year progressed Brian became more involved with his girlfriend and his interest in going to Peru waned accordingly. When he decided to get married the trip to Peru was off.

Not long after that I saw a recent travel (advertising) book all about Qantas going to Mexico on a new route it had pioneered. I immediately bought it and became fascinated with Mexico and the idea of going there. I was itching to get moving again, to go somewhere different. I hadn't been back that long from Europe and already I was missing the discovery of new places, new ideas, and new people to meet and talk with. Mexico seemed much more interesting than Peru, so I decided that if I was going to go somewhere it would be to Mexico.

A few days later Zara, who was still one of the dancers at The Lido, excitedly informed me that the next show at was to be called Tropicana and it was being billed as exotic Latin American entertainment.

'You should audition,' she suggested. 'Antonio is in it and they are looking for a conga drummer to be out front with the dancers. David (Hamilton) is very interested in featuring a drummer, you know like the lead drummers in the African Ballet.'

Antonio was a Brazilian friend. He had been a lead character dancer with the Katherine Dunham show when it came to Australia in the late 1950s, and he had stayed here, along with Albert Laguerre and a couple of others after the show had left the country. As mentioned earlier we spent a lot of time together playing drums at his art studio as well as at my place.

'That might be fun.'

'Bring your drums to rehearsal tomorrow, 2 pm. I'll tell the directors you are coming to audition.'

'Right, I'll be there.'

Antonio Rodriguez, Brazilian dancer who came to Australia with the Katherine Dunham Group.

I took two congas to the Lido and set them up on stage. I borrowed the drummer's stool from the orchestra pit so I could sit and play the congas. There were three people sitting and watching intently, one of whom was David Hamilton. The other two were assistants. There were others wandering around further back, setting tables and doing other stuff that needed doing in a restaurant theatre complex. The girls were backstage getting ready for their rehearsal. Behind me some workers were setting up scenery for the forthcoming show.

It was a bit nerve wracking at first since there was not going to be any accompaniment. I was to play solo. I briefly explained that I would play a variety of rhythm patterns with some improvisation so they could get an idea of the sound.

I started with a basic slow pattern as used for Cha Cha or slow Mambo and interspersed short variations to build complexity, then after about 30 seconds I doubled the speed to a fast Guaracha tempo again with a brief improvised segment, then suddenly changed it to a 6/8 pattern also with some variations. I paused a moment to explain that in African and Cuban drumming the tumbas and congas and djembe are always played in groups with each drummer having an assigned position within the structure of the group and of the rhythm. I demonstrated the base tumbao for guaguanco, the second part which is a counter point, then some improvised bits as would be played by a third drummer. I then explained that one drummer could play an imitation of the three parts by cutting parts out and isolating one hand from the other so one hand played the base tumbao while the other played the counterpoint with simple variations. If accompanied by another person playing sticks (clave or extended clave pattern) and played fast enough it would sound like multiple drummers playing.

They loved it, and I was hired immediately and told to start coming to rehearsals.

David explained he wanted me to be featured along with the girls dancing to the drums and for that I would have to be at all rehearsals. The other musicians would be coming in from the next day and I would have to work out some solo parts with the musical director, so his arrangements could include the conga drum solo parts. That meant I would have to create some specific 8 bar phrases that would remain unchanged but would appear to be spontaneous improvisations because the choreographers (one of whom was David Hamilton) wanted the girls to dance specific movements in time with the congas. During these so called solo bits the orchestra would stop playing and I would be alone (with the girls) on stage playing the parts to which their choreography matched.

It was great and I loved every minute of it. Unfortunately I had to wear one of those fluffy arm mid-riff shirts associated with tropical bands. I wore white trousers but remained barefoot on stage.

Tropicana was a sensational and exciting variety show with mime artists, acrobats, several singers, spectacular dancers, and of course the beautiful Lido Goddesses, the tall elegant practically naked ladies who posed provocatively onstage. No Lido show was ever presented without them.

Rehearsals went on for a couple of months before the show was performed. It ran for three months starting in April, 1967. The revues were generally good and in each one I was mentioned since I had been billed as '*The drumming star from Europe's Matecocos orchestra.*' My best line in the best review stated *'The music is insistent and the most important performer is the drummer, in this case, John Litchen.*' This appeared in The Age on the 6th of April 1967 and was written by Geoffrey Hutton. The Herald also on the same day reported '*Lively contributions come from top-line drummer John Litchen and Dancer Antonio Rodriguez.*' H A Standish.

On stage at The Lido playing the solo drum parts to which the chorus girls danced.

Shows don't always run smoothly, and opening night when the Flat Tops (comedy duo) were performing their mime to old pre-recorded music from Spike Jones and company, the tape broke and they had to rush offstage. They were half way through their segment with another four minutes to go. Suddenly there was mayhem backstage.

'Somebody, anybody…quick get out there… do something,' yelled the director. 'Antonio…'

Antonio Rodriguez, Zaid Affif from Indonesia and myself were billed as the Tropicana Trio, and we appeared to various degrees in most of the numbers involving singers and dancers but not in the feature acts of the Flat Tops, The Two Leslies (Adagio dance Sensationalists) or Robert McPhee's solo singing performances.

Antonio was dressed ready for his part in the next segment. I was ready, having done one segment and didn't need to change for the next.

The chorus girls weren't. They were half dressed and in a mad panic ran around looking for their cigar costumes while the showgirls, the Lido Goddesses, who as usual were naked except for their G-strings looked for their pasties to stick onto their nipples (since nipples were not allowed to be seen on stage). They all thought they had eight minutes and were only half ready. There was a lot of swearing and panicked yelling.

Antonio ran out onto the stage and started leaping about excitedly trying to fill the huge area with his dynamic dancing.

I ran out and grabbed a conga drum and followed him around the stage banging out improvised parts which I hoped matched the movements he made, much like I remember the African lead drummer doing in their recent performances at the Comedy Theatre.

I looked up towards the back and the Lido Goddesses leisurely sauntered onto the raised area to the rear. They came out slowly because they weren't allowed to move too much in case their boobs wobbled, but they helped fill space at the rear of the stage. Finally the chorus girls started coming out and they too improvised about on the stage helping to fill the space and having a great time, until all of them were ready.

The chorus girls sauntering out helped fill the stage. Zara is the second from the left.

Once all the girls had taken their place in the giant cigar box part of the set Antonio and I drifted off to our pre-arranged spots and the orchestra down in the pit came in with the music for the Havana Cigar sequence and we were all back on track.

No one in the audience realized for one moment what had happened and thought it was all part of the show. Perhaps that's why we got such spirited reviews.

The fabulous Lido girls during the show Tropicana

Fragments from my Life – and Science Fiction

Those three months of the Lido show were full on.

We did a show 6 nights a week and a matinee on Thursday afternoons at 1:30 pm without any more mishaps like that on opening night.

When I wasn't at the Lido I was working at Williamstown Dry Cleaners; there just wasn't time for anything else.

I had saved all the money I earned from the show and with that I went around to the Qantas office in the city and booked a round-the-world trip with stops in Tahiti, Acapulco, Bahamas, Miami, New York, Toronto, London and Stuttgart.

I left the return stops unspecified and would worry about that when the time came to come home.

I had a 6 months wait until departure in April 1968 and in the meantime Mum and Dad decided they would go to Europe with Qantas, so they beat me to Mexico. They only stayed there a week, whereas I stayed for almost a whole year.

The ticket I had was open and the way it worked was you could get off and stay at any stop and catch another flight the next week or month later. There was a flight once a week. Basically you could stay in any place as long as you liked before continuing on to the next stop. There was always someone getting off so it was easy to book a seat to continue the next leg. The only requirement was the round trip had to be completed by the end of 12 months.

What did I do in those six months apart from work at the dry cleaners? Nothing that I can recall. I would have read a few books. I was always reading something, but I can't remember anything in particular. Maybe there wasn't anything worth remembering published in the latter half of 1967.

Mum and Dad came back from their trip overseas with Dad looking quite ill. He had caught a bad dose of the Flu while in Albania and looked as ancient as an Egyptian Mummy when he walked off the plane.

'I wasn't going to die overseas,' he told us. 'I want to die at home.'

He must have been very sick if that's what he thought.

He recovered quickly enough though, once he got home, and then suddenly it was time for me to be off again, and once more we were all at the airport but this time they were waving me off instead of the other way around.

A lesson learned

I had learned a lesson during my previous trip and that was not to encumber myself with loads of luggage.

Travel light. Take only what you need.

So this time everything I needed, basically a few changes of clothes and some toiletries, was carried in one bag.

This meant I could take a camera with me (a Nikonos, which was an underwater as well as an above land camera) as well as my Bolex 16mm movie camera. The Nikonos had a wide angle lens to compensate for the magnification underwater due to refraction of light at the interface between the water outside and the air inside the camera, and when used out of the water it had a fantastic depth of field from quite close to very distant (almost infinity) which was fine except that if I wanted to photograph people I would have to get fairly close. However I would worry about that when I had to.

I had not taken a camera with me apart from the 16mm Bolex cine camera on my first trip to Europe and ended up buying heaps of postcards to send home with details of what I was doing. Mum saved them and put them in an album, but somehow they disappeared and were lost forever. This time I would come back with lots of photos, or at least I would get the film processed and bring back the negatives to be printed once I got home again

In Tahiti again

My first stop was Tahiti and this second time it was spectacular flying in to land at their new Airport. My plan was to stay there for a couple of weeks before going on to Mexico.

There seemed to be a lot of security checks at the airport, something I hadn't experienced the last time there. Coming in by ship we simply walked off and wandered around then went back on board when we wanted. We could come and go as we pleased. At the new airport however, my luggage was searched and they saw the Bolex cine camera and its Perspex housing they insisted on knowing what I was going to film. They wanted to see my ticket to make sure I was leaving in two weeks and that Mexico was my intended destination, that Tahiti was just a stop-over.

Eventually they let me through and as I walked across the new terminal to take a bus into town (Papeete) I felt as if they were staring at me. I couldn't help wondering are officials at airports always so paranoid? At that point I had never been overseas by plane or travelled anywhere in Europe by plane. I went by ship and had always taken busses and trains to get around in various countries.

Once again I found myself on the waterfront by the Vaima Café and settled into a small hotel that overlooked the yachts moored at the quayside across the street. A lovely spot...

It turned out the small two story hotel was a brothel and usually rented out rooms by the hour, so at night there was a lot of activity, noise, coming and going of people which made it hard to sleep at first, especially since none of the rooms had doors that could be closed; they only had a curtain that was drawn across for a semblance of privacy. But after a day or so I got used to it and it didn't bother me.

I rather liked the place because they didn't charge me much to stay there for a couple of weeks. In fact I felt they thought it was a great joke having a tourist stay as a guest at their hotel/brothel. They were very friendly and I shared a coffee and a croissant with the manageress every morning on the balcony of the upstairs floor. She could speak a bit of English and enjoyed practicing it with me.

I took a trip out to Moorea by boat and did some diving with an American friend I met, and the Bolex camera housing got flooded. There was a tiny crack in the Perspex which I had not noticed, and which probably happened as a result of rough treatment at the airport when passenger's luggage was unloaded, literally thrown down onto trailers to be towed inside for people to collect, and water quickly penetrated the housing as soon as I started to dive.

I rushed back up to the surface and got the camera out of the housing but it was too wet and very quickly seized up with salt from the sea

Paddling an outrigger canoe in the lagoon at Moorea.

water. It was now useless. I would have to wait until I got to Mexico to have it cleaned and serviced. There was nowhere in Papeete to get that done. As for the housing; I decided I wasn't going to lug that around if it was cracked, so I dumped it over the side and watched it sink slowly to the bottom of the lagoon a tiny trail of bubbles emanating from the crack in the Perspex.

I was starting to think that I might stay in Tahiti a bit longer than the two weeks originally planned so I bought a dictionary that was French/Tahitian – Tahitian/French. There were none in English, so I would have to brush up a bit on French if I wanted to use the dictionary. Most of the local people spoke Tahitian amongst themselves, (*I just loved the sound of their language — it was so musical*) and only used French when speaking to foreigners. French of course was the official language since Tahiti is a Department of France.

The day after my boat trip across to Moorea I became aware that there were a lot of police in and around the city and especially along the waterfront. There were two very large ships anchored way over where the Ellinis had been when I came to Tahiti 4 years earlier, but they were definitely not passenger ships. They had not been there the day before

*Back street in Papeete...
fishermen coming in with the day's catch...*

so they must have come in during the night. They were festooned with radio masts and satellite dishes.

There were quite a few Russians sitting at street side cafes and wandering about taking photos. Nobody liked Russians and viewed them with open hostility given the fact of the Cold War between them and America and the Space Race which they seemed to be dominating. Yet those sitting at cafes seemed quite ordinary, just like any other tourist.

A chance encounter

'John,' a female voice called excitedly as I walked past the tables set on the footpath in front of the Vaima Bar and café. And as I turned to see who could possibly have known me I saw a face I recognized. She was grinning widely. 'What are you doing here?'

I could have asked her the same question…and I did.

Isn't it odd how in a world where literally billions of people live and you go to somewhere reasonably remote from your own country, inevitably you will run into someone you know? I always find that astonishing.

The girl sitting at the table sipping her morning café au lait with a croissant was none other than the exotic dancer from Birdland whose giant snakes kept crawling towards my conga drums during the floor shows when she performed. I hadn't seen her for years.

'I hope you don't have your snakes with you,' I said as I joined her at the table.

She laughed at that. 'I gave them up a long time ago.'

And we chatted happily about old times.

When we'd finished our coffees she suddenly became serious. 'Can I ask a favour of you?'

I don't like it when people ask that. You can end up having all kinds of problems. What could she possibly want as a favour, here in Tahiti, after us not having seen each other for such a long time?

'You know I'm Russian…'

I had no idea. I rarely ask people who their antecedents are or what work they do; none of the usual stuff people ask that I find intrusive, especially when meeting for the first time. I take people at face value and believe first impressions of someone's character are always the best and most accurate. She was just the gorgeous dancer who did the floor shows with a six foot and a ten foot python. I never saw her at any other time than during those floor shows.

'At least my parents were,' she qualified. 'They were White Russian refugees. I was born in Australia but I can speak Russian.'

I wondered where this was going and what would be the favour she wanted.

'When I heard all these people talking in Russian I couldn't resist the temptation to speak to them. I hardly ever speak Russian to anyone in Australia apart from my parents.' She paused here and looked around. 'It felt so good to speak Russian and they joked about how old fashioned my language was. Anyway, they invited me to come on board for dinner and the chance to watch the Bolshoi Ballet perform.'

'The Bolshoi Ballet?'

She nodded. 'They are going to have a special broadcast live from the theatre in Moscow transmitted to the ship via satellite. You know, using one of their Sputniks.'

Could they do that? That's pretty advanced stuff. Were the Americans capable of doing anything like that? No wonder they were winning the Space Race.

'The trouble is all the crew on the ship, on both the ships, are male. I'm a bit scared to go on board being the only female. Would you come with me?'

Well that wasn't so bad. I could do that.

'I'd feel more comfortable with you there… and they would be less likely to do anything to me knowing I have a friend with me.'

I wasn't sure having me with her would make any difference if they really wanted to do anything, but I couldn't refuse an invitation by a beautiful girl to accompany her to dinner and ballet could I?

'I'd love to see the Ballet. I've never been on board a Russian ship so it could be interesting.'

Suddenly she was all smiles again. She stood up and said, 'Can we meet here at six o'clock tonight? I'll get one of the sailors who invited me to meet us and take us on board.'

'Not a problem,' I said and then she was off, skipping along the waterfront footpath like a happy child heading to a birthday party.

Well the dinner was typically Russian with the only thing standing out now in my memory being cabbage rolls and some kind of dumplings that were very tasty though a bit heavy, but with a few shots of vodka to wash it down it didn't seem bad at all.

They crew seemed rather nerdy to be a fishing crew but there were a few who looked like they could have been ex-marines or whatever the Russian equivalent was. They were quite rowdy after a few vodkas had been downed and made a big fuss over their lady visitor. I might as well have been invisible.

I do remember as we walked towards the ship it looked as if it was festooned with aerials and satellite dishes pointing up at various angles which seemed incongruous on a fishing vessel.

On the aft deck there was a large wheel with wound metal cable and the usual slab sided doors that trawlers drag along the ocean bed behind as they go fishing, but these looked as if they had never been used. The paint on them glistened with the lights along the dock shining on them. If they had been used regularly they would have been scratched and rusty.

The only part of the ship we saw apart from the deck beside the gang plank was the main dining room and an adjoining lounge where a huge television screen had been set up ready for the broadcast. We had been ushered in the moment we stepped on the deck and I got the impression that they didn't want us to linger and look around.

The huge TV was flickering with white noise and jagged lines as we settled down to watch. The Captain spoke into an intercom and presumably someone in the telecommunications control room connected the TV because suddenly it came to life with a long shot of the stage where the ballet was to be performed.

We settled into our chairs, sipped our vodka and waited for the performance.

As innovative as this might have been, I was disappointed at the poor quality of the image. It flickered and drifted in and out of focus so nothing was sharp. The screen was too big for the scanning lines to be invisible and they were quite obvious as dark bands that continually drifted down the screen.

The Russians however seemed to think it was fantastic and they laughed and cheered and drank heaps of vodka. When the ballet was over they thanked us for being their guests and escorted us back to the gang plank.

As we walked away from the ship towards the small security control room on the dock about two hundred metres ahead we could hear them calling out and saying goodbye in Russian.

A touch of paranoia

'**Well that was interesting,**' I said as we stepped into the security control room. It was brightly lit with a couple of desks and a passport control booth like you see at the airport. We had to go through this control room to exit the wharf's restricted area where the Russian ship was moored.

'What was interesting?' a voice asked in English as we entered the room.

There were other rooms adjoining the main area and there were a number of people there, even though it was just after midnight local time. Two of them were in what looked like a police uniform, but the man who had spoken was dressed casually with trousers and an open neck shirt. He wasn't smiling and didn't appear the least bit friendly.

The casually dressed man said something in French to a uniformed associate then stepped towards us. 'I asked you what was interesting. What were you doing on that Russian ship? Do either of you speak French?'

'Oui. Je parle francais,' my companion replied. Apparently she spoke as good French as she did Russian. I was impressed.

'Bon,' he said and proceeded to ask the same question again. He also indicated that he wanted to see our passports which we handed over. He studied them for a few moments flipping the pages over to see what stamps we had and then passed them to his uniformed associate.

He said something and looked at my companion. The only thing I could pick out of it was the name Mururoa which I thought was Moorea. Twelve nautical miles away from Tahiti there was nothing on this spectacular volcanic island other than a tourist resort.

'He wants to know if the people on the ship said anything about Mururoa.'

'What's that? Doesn't he mean Moorea?'

'No he was very specific about naming the place.'

'Tell him I've never heard of it. I couldn't understand anything the people on the ship said anyway. It was all in Russian. Did they say anything about it to you?'

'No, all they talked about was the ballet and how homesick they were. They've been out here doing research for more than 6 months.'

This conversation was relayed back in French and our inquisitor nodded as if he understood. Then he asked about what we had seen on the ship. Had we seen any equipment and could we describe what it looked like?

Everything he asked was in French, but I suspected he could understand English because from his expression it was clear he knew what we were talking about. He wasn't interested in the big TV which was the only equipment we had seen.

After about half an hour he was finally convinced that we were not spies and that we had been nothing more than innocent visitors to the ship, and that the reason was no more than my friend's joy at being able to converse in Russian which she hadn't done for years.

What he didn't do however was to return our passports.

He led us through the control room and on the wharf on the other side was a black expensive looking car.

'I will take you back to your hotels,' he said in English.

'What about our passports?' I asked him.

'They will be returned to you tomorrow,' he stated. 'You will come and see me at Police headquarters at 9 am.'

In the car on the way back into Papeete I asked him why he hadn't conducted the interview in English since it was obvious he spoke it very well.

'I wanted to see what you would talk about between yourselves if you thought I couldn't understand.' His English was good enough that there was barely any French accent to it.

'And...?'

'I was convinced you weren't on that ship for anything other than what you told me.'

After that he said nothing until he dropped me off in front of the yachts moored along the waterfront opposite the Vaima Bar which was still roaring with life. As usual the party there was only beginning.

'Tomorrow morning...' he reminded me as he drove off with my friend still in the car. She was staying at a more 'up-market' hotel than I was.

After the inquisition I was too tired to join the endless party at the

— Ephemeron —

Vaima Bar so I went upstairs to my room and tried to sleep. It took a long time because it was hot and humid and I was worried about getting my passport back.

'Here is your passport,' he said as he handed it back to me. 'I checked your airline itinerary and you are scheduled to leave on Friday. Please be on that plane or you will be deported.'

That came as a shock. I had been starting to think I would stay longer, since I had an open ticket. I was even thinking of learning the local language.

He stood up and extended his hand which I automatically shook.

'I hope you have enjoyed your stay with us, but you are no longer welcome to remain in Tahiti.'

And when I was about to ask why he anticipated the question with a vague response; 'The political situation here at the moment is delicate and we don't want any troublemakers upsetting things.'

I had no idea what he was talking about and also I had no choice. I put my passport into my pocket and left his office.

When I went around to the airline office to book my ongoing flight with Qantas I was told I would have to stay at least a week longer since there was a maintenance crew strike back in Australia and Qantas flights out of Sydney were grounded. They also told me they would pay for the hotel for the extra days I was to stay since they were responsible for my delay. I didn't mind staying a bit longer especially if the airline was paying for it, but I was concerned about what the security officer's reaction would be. He had been quite adamant that I was to leave.

I told the hotel manageress to make up my bill until Friday and I would pay it now. After that any extra days I stayed would be paid for by Qantas airlines. She was quite happy with that and immediately told me she would double the price for the days the airline was paying.

Good for you, I thought.

I thought the strike would only last a couple of days and that would be it.

On Friday the security inquisitor turned up and informed me that Qantas was on strike and it looked like it could last awhile. 'I've taken the liberty of booking you on the next flight out with Air France.' He definitely wanted me off the island. 'It leaves next Wednesday. Someone will come and escort you to the airport.'

'Air France doesn't fly to Mexico, to Acapulco,' I said but before I could add anything else he interjected.

'Not my concern. They fly to Los Angeles but they will guarantee you get to your destination.'

He went into the office of the manageress and came out a few moments later.

She came out after that and smiling happily she told me that the French Government would also be paying for the extra days so she had tripled the price.

I couldn't help chuckling at her audacity; charging Qantas double and the French Government triple.

'I like you,' she said, 'you good customer.'

There was nothing I could do other than sit around and wait, drinking coffee while enjoying the passing tourist parade along the waterfront.

The Russians from the research ship wandered about, and now that I was aware of them I also saw quite a few shifty looking French guys whom I assumed were security or 'secret service' people wandering about tailing the Russians. They didn't try to stay hidden, which they couldn't have anyway because they looked nothing like the locals and were always clearly visible. It seemed the Russians didn't care whether they were being followed or not. There was even one who followed me around. He looked bored and indifferent and I hoped he enjoyed watching me drink coffee as I sat reading or looking at the yachts and the fishing boats moored along the waterfront.

There was a lot of talk in the cafés about Mururoa Atoll and atomic bomb tests which explained the security and the nervousness about us visiting the Russian ship. None of this had been obvious to me before but having been stopped and questioned after leaving the ship I was now well aware of the excessive presence of these 'secret service' men. They wore bright coloured shirts over casual slacks in an attempt to blend in but they might as well have worn dark suits and sunglasses; they were that obvious.

I previously had no idea the French were testing atomic bombs in the Pacific. But everyone knew the Russians, the Americans and British had conducted atomic bomb tests in the atmosphere as well as underground, (The British did it in Australia) so it shouldn't have been a surprise to discover the French also were doing it.

Inadvertently I had blundered into this MAD espionage game and the result was to be kicked off the island. I didn't see my dancer friend anywhere so she may have already left. There were however a number of people sitting around drinking coffees or beers who seemed irritable or bored as if they too were waiting to leave but couldn't because of the Qantas maintenance crew strike.

Wednesday morning I was ready. I'd said goodbye to the manageress and was sitting and sipping a coffee out front when a dark vehicle pulled up. The security chief himself, still dressed as if he was a casual tourist, stepped out and seeing me sitting at a table waved me over.

I grabbed my camera bag and backpack and wandered over.

'Bon jour, I see you are ready' He handed me an airline ticket in a folder, and indicated I should get into the car.

They must have considered me someone special to have sent the 'boss' to pick me up and take me to the airport. Perhaps they were short of staff with everyone following the Russians about? I didn't ask.

On the way to the airport he said very little, other than the injunction to enjoy the flight.

'I do hope you enjoyed your stay and will come back again… but not too soon,' he said as I got out of the car which he parked in a no-standing zone by the front entrance.

I nodded to show I understood, and he drove off before I could thank him for his hospitality. I was going to tell him that I probably would never be coming back here again but I didn't get the chance to say it.

Then again one should 'never say never again' since I found I had to go through Tahiti on a couple of occasions while travelling by air to Easter Island and to South America some years later. I didn't actually stay over on those occasions but only spent a short time in transit while waiting to change planes. My passport was checked but no red flags came up to say I was a suspicious or an unwanted visitor.

The longest single stretch

It was a 13 hour flight from Tahiti to Los Angeles and was at that stage the longest single stretch I had ever taken. It started in the middle of the morning but it was late in the night when the plane landed and we were hustled through customs to a waiting bus which took those of us who were in transit to Mexico, specifically Acapulco, to a motel that was an hour's drive through endless streams of traffic. We were told we would be collected again at 8 am the next morning.

It was a hot humid night and the air had such a different smell to it, so unlike the lush half rotten tropical smell of Tahiti. I'm sure it was tinged with carbon dioxide from car exhausts and dust from the dry mountains along the Californian coast. It had the smell of a desert but one couldn't see that because everywhere was built-up with apartments, motels, and shopping malls. The sky was clear but too hazy to see any stars shining and it glowed from all the streetlights which made it bright enough to read a newspaper even at 2 am in the morning, which was about the time when we arrived at the motel. I had slept a bit on the plane so on arrival at the motel I thought I would go for a walk. I had never been in the US before so the least I could do was have a quick look around.

I walked along a footpath away from the motel amongst crowds of people who didn't really seem to be going anywhere, but were just walking around because it was too hot and humid to sleep. My lasting image is of the street lined with very tall palm trees silhouetted against a glowing hazy sky. I heard a lot of voices chattering in Spanish but at that stage I couldn't understand much of what they were saying. A couple of rough looking guys asked me for some money. I told them I had none to give. Perhaps it was my Australian accent or perhaps it appeared that I wasn't the least bit put off by how rough they looked, but they nodded and left me alone. It must have been about 3 am when I finally got back to the motel and went to sleep.

I was woken up by one of my fellow passengers banging on the door and staggered out dressed but half asleep. I did make sure I had my meagre luggage though. I must have fallen asleep on the bus, or at least sat there in dazed state because I remember nothing of that trip back or getting onto a Western Airlines flight from LA to Acapulco. I came awake half way through the flight. This is what flying long distances and crossing various time zones does to you. It throws your whole body-clock out of sequence so you don't know what time of day it is or when you should be asleep or awake. I had not experienced this jetlag before since all my previous travelling had been done at a leisurely pace aboard ships, trains, and busses.

I found myself sitting next to a French woman whom I remembered vaguely from having seen her a number of times sitting at a café over the road from where the yachts were moored in Papeete. I had often sat there observing the 'passing parade' while sipping coffees. It hadn't taken much effort to notice other regulars like myself who were doing the same. Although we never spoke to each other then, we sometimes acknowledged the other's presence with nod of the head or a brief smile of recognition.

'*Bon Jour,*' she said seeing that I was awake. '*Comment ca va?*'

'I'm good, thanks,' I replied automatically in English.

She looked at me for a second and I imagined I could see in her eyes a switch from one language to another. There was a momentary blankness then a sudden glint. She smiled and said in English, Australian English with a French accent overlaying it, 'I quite often saw you having breakfast down by the waterfront in Papeete.'

'Yeah, I remember seeing you too,' I said.

'It seems you had some problem with the security police…?'

'You noticed that. Well basically they kicked me off the island. I was intending to stay longer…' I shrugged. It was all unimportant now.

'I was booked to leave on the Qantas flight to Acapulco, on my way back to Paris, but it was cancelled so here I am on this one instead. There are quite a few from that cancelled flight on this one.'

And from then we chatted about Tahiti and what we expected to find in Acapulco.

'I'm only going to be there a couple of days before going on to Paris.'

'I don't know how long I'll be there. Depends on what I find I suppose. I have an open ticket and can stay as long as I like.'

Acapulco

Looking towards the centre of Acapulco from Caleta

The jetsetter's choice

Acapulco was the jetsetters choice for a getaway holiday.
Like several other places along the Pacific coastline (at that time) it was isolated from the rest of Mexico, sprawling around a magnificent harbour on the Pacific coast which was surrounded by the *Sierra Madre del Sur* mountain range. A narrow winding road, via Cuernavaca, Tasco and Chilpancingo, connected Acapulco to Mexico City.

The only way to get there was either by sea into the superb harbour, (*Think of something that looks like Rio de Janeiro only smaller.*) or by the narrow winding road from the capital. If you wanted to go to another small fishing village more than a few kilometres north or south from Acapulco, and there were quite a few of them scattered along the Pacific coast, you either had to go by boat, or you went back to Mexico City then took another winding road through the mountains to your new coastal destination.

A recent innovation *(in the 1960's)* was Acapulco's international airport which suddenly made it easy for the wealthy jetsetters to go there, and as a result some magnificent and super luxurious hotels were built. American film stars such as Kirk Douglas, Mamie Rogers and many others had constructed luxurious getaway homes tucked into the sides of mountainous rocky escarpments overlooking the harbour. Tour boat owners took people around the harbour so they could view these magnificent homes, a popular pastime with local as well as overseas visitors.

The Spanish Conquistadors made Acapulco their main port on the Pacific side of Mexico in 1532 and attacks led by Hurtado de Mendoza went from there to other parts of New Spain as they subjugated the natives down along the Central American and South American coastline.

Spanish galleons traded between the Philippines and Mexico carrying gold and other riches and they became targets for British and Dutch pirates who attacked the galleons without mercy. Eventually the Spanish went elsewhere to avoid the pirates and Acapulco declined, becoming a fishing village for a long time, until its spectacular beauty was rediscovered and it suddenly became a mecca for tourists. Once the airport was built it ceased to be a moribund fishing village and blossomed into a premier location that attracted the wealthiest from all around the world. Books were written about the place, and films were made.

I remember seeing a noir murder mystery film some years before I was aware of the place and the thing I remembered most from a few scenes in the film was a seemingly endless row of small palm trees with white painted trunks planted along the centre strip of the highway (*La Costera Aleman* or more correctly: *Avenida Miguel Aleman*)) that ran along the beach around the Bahia de Acapulco. I thought it was a beautiful looking place but had no idea of where it was at the time.

It didn't hit me until I was being driven in a taxi from the airport that the palm trees along the highway by the beach with their white painted trunks had been the same ones I saw in that old film from the late 1940s, only now in 1968 they were huge, 15 to 20 metres tall, and still with freshly painted white trunks.

Acapulco has many rocky headlands that overlook a myriad of small harbours with their own almost private beaches and these headlands all have luxurious hotels or resort type accommodation built on them. One of the most famous is La Quebrada and the hotel El Mirador.

This hotel overlooks a narrow split in the cliffs where ocean waves wash in and where the famous cliff divers thrill visitors each night by diving from the top of the 35 metre cliff down into the narrow gap where the waves wash in. It is brilliantly lit with floodlights and the show is on every night.

The water in the gap is quite shallow and the divers have to time their dive so that when they hit the water it is surging into the gap and thus cushions their entry into the water. If they hit the water when the wave is retreating they will most likely hit the rocky sand underneath and break their neck or kill themselves, so there is a lot of drama and suspense as the diver eyes the waves and times their movement in and out of the gap before leaping off the cliff top. Since it is not a vertical cliff face but slopes back, the higher up the diver begins the further out he must project himself to clear the jagged rocks at the cliff base.

The best view is from the overhanging balcony of the hotel but you must pay to go in there. During the day the divers practice from various levels up the side of the cliff and there is a viewing platform for those like me who couldn't afford to go into that luxurious hotel.

Sometime in the 60s Elvis Presley made a film (with lots of singing in it of course) where he played one of these divers who has a love affair with a tourist. I don't think I saw that film until after I came back from my stay in Mexico so the film could have been made in the early 70s. It was called *Acapulco Gold*, (also the name of a specific Mexican product that was extremely popular in the US at the time). It was an appropriate title because Acapulco was sun drenched all year round with many beautiful golden sandy beaches.

The only variation was in summer when it rained daily and was humid and windy for a couple of months (sub-tropical wet season) while the rest of the year was sunny and warm and always pleasant. *Acapulco Gold* was also the same title I gave to an unpublished novel I wrote while in Acapulco and finished after I came home, and so thinking back I couldn't have seen that film until sometime in the early 70s or I wouldn't have titled my piece with that name.

I fell in love with Acapulco from the moment I stepped out of the plane and could smell the tropical fragrance in the air. It was a much different smell than Tahiti, sweeter, more vibrant and there was none of that mouldy rotting vegetation-smell one associates with damp tropical places.

It was the beginning of April and it was the dry season and the sky was clear of clouds and a brilliant blue that was hard to look at. A slight cool breeze off the nearby Pacific Ocean ruffled the palm trees and the tops of the rain forest trees surrounding the airport, and there was a sense of excitement among the passengers as they disembarked from the plane. There seemed to be a vibrancy, an aliveness that was different from any I had experienced in other places.

Perhaps it was the thrill of arriving somewhere by plane, which was a comparatively new way to travel in the 1960s.

Whatever the reason, I just knew I was going to love this place.

Fitting in with the locals

As it turned out, it was the week before Easter and a long weekend, so Acapulco was packed with visitors and tourists from Mexico City and other international destinations. All the most popular accommodations were full. At least that is what the taxi driver and bus drivers told the disembarking passengers. Some of the people from Tahiti had bookings and called to see if they were still available. Others like myself and the French woman who had been sitting beside me had not any accommodation booked.

'Follow me,' I said and headed to the front entrance of the terminal. There was a long line of waiting taxis out front and I walked straight up to the first in line. The driver was leaning casually against the driver's side door, smoking a foul smelling black cigarette, or perhaps it was a miniature cigar. He flicked it away as I approached.

'*Habla usted Ingles?*' I asked.

'*Seguro que si,*' was his smiling response.

Relieved that I didn't have to make an attempt yet to use my laboriously slow Spanish I asked if he knew of a place where we could stay for a day or so.

'Let me make a quick call,' he said and went inside through the main entrance.

'I'll bet he has a friend or a cousin who just happens to have one spare room available,' I said as we watched him head for the row of public phones along a side wall not far from the main entrance.

He came back a few moments later with a big grin and announced 'I have found a place that does have a room available.'

I smiled. 'What a coincidence,' I said to my travelling companion.

The taxi driver looked at us questioningly. 'It is a very nice motel,' he added as an inducement.

'Of course it is. Shall we go and have a look?'

How many times do you hear something like that? He probably got a commission on customers he brought in. I could see that she was thinking the same thing. But we had to go somewhere. We couldn't stay at the airport. It was early afternoon, and it had been a long day so far.

'Do you want to share a room, at least for this one night, until we find somewhere else? She asked me.

'Yeah, I guess so.' It wasn't something I had considered but under the circumstances it did seem a viable option, if accommodation was as scarce as we had been told, and if this taxi driver could only find us a place with one room left.

We got into the taxi and the driver delivered us to a small motel on the main road half way around the harbour heading towards the town centre. It was a bit out of town on the beach side of the Costera Aleman, and was quite luxurious. (The beach here is La Condesa and is very popular with tourists from the larger hotels nearby.) The motel was expensive, but not unreasonable. We paid half each for the one night, and explained we weren't sure if we would stay longer at that stage, which was quite acceptable to the man behind the reception desk. 'Let me know before 11 am tomorrow if you are going to stay longer,' was all he said while handing over a key to the room.

I left my stuff in the room we were given while my companion said she wanted to freshen up. Every other room had a car of some kind parked in front and the larger car park further in on the property was also full. It did appear that the taxi driver was right about the place being packed with visitors for the Easter Weekend.

'I'm going to go for a walk along the beach. It looks pretty good out there.'

The motel was perched on a slight cliff and there were steps leading down to a wide long stretch of beach of golden sand with gentle surf washing against it. I saw about half a kilometre towards the town centre sticking up out of the water a huge clump of granite boulders washed smooth by the waves breaking against them. I could see a number of small boats anchored around them and people jumping off the boats into the water. On the beach facing the granite clumps were rows of thatched cabanas and behind them were what appeared to be some restaurants or bars.

I immediately wandered along the beach to see what was going on. As I got closer I started to hear 'Tropical' music. There was a band playing, and they sounded fabulous. This was my kind of music. They were playing a son montuno. I couldn't help walk a bit faster. The closer I got the better it sounded. Looking up as I reached the first of the cabanas on the beach I could see the tops of the heads of several couples who were dancing to the music. There was a wall around the edge of the restaurant or club perched on the cliff edge, obviously so no one would fall over and that obscured my view from the beach.

There were people laughing and enjoying themselves in the soft surf. Voices floated across the water from the people diving from the boats beside the granite outcrop a few hundred metres offshore. There was a group of tourists sitting under the nearest cabana sipping elegant cocktails while a Jarocha trio tried to induce them to pay for a song. But I had ears only for the band playing in the club on the cliff. There were steps leading up from the beach and I raced up them and stood at the top. A smooth concrete floor, polished over years by thousands of dancing feet stretched across to a white-washed wall against which the band, consisting of two congas, timbales, bass, piano, two trumpets, and a singer who played guiro as he sang were playing. Two couples were dancing. Only a few of the tables around the dance floor area were occupied. I imagined that the place would be jumping once it got close to what is euphemistically called 'the happy hour', but it was only early afternoon so not all that many were out and about.

I stood there entranced. I had not heard music like this since I had been in Paris four years ago with the Matecocos. When they finished and the dancers sat down I went over to the band and asked if they would play a *guaguanco* and if I could sit in and play congas. They were only too happy to oblige.

I used slowly pronounced Spanish; I had been studying a Spanish conversation course at a private college in Melbourne before leaving and this was the first chance I had to use it. One of them said something to me but it was too fast for me to grasp, but the piano player indicated the congas and the guy who had been playing them stepped aside with a smile.

The song they started to play was *Complicaciones*; a song I knew from a Mongo Santamaria album (*Our Man in Havana*) which had been written by Francisco Aguabella especially for the Tito Puente orchestra who also played it on my favourite album, one of the best Latin dance albums of all time, *Dance Mania*. The lead singer sang '*Yo no quiero mas complicaciones, la vida me traiciono…*' and I dropped into the *guaguanco* rhythm without any variations but played on two drums as if being played by two people. I could see the conga player was impressed by this. It turned out he had never seen *guaguanco* played that way, the way I had learnt it from JoJo Smith a few years back. I was having a great time. Right in my element, I indicated the conga player should come back and play the *tumbao* part, and as soon as he did I switched to the *repicador* part which I could then play with some embellishments. I didn't see whether anyone was dancing, I was so focussed on the music and playing as well as I could. It had been a long time since I had played any real Cuban music.

When the song was over they all wanted to shake my hand and asked where I was from and couldn't believe it was Australia. They wanted to know what I was doing that night and if I wanted to they had a party to perform at but needed a conga player. Well of course I was available.

'*No tengo congas,*' (I don't have any congas) I told them.

'*No te preocupes. Tenemos que venir aquí para coger los instrumentos a las siete. Si esperas aquí te llevamos a la fiesta. ¿Está bien?*'

'*Por seguro. Estaré aquí...*'

With that settled we played another song and then they took a break. I thought I should go back to the motel and freshen up, maybe have a brief nap or something so I would be fresh for the evening Gig. I was quite happy at the way things had worked out. Also I was amazed at how easy it was to fit in with the 'locals'. They didn't care who I was or where I came from; they simply accepted me as a fellow musician.

'At home' with the boys in the band at Playa Condesa. Behind the band was a steep drop down to a wide beach, filled with thatched huts where tourists sat out of the sun when not swimming.

A few weeks later in the street out front of the restaurant where I first sat in and played with the resident band. One of the band members is standing behind me.

The party and afterwards

The party was in a mansion overhanging a cliff with unbelievable views across the harbour towards the town centre. There was tons of food, plenty of booze and lots of people determined to have a great time. We set up the instruments and played all night with very few breaks. This is the way they wanted it.

The great thing about parties in Acapulco at that time is that they hardly ever played recorded music. There were always many itinerant musicians available to make up a *conjunto* or small band at the drop of a hat. Most of these musicians gravitated in the afternoons to the very same place I had discovered on my walk along the beach, where they would chat and socialize with each other, to catch up on what each had been doing. They also sat in with the resident band and jammed.

It was just my luck that I found this place, and sitting in, showed them I could play as well as any other local percussionist, and so I was offered a gig that first night there. Apparently several bands had been put together that afternoon to play at half a dozen different places around town. Acapulco was truly a party town for those with money. For me, it was Paradise.

I didn't have a watch or any idea of the time I was dropped off as the instruments were returned to the restaurant at La Condesa, but the sky was beginning to get lighter. By the time I had walked back to the motel the sun had already risen somewhere behind the *Sierra Madre del Sur* mountains. Long dark shadows stretched across the wide stretch of sand towards the waves that relentlessly pounded the beach. I imagined there would probably already be surfers out there somewhere, but I couldn't see them. It still wasn't bright enough.

I had had a few tequilas at the party where we played and this combined with having been awake from very early the morning before in Los Angeles when we were ferried out to the airport to take the flight down to Acapulco, absolutely knocked me out. I let myself into the motel room as quietly as possible and just collapsed on the bed in my clothes and immediately fell into a deep sleep.

A bossy lady

My French lady companion shook me awake.
'Wake up,' she seemed to shout as she shook my shoulder with considerable force.

I leapt up off the bed thinking there might be an earthquake. They do get them from time to time in Acapulco I had been told.

'It's 9 am and we have to check out in an hour or so.'
'You could have let me sleep a bit longer,' I grumbled.
'Non. You smell of sweat and alcohol and you need to take a shower.'
Well, what could I say? She was right.
'When you have finished you will find me in the foyer having a coffee and a Danish pastry. I've already packed my bag.'
'Okay, I get the hint. I'll meet you there in fifteen minutes.'
Were all French women as bossy as that?

The heart of Acapulco

***El malecon**, opposite the Zocalo, full of fishing boats used for big game fishing.*

We made arrangements with the motel clerk to leave our luggage in a side room off the foyer while we went downtown to look for another place to stay. The room we had occupied was already booked since we had not expressed any idea to stay longer, and the new occupants would be arriving soon. Besides this place was a bit expensive, obviously designed to fleece tourists, so we really needed to find somewhere cheaper. It probably didn't matter to my friend because she was going on to Paris the day after, but to me it did since I was planning to stay for some time.

I had read in one of those travel guides like *Mexico on $10 a day* that there were lots of reasonable small hotels and *pensiones* in the heart of Acapulco which catered for Mexican tourists coming down from Mexico City for weekend breaks, and that by our standards they were inexpensive.

We caught a local bus that stopped out the front of the motel and travelled in this to the town centre where the Zocalo was situated in front of a cathedral with bright blue cupolas glistening in the sun. The bus stopped right in front of the Zocalo which was shaded by huge trees (trunks again painted white) and was a charming place.

As the bus drove off I looked across the road to an extended waterfront quay (El Malecón) which had numerous fishing boats anchored along it. There were many brightly painted horse-drawn buggies lined up along the wide footpath in front of the moored boats with drivers casually chatting while they waited for tourists who wanted a ride around the older parts of the city.

Competing for tourist and other business were many small stalls, with big wheels like bicycle wheels so they could be moved from place to place, selling Chiclets (chewing gum) made from the milky juice of the Sapodilla tree *(apparently chewing gum originally came from Mexico. So did chocolate)*, cold drinks made from tropical fruits like cherimoya (custard apple), ice cream, quesadillas, tacos de carne, and many other varieties of food. One of the footpaths leading away from the Zocalo towards the other end of Acapulco from where we had come from was covered with stalls and canvas awnings. These stalls faced the shops and the space between them was like a tunnel dappled with shade and sunlight that came through the gaps between the awnings. These stalls sold millions of handmade items to passing tourists.

A young girl arrived with her mother, both having traversed the Zocalo. They were waiting to cross the street to go over to the malecón. They both carried stools and balanced big baskets of something they had cooked at home on their heads. They were searching for a good spot to set up shop. As it turned out they were selling home-made *quesadillas* (which looked like pasties but were filled with cheese). Not soon after them a woman walked by with a shallow metal bucket containing huge slices of watermelon balanced on her head. She spotted me doing something with my camera and waved her finger at me to say '*no fotos*' but kept walking on by.

A shaded footpath near the Zocalo, crowded with stalls selling every imaginable product. The woman in front is selling fresh oranges.

Even the children work hard...this boy is delivering parcels of sweets

At La Quebrada, a young boy selling souvenirs made from shells.

— *Ephemeron* —

Shoe shine boys relaxing beside the Malecon opposite the Zocalo while waiting for customers.

Boy with tray of chicklets balanced on his head walks past onlookers watching a fishing boat arrive.

I took photos with the Nikonos camera, surreptitiously holding the camera at waist height so it would not seem as if I was taking photos. The wide angle lens with its infinite focus should pick up what I was seeing without me having to look through the viewfinder. All I had to do was point the camera in the direction of the subject and push the shutter. Apart from the watermelon lady no one noticed what I was doing. I wouldn't know what I got though until the film could be processed, and that wouldn't happen until at least we had somewhere to stay for a while.

Both sides of the Zocalo were lined with cafes and coffee shops behind a narrow road. The other end was filled with the façade of the cathedral. Its main entrance opened onto the Zocalo. The road on both sides of the square went behind the Cathedral and many other narrow roads led away from this narrow ring road. This was an ideal place to start looking for somewhere to stay. According to the information I had the roads leading off from the Zocalo had many small family hotels popular with local tourists from Mexico City who came to Acapulco for a short or weekend holiday. These would be the kinds of places I could afford, places that catered for Mexicans and not for foreign tourists who nearly always went to the more glamorous hotels scattered along the Costera Aleman or to places like Las Brisas which had rooms built into the side of a sloping mountainside each with its own swimming pool and tiny jeep like a golf cart which guests could use to get around in, and which cost over US$1000 per day. Not the kind of place I would ever go to! Or could ever afford to go to.

Give me a little hotel tucked away down a side street where no one could speak a word of English and I would be happy.

Why go to a foreign country if everywhere you stayed people spoke your language and everything looked the same as what you could find in your own city? What a waste of time and money. Where is the spirit of adventure when you do this? You need to feel you are somewhere different. You need to be challenged to make yourself understood and to understand others; you need to open your mind and your brain's synapses to other ways of thinking, of seeing things and of expression of ideas, otherwise there is no reason to travel somewhere different.

Someone once said that the destination wasn't important, it was the act of travelling that was what was important.

It's all about who you meet and what you do on the way, because ultimately all travel always leads back home.

— *Ephemeron* —

The place we call home is the ultimate destination, and appreciation of that is always increased as you see see it with eyes and mind different from what they were before you left.

The best way to carry stuff is to balance it on your head, which goes a long way in explaining why these women have such good posture.

Selling quesadillas, cheeze pasties, under the shade of a palm tree near the Costera Aleman and the Zocalo.

A vendor selling bananas and mangosteen on the steps leading down to the viewing platform at La Quebrada. Below: watching a diver leaping out from the very top. Note the shrine where they pray before diving.

— Ephemeron —

La Quebrada

Most of the small hotels close to the Zocalo were full, so we wandered up the hill towards La Quebrada and found a two story hotel across the road from El Mirador. The El Mirador is built over and along the jagged cliff faces that drop into the ocean as well as having rooms that cascade down into the clefts between cliff faces and has fantastic views along the coast as well as of the cliffs the high divers use. It was very expensive and simply out of the question as far as I was concerned.

Between the two hotels, the up-market El Mirador and the very Mexican hotel (the name of which now escapes me) was a wide square with a set of steps leading down to a viewing platform, the flattened top of another jagged outcrop of rock directly opposite the cliff the divers use while practicing and performing their spectacular dives. The square thronged with people who all wanted to see the divers as well as the views along the coastline.

This less luxurious local hotel was popular with the slightly more affluent Mexican tourist but was well within what I could afford for a little while. There were several rooms available and we booked one for a couple of days, a large room with twin beds, an ensuite and a window overlooking the square across to where the steps went down to the public viewing platform.

The divers didn't perform during the day, but they often practiced as well as trained up and coming divers how to push off from the side of the cliff. They didn't dive from the highest points during these practice sessions but used various levels up the side of the cliff face. Crowds of people made their way down the many steps from the plaza at the top of the cliff to view the divers from a platform about half way down the opposite cliff face from the divers. From my window I could see a lot of people trying to go down the steps to the viewing platform so something was happening. I had to go down and have a look.

The viewing platform was crowded with tourists all wanting to see the divers. Two were perched precariously on a narrow ledge about the same height as the viewing platform and I had a clear view of them only ten metres away. They stood and stretched their arms over their heads, ostensibly ignoring those viewing them but nevertheless fully aware of the tourists watching. They pretended to start to dive and then would pull back for another look at the waves constantly surging up the narrow chasm between the two cliff faces. They had to time the dive so they hit the water as it rushed in, and not as it was retreating. The wave rushing in would lift them up as they entered the water so they wouldn't smash into the bottom. Timing was critical, even from a low height only a few metres above the water. The chasm was shallow and rocky and if there was not enough water to lift them as they hit, they would go straight through and smash into the bottom, breaking their neck or killing themselves. Timing the dive so they hit the water at the exact moment it surges highest was critical especially when diving from a height. Also critical was making enough distance out from the cliff face to clear the jagged rocky base. At the highest point at the top of the cliff, the distance out was a bit over three metres — a long distance to go out while falling, so they needed strong legs to push out hard. Training from lower heights taught them how hard they had to push into each dive to clear the bottom of the cliff. As they progressively dived from a higher position they had to push harder to make more distance.

This was what the crowd was watching. The divers practicing and learning how to clear the cliff bottom as well as how to time the entry into the water so they wouldn't smash into the sand and rocks underneath the surface.

Divers perched on the sides of the chasm.

These divers are practicing to dive from various heights and learning how to judge the infow of water into the narrow chasm as well as how hard to push off from the cliff to clear the rocky base where the sea rushes in.

left:
At the bottom of the cliff a novice diver practices clearing the rocky base.

The water here is not very deep and the space to dive into is narrow. It takes a lot skill and nerves to dive into such a narrow space from any height let alone from the top of the cliff.

From the public viewing platform tourists watch a diver about to enter the water during a prctice dive.

It was just as thrilling to watch these practice sessions as it was to see the night-time performance with nothing but a spotlight to show where the water was and the diver balanced on the top of the cliff preparing to dive.

— *Ephemeron* —

An unexpected question

After spending the day wandering around Acapulco we were exhausted. Apart from the areas adjacent to the beach and the harbour, everywhere else inland was very hilly. You were always walking up or down a steep slope. The further you went inland from the actual coast, the more extreme the hills became. The road from the square in front of our hotel on top of La Quebrada was half a kilometre at a thirty degree incline down to the Zocalo, or back up from the Zocalo. This road was the only access so we had to walk up or down it whenever we wanted to go somewhere.

That evening, a gentle sea breeze blew in from the window and we could hear the sound of the 'tropical' band playing in the open space of the El Mirador's outdoor dining and dancing venue which of course afforded a fabulous view of the famous divers' platform as well as the huge chasm they dived into where the waves below smashed onto the rocks with a hollow booming sound. Unfortunately from our window we couldn't see the divers or the gap they dived into, it was angled away in a more westerly direction which gave great views of the ocean but not anything of the divers. A full moon reflected on what appeared to be a calm ocean, but I could hear waves smashing onto the rocks below the edge of the cliff so it was rough down there; exactly what the divers wanted, a big surge washing in to cushion their entry into the water.

We had been watching them earlier in the day but the thought of climbing down several hundred steps to the viewing area amidst crowds of tourists here for the Semana Santa holiday, not to mention having to climb back up again after it was over, was off-putting. Acapulco was packed with people enjoying the Easter weekend, and it seemed like thousands had gravitated towards the cliff edge to see the divers' evening performance which was delayed because the water washing into the chasm was not deep enough. The tide had been out and was only just starting to come in. Besides, my friend had to get up early in the morning to catch her flight on to Paris, and since I was under no such compulsion I decided I would go down to the foyer and buy a beer from the vendor opposite the front entrance to the hotel while she had a shower and an early night.

I sat and sipped the beer, 4 equis, which was not too bad, chatted with the vendor and watched people arriving in small excited groups to see the evening performance. Across the square floodlights intermittently lit up the cliff face and the small shrine where the divers prayed before preparing to dive. There were no divers visible at that point. A taxi slowly entered the square and had trouble making a turn to let passengers out for the El Mirador, there were so many people pushing and shoving and moving about. Finally it made the turn and once the passengers had got out it moved cautiously back towards the crowded street leading down to the Zocalo. No other cars or taxis attempted to come up the street because of the crowd filling the square at the top of the cliff.

When I got back to the room the lights were out and my companion appeared to be asleep in the bed nearest the window, a light sheet pulled up to her shoulders.

Plenty of moonlight shone through the window so it wasn't really dark. I made my way to the ensuite and had a quick shower, used the toilet and quietly got into the other bed. The noise of the people outside impatiently waiting for the divers to perform drifted in though the open window and sometimes, when the breeze was right, a faint sound of the band from the El Mirador overlaid it. They were playing what I thought was the cha-cha, El Bodeguero, but the voices from the square often overwhelmed the sound of the music so it was hard to identify the song.

I was just drifting off to sleep when the sheets rustled in the other bed as she turned towards me.

'Do you not like women?' she asked me.

What?

I looked over and saw her sitting on the edge of the bed. She obviously slept naked, as did I because of the heat.

She stood up and stepped across to my bed and sat down on the edge.

'Do you not want to have sex with me?'

That was certainly unexpected and definitely not something I had even been thinking about.

My understanding was that we had shared the room the night before and this night as well because it was convenient in a city crowded with holidaymakers taking all available rooms in every imaginable hotel, and that we had been lucky to actually find a room. To find separate rooms would have been impossible so we had shared, that was all, no expectations of anything else.

The truth was I didn't find her particularly attractive. She was a traveling companion, someone I remembered seeing a few times in Tahiti and someone who sat next to me on the plane travelling to Acapulco. We hardly knew each other and I was stunned by her audacity.

I didn't know what to say. I was always shy around women when it came to sexual advances, and it seems the more forceful they were the more I retreated. I was inexperienced and being aware of this never helped.

She snuggled closer and made it very obvious what she wanted to do, and although I was nervous about it I managed to respond. It was hot and humid and we were sweaty and I felt the end result was not that satisfactory but she seemed to accept it and eventually moved back to her own bed and promptly fell asleep.

She was already up and moving about in the morning when I woke up. She had dressed and packed her bag.

I stared up at her. 'What time is it?'

'Six o'clock.'

'In the morning?' My eyes stung and I could hardly open them.

'Of course in the morning. I have already rung for a taxi. It should be here any minute now.'

The phone on her bedside table rang at that moment. ''allo,' she said into the phone, and then after a brief pause, 'Gracias'.

She leaned over and gave me a peck on the forehead since I was lying on my back. 'The taxi is downstairs. I have to go now.'

She grabbed her travelling bag, slung her purse over her shoulder, and headed for the door, where she paused after opening it. She gave me a big smile and said, 'I will send you a postcard when I get home. Enjoy Acapulco.' Then she was gone and the door closed softly behind her.

I promptly went back to sleep and was woken up by a loud knocking on the door it seemed only a few moments later.

Jumping out of bed I put on a pair of shorts and opened the door. The man from the reception the day before was standing there, and looking annoyed. 'It's checkout time,' he told me.

10 o'clock already… My companion had been gone for almost four hours and would be well on her way to Paris.

'I wasn't planning on leaving;' I said hesitantly 'I need a few more days at least…'

'Well you can't have this room; it's already booked. Come down to reception and we'll see what we can arrange.'

I threw on a shirt and followed him down.

As it turned out they did have a smaller room overlooking the front entrance by the street coming up from the Zocalo and it was now available for a week. I booked it, paid in advance and went back upstairs to shift my few things from the larger room into the smaller one. And that's where I stayed for the rest of the week.

Playa La Condesa

Every day for the next week I took a bus to La Condesa beach where I spent the afternoon having an occasional swim in the surf, swinging in a hammock while listening to one of the two bands that played in the clubs that overlooked the beach, but mostly sitting in and playing congas with the same group I first met who organized the gig at the party. Of course to sit in a hammock I had to buy a drink, which was usually a tequila cocktail, but sometimes I had a cold beer instead. Drinking tequila in the mid-afternoon was a bit much…

There were several of these club/restaurants along the top of the small cliffs overlooking the beach. The two I gravitated towards played 'tropical' music. This was also the place where Cuban musicians came to for relaxation, gossip and the possibility of organizing a gig. A couple of other clubs had rock bands, while another further along had a small mariachi band that alternated with a son jarocha group. These were popular with tourists while those with the rock bands were popular with the younger teenage Mexican crowd. All of these places had rows of thatched cabanas lined up on the beach in front of each place, and waiters were always running up and down steps from the clubs to their patrons sitting in the shade under those thatched rooves.

Divers came up onto the beach from the rocks offshore offering to cook fresh clams that they had collected for tourists sheltering under the cabanas. Often small mariachi bands or jarocha trios would wander along the beach trying to interest people in paying to hear them play.

above: Mariachis on the beach at La Condesa. It appears not everyone wants to listen to them.

right: Divers shucking oysters and selling them to passers-by.

A peanut seller waiting patiently in the shade for his next customer.

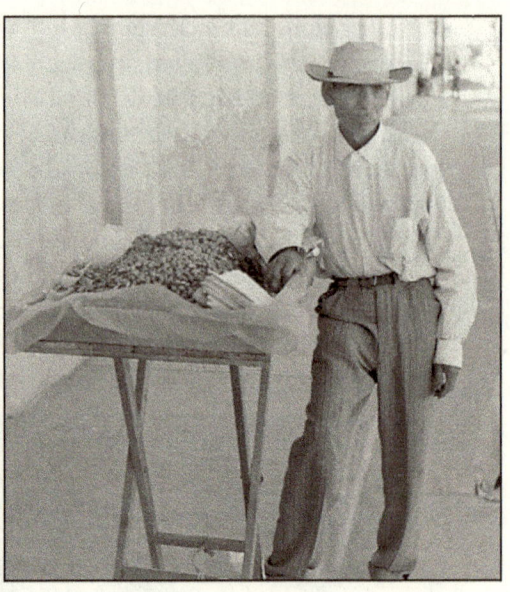

Private enterprise thrives along narrow streets in smaller towns throughout Mexico.

Left: a fruit stall outside a home.
below left: Selling a variety of beans and dried peppers.
below right: another fruit stall outside a home.

Boys selling souvenir necklaces and bracelets made of shells pestered tourists sitting in the shade. They weren't allowed up into the bars and restaurants, but the beach was open to everyone. Girls selling cut orange slices, watermelon pieces, or tacos and quesadillas were chased away by waiters who wanted the tourists to buy the food they sold in the restaurant above the beach. There was always someone on the beach who wanted to sell something; suntan oil, rides on a parachute towed by a speedboat, boat rides, big game fishing, scuba diving, although these people were more likely to be found in hotel foyers or along the Malecon downtown there was always someone willing to buy what they sold.

It was the same wherever I went in Mexico. Everyone tried to supplement their income by selling something, or made a meagre living selling whatever they could produce, or whatever extra that they had and didn't need they would try to sell. Often housewives would set up a small table outside their home and sell a bit of their evening meal to passers-by, or someone would pick fruit from a tree in their backyard and set up a stall in the street to sell it. I often saw women making and cooking tortillas on a small hotplate beside their front door. They would offer a fresh tortilla wrapped around a hot chili to anyone passing by in the street willing to buy it. Often I saw women sitting in the shade on the footpath surrounded by open bags of beans, herbs and spices, offering small quantities for sale. I never knew there could be so many different kinds of dried beans until I happened across a display like this.

More formally downtown there were roving stalls on wheels where you could buy tacos de carnitas cooked while you waited, fresh tamales, ceviche, piernas de pollo con mole, fruit salads sprinkled with chili powder, tropical drinks made from fruit with names unknown to me like chrirmoya, ice creams, in fact every kind of food imaginable. It was cheap and if you had a cast-iron stomach you could eat this fabulous food without having to spend a lot of money in restaurants where the food was often not as fresh or as good as what you could buy in the street or the local markets.

Seeing this should have been a cultural shock because there was nothing like this in Australia in the 1960s, but having read books by Jack Vance who often described strange food and restaurants on worlds populated by humans who were somewhat different from us it wasn't such a shock after all; to me it seemed perfectly normal. I was in another world, and although it wasn't on another planet, it could very well have

Cooking tortillas on small hotplates beside their front doors.

Home deliveries with a donkey drawn cart.

Milk being delivered with canisters strapped on the backs of donkeys.

been. Jack Vance travelled a lot and experienced many different cultures and the food produced by these cultures, and this obviously influenced his writing and his descriptions of exotic foods and customs in different places on far away planets scattered along the galactic arm beyond where our solar system resides. In fact many of his novels were written while he and his family lived for some time in Mexico near Guadalajara (for a while with Frank Herbert), and later in Morocco and Tahiti.

At the end of the first week I found a Pensión which was in the same street as the hotel but right down near the Zocalo and all the restaurants surrounding this tree shaded square. The weekly rate was half that what I was paying at the hotel. I could quite safely leave my stuff here and not worry about anything being stolen because the front door — an iron grill with a huge deadbolt lock — was always locked and residents had to use a key to get in.

Once sure my stuff was secure I bought a ticket on a bus to go to Mexico City (*simply referred to as Mexico by locals and hardly ever by its official name of Ciudad de Mexico*) where I knew there was an agent for Bolex cameras (*I got thier address from the yellow pages for Mexicco City at the locaal post office*). I was hoping they could repair and clean the mechanical parts of the camera to remove the salt that got in when the cracked underwater housing filled with sea water in Tahiti.

I found the place easy enough and was told it would take three days. I had to wait of course so I booked into a hotel near the heart of the city, not one of the fancy ones tourists used that filled the wide boulevards of the city, but one Mexicans themselves used. Three days would give me a chance to look around the city. It was also, on the second day that I experienced my first earthquake.

A small Earthquake...

I was asleep in my room on the fourth floor when the violent shaking of the bed awoke me. The noise was frightening. I leapt out of bed and rushed to the window. The whole building was vibrating. Barefoot I felt the vibrations through the wooden floor. Car horns sounded cacophonously in the street outside. Looking through the window I saw all the traffic in the street had stopped as close to the centre of the road as possible. There were people milling about looking up and around at the buildings on either side. Looking across to the building opposite I could see it shaking. Bits of masonry fell off and plummeted down to the sidewalk which was empty because anyone walking along was in the centre of the road.

'Shit, it's an earthquake!'

And I'm on the fourth floor.

I grabbed some clothes, thinking 'what if the building starts to collapse…?'

'How do I get out of here?'

But before I could finish getting a pair of pants on the shaking and the noise stopped.

It probably hadn't lasted more than thirty seconds, but it had seemed an awful lot longer than that. I had never been in an earthquake before.

Again looking through the window I saw all those who had been milling about in the centre of the street were once again on the sidewalks and on their way to wherever they had been going before. The honking of car horns had stopped and the traffic was moving along as if nothing had happened.

It was 6 am and I was already too awake to even think of going back to sleep so I finished getting dressed and went downstairs to see what damage had been done.

They told me it was nothing… 'nada más que un temblor, un pequeño terremoto… no se preocupe señor.'

Happens all the time apparently…

Mexico City is built over an ancient lake and the sandy soil underneath vibrates whenever there is a minor earthquake. A major event causes it to partially liquefy and buildings sink down into it because their support in that moment disappears. This is why many buildings are at various angles other than vertical because every time there is an earthquake they sink a little further into the ground. I was told some buildings had disappearded completely into this quake-formed quicksand, although that hasn't happened for a long time. Mostly they just collapse from violent shaking, or they sink a little each time.

The Cathedral in the huge Zocalo in Mexico City (in 1968) shows pronounced sinkage to one side caused by earthquakes.

It is also why you can't drink the water; the sewerage pipes and the water supply pipes have split in places or have broken and seepage from one into the other has infected the water. Locals can drink it but visitors will get a severe dose of the runs (or even cholera which is endemic) if they accidentally take even a sip of this water. Bottled purified water is available in every hotel and is the only water you should use.

Once I stepped outside it seemed as if nothing had happened.

Traffic was back to its chaotic scramble and pedestrians had returned to the sidewalks, stepping over any rubble that may have fallen without even noticing it. There weren't even any cracks in the pavement on the street so it couldn't have been much of an earthquake. But for me, those moments when the bed started shaking along with the incredible noise were terrifying. I decided then that I wasn't going to stay in Mexico City any longer than was absolutely neccessary.

Having called to ascertain whether my camera had been fixed, I was told it was, so I immediately went and collected it after which I took a bus back to Acapulco which was built on top of a granite base and, I hoped, was much safer in the event of an earthquake.

Mexico, along with the whole western coast of the American continent, sits along an earthquake zone and there are always earthquakes. Mexico has a number of volcanos as does South America and sometimes they are active while at other times they remain quiescent. I never thought about earthquakes and volcanos before because in Australia we don't have anything like that. I suppose there are always minor earthquakes but hardly anyone notices them. Australia is geologically stable, while South and North America are subjected to the Pacific Plate subducting all along their coastline, which forces the coastal mountains to rise higher and volcanos to periodically erupt. Mexico City has two volcanoes close by (*Ixtaccihuatl* and *Popocatepetl*) but while I was there they were both dormant and had been since the late 1880's.

Mexico City (*with about 8 million people in 1968*) seemed grey and dusty, overcrowded and not at all like I expected from having read 'Where the air is clear' by Carlos Fuentes which was set in Mexico City at an earlier period when there was not the same amount of industrial pollution nor the same population numbers. (*It was even worse 20 years later in 1989 when I went there again to find the city had swollen to over 20 million.*) Sure, there were a couple of nice clean looking tree-lined boulevards through the city and a beautiful park where guys festooned with colourful balloons wandered about hoping to sell them, but I found the streets dusty, smelly, often littered with garbage and not very pleasant. I couldn't wait to see the bright blue skies and sunlit beaches of Acapulco again.

Buried in a cloud of ballons ... one of the many balloon sellers in a Mexico City park.

Back in Acapulco...

Rodolfo Loredo Robles was a young man whom everyone called 'Rudy', Rudy Loredo. He played trumpet as well as piano and had written several songs one of which had been recorded on a 12 inch LP produced with him as leader a couple of years earlier in 1966. The liner notes talk about the popularity of tropical music and that Rudy was a great interpreter of such music. This was his first recording in which a number of songs popular at the time were presented including his own *guaracha, El Coquero*. None of the other musicians who congretated to play or socialize at La Condessa had been featutred as leader on a recording.

Rudy took a liking to me because firstly I was from somewhere he

Rudy playing trumpet at La Condessa. He started to grow a small beard because I had one... below: playing piano at a recording session in the restaurant at La Condessa.

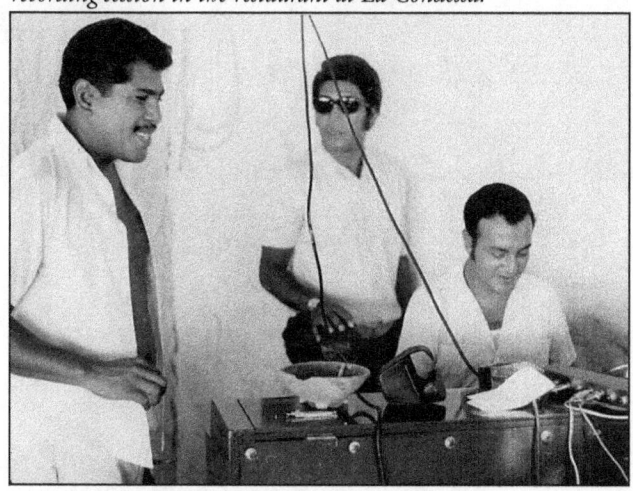

had hardly ever heard of, and I played cuban drums (*Congas*) in his view, better than all the local (*Mexican*) players, and at least as good as any of the expatriot Cuban players who lived in Acapulco. I also played them differently to the other players with the drums in a reversed position, and being able to isolate one hand from the other to play two rhythms simultaneously. (In particular, *Guaguanco* which none of them could play that way.)

And secondly, when I told him I had worked in Paris with *Pancho Cataneo* and his *Los Matecocos* he made me very welcome. He knew Pancho from time spent in Vera Cruz where there are a lot of expatriot Cubans with many fine musicians amongst them.

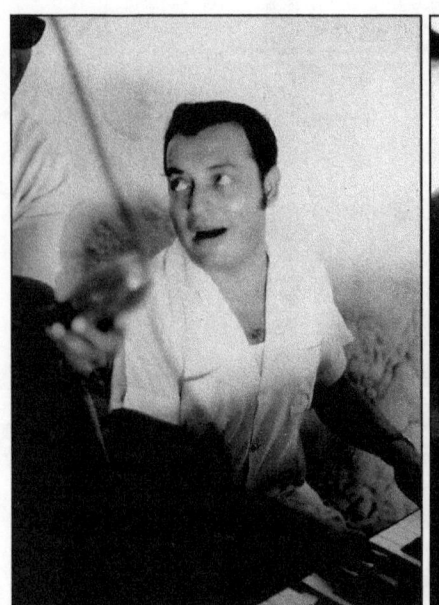

Above; Rudy singing the chorus, Nacho plays a Timbale solo.
Below Tabaquito soloing on congas, during a recording of El Coquero, which they taped especially for me to have as a souvenir.

El Tropicalismo de Rudy Loredo... this was the recording Rudy made in 1966. On a second trip to Mexico in 1990, 22 years later, I caught up with Rudy again and he inscribed this copy for me along with his most recent recording, **Musica Internacional a la manera de Rudy Loredo** his 1989 LP of famous boleros and other romantic songs.

Back cover of the 1966 album.

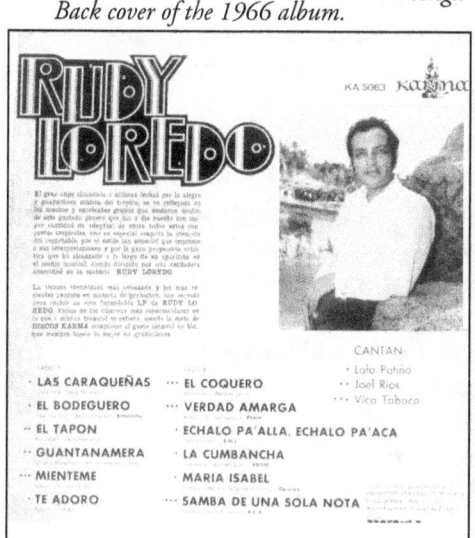

Moving into an apartment

At night Rudy played piano with a group hired by a luxury hotel. They played in a small intimate nightclub on the first floor of the hotel and I joined them to play conga drums. I wasn't paid but did it because it was a good opportunity to practice in a quiet relaxed way.

The music we played was mostly boleros and romantic songs which suited the venue. The group as well as the hotel management didn't mind me sitting in with them.

Rudy also played trumpet with one of the bands at the restaurant on the beach at *La Condessa* during the afternoons, which is where I met him the first day I arrived. The music there was much more tropical, danceable, mostly cha-cha, son montuno, mambos and guarachas, as befitting the venue and the location right on the beach.

Before moving to Acapulco he had played trumpet in a Mariachi Band in *Guadalajara*. He was originally from *San Luis Potosi* which is north and east of *La Ciudad de Mexico* (Mexico City), about as far north as Guadalajara but further to the east. Guadalajara is home to the best Mariachi bands in the country. It is located not far from a huge lake called Chapala where many foreign (mainly from the USA) residents have retired and bought properties because living on a pension is easier here than back home.

As it turned out, after I had been in my *pension* for a few weeks, Rudy told me he had separated some time ago from his wife, and was living alone in a two bedroom apartment behind the Cathedral near the Zocalo. He said he hated living alone and offered his spare bedroom to me. I was happy to move into the apartment and offered to share the rent.

He insisted that he would pay the rent as he had always done, but when I explained I felt awkward not contributing he then relented and said if I wanted I could pay the housemaid who came in and did the cleaning and washing five days a week. So that's what I did. The cost was hardly anything from my point of view so I gave her a bit more than Rudy had; ten dollars a week.

'Too much,' Rudy said.

He had been paying her the equivalent of 1 dollar a day. What I decided to pay her was double what Rudy had paid since she only worked five days a week.

She was certainly happy with that. She was a young woman from a village about 15 kilometres along the coast north of Acapulco. Most of the unmarried women from this close-by village worked as domestics in houses and flats all over Acapulco. Apart from the washing and cleaning she also did some shopping to keep the fridge stocked with milk butter, cold meats and salad greens for lunches. She was always there when I woke up in the morning, but she would leave about lunch time having done the washing and general cleaning by then. Before she left, if we wanted fresh bread she would run downstairs and get some rolls from a vendor in the street around the corner. The bread rolls they sold were always fantastic.

Mostly we ate the evening meal at a small restaurant along the Costera near the edge of the more urbanized part of Acapulco. It was on the way to the hotel where Rudy worked playing piano in a nightclub. It was where we were eating the time I experienced my second earthquake.

Baskets full of delicious fresh bread rolls for sale in the street just around the corner from the apartment.

You never tasted better bread than this!

Another Earthquake

Rudy and I were sitting at a small outdoor café having an evening meal. I could see across the *Costera Aleman* where traffic was not heavy to the beach and the sea beyond. It was calm and the sea appeared glassy with hardly any waves. Stars were beginning to sparkle brightly as the setting sun's light rapidly diminished. A warm breeze carried the scent of tropical flowers; a beautiful evening.

The specialty of the house was *Charky* or reconstituted dried beef lightly spiced with *jalapeño* peppers. The chefs were very friendly and after eating there regularly I got to know them well enough for them to allow me to sometimes help with the cooking on nights when they were busy, but this wasn't one of those nights.

Suddenly the air seemed heavy. I had an uneasy feeling and looked around but couldn't see anything out of the ordinary. I looked across towards the glassy sea and saw that it was agitated with choppy waves, strange waves because they were bouncing up and down and not rolling in towards the shore. There was no wind at all so there shouldn't have been choppy waves. Then I felt it through my feet before I heard it. They tingled with vibrations from the ground. I looked at Rudy who continued eating as if nothing was happening.

Then a deep groaning noise vibrated in my bones making my legs itch inside. Cars parked in the street started to bounce up and down or wobble from side to side. Traffic along the Costera slowed to a halt, and people walking along the sidewalk stopped wherever they were. The noise became louder. It sounded as if a piece of wood was slowly being torn in half lengthwise and magnified a thousand times. I could feel it through my whole body. as well as hear it. It was a very odd feeling. The audible part was almost ear-splitting. The café shook and for a moment I thought the roof that cantilevered out over the sidewalk would collapse. I was about to jump up and run out into the street when Rudy looked up and smiled.

'It's a small earthquake, Nothing to worry about,' he explained and continued eating.

The noise stopped suddenly, the parked cars stopped bouncing, traffic along the Costera stared to move again and beyond that the sea settled back into low swells with a glassy surface. It was all over in less than thirty seconds, but to me it seemed to have lasted much longer.

'Is there something wrong with the food?' he asked a moment later.
'No, the food's fine.'

I had forgotten to eat for that moment still thinking about the earthquake. As small as it had been, it was scary enough to make me want never to be in a real earthquake of such magnitude that buildings fall down and roads heave up and split and people are trapped under tonnes of rubble. Yet people here were used to these small earthquakes and hardly noticed them at all. Luckily there were no more of these for the rest of the time I spent in Mexico.

Lunch at Puerto Marquez

A 'First' for Mexico

I was vaguely aware of the fact that Mexico was to be the host of the XIX Summer Olympic Games, but never thought about it until one day a display of children's art was set up along the Malecon near the Zocalo in the centre of town. The art consisted of large posters designed by school children and it reflected their thoughts and desires for Mexico and the world during this year of the Olympiad, mostly expressing concepts of peace and friendship.

Even I, as a visitor, felt the pride the locals exhibited as they looked at these posters.

Mexico was unique in being the first Latin American country to be awarded the right to hold the Olympic Games. It was also the first time a Spanish speaking country held Olympic Games. Everyone, from children to adults, wanted these games to be special and different.

Mostly the games were going to be held in Mexico City, but the yachting events were to be held in Acapulco and there was a lot of excitement amongst people as they watched a plethora of yachts of various sizes practicing in the Bay of Acapulco. (Bahia de Acapulco)

Fragments from my Life – and Science Fiction

Two children working on their poster.

La Ciudad de Mexico would be problematic since it was situated some 2,240 metres above sea level, (7000 feet), and the air at this height was much thinner, and thus contained less oxygen, than the air at sea level. I imagined the athletes would have to acclimatize well before the games or they simply would not have the stamina for most of the major events. This was also the first time the Olympic Games were to be held at such a height above sea level.

Another first was the concept of simultaneously holding Una Olimpiada Cultural, or Cultural Olympics. The idea being that during the lead up to and perhaps even during the games themselves, countries participating would also have theatre, musical or dramatic groups performing in various venues around the city, to emphasize that there is more to life other than sports, and that entertaining people and enriching their minds was as important as winning medals or performing well at the games.

This cultural programmes was called Festival Internacional de Las Artes, and was presented by the Instituto de Bellas Artes. There were ballet, opera, musical theatre, and folkloric groups from around the world participating.

What excited me about this idea was the African Ballet, or *Ballet Africain du Guinea* was going to be in Mexico City, the very same African Ballet that had appeared a couple of years earlier in Melbourne. I couldn't wait to see them again since I knew most of the people involved in that company would be the same as those who were in Melbourne. This was to be the first time the African Ballet performed in Mexico and there was a lot of anticipation regarding their arrival. It was also the first time The Republic of Guinea had athletes competing in the Games. They had a football team (who played valiantly but didn't win any games and were eliminated after the first round). On the other hand, their ballet won accolades throughout the country.

As far as I can remember the two most popular theatre events were Ballet Folklorico de Mexico who performed every day at the Palacio de Bellas Artes and Ballet Africano who performed for a month at Teatro Ferrocarrilero, a huge theatre out of the centre of the city closer to the main sporting venue.

Everyone I encountered in Mexico City was talking about how spectacular the African Ballet was, how beautiful the girls were, and how incredible the music was. They had never seen anything like it before. Expatriate Cubans were fascinated by the drumming and the religious as well as secular aspects of the performances: they could see and hear where a lot of their own music originated from (before Spanish and Europeans influences changed it) and this fascinated them.

Mexico City was packed with visitors from around the world for the Summer Olympics with all the major hotels booked out for months in advance, yet I had no trouble at all in finding a small hotel down a side street not far from the hotel the African Ballet was at. There were a lot of these small hotels in side streets or minor throughways which catered not for foreigners but for locals who had to stay for a short while in town. Some of them didn't even look like hotels and so tourists never found them. I had been told by some friends in Acapulco where a few of these might be and had no trouble finding one once I got into Mexico City. By this time I had been in Mexico for more than six months and my ability to speak Spanish was quite fluent. Living in Rudy's flat and conversing only in Spanish with him since he didn't speak a word of English — neither did any of the musicians I played with at La Condesa and elsewhere — as well as chatting with the housemaid and her friends, none of whom spoke any English, soon had me conversing fluently. In fact the people at the small hotel I stayed in were surprised when I presented my Australian Passport to them; they had actually thought I was a Mexican visitor.

No sooner than I had checked in and put my stuff in the room, I went around to the Hotel Marlowe where the African Ballet were staying and caught up with Italo Zambo whom I encountered in the foyer

With Italo and the general manager of the African Ballet outside of their hotel 'Hotel Marlowe' in Mexico City (1968)

with the general manager of the ballet. Italo was one of the two Artistic directors of the ballet. The other was Hamidou Bangoura. Perhaps they both had been Artistic directors when they were in Melbourne a couple of years earlier but I was unaware of that at the time. Someone lent us Mariachi hats and a picture of the three of us was taken outside the hotel.

'What are you doing here?' Italo kept asking me.

'I'm living in Acapulco for the time being, playing drums."

'Well this certainly is a surprise.'

The company had already done several performances and Italo wanted to know what I had thought of them. They had made many changes to what was performed in Melbourne so in effect it was a whole new ballet. They also had a few different dancers, although the drummers and lead musicians were the same.

'I only just got here. I haven't seen anything yet.'

You'll have to come tonight.'

'It's booked out. Every performance has been booked out.'

The first thing I did on arrival in Mexico City was go to buy a ticket for the evening's performance only to discover all the performances for the entire season were sold out.

'You come with us. You don't need a ticket. I will arrange a backstage pass.'

The cover from the programme of the African Ballet's part in the **Programa Cultural De La XIX Olimpiada**

Photo of the lead drummer from the official programme booklet.

The lead drummer was also delighted to see me again.

'I want you to listen well to us tonight,' he told me in French. 'We have incorporated the rhythm you showed me in Melbourne.'

'Guaguancó.'

'Oui. That one.'

Now that I did want to hear...

I was delighted to see how well this more modern rhythm fitted into their traditional music, because guaguancó, although Cuban, didn't originate in Guinea, Mali, or Senegal, but came from Nigeria where the music is very different from that of the formally French-occupied African countries, and it wasn't until some of the rhythms from Nigeria underwent a metamorphosis which included a Spanish influence that guaguancó and other forms of rumba developed. To hear how well it fitted into a different African tradition was exciting.

That night after the performance a few of us went to a Cuban nightclub where those present stood up and applauded the African Ballet drummers when they walked in. After we had sat down and had something to eat I went to the conga drummer of the house band and asked if the lead drummer from the ballet could play something. His name was 'El Gallego' and he was only too happy to have another drummer sit in and play.

I called the lead drummer over and he stood behind the quinto and gestured to me to play the deeper tumbadora. I looked at El Gallego who nodded and smiled. The drums were on stands so we had to stand up to play them. I started with the second rhythm from a group of rhythms loosely called Bembé, a 6/8 counterpoint rhythm and the lead drummer immediately began a solo which fitted around the drum pattern I was playing. Almost immediately El Gallego grabbed a cowbell and started to play the 6/8 stick pattern. He also sang from the Yoruba tradition, songs every Cuban who was Santo Lucumi knew. Quite a few seated at nearby tables joined in to make a chorus which enriched the songs. The singing obviously inspired the African lead drummer to play some incredible riffs on the quinto which in turn enticed a couple of guests in the nightclub to get up and dance as if they were possessed. Someone else from the house band added a shekere to the mix. It was a fantastic session and it lasted about twenty minutes before the lead drummer nodded to El Gallego and me and at the end of the next cowbell pattern we all stopped abruptly.

Over the deafening applause El Gallego asked me, '*Donde aprendiste tocar asi?*'

'*En Australia,*' I told him.

'*Hay muchos Cubanos ahi?*'

'*Ninguno,*' I answered.

And when he looked puzzled I explained that I had learned these rhythms from various congueros visiting Australia, like Armando Peraza who came out with George Shearing, with Francisco Aguabella, who was with the Katherine Dunham group touring Australia, and others who came also with various musical groups and dance companies. He knew the names I mentioned and clapped me hard on the shoulders. He couldn't stop nodding and smiling.

What a night: after that I don't remember much because I drank too much tequila. But it was like that for a month. I would watch the performance of the ballet in the theatre and afterwards we would go for something to eat and inevitably finish up in a nightclub where we would sit in and play until early hours of the morning.

Back again in Acapulco having fun on a night time cruise around the harbour with a friend from San Francisco, and battling a pirate who came on board to hold the passengers for ransom. Lots of fun...

In 1968 it was a fantasy, but in recent years this has become a reality with gangs attacking locals and tourists alike travelling by bus, and sometimes killing them when they are too slow to cooperate in handing over their valuables.

— *Ephemeron* —

Time flew by...

Back in Acapulco time flew by. I met a lovely girl from San Francisco who was on holidays and we did the tourist things like taking an evening boat ride on the harbour during which the boat was supposedly hijacked by pirates one of which I fought off with a cutlass. After the pirates left we had dinner and a band played music so the passengers could dance the evening away. The sea was dead calm unlike it would be in a couple of weeks as the wet season approached. Few foreigners came to Acapulco during the summer; the wet season was hot and sultry, and there storms blew in from the ocean bringing big waves and rough seas leaving the beaches deserted. The only visitors were people from Mexico City who came down for their holidays. They didn't mind the sultry weather on the coast; it was so much better than Mexico City where humidity and pollution were trapped over the city by the surrounding mountains.

(It was bad enough in 1968, but when I returned in 1990 I was stunned to find it so bad that I couldn't see more than a couple of hundred metres. It was brownish in colour, a thick fog of exhaust fumes, dust, dried excrement from feral dogs and cats and people living in the streets, smoke from small factories, rotting food scraps and other detritus floating heavily in the air. I couldn't wait to get out of this city and head down to the coast and Acapulco where I hoped to find some old friends.)

I ate regularly at a café called La Cucaracha, (quite possibly named for the huge cockroaches that could often be seen running across the floor or up and down walls) and conversed a lot with a girl called Ofelia who worked as a waitress and eventually she agreed to spend an afternoon with me at Playa Condesa. She was reluctant to go out with a foreigner, which is what I was no matter how well I spoke Spanish or how much I fitted in with the locals. As it turned out she was reluctant to go out with anybody because she had a son to look after. It surprised me when she arrived at our agreed meeting place with her young son.

This was not something I had expected and didn't quite know how to react.

I wasn't prepared for the responsibility of being involved with someone with a young son (having been through that after coming back from Europe) so although we had a lovely time our relationship didn't progress beyond being friendly and having conversations at La Cucaracha whenever I went there for a meal.

Ofelia at Playa La Condesa and myself with Ofelia and her son.

A new Visa...

And suddenly I discovered I had been in Mexico for 6 months. My visa was about to expire, after which I would become an illegal visitor. There was too much red tape involved in extending my current visa so my best option was to leave the country and return after a couple of weeks. On entering Mexico again I would automatically be given another tourist visa for 6 months. That's what happened the first time I entered so I thought it would be just as simple second time around.

Of course it wasn't.

'I have to leave to get a new visa,' I told Rudy shortly after I realised how long I had already been there.

'And the easiest way is to go to *Estados Unidos* for a few days before coming back. I should get a new visa for six months when I come back into Mexico.'

He looked thoughtful for a moment. *'Posiblemente es más complicado que piensas.'*

'I don't think there will be any problems. I was told it was the easiest way to extend the visa.'

'Puede ser…'

An unexpected road trip

The next morning Rudy told me he thought it was time to visit his family in San Miguel de Allende and that he was going to go there with Raul, the Bass player from one of the groups at La Condesa, who had a car, and who wanted to go to Monterrey to visit his family… and if I wanted I could accompany them as far as San Miguel, and then on to Monterrey. After that I could take a bus to the border town of Nuevo Laredo where I could cross into the US. I thought that was a fabulous idea.

'You never mentioned going to San Miguel before. Are you doing this for me? You don't have to. I can take a bus to Mexico City and then another one from there to the US.'

'We were thinking of doing this a bit later, but since you have to go within the next couple of weeks I spoke to Raul and he agreed we could bring the trip forward. We could go tomorrow.'

That was unexpected.

'Está bien?'

'That's fine. I don't need to take much with me, just some changes of clothes, passport… that's about it.'

And off we went bright and early the next mornung in a little car that climbed laboriously up the steep and winding roads that crossed the Mountain Range called *Sierra Madre del Sur* that separated Acapulco from Mexico City.

We stopped at Chilpancingo (*the Capitol of the state of Guerrero*) for a toilet break, and again in Tasco (*the city famous for its silver mines*) where we had something to eat, then continued on to Mexico City.

There was no way we could avoid going there since the road from Acapulco went there without joining any of the other highways north or south all of which emanated from Mexico City. It was late evening when we arrived and Rudy wanted to stop at a special place he knew well, a market plaza where Mariachi groups would meet, play, and talk about their activities. It was a bit like *Playa La Condesa* where bands and musicians hung about and anyone wanting a band for party or a function went there to listen to them playing after which they could decide whether to hire them or not. Rudy knew people here and wanted to catch up for a while. Raul and I had something to eat and listened to the Mariachi music while Rudy gossiped with old amigos.

After that it took a couple of hours to negotiate the horrendous night time traffic in the Capital, and before we found the highway to San Miguel de Allende it was about three in the morning. When we finally got onto the highway we again drove through the rest of the night and all the following day without stopping, arriving in San Miguel late in the afternoon where long shadows from a beautiful cathedral spread across the Zocalo. We would leave Rudy here and and after a short walk to stretch our legs Raul and I continued on across to Guanajuato and then onto Monterrey much further the the north.

Rudy and Raul shortly after arriving at San Miguel de Allende.

– *Ephemeron* –

Rudy in front of the cathedral inSan Miguel de Allende.

Guanajuato...

Guanajuato is a name I remembered from a frightening Ray Bradbury story relating to *El Día de Los Muertos*, The Day of the Dead, which is celebrated throughout Mexico but in particular in Guanajuato which is famous for its catacombs where one hundred and eleven mummies were entombed. They are now on display at a special museum.

I am not sure now whether I read this story before going to Mexico or after I got back home, because the catacombs that Bradbury visited were only officially opened in 1969, and that was the year after I spent eleven months in Mexico. But the mummies could still be visited before then; people had been paying to see them as far back as the late 1870s, so Ray Bradbury could have seen them before they were placed in their new museum

The story was called *The Next in Line* which he wrote after visiting the mummies. The sight of these naturally desiccated bodies stored and displayed for public viewing terrified him so much that he suffered horrific nightmares and felt compelled to leave Mexico immediately. As soon as he got home he wrote *The Next in Line*, after which his nightmares disappeared.

Apparently the mummies resulted from the local government enacting a law in 1870 which required families to pay a burial tax after a year to keep the body buried. Poor families couldn't pay so they disinterred the bodies and because the air in Guanajuato is so dry the bodies were naturally mummified. They were stored in a nearby building. Not long after visitors to the city heard about this and paid a small fee to visit the bodies, and this has been going on since then. In 1969 a museum was established where the one hundred and eleven bodies are on permanent display.

Side streets and markets in Guanajuato which tourists rarely see. Many of these little streets would be too narrow for motor vehicles even if they were paved, but some, strewn with rocks and boulders, would have challenged a mountain goat. Yet as can be seen, people used them without problems.

We spent a couple of hours in Guanajuato without visiting the catacombs which at that time I had the impression were natural caves where the bodies had been placed after disinterring them — Raul wasn't interested in seeing them. 'That's for the tourists,' he said disparagingly, — before we headed off to Monterrey, almost a 1000 kilometres further north, a long drive through Mexico's high barren desert country where small towns mostly built of adobe were almost invisible from a distance until suddenly they would appear as if growing up out of the ground right in front of us. The streets we drove through in these towns appeared deserted, dusty, often unpaved, with all the buildings closed off from the street. No doubt they were more pleasant inside with private courtyards than their external street façade indicated. None of them seemed like nice places to stop, so we didn't.

The outskirts of Monterrey were also almost invisible until we got close but the smudge of dirty grey air hovering above the city gave it away from a distance long before we saw any outskirts.

The cobblestoned main road through a small country town on the way to Monterrey.

San Antonio and the Alamo

Raul left me at a central bus terminal where I bought a ticket to Nuevo Laredo. I promptly fell asleep on the bus and saw nothing until I woke up at the terminal before the crossing into America. There were a lot of busses and lots of people getting on or off them. Long lines of cars and trucks waited to go through the border control into the USA. As each vehicle was searched and allowed to continue across the others behind slowly inched forward. I went through customs check and had the entry date stamped in my passport beside the four year visa, and followed a path across the bridge over the Rio Grande into a very much cleaner and neater city, Laredo in Texas. I found a Greyhound bus to take me to San Antonio and once again was on the highway.

I suppose I could have stayed a few days in Laredo and then went back, but I had seen a couple of movies about San Antonio and The Alamo (the most recent one being with John Wayne and Richard Widmark in 1960) that I thought it would be nice to visit The Alamo while I was so close.

Several times the bus was stopped by American Border Officials and every person on board had their passports or papers checked to see if they were legally allowed to be in the USA. This felt intrusive to me, coming from Australia where no one had to show papers or any sort of ID no matter where they went within the country. Even though I had to carry a passport in lieu of other ID papers when in Europe, it still felt strange and intrusive to have to do this in America.

Two things astonished me about San Antonio: it was so clean the footpaths (sidewalks) and streets seemed as if they had been washed and polished overnight to appear spotless and fresh in the morning when people emerged into the day. Everywhere I looked I imagined I was looking at a living glossy postcard. The people in the street also appeared as clean and immaculately dressed as if modelling the latest fashions, like the whole town was a museum and everyone who lived there were actors playing a role.

And the other thing was how small The Alamo actually was.

I had the impression from seeing the film with John Wayne, that it was enormous, a huge edifice, but the reality was a disappointment, low crumbling walls that could easily be climbed. Apparently for the film a large scale duplicate of the actual Alamo was built on ranch nearby where the filming took place. I never got to see that.

For me, San Antonio was too clean. Even the water in the narrow canals which people made such a fuss about looked filtered like water in a fishpond; I imagined if I took a closer look I would see goldfish swimming there.

Instead of staying a few days as I had planned, I took another Greyhound bus back to Laredo the next morning. I couldn't wait to get back into Mexico where things seemed more natural than the artificiality of San Antonio.

An incident at the border

Leaving Laredo behind me I crossed over the Rio Grande into the Nuevo Laredo Customs and Passport control. I asked for a new visitor's visa and this was placed in my passport without charge.

I thought nothing of this and boarded one of many busses lined up heading south to Monterrey. I had bought a ticket before boarding. The bus started to fill with passengers when two uniformed Policia Federales boarded and came straight to me.

'*Pasaporte por favor,*' one of them demanded politely.

I handed it to him and they both looked at it.

'Come with us,' the other one said in English.

I followed them off the bus wondering what the hell I had done wrong.

We went back inside the building.

Inside the man with the passport handed it to another official behind a desk. He spent some time looking at it while I kept looking back to see if the bus had left. My small overnight bag was on board and I didn't want to lose it.

Nobody said anything and I was wondering what would happen next. Should I offer some kind of bribe? I had heard you had to do this, but then I was concerned that if I did they could claim I was trying to bribe a government official and would be refused entry which would be awkward because everything I had was back in Acapulco apart from the overnight bag on the bus.

One of the two policía said, '*Señor,* the bus is waiting.'

'Yes,' the man at the desk said while still holding my passport.

'If you could perhaps pay a small fee, we could facilitate the stamping of your passport.'

'You do need a stamp indicating time and date of entry into Mexico' the man at the desk added.

'A small fee…?'

'Yes…' The three men looked at each other then turned and smiled at me.

'Perhaps one hundred dollars…?' the one who spoke English suggested.

'Well,' I smiled back at them, 'I don't carry much money with me when travelling. There are thieves everywhere…'

They smiled and nodded understandingly. I took out my wallet and showed them I had no more than fifty dollars in small denominations.

'Fifty dollars is all I have at the moment, plus a few coins.'

They looked at each other.

I half pulled the fifty dollars out of my wallet so they could clearly see it and that the wallet was empty. I passed it to the one who had spoken in English.

'How do you travel with so little money?' he said, holding my wallet as if it would burn his hand.

'I have a bank account in Acapulco with Banco Nacional. If I need some I can draw it out from other branches. Is there one here?' I knew there wasn't, at least not anywhere nearby.

'*No señor.*'

'Is that not enough?' I pointed to the fifty dollars in my wallet.

They quietly conferred and suddenly the other policía took the money from my wallet and passed the wallet back to me. He turned to the man at the desk and with a great deal of over-acting he snapped at him, '*apure té hombre… el bus está esperando…*' 'What the hell are you doing holding him up like this?' 'Hurry up, the bus is waiting.'

'*Lo siento…*' and with a smile the man sitting at the desk pulled out a stamp pad and a large lump of a stamp and thumped it onto the page in my passport where the new visa was. With a magnanimous gesture he handed my passport to me. '*Bienvenidos a Mexico*, please enjoy your stay.'

I hurried back to the bus.

The driver smiled at me as I got back in. '*Cuanto te cobro?*' he asked.

'*Cincuenta dólares.*'

'*Bien barato*,' he said and with a flourish he started the engine.

A moment later the bust moved out of the terminal and onto the road to Monterrey.

Apart from the trip with Rudy and Raul in his car, everywhere else I went in Mexico was by local bus, not those air conditioned sealed tourists monsters, but the ones the people used to go from town to town on regular service routes. This was the way to see the country and to get a feeling of how ordinary people lived. I loved these local busses.

About half way to Monterrey the bus pulled in to a service centre and before the light desert wind could blow away the dust churned up by the bus it was surrounded by *vendedores*. They held what they were selling up to the open windows so the passengers could see what they were offering.

Everyone was shouting at the same time, the passengers and the *vendedores*. There were kids inside the bus telling their parents they were hungry or that they wanted to go to the toilet. The aisle between the two rows of seats was jammed with people standing up while attempting to pull bags down from overhead storage racks. Others were leaning out of the windows to negotiate with the vendedores. The bus doors were open and people desperate to get off for a toilet break pushed through them out into the vendedores crowding around.

'*Tacos, tacos…nieves…dulces…cajetas…tacos, un pesito…cinco por un peso…*' a cacophony of voices filled the air.

'*Deme un pesito,*' a man leaning out a window called as I struggled to get out of the bus.

The tacos were passed in through the open window and the peso dropped into the upheld hand. Someone had managed to get onto the bus with a guitar and was singing and playing.

Most of the passengers who had gotten off were standing in the shade of a huge tree near the service building, eating and drinking whatever they had bought.

'*Nieves,*' a nearby voice shouted as the man pushing a small cart passed in front of the crowd in the shade. '*Tengo de limón, nuez, coco y fresa...*'

I could still hear singing inside the bus.

All too soon the short break was over. '*VAMONOS*' the driver called out and started honking his horn.

I bought some *tacos de carnitas* because I was hungry and an orange drink to wash them down and got back on the bus. The man with the guitar was holding out his hat as he pushed his way off the bus against those trying to get back on. '*Regálame lo que quiera, lo que pueda,*' he chanted. I dropped some change into his hat as he passed.

'*Vámonos.*'

Another bus had arrived pulling up behind us in another cloud of dust and the *vendedores* deserted us to assail the newcomers.

The driver started the motor and revved it so loud I thought it would fall apart. He honked the horn a few times and received an answering honk from the bus behind. He started to move forward as the last couple of stragglers jumped aboard with hands full of food and soft drinks. Finally when he was sure all were aboard he closed the doors and the bus moved rapidly back onto the dusty highway to continue on the Monterrey.

Guadalajara

In Monterrey I transferred almost immediately to another bus going south to Guadalajara, a city that was home to the greatest Mariachi bands in Mexico. It was a centre for Mariachi music and was a place I had always wanted to see.

It was a three day trip diagonally across Northern Mexico, with a couple of changes of bus to make the connection to Guadalajara. All the buses had hard back-breaking seats which made it impossible to sleep so when I got there I was exhausted. I wandered through the centre of the city looking for somewhere to stay and came across an enormous

park with paved and grassed areas interspersed with large shady trees. It looked cool and peaceful and I decided to walk through it but was stunned and annoyed because everywhere I went it was filled with horribly distorted music coming from loudspeakers hidden in the trees or stuck on top of posts beside the pathways people walked along. It wasn't even traditional Mexican music, it was pop drivel — Muzak! This was my first encounter with this horrible stuff that was beginning to permeate all the nooks and crannies of big cities.

I hadn't been aware of it in Melbourne even though I had been paid on several occasions to be part of an orchestra recording music to be played in supermarkets and other public spaces, probably because it was something relatively new. I didn't like it much but a job was a job. You came expect it in supermarkets and shopping centres because they have this idea that people need to be relaxed so they will be more conducive to buying stuff, and what better way to do that than to have soft non-descript music playing in the background. But hearing it in a park where you go for some peace and quiet was not something I expected. It was loud, strident, and obtrusive. Perhaps the city council decided to use it in the park thinking because expatriate Americans were living in the city and the countryside, especially at nearby Lago de Chapala, muzak piped through the city's open spaces would make them feel at home. Did it not occur to them that one of the reasons people moved from the US to live in Mexico was to get away from that stuff? Of course muzak was relatively new in 1968 and the city fathers must have thought they were being innovative.

I headed for the exit where there was no muzak but on a small elevated bridge there was a one-man-band playing a popular Mexican song with a young girl singing to the music he produced. I quite enjoyed that.

A father with his daughter busking in Guadalajara.

After leaving the park I decided Guadalajara was just like any other big city and as such I wasn't particularly interested in staying there, so I took a bus to Chapala which was about a half hour from Guadalajara. I was dropped off in front of a beautiful hotel overlooking a long expanse of water. There were hundreds of brightly painted small paddle boats lined up along a rough sandy beach fronting the hotel. They bumped softly against each other as choppy waves lapped the shore. A cool breeze caused a number of flags on tall poles to flap and rattle like the rigging on yachts moored in a harbour.

It was off-season and there were not many staying at the hotel so I had a magnificent room overlooking the lake and the colourful little boats. After a dinner of enchiladas with fruit salad for desert I retired early and slept the best I had for several days. I got up at seven in the morning and after a breakfast of huevos rancheros with lots of coffee I took a bus heading south along the lake.

Lago de Chapala is one of the largest lakes in Mexico and it took almost all day to drive south along its shoreline. Occasionally I caught a glimpse of fishermen standing in narrow canoe like boats, balancing easily while they hurled a circular fishing net out over the water. The lake was full of fish and there was an abundance of aquatic birds along the edges of the water where often reeds and grasses obscured the shoreline.

I couldn't get enough of looking at that beautiful lake. Most of the land I had traversed from the US border was dry and barren and full of desert dust, or rocky and mountainous with scrawny bushes and ragged cacti, but here in the long high plains between the two mountain ranges that traversed the length of Mexico it was like a Garden of Eden, a paradise, green and fertile.

I Finished in Celaya where I stayed a night before making my way back to Mexico City and then down to the coast to Acapulco.

People used to ask me did I see the temples in the jungle and I had to tell them that Mexico is an enormous country and it is difficult to get around. So the answer is no, I didn't go East of Mexico City to Vera Cruz or further South to Chiapas or the Yucatan Peninsula where the Olmec and Mayan ruins are located in the jungles. I was content to be in Acapulco primarily because I was playing the kind of music I loved and because I had very good friends there after having been there for more than six months. I just never had the desire to go and see those ancient ruins at that stage in my life. I did go to Tehuantepec, the Aztec city which covers a couple of square kilometres and is located 50 or so kilometres out of Mexico City when I went back to Mexico some twenty years later, but even then I didn't go across to Yucatan and Chiapas. One day I will have to do that.

A difficult decision

Back in Acapulco it was still the end of the wet season with huge broken waves pounding the beaches, strong winds encouraging massive rainstorms and minor flooding keeping foreign tourists away. But for me it was like coming home after a long absence; I felt comfortable and relaxed and couldn't wait to join Rudy at the hotel club where he played six nights a week.

Someone I had seen and heard singing romantic songs often enough in the club lounge where Rudy played, a lothario who had a different girl every time I saw him, and who always sang boleros (romantic songs) to them, came up to me one night and said in perfect English 'If you want I can organize to get you a residential visa so you can stay here permanently.'

I was flabbergasted. He spoke with an 'Oxford' accent, and it turned out he was English not Mexican as I had thought he was. He had been there for years and was as much a part of the local scene as anyone who had been born there. His Mexican Spanish was impeccable and unless he told you he was English you would never think he was anything other than Mexican. I had only ever heard him speaking Spanish before.

'Well…' I had no idea what to say. 'I'll have to think about that,' I finished lamely.

'You fit right in. Everyone here likes you, so think about it, and let me know.'

'Okay.'

He nodded and went to Rudy at the piano to request a particular bolero, which when we started to play he sang like a pro. He was super smooth and sounded a bit like Tito Rodriguez, who after his initial rivalry with Tito Puente, went on to become a famous romantic singer that women everywhere swooned over. I could see the girl at his table was very impressed.

If I had a girlfriend or was involved with someone I would certainly have taken him up on his offer. But the truth is, all I could do in Mexico was play drums, and for musicians, there is never sufficient work for them to live comfortably with too many competing for the same few gigs that could come up. And apart from that, musical tastes were changing and the kind of music I played was becoming rarer as young Mexicans preferred the local Rock bands which started to dominate the club scene. Just like back home in Melbourne, the writing was on the wall. I was also obligated to return home after my year was up so Phillip could take some time off from the dry cleaning factory. Once he had done that Dad was going to retire and sell us the business, so I really couldn't stay no matter how much I wanted to.

But I really was tempted. I thought long and hard and finally decided I would leave a couple of months before my second visa expired because my *round-the-world* flight would have to be completed by the end of March (1969). If I didn't complete the trip within the time limit the fare would be lost and I would have to pay for new airfares to travel after that date, and I certainly didn't have money to do that.

I decided to go in January, to allow enough time to visit New York where I planned to buy recordings from Fania Records as well as visit Mum's relatives in Toronto in Canada. I would finish with a few days in Germany with my brother in law's parents, (who were expecting a visit from their wayward son after twenty years of not seeing him) before going to Rome and then to Nairobi, and Johannesburg in Africa, finally arriving back in Perth, West Australia via the Mauritius Islands. From Perth I would fly direct to Melbourne.

Unfortunately I could only allow a couple of days in each place or I would never complete the round trip in time. It would be a pity because most of those places I wanted to see, but having spent so much time in Mexico, which I didn't regret for a moment, meant that I had to forego time in those other places.

I sttill wanted to stay in Mexico as long as possible, so that's what I did.

The elegant way to carry a heavy load...

A sense of belonging...

If you stay in a place long enough you grow accustomed to it and after a while it feels as if you belong there. That's how I felt about Acapulco. People recognized me and said hello as I passed them on the street; often they stopped for a chat. I was no longer a tourist, but a resident.

The second floor apartment which I shared with Rudy was situated in a backstreet a block away from the Zocalo and the Cathedral and there was always a lot of traffic, vehicular as well as on foot, in the street. I would sit on the balcony after breakfast and watch the goings on in the street below. It fascinated me how people could carry often huge loads of things in baskets balanced on their heads. Men usually carried loads on their shoulder balancing it with one arm while almost always the women carried the load on their heads, sometimes holding it gently with one hand, or other times not holding the load at all. They walked with grace and balance, maintaining their load seemingly effortlessly. Models struggle to attain this natural grace that these women have. I once saw a guy carrying a load of bread rolls in a basket on his head while pedalling a bicycle through pedestrians in the street, weaving in and out between groups of people and never once touching the basket so perfectly balanced on his head.

A father and his daughter heading to market with their produce.

— *Ephemeron* —

I got on quite well with the two girls who alternated with doing our washing and cleaning and talking with them helped improve my Spanish and made it street fluent. They invited me to visit their village one weekend and I was more than happy to accept.

We took a local bus which dropped us off on the coast road not far from the village and we walked the rest of the way in. The village itself was on the inland side of the coastal road, a long way from the beach. It consisted mainly of adobe buildings, the ones in the centre of the town rendered and painted, while those more on the outskirts were never as finished and you could see the sticks and mud they were constructed with. All had palm thatched rooves.

The two girls and two of their friends accompanied me. It must have been quite a sight, me an obvious extranjero, with four girls walking along the dirt road through the centre of the village. The road was covered with piles of coconuts being chopped in half by guys wielding machetes. Working with coconuts was the only income this village had and it was a collective effort. What they actually produced apart from dried and desiccated coconut I have no idea. A couple of naked kids and some scrawny dogs followed us as we walked along the street.

We walked towards the other end of the village where there was a hill sparsely covered with small trees. In the shade of these trees several women were labouring over huge metal pots preparing food for everyone. Again I am not certain if this was for a special event (to which I had been invited) or simply this was what they did every day: the men worked with the coconuts while the women prepared the food for all of them.

They stopped what they were doing when we arrived and the girls embraced the women around the pots one by one. They introduced me not in Spanish but in a native dialect. I was invited to assist with the cooking by helping to stir the giant pots. I had no idea what was in them but it sure smelled good. It was a great day and the food was fabulous. God knows what it was we ate, but it is always best not to know if it tastes good. Just eat it and enjoy it.

Feeling right at home in the village

– *Ephemeron* –

Last days...

After that visit to the village I hung around the Zocalo, always full of noisy activity. Mexicans loved making noise. Cars swirled around the outskirts of the Zocalo, horns honking, with radios screeching raucous versions of Happy Birthday or Never on Sunday (very popular the time) or mariachi music or some kind of tropical music (later to be called salsa). Shoe shiners filled one side of the shaded Zocalo entreating passers-by have their shoes made better than new, while other vendedores offered everything from chiclets to tacos.

My sister Christine came ashore from a passenger liner anchored in the harbour. She was with her friend Yvonne and they had one day in Acapulco before going on to England where they were hoping to work for a while. It was great to see them and I took her all over Acapulco's touristy spots because that's all there was time for. My uncle Eddie with his second wife and a new family also turned up on a ship for one day while on their way to Germany. I showed them around the town like the proud resident that I was and we had a lovely time. Other than that not much else happened over the last two months I spent there.

There were always two sides to Acapulco; one the tourists saw which was bright and sparkling and glitzy with beautiful people inhabiting expensive hotels, visiting fancy boutiques and high-priced restaurants and clubs where they could party and dance as well as eat fine food, and the other side which these tourists never saw, the poor side where people washed their clothes in a river that was more a drain for houses high on the surrounding hills after which they draped the clothes over bushes to dry in the sun, where they ate food in the market place or from stalls along the roadside, where little kids had to work selling stuff to tourists because their parents had no money or had abandoned them. This was a side few visitors saw, but nevertheless it coexisted with the jetsetters glamourous Acapulco and it had a character and beauty of its own. It was this side of Acapulco that I liked and it was this side of it that I would miss when I left— not the glitz and glamour; that you can find anywhere in any country, but the other side the tourists don't or can't see, that was unique.

Washing clothes in the drainage channel everyone called 'the river'

My uncle Eddie, his wife Renata, and their children Iris and Manuela disembarcing for a day in Acapulco.

Uncle Eddie and me near the Zocalo.

— *Ephemeron* —

An International Film Festival

December came and posters advertising Acapulco's International Film Festival appeared all over the place. My recollection is that this was the first time there had been a film festival in Acapulco and everyone was excited about it. The list of films was impressive and there were two that I definitely wanted to see: *Rosemary's Baby* directed by Roman Polanski and starring John Cassavetes with Mia Farrow, and on the last day of the festival was *2001* directed by Stanley Kubrick and Arthur C Clarke. The added bonus was that these films were in English which meant I could ignore the Spanish subtitles. All the other films were French, Spanish, or from other European countries. All would have Spanish subtitles which I would have not had the ability to read fast enough to make sense of the films, so I bought tickets for the only two films spoken in English.

Rosemary's Baby was near the start of the programme and was shown in a theatre which had an open roof so cool tropical air filled the theatre with fragrant freshness. The film was frightening, after starting out seemingly ordinary it soon became creepy, scary and definitely upsetting for anyone with a religious bent. Set in a gothic apartment building in Manhattan it quickly became clear that the over-friendly neighbours of the recent newlyweds were not what they seemed. They were Satanists and had decided Rosemary would be the one to give birth to the Devil's son. Shot from Rosemary's viewpoint, the audience gradually becomes more and more uneasy as they realise what Rosemary realizes, that she is going to give birth to something horrible, but worse than that, her husband is also a Satanist and is part of the scheme to bring to the world the Devil's son, and she is all alone with no escape from the forthcoming birth. A stunning film…

It was a coup for Acapulco to secure this film since Roman Polanski had resigned from the Jury in Cannes and along with three other members they also withdrew their films from exhibition at the Cannes Festival.

Of course being an aficionado of Science Fiction books and films I just had to see **2001 A Space Odyssey**, having read about it being in production some time back and how it was based on a short story, The Sentinel by Arthur C Clarke, where a group of astronauts on the moon discover a black monolith half buried in the regolith and inadvertently cause it to send a message to outer space and are left wondering where the message went and who or what it will attract as a reply. That story finished with the words I don't think we will have long to wait.

Kubrick loved the idea and wanted to develop it into a film so he got Arthur C Clarke to collaborate on a script that expanded the story into a magnificently realistic depiction of everyday activities in space and on the moon. The second part of the film was completely enigmatic and abstract leaving everyone for years, even today, trying to work out what it meant. (*Years later Arthur C Clarke said something to the effect that if anyone understood it then they hadn't done their job right as filmmakers.*)

The film begins with a depiction of primitive hominids fighting and arguing with each other as mysteriously a huge black monolith appears near them in the morning. Tentatively one of them touches it. Not long after this there is a stunning jump cut to our future in Space as one of the hominids throws a large leg bone up into the air. The bone morphs into a space vehicle approaching a huge space station in orbit around the Earth. Everyone now knows this story of how another monolith is discovered on the moon and when an astronaut touches it a message is sent into space in the direction of Jupiter. Soon after an expedition is sent to Jupiter to find out what is there and where the message went. They discover another monolith orbiting Jupiter and from this point on the film becomes weird and abstract as one of the astronauts is taken through the monolith, which is some kind of gateway, and enigmatically he is reborn as a space child and sent back to Earth.

What helped to lift this film out of the 'B grade' category and into first class 'A grade' (apart from superb photography) was the use of classical and light classical music instead of weird electronic noise as earlier films had used, as well as absolute silence when showing scenes externally on the Moon and in space. There is no air there to carry sound so no sound at all was used. Earlier films always had swishing wind noises to indicate movement. Kubrick never did that. And the detail of the space shots, made even better by being shown in Cinerama and later 70 mm Cinemascope truly gave an impression of the vastness of space that no other film had done before it. And then there is the problem of artificial intelligence and computer controlled systems that decide humans may be irrelevant and how to deal with something that is trying to eliminate you. We have yet to confront this problem but I don't think it will be too far off now, the way computers and computer controlled systems have been evolving and insinuating into everything we take for granted. One day the human race will experience a rude awakening.

One has to see this film several times to appreciate the incredible detail that is in it which one does not see at first.

What made this film truly memorable for me was that it happened to be shown on the 24th of December, and halfway through the film's one and only evening session it stopped, and before the audience could start protesting about the break in the film an announcement was made through the theatre's sound system that three American astronauts had just arrived at the Moon and were at this moment orbiting it. It was the very first time humans had left the planet and traversed empty space to another celestial body. Previously manned flights only stayed in orbit around Earth. Only unmanned probes had been sent out into space beyond Earth.

I felt incredibly excited and energised. We had done it...we had gone to the Moon...Mars would be next after establishing a moon base...and then the rest of the solar system was open to human exploration.. I could imagine it all happening in the near future and at just 28 years of age I would get to see it all... I could barely contain myself.

Frank Borman, James Lovell, and William Anders were the astronauts. They didn't land because they couldn't, the landing module had not been ready, but there was pressure to launch for the Moon ahead of the Russians who were attempting to send a cosmonaut around the Moon early in 1969. The Americans couldn't let them be first so they launched and got to the Moon within President Kennedy's deadline and achieved a spectacular win against the Russians for America, finally achieving a true milestone.

They broadcast a Christmas message of peace to the whole World from the Moon and everyone in the theatre cheered and clapped. About half an hour later, once the excitement had died down, they continued to project the film, the rest of which left the audience totally bewildered.

Apollo 8 made ten orbits around the moon and the photos they took of Earth rising above the Moon appeared not long after in newspapers all over the World. Those three astronauts were the very first humans to see the Earth rise like that beyond the Moon and it profoundly affected them. On Christmas day (1968) on their return journey they broadcast another message to the people of Earth in which they read verses from the Book of Genesis.

On my way

All too soon it was early January and I boarded the plane to Mexico City where I changed to a short flight to the Bahamas. I had checked in my suitcase in Acapulco. Arriving in the Bahamas late at night I waited for my luggage to arrive on the carousel but it didn't appear. No one knew where it had gone. After a lot of mucking about I eventually left and found a hotel for the night.

I flew to Miami the next morning still wearing what I had worn since leaving Acapulco. All my other clothes were in the missing suitcase.

At the airline office in Miami they told me they had sent my luggage to Bermuda instead of the Bahamas. It could be a week before they would get it back. I explained I wasn't going to be there that long and would be in New York for a couple of days before going on to Toronto and then Europe. 'Send my luggage to Germany,' I told them and gave them the address of Fred's parents in Backnang.

The airline also offered to pay for winter clothing since they had lost my luggage and I would need warm clothes for New York where it was minus 8 degrees as well as even colder in Toronto. And of course it was winter in Germany also with zero or less degrees. I would certainly need warmer clothes than the sandals, shorts and T shit I was wearing when I landed in Miami. I happily accepted their offer and bought an overcoat, thick winter trousers, fur lined boots and a few other bits and pieces all paid for with the voucher they gave me.

For some obscure reason they told me I had to hand over my boots to them when I got back to Melbourne, Their insurance company insisted on it, which didn't make sense since I was allowed to keep the other items bought.

In New York I went to a record warehouse and bought 200 records of music not available anywhere in Australia. It was mostly what is now called Salsa. I had them shipped to my home address via cargo ship which meant I would be home long before they arrived.

I stayed a couple of days in Toronto visiting my mother's aunt but I couldn't stay there because it was too cold for me after a year in sub tropical Acapulco. It might as well have been the North Pole as far as I was concerned. I left anf flew to Germany where it was still below freezing but nothing at all like it had been in Toronto.

They knew I was coming when I got to Backnang because my luggage had already arrived. I got there a couple of days before Zara and Fred. Christine and Yvonne came over from England to surprise them. I went to the airport with Fred's parents and when we got back with them Christine and Yvonne jumped out from behind the door where they had been hiding as we entered, and Zara nearly fell over in surprise. It was a wonderful family reunion.

Two days later I left.

I went first to Bonn to visit my uncle Eddie after which I flew to Rome on the first leg of the return trip. The only thing I remember about Rome was that the Coliseum was much smaller than I thought it would be. I was sitting at a roadside café opposite, across a wide boulevard and watched endless traffic swirl past it. A taxi was on its way to collect me to take me to the airport so there really wasn't time to go and have a closer look at it.

I had a week and a half to complete the round the trip so I could not stay any longer than overnight in any place once leaving Germany and that included Rome.

I spent one night in Nairobi, one night in Johannesburg, and one night in the Mauritius. I arrived in Perth about 2 am and waited at the airport until the first flight left for Melbourne around 5 am. 5 or 6 seemingly endless hours later I was back in Melbourne, exhausted and feeling totally drained of energy, and that was the end of my second round-the-world trip.